Strengths-Based Engagement and Practice

Creating Effective Helping Relationships

Bob Bertolino

Maryville University

and

Youth In Need, Inc.

Allyn & Bacon

Boston   New York   San Francisco

Mexico City   Montreal   Toronto   London   Madrid   Munich   Paris

Hong Kong   Singapore   Tokyo   Cape Town   Sydney

In memory of

Tom Conran (1956–2008)
and
Megan Piontek (1985–2008)

"Love and compassion
know no bounds."

Senior Acquisitions Editor: Patricia Quinlin
Series Editorial Assistant: Carly Czech
Senior Marketing Manager: Wendy Albert
Production Editor: Pat Torelli

Editorial Production Service: TexTech
Manufacturing Buyer: Debbie Rossi
Electronic Composition: TexTech
Cover Designer: Joel Gendron

Library of Congress Cataloging-in-Publication Data

Bertolino, Bob
    Strengths-based engagement and practice : creating effective helping
relationships / Bob Bertolino and Youth in Need, Inc.
        p. cm.
    ISBN-13: 978-0-205-56904-5
    ISBN-10: 0-205-56904-8
  1. Psychotherapist and patient.   2. Psychotherapy.   I. Youth in Need, Inc.
II. Title.

    RC480.8.B47 2010
    616.89'14—dc22   2008049503

10 9 8 7 6 5 4 3 2 1   RRD-VA   13 12 11 10 09

Allyn & Bacon
is an imprint of

www.pearsonhighered.com

ISBN-10: 0-205-56904-8

ISBN-13: 978-0-205-56904-5

Contents

PART II

PART III

PART IV

PART V

PART VI

Chapter 13 Evolution in Context: Constructing New Worlds through Respect and Integrity 347

I began this book in the fall of 2006. From that time until its completion in the spring of 2008, different parts were written in fourteen states and five countries. The process was an exciting and often exhilarating one, although not without challenge—such as when part of a hand-edited version of the manuscript was whisked away by the wind only to end up in the Mississippi River. Despite the efforts of several passersby who desperately tried to retrieve drenched pages from the river, several sections were lost. Then there was the time nearly 20 pages inexplicably disappeared from a flash drive—never to be seen again. Things became even more interesting when I left key reference materials and research summaries on an airplane in Tokyo, Japan. Perhaps a few passengers or airline personnel found some unexpected and surely riveting reading materials on their flights. I admit to missing the humor in these events as they occurred, yet I have no doubt that they contributed to my experiencing the world in new and more meaningful ways.

It has been said that we are each representations of our experiences. In my estimation, this book, although situated in research, is about experience. Therapy is a personal and experiential endeavor and one that involves the continuous creation and re-creation of new meanings. It is my hope that the pages of this volume resonate with you in some way and perhaps contribute to your personal and professional evolution.

A Field of Change

As psychotherapy and family therapy have matured, much has been learned about conditions and factors that influence successful outcomes. The purpose of this volume is to capture and expound on these findings, enhancing current practices in helping relationships and psychotherapy in particular. A secondary but equally important purpose of this volume is to address the necessity of increasing accountability in therapy. It is imperative that therapists incorporate ways to monitor and improve therapy outcomes. There is great news on this front. Despite the ongoing, often complex debates that surround psychotherapy research, there is much to be gleaned from the data about successful practice.

As a vehicle for articulating these ideas, I offer an overarching philosophical posture—*strengths-based engagement* (SBE). This stance is firmly grounded in what has been known for years by practitioners and is now supported empirically: the importance of identifying and building on client strengths to help them resolve concerns, heal, and achieve desired changes. This is more than just a passing idea: a strengths-based focus makes sense to those who work each day to make a difference in the lives of others. It is characterized by respect, collaboration, competency, and an unwavering faith in the possibilities that exist when people are seen as capable.

The core principles of SBE are not random. They are based on a convergence of evidence by leading researchers. I have chosen to explore how primary research perspectives intersect and share common ground for the benefit of both clients and therapists. It should also be noted that the specific framework of SBE represents a posture that continues to be taught and implemented in clinical (including both public and private sectors) and academic settings. The ideas in this book are meant to be practiced in the "everyday" settings in which counselors, social workers, therapists, psychologists, and those in mental health, social services, educational, and health settings provide services.

This book is intended to help practitioners examine new ways to engage clients through respectful processes to build on their capacities and to enhance the possibilities for positive change. It is not meant to address any one circumstance, diagnosis, or issue. Numerous wonderful resources are available to therapists who are in search of increased knowledge about specific issues. Instead, this book assists therapists in thinking about and exploring processes that are essential to improving the effectiveness of therapy, no matter the issue or concern.

Language and Terminology

It is acknowledged that education, discipline, setting, and role determine professional identity. For the purposes of this book, the terms *therapist, counselor, social worker, clinician, practitioner,* and *student* are used at different junctures. Similarly, the contexts in which those in helping professions work is a factor in determining the language used. Ideally, people are consulted about language and asked how they would like to be referred to (e.g., as a client, consumer, patient). In this book, the word *client* is used in reference to people who are seen in therapy. When referring to those persons who may or may not be involved in therapy yet care for clients, the words *parent, guardian,* and *caregiver* are used. Finally, several terms have been chosen when describing services including *counseling, therapy, prevention, education,* and *case management.* In addition, words such as *interactions, meetings, sessions, appointments,* and *intakes* also appear when referring to the arrangements in which people might be met for services. Although the terminology may need to be adjusted given different contexts, again it is the ideas that are paramount. Believe in and live the ideas, and the techniques will evolve out of those philosophical underpinnings. It has been said that if you practice something long enough, it becomes yours. This is an invitation to take the pages of this book and transform them into something that fits for you and the context(s) within which you work. Please make these ideas and practices your own.

Arrangement of This Volume

This book is arranged in six parts and thirteen chapters. Each part addresses specific components of SBE and contributes to an overall philosophy aimed at increasing the effectiveness of each therapeutic encounter.

Part I comprises the first two chapters, "The Atmosphere of Practice" and "An Ecology of Ideas: Foundations and Core Principles of Strengths-Based Engagement." The premise of Chapter 1 is to acknowledge many of the larger contextual factors that affect all practitioners and to introduce readers to what it means to be strengths based. Chapter 2 delves into discussion about the primary agendas of psychotherapy research and how agendas converge to contribute to the core principles of SBE, which are outlined in the chapter.

Part II includes Chapters 3, "Keys to Collaborative Partnerships: First Steps in Client–Therapist Engagement" and 4, "Active Client Engagement: The Language of Change." Chapter 3 focuses on how therapists can begin to encourage collaborative partnerships, both prior to the start of and early in initial interactions and sessions. Chapter 4 delves into numerous ways to use language as a vehicle for promoting change.

Part III presents chapters on gaining direction and focus in therapy by further tuning into clients' perspectives. Chapter 5, "Establishing Structure and Direction: Using Information–Gathering Processes," focuses specifically on using formal and informal processes for gathering information and establishing goals. Chapter 6, "Mapping the Topography of Change: Understanding Clients' Orientations," involves discussion of how to tune into clients' orientations, including the influence of their concerns and ideas about change. This helps to assist with selecting and

using the more advanced methods described in Chapters 7–10.

Part IV comprises four chapters. Chapters 7, "Changing Views and Perspectives, Part I: Exceptions and Differences," and 8, "Changing Views and Perspectives, Part II: Patterns of Attention," focus on processes and practices that assist with helping clients to develop new meanings and understandings as well as change perceptions and patterns of thinking and attention. Ideas for using consulting teams are also offered. Chapters 9, "Changing Actions and Interactions, Part I: Identifying and Altering Repetitive Patterns," and 10, "Changing Actions and Interactions, Part II: Identifying and Amplifying Solution Patterns," detail ways to collaborate with clients to change individual patterns and interactions that occur among people.

Part V includes two chapters: 11, "Future Interactions and Sessions: Patterns of Client Responses," and 12, "Emerging and Evolving Stories: Building on Progress and Change." This part delves into subsequent sessions, offering means of tracking, monitoring, and responding to client change. Chapter 11 specifically focuses on clarifying and negotiating points of impasse. Chapter 12 offers ideas for amplifying and building on changes and for helping clients to transition to less intensive forms of therapy or out of therapy altogether.

Part VI comprises the final chapter, Chapter 13, "Evolution in Context: Constructing New Worlds through Respect and Integrity." This chapter outlines ideas for approaching supervision and developing a strengths-based culture in organizations.

To enhance the experience of readers, case examples, dialogues, and clinical vignettes have been used to illustrate different ideas, processes, and practices. Although identifying characteristics have been changed, the majority of the examples are from actual client–therapist dialogues. Also included are sample questions, stories, and exercises that are intended to deepen readers' understandings of SBE. Finally, an appendix that offers a brief synopsis of the three "waves" of psychotherapy has been provided. This historical timeline outlines major theoretical developments that inform SBE.

You are now invited to engage in a journey of both intellectual and emotional exploration. It is my hope that you will be encouraged and inspired to further explore your personal beliefs about people, change, and the ideas that underscore your approach to helping relationships. You are an important catalyst in facilitating change in others' lives and can make a difference in each and every interaction.

Acknowledgments

This book represents an evolution of learning and experience. The most profound aspect of life experience, in my estimation, involves relationships. I would like to express my appreciation and gratitude to my colleagues, family, and friends, whose support and kindness have helped me to evolve both personally and professionally. Their contributions to my life have served as a lifeline in turning what began as a vision into this book.

First and foremost, none of this would have been written without the love and support of my family. Thank you to my mom, dad, stepmom, brothers, and sisters for always being there and showing interest in whatever I'm doing at the moment. Your words, no matter how small to you, have always been what has mattered the most to me. And to my daughter, Morgan, who watched me pore through what must have seemed like truckloads of therapy-related articles and books, thank you for introducing me to the finer side of literature through *Harry Potter* and *The Golden Compass*. I'm very teachable. I love you all.

I would particularly like to thank Barbara Parker, Michael Kiener, and Gina Oswald, my colleagues in the Rehabilitation Counseling program at Maryville University, whose words of encouragement and excitement about the

book were just what I needed to see it through. A special thank you to Chuck Gulas, Dean of the School of Health Professions, for recognizing my passion for developing the ideas in this book and for being flexible with my schedule so I could complete the necessary research and writing; and to Mary Ellen Finch, Vice President of Academic Affairs, who perhaps unknowingly has influenced me through her commitment to learning, education, and the exploration of "the new." I would also like to express my appreciation to the faculty in the School of Health Professions at Maryville University, who listened to and supported my ideas and saw them as applicable to professionals beyond the fields of counseling, psychology, and social work; and to the students at Maryville University, who have participated in my courses. Thank you for opening your minds and hearts and for a willingness to challenge yourself to grow. I have learned so much from you.

For nearly two decades I have had the great fortune of doing my community work at Youth In Need (YIN), Inc., in St. Charles, Missouri. What I have learned from the staff, clients, and community has indelibly shaped my life and how I view relationships and the capacity to change that people have. During my entire tenure at YIN, I have had the full support of Jim Braun, President and CEO, and Pat Holterman-Hommes, Senior Vice President of Youth Programs. Both have always seen the value of my contributions and encouraged me to take our programs to new heights. The trust you have placed in me has provided numerous opportunities to connect research to practice, which is a cornerstone of this book. Thank you for your unwavering belief in me.

I cannot fully convey my sincere gratitude to the outclient clinical team at YIN, who epitomize what it means to be strengths based and exemplify the ideas in this book. Each day I am inspired by the creativity and loyalty of this group of people who are my family away from home. To Ryan Patterson, Amy Brown Gander, Melanie Watkins, David Salvatierra, Lisa Hinni, Rachel Berkowitz, Tiffany Flaherty, and Jeff Homan: I am blessed to have you in my life. Thank you for your commitment to children, youth, and families, YIN, and to each other. You are an example of what a group of people with a unified mission and vision can do to positively impact the lives of others.

Thank you to the entire staff at YIN for embracing a strengths-based philosophy and in "walking the talk." Ideas mean little if they are not put into motion. In particular, I would like to express my gratitude to Michelle Gorman, Katie Goetz, Katrina Peoples, Taedra Rutlin, Stephanie Flake, and the YIN executive management and emergency shelter teams with whom I have worked closely in creating a climate for change at YIN. The work you do will continue to affect lives beyond imagination.

Many colleagues have taken the time to comment on this manuscript, encourage the ideas behind it, and challenge me to do my part in moving the field forward. I would particularly like to thank Bill O'Hanlon, Adrian Blow, Jay Memmott, Monte Bobele, Charlie Appelstein, Scott Miller, William Madsen, Tom Conran, Bill Heusler, and the numerous peers and colleagues who have embraced these ideas and taken their time to offer feedback. I would also like to acknowledge the groundbreaking work of luminaries such as Michael Lambert, Bruce Wampold, John Norcross, Larry Beutler, James Prochaska, and Carlo DiClemente, along with others unmentioned here, whose ideas have influenced this volume.

My thanks also go to the reviewers of this book while it was in the manuscript stage for their insightful comments. They are Adrian Blow, Michigan State University; Monte Bobele, Our Lady of the Lake University; David A. Dia, University of Tennessee, Memphis; Jay Memmott, Washburn University; and Penny S. Tropman, University of Michigan, Ann Arbor. I would also like to express my gratitude to Gearoid Carey for continuing the legacy of the ideas in this book and assisting with the development of the supplemental materials.

Finally, I am deeply grateful to Patricia Quinlin, Senior Acquisitions Editor, Social Work/Family Therapy at Pearson/Allyn & Bacon Publishers, who saw this book as an important contribution to the field. Thank you for your vision and commitment. To David Estrin, my editor in New York, who demonstrated enormous patience and provided poignant feedback throughout the development of the manuscript: thank you for knowing what to say and how to say it. And thank you to Carly Czech and the rest of the editorial and creative staff at Pearson/Allyn & Bacon and to John Shannon and the staff at TexTech, Inc. for your work on this book.

BOB BERTOLINO
St. Louis, Missouri

PART ONE

Chapter 1

The Atmosphere of Practice

■ Strengths-based engagement (SBE) is a philosophical stance that emphasizes a way of being in relationship to and interaction with others. This relational posture influences how we think about change and change-effecting processes. As you will learn throughout this book, the foundational principles of SBE are based on decades of research and empirical findings that have been demonstrated as influential in therapeutic outcomes. More important, however, SBE is characterized by a respectful "attitude" toward others that is distinguishable by five C's: culturally sensitive, collaborative, client informed, competency based, and change oriented, each of which is imparted in all aspects of helping relationships. Although subsequent chapters will include an extensive exploration of methods and techniques associated with the principles outlined, this SBE philosophical stance provides the connective tissue and fabric of change.

Before delving into the core foundational principles of SBE outlined in Chapter 2, it is important to consider both macro- and microfactors and their potential affect on helping relationships. *Macrofactors* are those more general overarching factors that shape the culture of practice. This class of factors represents considerations for all

counselors regardless of their theoretical alliances. *Microfactors* relate to therapists' personal philosophies or worldviews.

This chapter begins with a discussion of several macrofactors that are considered along the road of effective practice. The role and potential impact of each on helping relationships are discussed. Following the discussion of macrofactors, you will embark on what will be an ongoing exploration of personal philosophy as it relates to helping relationships, change processes, and strengths-based practice. This discussion leads into the final part of the chapter that explores the concept of what it means to be "strengths based."

The Big Picture: Macrofactors and Helping Relationships

Of the many factors that shape the culture of practice, some are more reflective of the climate in which helping relationships are embedded. We will refer to these as macrofactors. The macrofactors include:

- the general efficacy of psychotherapy
- professional discipline
- competency and effectiveness

- the scientist-practitioner
- the reflective practitioner
- therapist effects
- practice and setting

Because of their potential influence on numerous aspects of helping relationships, each of these areas will be explored here briefly and then expanded upon in later chapters. It is important for therapists to be aware of these factors and their potential influence on clinical practice.

The General Efficacy of Psychotherapy

Psychotherapy has evolved significantly since its creation in the early 1900s. Rich with tradition, it has been brought to life by prominent figures and their groundbreaking models. Spanning different "waves" of psychotherapy (Bertolino & O'Hanlon, 2002) (see the Appendix at the end of this text) and epistemological viewpoints (in other words, different ways to conceptualize "reality"), numerous luminaries and their innovations have paved the way for the emergence of new approaches. Amid these many contributions, a question has remained: Does psychotherapy work? The answer is yes.

Whether provided by counselors, therapists, social workers, psychologists, or other professionals, research has legitimized psychotherapy as an efficacious treatment (Asay & Lambert, 1999; Lambert & Bergin, 1994; Lambert & Ogles, 2004; Lipsey & Wilson, 1993; Smith, Glass, & Miller, 1980). Although data regarding couples and family therapy are more limited than those on psychotherapy, available data indicate that such therapies are consistent with those of individual psychotherapy (Sexton, Alexander, & Mease, 2004; Shadish, Ragsdale, Glaser, & Montgomery,

1995). Gains made by clients who engaged in therapy are statistically significant, clinically meaningful, and surpass those of clients who received placebos or went untreated (Lambert & Ogles, 2004). Lambert and Ogles (2004) stated:

> Psychotherapy facilitates the remission of symptoms and improves functioning. It not only speeds up the natural healing process but also often provides additional coping strategies and methods for dealing with future problems. Providers as well as patients can be assured that a broad range of therapies, when offered by skillful, wise and stable therapists, are likely to result in appreciable gains for the client (p. 180).

Beyond the potential benefits to individual well-being, close interpersonal relationships, and social role functioning (i.e., friendships, career), research findings indicate that psychotherapy can be cost effective in reducing inpatient stays, consultations with primary-care physicians, use of medications, care provided by relatives, and general health care expenditures by 60 to 90% (Chiles, Lambert, & Hatch, 1999; Gabbard, Lazar, Hornberger, & Speigel, 1997; Guthrie et al., 1999; Kraft, Puschner, Lambert, & Kordy, 2006). Referred to as *medical cost offset* research, these findings have been demonstrated with persons with high utilization rates of medical and health-related services who received individual, family, and marital therapy (Cummings, 2007; Cummings, Cummings, & Johnson, 1997; Cummings, O'Donohue, & Ferguson, 2002; Law, Crane, & Berge, 2003). Although further research is necessary to determine the variables effecting medical utilization (for example, client age or length of therapy), the implication that psychotherapy can contribute to a reduction in health care expenditures is promising.

With psychotherapy established as efficacious, research focus has turned to identifying the various elements that influence outcomes and account for client improvement. Although this identification has proven challenging (Castonguay & Holtforth, 2005; Craighead, Bjornsson, & Amarson, 2005; DeRubries, Brotman, & Gibbons, 2005; Kazdin, 2005; Wampold, 2005), much has been learned about what makes therapy effective. This research will be addressed and discussed in detail in Chapter 2. It is important that therapists educate themselves on, maintain an awareness of, and incorporate these findings in clinical practice as a means to maximize the benefits to clients.

Professional Discipline

Mental health and social service workers practice in an ever-growing array of professional settings. Practitioners are counted on to perform a wide range of tasks from case management to respite care to psychological testing to counseling that impact the lives of others (Boyle, Smith, Farley, & Hull, 2008). Regardless of the practitioner's discipline (for example, counseling, marriage and family therapy, social work, psychology), those in the helping professions consistently work in the same contexts with the same clientele. Psychotherapy is the most common intersection of service provision between professional helping disciplines. This commonality between fields has perpetuated comparisons. Psychologist Michael Lambert (2004) noted that beliefs regarding the effectiveness of one discipline versus another are more fiction than fact: "On the basis of much research evidence, no one profession can claim a monopoly on superior service" (p. 5). When it comes to actual psychotherapy practice, distinctions between professional degrees and disciplines matter little (Wampold & Brown, 2005).

The education and training of students and practitioners can vary greatly, not only according to a person's chosen professional discipline but also within respective programs and settings. Instructors and trainers in different programs emphasize different principles, practices, and models. Some approaches are valued and privileged more than others and included as part of counseling curricula; others are given less attention or excluded altogether. An implication is that two people who attend different graduate programs (in social work, counseling, or marriage and family therapy) are likely to receive different training and, perhaps, more or fewer courses in counseling skills and theory. Although differences in curricula exist in many disciplines, considerable variance exists as to what constitutes acceptable coursework and training when it comes to preparing students to practice as therapists. This is a crucial point because no matter the educational path and professional discipline, those who choose to work as therapists will more often than not work in the same settings, performing the same or similar tasks.

Differences between professional disciplines are exemplified elsewhere as it is common for practitioners to stay within the boundaries of their respective fields when exploring postdegree training opportunities and in utilizing academic and professional resources. For example, both psychologists and social workers tend to refer almost exclusively to research in their respective fields. Although differences exist between disciplines, including what to study, how to conduct studies, and the language and terminology to use, delving into related fields frequently reveals new ideas and directions that result from this type of cross-fertilization. A challenge for both current and future therapists is to maintain an openness to and awareness of research outside their respective disciplines.

Through training and education, therapists become active participants who can benefit significantly by learning from others in adjacent disciplines. In accordance, it is important that therapists be as prepared as possible to work collaboratively with others from within and outside their disciplines. Maintaining this kind of openness allows further opportunities for the cross-fertilization of ideas, multidisciplinary learning, and growth. As you will see in Chapter 2, accessing knowledge from different disciplines and perspectives increases therapeutic possibilities. You will learn that no matter the discipline, universal ideas, processes, and practices cross disciplines and underscore effectiveness. Given their influence on helping relationships, all practitioners should be skilled in these areas.

Competency and Effectiveness

The concept of *competence* for therapists varies according to the clientele served, setting, code of ethics, and licensure laws. Certain areas of competence are, however, consistent within helping relationships. These areas include but are not limited to cultural competency as reflected in the knowledge of issues affecting clients and culturally sensitive practices; awareness of personal values and biases, appropriate ethical behavior, and professional conduct in fulfilling roles and responsibilities; and sound communication and therapeutic counseling skills. Each of these overarching competencies and corresponding ones are vital to both therapists and clients.

Historically, therapist competence has been demonstrated through meeting educational requirements, participating in supervised programs, and passing a licensure examination. Consistent with scope of knowledge and ability to practice skillfully, both of which reflect general measures of competency, a prevailing assumption is that the more training clinicians receive, the more competent they will be. This notion makes good sense when it comes to developing areas such as cultural competency and therapist awareness. It is imperative that therapists continue to develop and increase their knowledge.

When the issue of therapist effectiveness is considered, however, competence takes on new meaning. In particular, the more competent the practitioner, the more effective (in achieving positive results) the practitioner is assumed to be. Considerable research suggests, however, the contrary: *The more training, the less effective therapists may be* (Atkins & Christensen, 2001; Christenson & Jacobson, 1994; Lambert & Ogles, 2004). This finding is complicated and debatable and has several implications for consideration. The first relates to service provision. That is, a person could be well versed and knowledgeable about a particular field or model, be competent in practice, and yet be ineffective. Competence does not necessarily equate to effectiveness, and not all knowledge is equal. This leads to a second implication. Although the major ethical codes clearly delineate standards for competence, less attention has been given to establishing standards for clinician effectiveness.

A final consideration, which corresponds to the previously mentioned research finding on competence, is the type of training for practitioners. When it comes to therapeutic practice, training tends to focus on specific issues or models and methods with the intent on increasing those forms of competency. This, however, represents just one form of competency. Another relates to therapists' effectiveness. Because it is imperative that practitioners be both competent *and* effective, those designing and implementing supervision and training programs must expand training programs to include a focus on building competencies that will increase effective practice and therapy outcomes. In Chapter 2, you will learn about various directions in research that address this need through processes that involve tracking and monitoring client progress and improvement. Subsequent chapters will articulate practices that assist with the implementation of therapeutic work that is client informed and outcome oriented—both of which are essential to the viability of therapy and are central to a strengths-based philosophy.

The Scientist-Practitioner

Consistent with the previous macrofactor, the legitimacy of helping relationships and therapy, in particular, is based on evidence supporting its effectiveness. This leads to a fourth factor—the role of research in clinical work, and with it, two adjoining points. The first point is the impact of having no knowledge or incorrect knowledge. The gap between what clinicians do not know and assume to know presents multiple pitfalls (Boisvert & Faust, 2006). For example, research has consistently demonstrated that most clients achieve some form of change early in therapy (Kopta, Howard, Lowry, & Beutler, 1994). Furthermore, therapists can employ processes to monitor for these changes and corresponding systems of response depending on the feedback. Therapists without this knowledge are at a disadvantage, one that can contribute to decreased effectiveness and increased rates of dropout. While it is not possible nor is it suggested that therapists have endless reservoirs of research knowledge, some findings (many of which will be outlined in later chapters) are crucial to all therapists, no matter their theoretical approach.

What therapists claim to know and/or believe to be correct can also have unfavorable consequences. Misinformation and incorrect assumptions derived from sources such as poorly designed studies, misinterpretation of research, or training or supervision can contribute to therapists practicing in ways that negatively affect clients and outcome. For example, a common misconception is that specific techniques account for the majority of the variance in outcome. Under this assumption, therapists may routinely use specific methods or interventions they believe are responsible for change without exploring alternatives or options that are equally effective and may provide a better fit for clients. Although familiarity with research does not guarantee improved outcome, its absence precludes that possibility (Boisvert & Faust, 2006).

The second adjoining point relates to therapists engaging in evaluation strategies aimed at improving clinical practice and client outcomes. Primary hurdles to such strategies include negative attitude and fear; in addition, some therapists may see research as irrelevant, unhelpful, having a negative impact on the therapeutic relationship, disrupting the flow of therapy, and being too cumbersome. While upcoming chapters will address these concerns as well as others, a mindset in which the study of one's effectiveness (research) is valued represents an important point for practitioners.

Because effective helping relationships rely on a crossover between practice and research as well as art (in other words, creativity) and science, understanding how research enhances practice is necessary. Keeping up to date on professional developments and trends translates to therapists showing interest in their clinical outcomes including whether or not and to what degree clients may or may not be benefiting from therapy. Therapists need to embrace research as an integral part of practice and actively employ strategies to monitor progress to improve the effectiveness of services rendered.

The Reflective Practitioner

Training and education, competency and effectiveness, and a focus on science and practice are all variables that can greatly affect how therapists function. In addition, state licensing boards, accrediting bodies, insurance panels, and professional associations create, maintain, and monitor standards of care and practice. Law and ethics necessitate personal accountability for every person who works as or is working toward a career as a therapist. Each current or therapist in training is responsible for maintaining an understanding and awareness of legal and ethical factors and how they affect the scope of practice.

Awareness of these and other factors that can affect practice is critical to personal and professional growth. Awareness requires self-reflection. *Reflective practitioners* consider both how they influence and how the therapeutic milieu influences them. Reflective practitioners develop and maintain ongoing awareness of matters including but not limited to personal biases and issues, philosophical worldviews, selection of strategies and methods, and demonstration of interest in their effectiveness as therapists.

Reflective practitioners also take the initiative to keep up on professional issues through education, training, and practice. They build time in their practice to reflect on their experiences in all contexts, expand on existing expertise, and accept that professional identity and practice evolves over time. Reflective practitioners also seek new opportunities to learn and grow, understanding the interrelatedness between personal and professional realms.

It has been argued that the ability to critically self-reflect is the most important distinction between therapists who continue to grow and develop professionally versus those who face professional stagnation and burnout (Skovholt & Jennings, 2005; Skovholt & Rønnestad, 2001). This argument is of central importance given the influence of the person of the therapist in the therapeutic milieu. Therapists who are lifelong learners and embrace opportunities to critically reflect on their own work are engaging in processes that benefit not only clients but also themselves. Lifelong learning and reflection are of particular importance given the enormity of therapists' influence in therapy—the next topic discussed.

Therapist Effects

As previously mentioned, a common belief is that change during therapy is largely contingent on the interventions that practitioners utilize. This belief is consistent with an emphasis on training clinicians in the most recent "discoveries," most often in the form of methods, models, and techniques (MMTs), as a means to increase competence. As you will learn, empirical evidence does not support the assumption that MMTs are responsible for change. In contrast, therapist effects have demonstrated modest to large contributions to the variability in outcome (Blatt, Sanislow, Zuroff, & Pilkonis, 1996; Crits-Christoph & Mintz, 1991; Luborsky et al., 1997; Project MATCH Research Group, 1997) and contribute three to four times *more* to outcome than different forms of treatment (Luborksy et al., 1986). Wampold (2001) stated, "A preponderance of the evidence indicates that there are large therapist effects (in the range of 6–9% of the variance in outcomes accounted for by therapists) and that these effects greatly exceed treatment effects" (p. 200).

No discernable differences between professional disciplines exist; however, a growing body of data indicates that some therapists are more effective than others, even when addressing a broad range of initial symptomology (Okiishi, Lambert, Nielsen, & Ogles, 2003; Orlinksy & Howard, 1980; Wampold & Brown, 2005). Wampold and Brown (2005) reported a study of 581 licensed providers, including psychologists, psychiatrists, and master's level therapists, who treated a diverse sample of more than 6,000 clients. The researchers found that clients of the most effective therapists in the sample improved at a rate at least 50% higher and dropped out at a rate at least 50% lower than those assigned to the least effective therapists in the sample. The evidence appears incontrovertible: *Who* provides the therapy is a much more important determinant of success than *what* treatment approach is provided (Miller, Hubble, & Duncan, 2007).

Although numerous variables (for example, age, gender, race, culture, personality, values, style, experience) contribute to difference in therapists' *practicing* (Beutler et al., 2004), these influences and others (for example, level or type of training, theoretical orientation) have shown to have little or no relationship with therapist effectiveness (Wampold & Brown, 2005). After a study of more than 1,700 clients seen by 56 therapists over a two-year span, Okiishi et al. (2003) determined, "Even though graduate school training and managed health care tend to focus on training in specific techniques, something else, perhaps the individual therapists themselves are responsible for the variation in client outcomes" (p. 370).

Whereas treatments have little effect on outcomes, the person of the therapist is a crucial factor in the success of therapy (Wampold, 2001). Despite these findings, studies on therapist variables remain underrepresented when compared to the attention given to models (Blow, Sprenkle, & Davis, 2007). Lebow

(2006) commented, "Psychotherapy researchers typically focus on different clinical interventions while ignoring the therapists that make use of them. It's as if treatment methods were like pills, in no way affected by the person administering them" (p. 131–132). It is clear that as this underresearched yet fertile area of future study is given adequate attention, additional data will emerge, leading to a better understanding of therapist dimensions and contributions to change. What has been gleaned thus far from the data will be discussed in subsequent chapters in exploring ways to increase effectiveness and outcome.

Practice and Setting

A final macrofactor includes variables that may differ in terms of their influence but affect all who provide direct services. These factors include, but are not limited to, ethical and legal responsibilities, operational guidelines and regulations within practice settings, supervisors and mentors, third-party payers and other funding sources (predominately found in managed care), and diagnostic classification. Given that psychotherapy is a prominent aspect of mental health and social services, these influences cannot be understated or viewed in isolation from one another—they can, and often do, affect service provision. Each practitioner must meet and/or negotiate, often on an ongoing basis, the parameters and requirements that are relative to the context in which he or she provides services.

Just as not all therapists are equally effective, some settings produce better overall outcomes than others. Clinicians can better prepare themselves by investigating practice and setting factors prior to interviewing for jobs, changing roles, or considering moves to different contexts. They can do this through processes such as researching potential employers, asking others who have worked in them about the contexts being considered, and preparing interview questions to ask a potential employer. Therapists also consider the kind of support they believe will help them to grow and evolve. Skovholt and Rønnestad (1995) stated:

> It is important to have an environment supportive of one's search, an environment where the person is connected to other professional searchers. Such an environment is not dogmatic or rigid but is supportive of professional development and increased competence. Such an environment values high standards of performance and a searching process as opposed to the process of total acceptance of a preordained set of ideological principles. Such an environment supports an exploratory, investigative approach. Such an environment values diversity and has an opening up stance versus a simplification of the complex world, i.e., in working with a client case, such an environment will encourage looking for as many associations on a case as possible versus reinforcing only a narrow, prescribed theory or method (pp. 106–107).

Because the context of practice can vary greatly, some contextual factors may not be immediately evident to newer practitioners. Thus, it is critical that therapists learn how to work within parameters that are less flexible while searching for ways to initiate change in those areas that are more malleable.

While its respective influence will vary, each macrofactor discussed plays a role in shaping the culture of therapy practice and helping relationships. Next we move to a microlevel by exploring how worldviews, which we will refer to as our "personal philosophies," affect therapy and change processes.

Personal Philosophy and Worldview

Often referred to as one's *worldview, personal philosophy* represents the evolution of collective experience and is shaped by *microfactors* or influences such as culture, gender, education, environment, family history, genetics, physiology, religion/spirituality, sexual orientation, politics, economics, and social relationships. Our personal and professional experiences filter these influences. Although some influences are (or will be) more meaningful than others, each makes a contribution to the formation of our respective personal philosophies. These philosophies affect change and precede therapy theories and practices. Consistent with Madsen (2007), philosophy maintains the first-order position in a three-level system for understanding how we approach therapy and change. It can be understood graphically in the following way:

Personal Philosophies ▸ Theory/Models ▸ Practices
"How we are"   "How we think"   "What we do"

Personal philosophies represent our underlying belief systems and ways to understand the world. Theories and models are higher-level maps and systems that serve as conceptual templates for how we think about clients and their concerns. Last, practices represent the specific means or how we go about facilitating change. Because personal philosophies precede both theory and practice, the influence of such philosophies is significant. One's philosophy can open up pathways with possibilities or close down such avenues. To gain a more intimate understanding of the impact of philosophy, you are invited to complete Exercise 1.1, A Philosophical Inventory.

Exercise 1.1

A Philosophical Inventory

(Please use the space below to write any ideas, thoughts, or comments you may have for each question.)

- What core beliefs or assumptions do you have about people and change?

  _____

  _____

- How have you come to believe what you believe and know what you know?

  _____

  _____

- What have been the most significant influences on your beliefs?

  _____

  _____

- To the best of your knowledge, how have your beliefs and assumptions affected your work with people? with colleagues? with the community?

  _____

  _____

- Do you believe that positive change is possible even with the most "difficult" and "challenging" people? (If you answered "yes," answer the next question.) (If you answered "no," skip the next two questions.)

  _____

  _____

- How do you believe that change occurs?

  _____

  _____

- What do you do to promote change? (If you answered this question, end here.)

  _____

  _____

- How do you work with others with whom you believe cannot change?

  _____

  _____

(continued)

Exercise 1.1 *(continued)*

- If you do not believe that the people with whom you work can change, what keeps you in the field?

  _____

  _____

  After completing this exercise, consider the following questions:

- What did you learn about yourself?

  _____

  _____

- What did you learn about your philosophy of change?

  _____

  _____

- How do you think your views impact your work in helping relationships?

  _____

  _____

- What, if any, new thoughts do you have about how your philosophy could become more effective as a vehicle for change for you and the people with whom you work or will work in the future?

  _____

  _____

- What might you do with this information?

  _____

  _____

Because personal philosophies are constantly evolving, it is crucial for us as practitioners to remain open to the process of reexamining our beliefs. Checking in with our ideology does not mean compromising individual belief systems: Each of us has a right to believe what we believe. The primary purpose of this exploration is to understand the impact that our individual philosophies have on change processes. What we believe is not random, nor does it exist in a vacuum. It affects what we perceive and how we exist in relationship to and work with others.

We acknowledge that physical, cognitive, emotional, developmental, and other hurdles and/or limitations must be considered and addressed in any form of human, social, educational, or mental health services. Philosophy, the blueprint of our belief systems, however, is frequently the point from which impossibility originates. It arguably poses the most significant threat to helping relationships. It can lead to decreased job motivation and effectiveness as well as increased stress, dissatisfaction, resentment, anxiety, depression, physical illness, burnout, and, ultimately, the loss of hope.

Some philosophies open up possibilities for change, whereas others close them down and can threaten both those providing and those receiving services (Bertolino, 2003). The following story illustrates this idea.

> A particular class of students had become unmanageable. The teacher, who was nearing retirement, decided she had had enough and took early retirement rather than spend her last year in a constant battle with the class. The class was then emboldened by the fact that members had been able to drive the original teacher into retirement. Another teacher from the school was brought in and was also quickly defeated. This second teacher resigned rather than continue with this class.
>
> In desperation, the school called a teacher who had recently finished her student teaching, was just fresh from university, and had applied for a job but hadn't received one. The principal feared that if this new teacher were told the true nature of the class she was getting, she wouldn't accept the job, so he said nothing about the previous problems with the class.
>
> After about a month, his guilt finally got to him and he decided to do a class visit. To his amazement, the class was very well behaved. He stayed after the students left and told the teacher that he was very impressed with the results she had shown with the class. She demurred and thanked him for making it so easy by giving her such a great group of kids for her first real teaching job. He asked her what had given her the idea that they were a great group. She smiled and told him that she had discovered his secret on her first day with the class; she then opened the desk drawer and pointed to a list for the students in the class followed by numbers from 135–170. "I found this list of their IQ scores the first day. I realized that these were gifted children who really needed to be engaged in a challenging way or else they would be bored and troublesome, so I completely changed my teaching plan with them. They responded very well after a few days of being rambunctious." The principal looked at the list and responded with incredulity, "But those are their locker numbers, not their IQ scores!" No matter. The teacher had already acted on her perceptions and changed the classroom situation for the better.

An antidote to worldviews that close down change is a strengths-based philosophy. This perspective reflects core values such as respect, compassion, competency, hope, and change. Martin Seligman, former president of the American Psychological Association, and Mihaly Csikszentmihalyi (2000) remarked:

> What we have learned over 50 years is that the disease model does not move us closer to the prevention of these serious problems. Indeed the major strides in prevention have largely come from a perspective focused on systematically building competency, not correcting weakness. Prevention researchers have discovered that there are human strengths that act as buffers against mental illness: courage, future-mindedness, optimism, interpersonal skill, faith, work ethic, hope, honesty, perseverance, the capacity for flow and insight, to name several. Much of the task of prevention in this new century will be to create a science of human strength whose mission will be to understand and learn how to foster these virtues in young people. Working exclusively on personal weakness and on the damaged

brains, however, has rendered science poorly equipped to do effective prevention. We need now to call for massive research on human strength and virtue. We need to ask practitioners to recognize that much of the best work they already do in the consulting room is to amplify strengths rather than repair the weaknesses of their clients (pp. 6–7).

A strengths-based philosophy provides a practical, respectful foundation that informs helping relationships. If you hold the philosophy that people can change, that they have strengths, and that each interaction can make a difference to them, your ability to fully participate in and positively affect the lives of others will significantly increase. Furthermore, if you believe in yourself, your abilities, and in what you do, you will experience more possibilities for yourself and the people with whom you interact.

Opportunity for Change: Becoming Strengths Based

Historically, the term *strengths based* has been used generically, resulting in criticisms about its definition and inconsistencies in how it is practiced (McMillen, Morris, & Sherraden, 2004; Staudt, Howard, & Drake, 2001). This dilemma is in part due to efforts to categorize a strengths-based perspective as a model or theory as opposed to a philosophical position. A strengths-based perspective is not a theory but an overarching philosophical perspective that sees people as having capabilities and resources within themselves and their social systems. When cultivated, activated, and integrated with new experiences, understandings, ideas, and skills, these strengths help people to

reduce pain and suffering, resolve concerns and conflicts, and cope more effectively with life stressors. This contributes to improved sense of well-being and quality of life as well as higher levels of relational and social functioning. Strengths-based practitioners promote change through respectful educational, therapeutic, and operational processes in addition to practices that encourage and empower others.

In recent years, numerous efforts have been undertaken to clarify what it means to be strengths-based. The ideas identified in these efforts have been applied to multiple contexts and services (Bertolino & O'Hanlon, 2002; Madsen, 2007; Rapp, 1998; Saleeby, 2006). Despite this, a strengths-based perspective has been criticized as lacking empirical viability. This criticism again is in part due to an emphasis on classifying a strengths-based perspective as a specific psychological theory as opposed to an overarching framework or metaview. Through the latter lens, each aspect of a strengths-based perspective is in fact clearly rooted in decades of empirical evidence regarding the components of effective and successful services. The interplay of these elements is crucial to outcome and will be discussed throughout this book.

A strengths orientation is also at risk of being misinterpreted. It has become commonplace for so-called competency-based and collaborative frameworks to focus almost exclusively on strengths. The idea is that people have all of the strengths they need to resolve any problems they encounter. This idea not only is a misrepresentation of what strengths based means but also can be invalidating to those who desperately need helpers to thoroughly understand the different hardships and risks they are facing. Being strengths based does not mean being "problem phobic," nor does it suggest forcing solution-talk (Nylund & Corsiglia, 1994) (see the Appendix). Understanding the problems others face while keeping an eye on strengths that can be useful in resolving their concerns is crucial. Nevertheless, people are not bottomless reservoirs of ability who have every answer to every life problem. Such belief is unrealistic and a potentially hazardous idea that can lead to overlooking serious threats to clients' well-being. A strengths-based philosophy involves identifying such threats while focusing on both the evocation of strengths and abilities *and* education in the service of change. The latter focus relates to creating situations in which clients can acquire new information and develop new skills, which reflects an emphasis on lifelong learning.

A strengths-based approach is not based on positive thinking or seeing the proverbial glass as being half full, both of which represent oversimplistic points of view. Being strengths based means looking beyond what is immediately observed or believed to be true and making the investment in others to know more about them. Madsen (2007) has referred to this through the notion of being "appreciative allies," a concept that translates to first acknowledging the negative emotional reactions we may have to clients whose actions we find intolerable or offensive. In doing so, we open ourselves up to finding something, however small, that we can appreciate and respect about our clients. These granules contribute to the foundation for subsequent work and reflect our faith that positive change and successful outcome are possible even in the most challenging situations. Such a perspective can circumvent services by freeing clinicians from predetermined theoretical restraints that suggest impossibility. The Clinical Vignette on page 14 illustrates this idea.

Erickson viewed people as capable of change, tailoring his approach to fit his patients. He worked to create possibilities by accessing their abilities while creating opportunities for learning and trying out new skills and behaviors. Method was secondary to Erickson's approach. He understood that methods and techniques were vitamins that fortify the seeds of change, not *the way* to bring about change. To see possibilities, we must cultivate a new mindset, immersing ourselves in ways of thinking that dissolve preexisting boundaries.

A strengths-based philosophy relies on creating and embracing contexts in which methods and techniques increase the prospects of change. Methods and techniques that are used randomly and without sound rationale are more likely to fail and/or contribute to negative consequences and outcomes. Conversely, by better understanding with whom, how, when, and under what circumstances certain methods should be considered, we significantly increase our "factor of fit" with clients. This increases the chances of positive change.

A strengths-based philosophy is characterized by *hope* (Snyder, 2000). It has been said that the absence of hope is the most devastating experience one can have. Its presence, on the other hand, can lead to new possibilities in how people experience themselves, the world, and in the actions they take. Although hope is just one aspect of the change equation, it is a necessary catalyst without which we have no art, no science, no education, no imagination, no accountability, and no sense of opportunity. Lack of opportunity breeds hopelessness; loss of hope can close down opportunities. What affects one affects the other. Practitioners who maintain their sense of hope are better able to envision possibilities for change and create opportunities in their interactions with others. See Table 1.1 for several important elements of hope.

CLINICAL VIGNETTE

A former patient of Dr. Milton Erickson had an aunt living in Milwaukee who had become quite seriously depressed and perhaps suicidal. The man spoke with the psychiatrist and asked if he would stop in and see her when he came to the area to give a lecture. Dr. Erickson agreed.

The woman, who had inherited a fortune from her family, was secure financially. She lived alone in a mansion, had never married, and had lost most of her close friends and relatives. Now in her 60s, she had developed some medical problems that required her to use a wheelchair. This had significantly altered her social activities.

Dr. Erickson arrived at the woman's house following his lecture. She was expecting him as her nephew had told her that he was coming. Upon his arrival, the two met and she began to give him a tour of her home. Although the woman had had some changes made to her home to make it more wheelchair accessible, it appeared to be largely unchanged from its original 1890s structure and décor. The house showed faded glory and the scent of musk. Dr. Erickson was struck by the fact that the curtains were drawn, contributing to an overall feeling of darkness. It was as if the majestic old home was a place of depression instead of happiness.

But the woman saved the best part of the tour for last. She finished by showing Dr. Erickson her pride and joy—a greenhouse nursery that was attached to the house. It was in this greenhouse that the woman had spent many tireless, happy hours working with her plants. As the two admired the flowers and plants, she showed Dr. Erickson her most recent project, which was to take clippings of African violet plants and grow new plants from them.

Following the tour, the two continued to speak. Dr. Erickson learned from the woman that although she was isolated, at one time she had been quite active in her local church. But since she began using a wheelchair, she attended only Sunday services. The woman described how she had hired her handyman to take her to and from church and because the church was not wheelchair accessible, he would lift her in and out of the building. Worried about blocking foot traffic, the woman told Dr. Erickson that she would arrive late and leave early.

After hearing the woman's story, Dr. Erickson told her that her nephew was worried about how depressed she had become. She admitted that the situation had become quite serious. But Dr. Erickson told the woman that he did not think that depression was the problem. Instead, what had become clear to him was that she had not been being a very good Christian. The woman was immediately taken aback by this comment, aghast that he would say such a thing.

Dr. Erickson continued, "Here you are with all this money, time on your hands, and a green thumb. And it's all going to waste. What I recommend is that you get a copy of the church directory and then look in the latest church bulletin. You'll find announcements of births, deaths, graduations, engagements, and marriages in there—all the happy and sad events in the lives of people in your congregation. Make a number of African violet cuttings and get them well-established. Then repot them into gift pots and have your handyman drive you to the homes of people who are affected by these happy or sad events. Bring them a plant and your congratulations or condolences and comfort, whichever is appropriate to the situation." After hearing Dr. Erickson's recommendation, she agreed that perhaps she had fallen down on her Christian duty and agreed to do more.

About 10 years later an article appeared in a local Milwaukee newspaper. It was a feature story with a headline that read, "African Violet Queen of Milwaukee Dies, Mourned by Thousands." The article detailed the life of this incredibly caring woman who had become famous for her trademark flowers and her charitable work with people in the community.

When Dr. Erickson was asked why he had chosen to focus on the African violet plants as opposed to the depression, he replied, "As I walked through the house the only sign of life I saw was the African violet plants and the nursery. I thought it would be much easier to grow the African violet part of her life than to weed out the depression."

Table 1.1

H.O.P.E.: An Acronym for Change

Humanism relates to the importance of the human condition, relationships, and connection. It is important that people experience competency, feel good about themselves, and have strong relationships that connect them to other individuals and communities at large. Virtually every story of someone who overcomes an obstacle or achieves positive change involves at least one supportive individual who was instrumental in helping the person to succeed.

Optimism reflects the true essence of hope. Optimism helps people to persevere through adversity, face challenges, and recognize that change is possible in even the most difficult of situations. Although optimism and the hope that accompanies it are essential to change, being optimistic does not mean being "positive." Optimism must be paired with *possibilities*—which include specific ideas and ways to identify solutions and solve problems.

Possibilities relate to the myriad of ways that people change. It involves searching for new ways to view situations, take action, or change interactions and relationships to find solutions to problems. People who are struggling and perhaps suffering and in pain need practical, commonsense ideas and methods that open up possibilities for change and ultimately produce results.

Expectancy is core to hope and change. One of the primary reasons people try new ideas and methods is that the latter offer some glimmer of hope, however small, that positive change might result. Therefore, the expectation that change can occur precedes any attempts to bring about change. People who expect positive change are more likely to notice it when it occurs.

Creation of a Culture of Care and Respect

Albert Einstein once said, "It has become appallingly clear that our technology has surpassed our humanity." A strengths-based philosophy emphasizes the human element of human services and helping relationships, forming a culture of care and respect (CCR) (Bertolino, 2003). A CCR represents both experiential and physical climates in which safe, secure, nurturing contexts are created through helping relationships. Such climates help clients to learn, grow, and develop at each level of services—prevention through treatment—through the lifespan.

A CCR also serves as an atmosphere in which practitioners can expand their individual potentials as a means to grow and evolve. The growth and evolution occur through seeing what is possible as opposed to what is not. CCR is both a personal *and* professional philosophy and a way of "being." To see possibilities, we must live them. Although context will dictate different responsibility and action, we are the same people whether in grocery stores, at our homes, or at our respective jobs.

This chapter has explored various factors that affect helping relationships, the role of philosophy in such relationships, and what it means to be strengths based. The next chapter undertakes an in-depth investigation of the research influences and core foundational principles of SBE.

SUMMARY POINTS

- Strengths-based engagement (SBE) is a philosophical stance that emphasizes a way of being in relationship to and interacting with others, influencing how we think about change and change-effecting processes.
- Therapists consider various overarching micro- and macrofactors. Microfactors relate to therapists' personal philosophies or worldviews. Macrofactors are those that can significantly shape practice and impact services.
  - *The general efficacy of psychotherapy* indicates that psycholtherapy has been determined to be efficacious in facilitating the remission of symptoms and in improving functioning. Results in family and couples therapy have been consistent with these findings.
  - Regardless of the *professional discipline,* the most common point of intersection between professional helping disciplines is therapy. Despite differences in therapists' education and training, no discernable differences in effectiveness of one discipline versus another exist.
  - *Competency and effectiveness* refer to the fact that it is important that therapists not only are competent, as demonstrated through skills and knowledge, but also show interest in and monitor their effectiveness.
  - *The scientist-practitioner* macrofactor posits that therapists assume the posture of researchers who use empirical means to support, give direction to, and study their clinical work *and* of practitioners who provide direct services to improve the lives of others.
  - *The reflective practitioner* indicates that therapists develop their awareness through self-reflection and continue to evolve by considering how they are both influenced by and influence the world around them.
  - *Therapist effects* refer to the fact that therapists contribute significantly to therapeutic outcome. Although therapist variables such as gender, race, and culture have been shown to have little or no correlation with their effectiveness, it is clear that some therapists are more effective than others.
  - The term *practice and setting* suggests that numerous variables related to practice settings can affect how therapists provide services. Therapists prepare for their roles in such environments by investigat-

ing potential influences prior to accepting new roles and maintain flexibility and adjust as changes occur on the job.

- Numerous microfactors (for example, culture, education, environment, religion/ spirituality) influence one's philosophy or worldview.
- Therapists' philosophies affect change; some close down or open up possibilities for change.
- A continuous reexamination of one's beliefs is necessary to identify and address potential blind spots and to grow both personally and professionally.
- A *strengths-based* perspective is not a theory but an overarching philosophical position in which people are seen as having capabilities and resources within themselves and their social systems.
- Strengths-based practitioners promote change through respectful educational, therapeutic, and operational processes that encourage and empower others.
- A strengths-based philosophy is characterized by *hope,* the increased presence of which can be a catalyst for change.
- A strengths-based philosophy is an essential part of a culture of care and respect (CCR), which represents both experiential and physical climates in which safe, secure, nurturing contexts are created through helping relationships.

DISCUSSION QUESTIONS

1. In what ways might the macrofactors discussed in this chapter impact your work as a therapist?

2. What questions might you ask a prospective employer to learn more about a practice setting during a job interview for a therapist position?

3. In what ways has your educational background prepared you to work as a therapist?

4. What kinds of knowledge do you believe competent therapists should have? Please provide rationale for your choices.

5. What are ways that you could monitor your effectiveness as a therapist?

6. How might you become a more reflective practitioner?

7. Given that the person of the therapist contributes significantly to the variance in outcome, what are the characteristics and qualities you possess that are strengths in increasing your effectiveness as a practitioner?

Chapter 2

An Ecology of Ideas

Foundations and Core Principles of Strengths-Based Engagement

■ With the efficacy of psychotherapy established, researchers have focused intently on this question: What makes therapy *effective?* Divergent agendas in research have been formulated in attempting to answer this and other questions addressing the issue of "what works." Although there are few definitive answers, conclusions, or "truths" are to be gleaned from the data, research has significantly expanded our knowledge about the conditions, factors, and processes that underscore successful therapy outcomes.

This chapter explores the various primary research agendas that contribute to the efficacy of therapy. Following this exploration is a discussion of the core principles that emerge from these agendas and form the foundation of SBE. These principles can be applied across a variety of contexts and offer possibilities for *how* therapists can create effective helping relationships and monitor that effectiveness throughout services.

The idea of tapping into and integrating ideas from different disciplines and realms of thought is a common one. In his landmark book, *Steps to an Ecology of Mind,* British Anthropologist Gregory Bateson (1972) discussed the necessity of assuming an ecological perspective in attempting to understand the world around:

> Such matters as the bilateral symmetry of an animal, the patterned arrangement of leaves in a plant, the escalation of an armaments race, the processes of courtship, the nature of play, the grammar of a sentence, the mystery of biological evolution, and the contemporary crisis of man's relationship to his environment can only be understood in terms of such an ecology of ideas (p. xv).

The incorporation of multiple perspectives has proven productive in a variety of fields including physical sciences, education, and health and is represented in a growing constellation of professional and popular literature. In *The Medici Effect,* Frans Johansson (2002) discussed how varying, independent perspectives and disciplines intersect leading to the resolution of problems—many of which are global. Although individual disciplines and theories within those disciplines maintain their integrity and usefulness as stand-alone approaches (i.e., an approach may provide a good fit for a particular person or situation in which there is a specific, well-defined concern), collectively each viewpoint contributes to an expanded perspective with potentially far greater benefits.

Multiple Perspectives and Ecology

Because multiple factors influence client concerns, therapists need to use an ecological perspective and draw on ideas from different influences and disciplines. This creates space for the coexistence of multiple perspectives and a broader scope for understanding the concerns and problems for which people come to therapy. An ecological perspective also encourages a more encompassing view of human beings and change processes, which provides therapists increased latitude in selecting practices aimed at maximizing individual, relational, and systemic change.

In psychotherapy, practitioners routinely draw on other disciplines such as anthropology, art, education, religion, and sociology. Merging multiple perspectives opens for both clients and clinicians a panorama of opportunities for understanding problems and exploring potential solutions. This is further evidenced within psychotherapy itself in which numerous explorations of various theoretical combinations have attempted to address the limitations of single perspectives. These efforts can be categorized into three forms of "hybrid" frameworks: *technical eclecticism, theoretical integration,* and *assimilative integration.* Next is a brief discussion of each.

Hybrid Responses: Eclecticism and Integration

According to *technical eclecticism,* the therapist relies on previous experience and knowledge of data about what has worked best for others in the past. Determining this through research helps the therapist to choose the best treatment for the person and the problem (Beutler, Consoli, & Lane, 2005; Lazarus, 2005; Norcross & Goldfried, 2005). Lazarus (1992) states, "The technical eclectic uses procedures drawn from different sources without necessarily subscribing to the theories or disciplines that spawned them" (p. 323). By virtue of avoiding alignment with any one theoretical perspective, technical eclecticism stands in stark contrast to models, which adhere strictly to the theoretical principles underlying the models.

Theoretical integration, sometimes referred to as *theoretical synthesis,* involves merging two or more theoretical perspectives into a designed framework that will be better than each constituent therapy alone (Norcross & Goldfried, 2005). This is the most difficult level at which to achieve integration because it requires combining theoretical concepts from various approaches, which may differ in their fundamental philosophy about human behavior. It has been suggested that proponents of theoretical integration are interested in creating a single, grand, unified "metatheory" (Allen, 2007). In fact, however, they seek ways to combine theories to generate new hypotheses distinct from the individual theories that were integrated in the first place (Arkowitz, 1992). This search for new hypotheses has lead to the development of numerous integrative frameworks (Breunlin, Schwartz, & Mac Kune-Karrer, 1992; Norcross & Goldfried, 2005; Pinsoff, 1995, 2005; Prochaska & DiClemente, 2005; Sexton, Ridley, & Kleiner, 2004; Stricker & Gold, 1993). Specific examples of theoretical integration include *cyclical psychodynamics* which integrates psychodynamic, behavioral, and systemic theories (Wachtel, Kruk, & McKinney, 2005) and *cognitive analytic therapy* in which object relations and cognitive therapies are combined (Ryle, 2005).

Assimilative integration, the third type of hybrid framework, offers a way to bridge technical eclecticism and theoretical integration. The therapist using assimilative integration has a commitment to one theoretical model but is willing to use techniques from other therapeutic approaches (Messer, 1992). Assimilative integration has become increasingly popular among practitioners who maintain strong theoretical ties yet seek innovative techniques that enhance those theoretical frameworks.

Hybrid frameworks offer flexible alternatives to individual models but have not escaped criticism. Technical eclecticism has been challenged for lacking a sound theoretical foundation and relying primarily on the success of its techniques. Theoretical integration has been criticized regarding continuity. With nearly 500 models available and hundreds of potential combinations, an infinite number of new integrative approaches could be developed (Lambert, 2004). Finally, proponents of assimilative integration have been challenged on the grounds that too much emphasis on or variance in technique detracts from and/or changes the models from which they originate. Criticisms aside, hybrid frameworks offer therapists flexible, broader alternatives to pure models while maintaining a focus on improving effectiveness.

Beyond Integration

Because clients and their concerns can vary significantly, integration, both at macro- (i.e., employing ideas from disciplines outside psychotherapy) and micro- (i.e., combining specific theories and methods within psychotherapy) levels, provides therapists greater degrees of flexibility in meeting clients' needs. The attraction of practitioners to integrative and eclectic approaches is evident. A study of 423 clinical psychologists, marriage and family therapists, social workers, and psychiatrists by Jensen, Bergin, and Greaves (1990) found that 68% identified themselves as eclectics. Other studies have shown that one-quarter to one-half of mental health professionals claim to be either eclectic or integrative and to use a "mixture" of techniques in an effort to do "whatever works" (Bechtoldt et al., 2001; Norcross, Karpiak, & Lister, 2005).

Although providing increased flexibility, attempts at integration have suffered from problems similar to those of individual approaches. One problem is that many integrative models simply have not been researched sufficiently. Another problem, as you will learn, is that with few exceptions, comparative analyses (i.e., studies involving the pairing of one model against another) have failed to consistently demonstrate differential efficacy—the superiority of one approach over another. This corresponds to a third dilemma regarding integration in therapy. Despite the presence of several well-formulated agendas, empirical support has predominantly come from one form of research—model-based research. The lack of effort to acknowledge and incorporate findings from other directions in research has proven perplexing because the major agendas in research most frequently interpret *the same studies and the same body of research* (Beutler & Castonguay, 2006). Because the major "platforms" have operated primarily in isolation and often at odds with one another, ascertaining what research as a whole demonstrates regarding the impact of psychotherapy has been difficult.

To address this issue, it is necessary to move beyond the macro- and microlevels of integration to identify elements that are consistently correlated with successful outcomes and common across research agendas. Identifying these elements provides further rationale and credibility to the efficacy of psychotherapy. The next section begins an exploration of these research agendas by identifying what they reveal about effective therapy and how the findings from this exploration form the foundation of SBE.

Primary Agendas in Research

Various attempts have been made to understand the effects and impact of psychotherapy both as a general approach and in regard to specific models. The four primary research agendas discussed here include *empirically supported treatments* (ESTs), *common factors* (CF), *empirically supported relationships* (ESRs), and *outcomes management* (OM). Each agenda represents an effort to further legitimize the field of psychotherapy by recommending directions for practice and standards of care. Although each agenda has its own shortcomings and strengths, it is important to note that the first two agendas discussed in this section—ESTs and CF—are more well formulated than the other two. Nonetheless, ESRs and OM make significant contributions and are included because of their importance and relevance to SBE.

Agenda 1: Empirically Supported Treatments and Evidenced-Based Practices (Model-Based Research)

As a means to advance understanding and the viability of talk therapies, researchers have addressed the question first posed by Paul in 1967: "What treatment, by whom, is most effective for this individual with that specific problem, under which set of circumstances" (p. 111). This question spawned concentrated movements to identify models that when practiced competently and consistently produce results that are reliably superior to others. With numerous models fitting the criteria for more than one classification, these general movements have included ESTs [formerly *empirically validated treatments* (EVTs)] (Chambless, 1996; Chambless & Holon, 1998; Christophersen & Mortweet, 2001; TFPP, 1995), EBPs (Drake, Merrens, & Lynde, 2005; Fisher & O'Donohue, 2006; Freeman & Power, 2007; Kazdin, 2000; Kazdin & Weisz, 2003; Norcross, Beutler, & Levant, 2005; Weisz, 2004), and *what works/treatments that work* (Carr, 2001; Fonagy et al., 2002; Goodheart, Kazdin, & Sternberg, 2006; Nathan & Gorman, 2007; Roth & Fonagy, 2004).

It is noteworthy that criteria for the various movements of model-based research are both similar and different. More often commentaries have referred to these movements synonymously, whereas others have aimed at making distinctions, particularly between ESTs and EBPs (Westen, Novotny, & Thompson-Brenner, 2005). The discussion here emphasizes the shared theme of identifying treatment methodologies for which there is scientifically collected evidence that treatments work. Although the terms EST and EBP will both be referred to, EST will be the primary term used given its historical legacy.

Several significant efforts within the first agenda have been made. The first effort was the Task Force on Promotion and Dissemination of Psychological Procedures (TFPP, 1995), a report adopted by Division 12 of the American Psychological Association (APA). The Task Force on Promotion and Dissemination of Psychological Procedures (TFPP) was created to verify the use of specific treatment approaches for specific mental health disorders by using stringent, clinically based, empirical studies. The TFPP was to "consider methods for educating clinical psychologists, third-party payers, and the public about effective psychotherapies" (p. 3). The TFPP was designed to identify superior treatment approaches primarily for adults and was later reformulated as the Committee on Science and Practice to continue the effort of establishing a list of empirically supported treatments and standards of practice.

A second but less known effort to identify efficacious treatments also contributed to the growing body of research concerning psychotherapy models. According to Nathan and Gorman (2007), the purpose of this effort was to determine what treatments had been scientifically validated, what treatments a large number of experts believed to be valuable but have not been properly scientifically examined, and what treatments were known to be of little value. Consistent with the APA research, this effort also focused primarily on disorders of adulthood.

Mental Disorders and Model-Based Research

Most frequently based on randomized clinical trials (RCT), model-based research involves pairing treatment modalities with "disorders" or clusters of problems defined by preestablished criteria. Proponents of this research, Chambless and Hollon (1998), stated, "We do not ask whether a treatment is efficacious: rather, we ask whether it is efficacious for a specific problem" (p. 9). "Problems" are most commonly considered some form of mental disorder. In evidence-based research, the *Diagnostic and Statistical Manual for Mental Disorders,* fourth edition (*DSM-IV-TR*) (American Psychiatric Association, 2000) is the standard nosology for assigning disorders although other forms of identifying and categorizing pathology and dysfunction have also been employed (Chambless & Holon, 1998; DeRubeis & Crits-Christoph, 1998).

Through model-based research it has been hypothesized that once identified, efficacious treatment models can be used in a prescriptive manner that can be replicated. Services can then be delivered in structured, manualized ways, which would theoretically lead to better and more consistent outcomes. Central to this philosophy is the notion that methods and models are what make therapy "work."

The No-Treatment Alternative or Placebo Condition

Model-driven research is based on the medical model of pairing treatment approaches with specific diagnoses or clinical problems. To be deemed "empirically supported," a model must be tested in two separate, independent studies (most commonly RCTs) and outperform a no-treatment alternative or placebo condition. This research is important because it establishes a context in which to test models under stringent conditions. It also provides empirical rationale for understanding the available psychotherapeutic options given a particular problem or disorder.

Conversely, the results of single studies and RCTs in particular are often easily refuted. Just about any treatment, although not statistically significant, may be better than no treatment. Demonstrating efficacy over a placebo condition is not the same as demonstrating efficacy over other treatment approaches. It says little about an approach except that it is better than the status quo. Therefore, a minimal level of empirical data could lend efficacy and validation to a model.

The medical model as a standard for psychological research continues to be challenged on many levels. Perhaps most compelling, however, is the distinct lack of evidence produced by model-based research. Referring back to the question asked by Paul (1967) about the best treatment for whom with a specific problem under a set of circumstances, Wampold (2001) stated that in the last 30 years "not one interaction theoretically derived from hypothesized client deficits has been documented robustly, casting doubt on the specificity of psychological treatments" (p. 147). Those who disagree with Wampold's assertion maintain that some models—mainly those that are cognitively and behaviorally oriented—are more effective than others. This argument is viable given that the majority of treatments researched represent cognitive and behaviorally oriented therapies. These are also approaches most likely to be practiced in settings that support research endeavors and are able to secure funding, thus revealing the influence of political and economic factors.

Although attempts have been made to monitor factors and variables that affect validity and reliability in model-based research, other issues remain. One such issue is diagnosis. Accurate diagnosis is critical for inclusion in studies. Mental health professionals with expertise in diagnostic procedures, however, can disagree, be inconsistent, and misdiagnose patients. It is not uncommon for clinicians to diagnose the same clients differently. This is complicated by the complexity of problems experienced by clients. Diagnosis rarely, if ever, captures the essence of clients' struggles. Few situations pertaining to human beings can be reduced to single explanations.

Diagnoses also clearly change with the times and tend to reflect political and economic factors and societal tolerances (Beutler & Clarkin, 1990). Examples of such diagnoses relate to homosexuality, which was once considered a mental disease, and post-traumatic stress disorder (PTSD), which was not included in the *DSM* until its third edition. More evidence of changes in diagnosis is the fact that between the first and fourth editions of the *DSM,* the number of diagnoses for mental disorders increased by 300% (Houts, 2002). Although alternative nosologies such as the *dimensional model* (i.e., recognition that mental disorders lie on a continuum with a client's situation identified in terms of his or her positions on specific dimensions of cognitive or affective capacity rather than placed in a categorical boxes), particularly for the diagnosis of personality disorders (Tackett et al., 2008; Widiger & Trull, 2007), have been suggested, these movements remain in developmental stages and face considerable criticism (Garb, 2008).

Another concern about model-based research relates to efficacy versus effectiveness studies. *Efficacy studies* are laboratory-based experimental trials conducted in research settings. In these settings, controlling variables that may affect outcome is feasible. *Effectiveness studies* test the impact of treatment or services in naturalistic or "real-life" clinical settings.

Of question is the generalization and transferability of results from studies conducted in research settings to community-based settings. In relation to psychotherapy treatments with children, adolescents, and families, researcher Alan Kazdin (2000) stated:

> There is little or no evidence that these treatments work in clinical settings. That is, an empirically supported treatment, when applied to clinically referred children and families, as administered by clinicians in practice and under conditions where treatment delivery is not so well monitored, has unknown effects (pp. 85–86).

Even if transferring findings from efficacy to effectiveness settings were a simple process, few therapists work with clients in laboratory-based settings, nor do they use manualized procedures and protocols, which are staples of ESTs. More research is needed into those settings for which services are provided on an everyday basis. Lambert (2004) offered the following advice:

> The dissemination or transportability of efficacious treatments may be one of the most fertile areas of study for the next decade. With diminishing resources and increasing accountability, those who fund the delivery of mental health services are clamoring for "best practices" and empirically supported interventions. The ability of researchers and evaluators to demonstrate that laboratory treatments also work in the real world will eventually lead to a better understanding of the effects of therapy as it is typically offered (p. 160).

Comparative Analyses

Head-to-head comparison of models provides inconclusive results. With few exceptions (for example, small differences in cognitive and behavioral therapies have been found), the vast majority of differences between models used in comparative studies are relatively small or nonexistent (Elkin, Shea, & Watkins, 1989; Lambert, 2004; Shadish et al., 1995; Smith, Glass, & Miller, 1980; Wampold, 2001). Forty years of outcome research has demonstrated that although most models effect change, no one approach is significantly and consistently more effective than another (Lambert, 1992, 2004; Lambert & Bergin, 1994; Lambert, Shapiro, & Bergin, 1986; Luborksy, Singer, & Luborsky, 1975; Project MATCH Research Group, 1997; Shadish et al., 1995; Smith, Glass, & Miller, 1980).

Differences between approaches, including those found in studies with cognitive and behavior therapies, are generally no more than is to be expected by chance (Wampold, 2001) and result from methodological factors such as more reactive criteria, therapists effects, or the allegiance effect (Lambert & Ogles, 2004; Luborsky et al., 1999). The *allegiance effect* factors in the influence of the researcher's allegiance to a particular model within a study. The more researchers believe in, practice, and support particular models, the greater the likelihood that those models will show favorable results in studies involving those models (Wampold, 2001). The allegiance effect is worthy of attention given the process undertaken to determine models chosen for study and how those studies are then conducted. Although a complex issue, the allegiance effect could occur if the researcher were a proponent of one of the treatments administered in a study. Indirectly, mental health professionals are subject to the influence of entities or organizations with allegiances or ties to particular treatment approaches. These could be in the form of, for example, funding sources, third-party payers, or political associations.

Although research on marital and family therapy is in its infancy, Shadish et al. (1995)

stated that based on the most comprehensive meta-analysis to date, "Despite some superficial evidence apparently favoring some orientations over others, no orientation is yet demonstrably superior to any other. This finding parallels the psychotherapy literature generally" (p. 348). *Meta-analysis* is an efficient and objective process of pooling or clustering various studies that meet predefined inclusion criteria. Several studies have demonstrated the benefits of certain treatment models with adolescents with specific disorders; however, these studies are subject to the same issues described previously, suggesting that any conclusions be made on a cautionary basis. Therefore, available empirical data do not support overall claims of differential efficacy with family therapy models.

Findings from comparative analyses in both psychotherapy and family therapy have evoked eerie references to the "Dodo Bird Verdict" from *Alice in Wonderland*: "Everybody has won and all must have prizes" (Duncan, Miller, & Sparks, 2004; Luborsky, Singer, & Luborsky, 1975; Rosenzweig, 1936). The implication is that all approaches work, an extreme point of view given that research findings have not demonstrated that *all* models are equal, effective, and valid (Shadish & Baldwin, 2002; Wampold, 2001). The assertion suggesting that everything works and anything will do is also potentially harmful. This assertion delegitimizes the profession as a whole and puts well-researched and supported models on the same level as palm reading, tarot cards, and Ouija boards (Sprenkle & Blow, 2004).

Key figures in psychology and psychotherapy including Sigmund Freud, Aaron Beck, B. F. Skinner, Joseph Wolpe, and Carl Rogers believed that different forms of psychotherapy could be effective. That some approaches provide a better therapeutic fit for some clients, under some circumstances, and therefore yield meaningful outcomes is a reasonable assumption (Sprenkle & Blow, 2004). It is equally reasonable that some therapies may have potentially harmful side effects. Although the Food and Drug Administration monitors the potential negative effects of psychotropic medications, psychological and relational therapies have no equivalent governing body. Furthermore, professional literature includes little discussion of the topic, leading to suggestions that the field of mental health, and psychology in particular, has been reluctant to police itself (Lilienfeld, 2007; Meehl, 1993).

In response to this and in accordance with a well-accepted tenet of the major ethical codes within helping professions, "first, do no harm," Lilienfeld (2007) has suggested that *potentially harmful therapies* (PHTs) be identified, listed, and disseminated. PHTs have met the following conjunctive criteria:

1. They have demonstrated harmful psychological or physical effects in clients or others (for example, relatives).

2. The harmful effects are enduring and do not merely reflect a short-term exacerbation of symptoms during treatment.

3. The harmful effects have been replicated by independent investigative teams. (p. 57)

Although this is an endeavor that would require answering questions about identification, the strength of evidence concerning such approaches, therapist and client variables, context, and so on, doing so would place impetus on exploring the notion that at worst therapy is innocuous (Lilienfeld, Lynn, & Lohr, 2003). This, according to Lilienfeld (2007), would help well-intentioned therapists "to avoid procedures that place clients at undue risk of deterioration" and clients to make more informed decisions regarding therapies with known negative side effects (p. 54). This would also address what has been referred to as *iatrogenic injury* or therapist-induced injury which refers to methods, techniques, assessment procedures, explanations, or interventions that harm, discourage, invalidate, show disrespect, or close down the possibilities for change (Bertolino & O'Hanlon, 2002). The identification of PHTs could provide valuable insight into mechanisms or mediators that may underlie client deterioration including regression, slow improvement, and premature dropout.

Agenda 2: Common Factors

The second agenda regarding common factors is based primarily on meta-analytic studies, not RCTs. These studies are then evaluated statistically to identify quantitative relationships between study features and results obtained. Meta-analysis has been used to explore the effects of specific treatment approaches on diagnoses such as depression and anxiety (see Lambert, 2004) and in a broader sense to determine the general benefits of psychotherapy regardless of the model employed (Lambert, 1992; Smith & Glass, 1977; Smith, Glass, & Miller, 1980; Wampold, 2001). Arguments against using a meta-analysis focus on its mix of dissimilar studies, publication bias, and inclusion of poor quality studies (Sharpe, 1997). Steps have been taken in recent years to address these concerns.

Although criticized by some, the findings of meta-analytic studies have been intriguing. Arguably, the most compelling finding is the hypothesis that successful therapeutic outcome is more contingent on *general effects*[1] or "common factors" than on methods, models, or what researchers refer to as *specific effects* or *ingredients*. *General effects* is a term used to refer to the benefits produced by nontheory-specific aspects (i.e, those that are not unique to any one model or approach). Rather, these effects are common among effective modalities and account for a significant portion of positive change (Hubble, Duncan, & Miller, 1999; Lambert, 1992; Wampold, 2001). *Specific effects* or *ingredients* refer to the benefits of specific actions (for example, techniques, methods, models) considered necessary for the success of treatment (Wampold, 2001). In other words, when positive change occurs, the majority of that change can be traced to general or nontheory-based effects as opposed to specific treatment models.

Saul Rosenzweig hypothesized the idea of commonalities among treatment approaches as early as 1936. He suggested that although diverse methods of psychotherapy could look different, they had the same effective factors. Jerome Frank (1973; Frank & Frank, 1991) was one of the first to describe components shared by all models of psychotherapy. This notion was explored further by Michael Lambert (1992), who identified four specific factors affecting outcome. Lambert originally estimated that the major contributors to outcome, in order of their significance, were *extratherapeutic change (client factors), therapeutic relationship, expectancy (placebo effects),* and *techniques.* The four common factors have since been examined in-depth and have gone through some revisions since first being hypothesized.

Client Factors

Client factors represent the resources that individuals bring to therapy, including their internal strengths, abilities, resources, and social

---

[1]The terms *common factors, general effects,* and *incidental aspects* will be used interchangeably to refer to nontheory-based contributions to psychotherapy outcome.

support systems as well as faith, family relationships, and membership in a community or religious sect. These factors account for the most significant portion of improvement that occurs in any form of psychotherapy. Lambert (1992) estimated that client factors account for up to 40% of the variance in the outcome of therapy. Other research indicates that the client is the single most potent contributor to outcome in therapy (Tallman & Bohart, 1999).

Client factors also include external influences such as spontaneous, chance events outside of therapy during it but typically have little or no correlation with the treatment itself. Other essential client factors include resilience and protective factors and having a change focus. *Resilience* and *protective factors* refer to those qualities and actions on the part of clients that allow them to meet and survive the difficulties and challenges of life.

Therapeutic Relationship Factors

The therapeutic relationship between the client and the professional is a central factor in successful therapy. It has been estimated that as much as 30% of the variance in treatment outcome can be attributed to relationships factors (Lambert, 1992). Perhaps the two most significant aspects of this factor are the quality of clients' participation and the degree to which they are motivated, engaged, and join in the therapeutic work (Orlinsky, Grawe, & Parks, 1994; Prochaska, DiClemente, & Norcross, 1992).

Clients who are engaged and connected with therapists may benefit most from therapy. However, the strength of the therapeutic bond is not highly correlated with the length of treatment or number of sessions (Horvath & Luborsky, 1993). In other words, the formulation of an instant bond between the therapist and client is commonplace. Most critical here

are clients' perceptions of the therapeutic relationship. In fact, client ratings of therapists as empathic, trustworthy, and nonjudgmental are better predictors of positive therapy outcome than are ratings of the therapist, diagnosis, approach, or any other variable (Horvath & Symonds, 1991; Lambert & Bergin, 1994).

The therapeutic relationship has been expanded to a broad concept known as the *therapeutic "alliance,"* a term that emphasizes collaborative partnership between clients and therapists (Horvath, 2001; Horvath & Bedi, 2002). Therapists can promote the therapeutic alliance by accommodating treatment to the client's motivational level, view of the therapeutic relationship, goals and preferred outcomes for therapy, and tasks to accomplish those goals and outcomes.

Expectancy Factors and Placebo Condition

Expectancy factors and placebo condition relate to the portion of improvement derived from clients' knowledge of being helped, having hope instilled, and possessing pretreatment expectancy as well as their recognition of therapist confidence, enthusiasm, and use of credible methods and techniques. *Expectancy* includes clients' expectations upon beginning therapy. Commonly referred to as *pretreatment expectancy,* the term refers to clients' faith and beliefs that therapy can help them with their concerns and problems (Mueller & Pekarik, 2000; Safren, Heimberg, & Juster 1997; Schneider & Klauer, 2001). Expectancy also includes the belief of both the client and therapist in the restorative power of the treatment, including its procedures. Simply expecting therapy to help can serve as a placebo and counteract demoralization, activate hope, and advance improvement (Frank & Frank, 1991).

Significant is the expectation of change and hope that accompanies processes and procedures, not the methods and techniques themselves. Lambert (1992; Asay & Lambert, 1999) initially estimated that expectancy and placebo in therapy contributed approximately 15% of the variance in therapeutic outcome. Because Lambert's original estimate was based on a narrow definition (in other words, primarily on the client's knowledge of being treated and the credibility of the treatment approach), this category of factors may account for a significantly higher portion of the variance in outcomes.

Model and Technique Factors

All therapeutic models involve the use of techniques and procedures. For example, behaviorists use methods associated with conditioning, Freudian analysts use analysis of transference, structural family therapists use enactment, solution-focused therapists use the miracle question, and narrative therapists use externalization. Techniques and procedures include but are not limited to asking particular questions, using specific interventions, assigning tasks, making interpretations, and teaching skills. Most techniques or procedures are designed to get clients to do something different such as experience emotions, face fears, change patterns of thinking or behavior, and develop new understandings or meanings.

Lambert (1992) suggested that model and technique contribute the same percentage to outcome variance as do expectancy and placebo factors—about 15%. More recently, others have determined that specific ingredients such as techniques contribute even less to therapeutic outcomes (Wampold, 2001). This is in part due to the fact that therapists are more interested than clients in techniques. When asked about what is helpful about therapy, clients rarely mention therapeutic interventions or techniques.

It is important to note that the percentages Lambert (1992) initially assigned to the variance in treatment outcomes of the four common factors were based on an interpretation of, not a statistical analysis of, 40 years of data. Nearly a decade later, psychologist Bruce Wampold (2001) completed a scientific evaluation and statistical analysis of the data. He found that Lambert had correctly interpreted that the significant portion of the variance in psychotherapeutic outcomes is due to general effects. Wampold found that ingredients such as model effects accounted for at most 8% of the variance and that only 1% of the overall variance could be assigned to specific technique. This leaves approximately 22% in variance unexplained. According to Wampold (2001), this variability is due in part to client differences:

> Whatever the source of the unexplained variance, it is clearly not related to specific ingredients. . . . Lest there be any ambiguity about the profound contrast between general and specific effects, it must be noted that the 1% of the variability in outcomes due to specific ingredients is likely a gross upper bound. Clearly, the preponderance of the benefits of psychotherapy are due to factors incidental to the particular theoretical approach administered and dwarf the effects due to theoretically derived techniques (pp. 207–209).

Wampold's (2001) findings suggest that nontheory-based elements, which contribute 70–92% (or more) of the outcome variance, are by far the most significant contributors to therapeutic outcome. Despite an emphasis on specific ingredients associated with various psychotherapeutic perspectives, the preponderance of empirical evidence indicates that these ingredients account for little of the variance in outcomes (Lambert, 1994; Wampold, 2001).

Research has not found any one model, method, or package of techniques to be reliably superior (Elkin, 1994; Lambert, 1992, 2004; Lambert & Bergin, 1994; Lambert, Shapiro, & Bergin, 1986; Project MATCH Research Group, 1997; Smith, Glass, & Miller, 1980; Wampold, 2001; Wampold, et al., 1997). This fact raises important questions about hypotheses and suggests that models are the "sparkplugs" of change. Miller, Duncan, and Hubble (1997) stated:

> The evidence makes it clear that **similarities** rather than **differences** between therapy models account for most of the change that clients experience in treatment. What emerges from examining these similarities is a group of common factors that can be brought together to form a more **unifying language for psychotherapy practice**: a language that contrasts sharply with the current emphasis on difference characterizing most professional discussion and activity (p. 15).

The common factors hypothesis has been criticized for being vague, theoryless, and difficult to articulate. Critics have also noted that the common factors position offers little direction in terms of determining which approaches are best for whom and under what conditions. As previously mentioned, a few studies have demonstrated that some approaches may be more indicated with certain conditions than others (Castonguay & Beutler, 2006a). Perhaps common ground can be found in the notion that effective models are carriers of common factors. That is, models are the vehicles through which common factors operate. Models and methods merely offer different and sometimes unique ways to activate the common factors and that the effectiveness of such models and methods is contingent on how well they fit with clients.

Agenda 3: Empirically Supported Relationships

In response to growing evidence regarding the influence of the therapeutic relationship and shortcomings identified with research on ESTs, the APA created an additional task force, the Division of Psychotherapy (Division 29). This task force was formed to identify elements of effective therapy relationships that affect treatment outcomes and to determine efficacious methods of customizing therapy to individuals on the basis of their personal characteristics (Norcross, 2002). This meant including client and therapist factors and variables that influence relationships and affect change (Beutler & Castonguay, 2006).

Division 29 clearly delineated between its efforts and those of Division 12 (Norcross, 2002). In addition to shifting from focusing on treatments and technical interventions to researching elements of therapy relationships and client and therapist characteristics, Division 29 researchers examined different forms of methodological design. These forms included RCTs as well as naturalistic, process-outcome, and correlational studies. In its conclusions and findings, the Division 29 Steering Committee (Steering Committee, 2001) stated:

> The therapy relationship makes substantial and consistent contributions to psychotherapy outcome independent of the specific type of treatment. . . . Efforts to promulgate practice guidelines or evidence-based lists of effective psychotherapy without including the therapy relationship are seriously incomplete and potentially misleading on both clinical and empirical grounds (p. 495).

Based on its findings, the task force set forth a series of conclusions and recommendations for practice, training, research, and policy (Steering Committee, 2001). Central to these recommendations was that practitioners should adapt therapy relationships to specific client characteristics and routinely monitor clients' responses to therapy and ongoing treatment. The steering committee also proposed that "training programs in psychotherapy are encouraged to provide explicit and competency-based training in the effective elements of the therapy relationship" (p. 496). A decade prior to Division 29 and Norcross's pioneering efforts, Lambert and Bergin (1992) stated, "Of all of the common factors investigated in psychotherapy, none has received more attention and conformation than the importance of the therapeutic relationship" (p. 371).

Criticisms of ESRs parallel those of the common factors agenda, which emphasize the importance of the therapeutic relationship as opposed to methods and technique. Proponents of ESRs argue that although the therapeutic relationship provides healing qualities, its contribution to change is relative to the client or patient and is a more complex issue. Castonguay and Beutler (2006b) remarked:

> Even for those who are convinced that the therapeutic relationship is healing by and of itself, there are strategies that can foster its impact. In other words, since not all kinds of relationships are likely to bring about change, one needs to be aware of interventions (including modes of relating) that should be encouraged or avoided for the relationship to become a corrective experience (p. 353).

Consistent with this point of view is that relationship factors for some clients will contribute more or less to the variance of change. Furthermore, relationships can be ruptured,

damaged, or strengthened through therapeutic processes. It is therefore essential that clinicians be adept at skills that enhance relationships and are responsive to ongoing changes in the therapeutic milieu.

Agenda 4: Outcomes Management

The final research agenda to be discussed is outcomes management, which has gained notoriety and is sometimes referred to as *patient* or *client based*. Operationalized through outcomes measurement, outcomes management involves monitoring the responses of those receiving services.

Distinguishing between outcomes measurement and outcomes management is important. According to Brown et al. (2001), "Outcomes measurement involves assessing clinical outcome of treatment though the use of standardized measures of clinical severity" (p. 925). This is done by calculating change from at least two different data points, most often one at the beginning of treatment and another at some later time such as the conclusion or in follow-up. Outcomes management, however, is a more comprehensive system of monitoring and tracking data and of *using* that data to improve services. Brown et al. (2001) stated:

> Outcomes management is an effort to improve the effectiveness of treatment services throughout a health care system by evaluating outcomes data. The key performance indicator for an outcomes management program is its ability to make a difference over time—that is, to measurably improve outcomes. Although reliable and valid outcomes measurement is an essential element of an outcomes management program, if this approach is to be effective it must go well beyond simple storage and tabulation of data. (p. 925)

Outcome is generally measured according to alliance and outcome strategies. *Alliance (process) measures* track clients' ratings of the therapeutic relationship. *Outcome measures* track clients' ratings of the impact of services on major dimensions of life functioning. These dimensions include individual functioning (personal and symptomatic distress), interpersonal (close, intimate) relationships and well-being, and social role functioning (for example, satisfaction with work, school, and relationships outside of family).

Therapists use alliance and outcome measures on a consistent basis, often in every session or interaction. Information gleaned from ongoing, "built-in" feedback mechanisms is incorporated directly into sessions and shapes the approach that therapists utilize. Therefore, the approach employed in any given situation and frequently in single interactions is client driven and largely determined through real-time processes. This makes for "practice-based evidence," which increases the factor of fit between providers and clients and allows for greater malleability in service provision (Duncan, Miller, & Sparks, 2004). Practice-based evidence, then, involves the ongoing integration of information gathered through alliance and outcome measures into treatment.

Outcomes-Management Methods

Although outcomes management is a relatively new movement, its methods are being applied in numerous settings and have been shown to enhance treatment outcome (Lambert, 2004; Lambert et al., 2001; Lambert et al., 2002). For example, Lambert et al. (2003) conducted a meta-analysis of three studies involving a total of about 1,000 clients indicated that clients who were predicted to have a poor treatment outcome. Clients whose therapists had access to feedback showed less

deterioration (13%) than those in the non-feedback condition (21%). Furthermore, the baseline rates of reliable and clinically significant change (see Chapter 11) improved from 21% in the nonfeedback condition to 35% in the feedback condition. These findings support the value of feedback processes, which include monitoring client ratings of the therapeutic relationship and alliance as well as tracking improvement through outcomes. Perhaps even more compelling to practitioners is that these methods can be integrated into routine practice with little disruption, thus narrowing the gap between practice and research.

Criticisms of outcome management primarily emphasize the point that client ratings of relationships and improvement do not always accurately represent a change. Clients may try to please their therapists or report results that are skewed in order to benefit themselves in some way (for example, to end services early if mandated). This fact implies that a reliance on client feedback numbers can inadvertently lead to "false positives" or indicators of success. These false positives could result in premature termination of therapy, leaving more profound or deeper issues unaddressed. What becomes clear is that outcome management is just one aspect of a process that can lead to increased effectiveness.

Intersection and Convergence in Research

As psychotherapy research matures and continues to evolve, the evidence underscoring effective practice becomes more apparent. Although much will be learned in the future, what has already been learned about effective practice is substantial. This knowledge serves as a major vehicle for promoting change in the current context and needs to be more actively integrated into practice and training regimens devoted to helping individuals, couples, and families.

As you have learned, whether analyzed in comparison or in isolation, the four research agendas have both strengths and shortcomings. In studying the question of "what works" from a different angle, it is apparent that the four agendas share numerous and consistent points of intersection, revealing significant common ground and agreement about the underpinnings of successful practice. See Figure 2.1 for a visualization of the intersections of these research agendas. Table 2.1 is a list, although not an exhaustive one, of the general areas of intersection across the research agendas. This theme of the intersection of perspectives suggests that effective therapy is characterized by universal threads and principles that increase the likelihood of positive outcomes.

Effective Therapy and Universal Principles

The concept of unifying principles that inform practice is a growing one. For example, Castonguay and Beutler (2006b) suggest that a focus on empirically supported "principles of change" (ESPs) that encompass a variety of therapeutic factors is overdue. The researchers' position is clear: "We think that psychotherapy research has produced enough knowledge to begin to define the basic principles that govern therapeutic change in a way that is not tied to

Figure 2.1

Intersection of Research Agendas

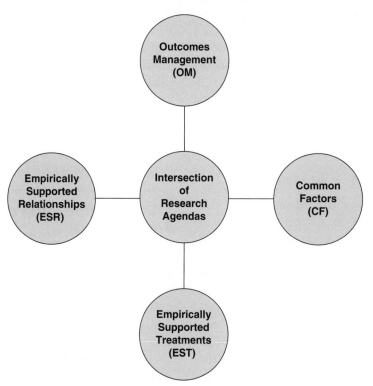

Table 2.1

Areas of Intersection in Primary Research Agendas

The major research agendas in psychology and family therapy—EST/EBP, CF, ESR, and OM—intersect to reveal common ground. Beyond their individual contributions are general points of convergence and consensus among these agendas. These include the importance of:

- viewing the client(s) as a primary factor in change (i.e., identifying and building on internal strengths and social support systems)

- therapeutic relationship and alliance (the strength of the alliance)

- empathy

- positive regard

- congruence/genuineness

- client-therapist match

- sensitivity to and respect for the unique cultural and contextual characteristics of each client

- creation of a respectful therapeutic climate in which clients are able to explore and express their personal stories or narratives and associated emotions

- inclusion of clients in therapy processes (i.e., preferences, goal setting, tasks.)

- selection and matching of therapy methods with clients according to factors such as preferences, level of need, state of readiness, level of distress/impairment, and coping style

- use of educational and developmental processes that increase social skills, coping skills, and self-regulation

- client-therapist feedback loops (i.e., the role of the therapist in monitoring the strength of the alliance and outcome or the subjective impact of therapy)

- attention to alliance ruptures

- therapist contributions to change (e.g., expectations, preferences, level of personal awareness, patience)

- structure/focus in sessions/interactions

- client expectations

- creation or rehabilitation of hope

- future focus

- therapist self-disclosure

any specific theory, treatment model, or narrowly defined set of concepts" (p. 5). This position is echoed by others who have recommended that common principles of practice that underscore effective services be outlined and disseminated (Duncan, Miller, & Sparks, 2004; Rosen & Davison, 2003; Wampold, 2001).

This recommendation reflects not just an acknowledgement of methods and models typically seen as competing with one another but also emphasizes points of crossover and commonality. The recommendation also draws attention to the integration of variables previously given little or no recognition for their influence in change processes. The APA espouses this perspective; in 2005, it established a task force on evidence-based practice in psychology (EBPP) (APA Presidential Task Force on Evidence-Based Practice, 2006). In response to criticisms of both ESTs and Division 12 and reflecting a broadening perspective, the task force defined EBPP as "the integration of the best available research with clinical expertise in the context of patient characteristics, culture, and preferences" (p. 273). Wampold, Goodheart, and Levant (2007) further commented on this progression, stating that EBPP "is a general framework that subsumes various forms of evidence drawn from various data sources for particular purposes" (p. 617).

This more recent definition of EBPP represents the broadest characterization to date of what constitutes evidence-based practice, closely resembling the definition of EBP adopted by the Institute of Medicine, which states: "Evidence-based practice is the integration of best research evidence with clinical expertise and patient values" (Sackett, et al., 2000). It acknowledges previous factors, including client characteristics and variables that have been noticeably absent in past definitions while underscoring the importance of convergence among adjoining disciplines. Physician Jerome Groopman echoed this more liberal depiction. In his book, *How Doctors Think* (2007), he both acknowledged and challenged the role of EBPs:

A movement is afoot to base all treatment decisions strictly on statistically proven data. This so-called evidence-based medicine is rapidly becoming the canon in many hospitals. Treatments outside the statistically proven are considered taboo until a sufficient body of data can be generated from clinical trials. Of course, every doctor should consider research studies in choosing a therapy. But today's rigid reliance on evidence-based medicine risks having the doctor choose care passively, solely by the numbers. Statistics cannot substitute for the human being before you; statistics embody averages, not individuals. Numbers can only complement a physician's personal experience with a drug or a procedure, as well as his knowledge of whether a "best" therapy from a clinical trail fits a patient's particular needs and values. (pp. 5–6)

While criticisms remain (Stuart & Lilienfeld, 2007), there are indications that the gap between the four research agendas outlined in this chapter is closing. For example, whereas RCTs were at one time considered *the* standard in psychological research, support is growing for other forms of research that reflect a multiplicity of viewpoints and methodologies. Another indication of this support is a strong movement toward the recognition of outcomes management as an EBP. These examples represent the emergence of a more comprehensive metaview of therapy specifically and helping relationships in general.

A series of common principles of change that form the foundation of SBE underscores this metaview. These principles are general statements regarding client characteristics, relational factors, therapist variables, and other contextual influences that have been demonstrated through research as essential to strengthening therapy relationships and have been correlated with successful outcomes. They are shared by, yet are not the province of, any one research agenda but reflect "what works" therapeutically.

Reflection on Philosophy and Research

Before we delve into the foundational premises of SBE, please take a moment to review your responses in Exercise 1.1. Next consider the research trends discussed in this chapter. Then please complete Exercise 2.1, Ideas about Change.

As mental health professionals, we will continue to reexamine our personal philosophies because of their impact on helping relationships and change. This ongoing process can be invaluable no matter what your role in the profession and whether you are experienced or new to it. We all have ideas and assumptions that can positively or negatively affect change processes. By continuing to reevaluate our personal perceptions and principles of change, we can remain aware of threats to the integrity and effectiveness of helping relationships.

Core Principles of SBE

As stated, effective therapy approaches are more similar than different. Effective helpers engage in processes that are change-oriented, client informed, collaborative, strengths based, and outcome oriented, although these are not the only characteristics. These elements are reflected in six core principles that form the foundation of SBE:

- client contributions
- therapeutic relationship and alliance
- cultural competence
- change as a process

- expectancy and hope
- method and factor of fit

Client Contributions

Clients are what make therapy work and are the single most important contributors to outcome (Tallman & Bohart, 1999). Estimates are that client factors provide between one-third and one-half of the overall variance in outcome (Lambert, 1992; Wampold, 2001). Although therapists are facilitators in change processes, clients' abilities as self-healers make them the engineers of change. Effective therapeutic approaches identify, highlight, and encourage client contributions to change.

Client factors comprise internal strengths and external resources including support systems. *Internal strengths* include optimism, persistence, resilience, protective factors, coping skills, and abilities utilized in vocational, educational, and social settings. *Resilience* and *protective factors* refer to clients' qualities and actions that allow them to meet the difficulties and challenges of life. Related to resiliency, *growth* and *maturation* relate to the client's ability to move through or mature out of individual and lifecycle developmental phases, manage the trials and tribulations of life, overcome problems, and find viable solutions (Carter & McGoldrick, 1999/2005). Clients experience ups and downs, transitions, and movement through different phases of life. It is important to learn about the meanings that clients attach to their experiences and invite them into conversations in which they can explore the relevance of developmental, maturational, and transitional processes and changes. In doing so, therapists take care not to impose personal beliefs but work to normalize client experiences and offer alternative possibilities that may promote positive change.

Exercise 2.1

Ideas About Change

- Review Exercise 1.1, A Philosophical Inventory. What do you notice most about your responses?

  _____

  _____

  _____

- What, if anything, would you change about your responses in Exercise 1.1?

  _____

  _____

  _____

- What struck you most about the research findings discussed in Chapter 2?

  _____

  _____

  _____

- Based on the research findings and what you have read to this point, list four to six general ideas about change.

  1. _____

  2. _____

  3. _____

  4. _____

  5. _____

  6. _____

- How might these ideas about change affect your work as a therapist?

  _____

  _____

  _____

- How might these ideas about change benefit your current or future clients?

  _____

  _____

  _____

Exercise 2.1 *(continued)*

- How might these ideas present challenges?

_____

_____

_____

External resources refer to relationships, social networks, and systems that provide support and opportunities. Examples are family, friends, employment, and educational, community, and religious supports. External resources also include affiliation or membership in groups or associations that provide connection and stability. Client support systems are central in maintaining long-term change; focusing on processes that tap into, develop, and encourage such capacities is a key aspect of SBE.

Effective therapists elicit client strengths and use psychoeducational processes to facilitate change. They view clients as having competencies—internal and external resources that have been helpful in the past in similar or different contexts. Effective therapists emphasize evoking those abilities so the client can utilize them with present and future concerns. In addition, therapists assist clients by using educational and experiential activities in learning and developing new understandings and skills and by creating educational experiences and opportunities to develop new meanings.

Internal strengths and external resources provide the fuel for change. To better understand the value of client contributions to change, please focus on your abilities by completing Exercise 2.2, Understanding Strengths, Abilities, Capacities, and Competencies. This exercise can also be completed with others as a therapeutic or role-playing exercise.

Tapping into client contributions involves respecting their motivations. This is not an either/or proposition (i.e., either they are or they are not motivated). Motivation exists on a continuum. Clients often appear to lack motivation or be resistant because they have little interest in working on the identified directions or goals. Duncan, Hubble, and Miller (1997a) stated:

> There is no such individual as an unmotivated client. Clients may not, as we have found all too often, share ours, but they certainly hold strong motivations of their own. An unproductive and futile therapy can come about by mistaking or overlooking what the client wants to accomplish, misapprehending the client's readiness for change, or pursuing a personal motivation (p. 11).

Clients have different motivations. For example, adolescents are typically motivated to achieve desired experiences or goals (for example, money, freedom) and to avoid unpleasant or unwanted experiences (for example, boredom, restrictions) (Bertolino, 1999). The same can be said for their parents or caregivers. Matching levels of motivation with methods is crucial. Doing so corresponds to learning how clients situate themselves (for example, involved, not involved) in relation to their concerns (their problems, other people's

Exercise 2.2

Understanding, Strengths, Abilities, Capacities, and Competencies

- What are your best qualities?

  _____

  _____

- In what way(s) are these qualities a resource for you?

  _____

  _____

- What are your qualities (same or different than in the preceding question) that allow you to manage adversity and persevere through difficult problems, situations, and times?

  _____

  _____

- How have the qualities in the preceding question helped you to persevere?

  _____

  _____

- What does the fact that you have been able to manage and perhaps overcome adversity in your life say about you as a person?

  _____

  _____

- What specific internal strengths and abilities are you aware of that you have found useful in managing problems?

  _____

  _____

- How specifically have you used those strengths and abilities to be more resilient and/or resolve concerns?

  _____

  _____

- What is an ability that you have in a nonproblem area that you could use more often in a problem area? (Example: How could the fact that you are artistic be useful if you experience a conflict with a close friend?)

  _____

  _____

- Who in your life (past or present) have been sources of support for you?

  _____

  _____

Exercise 2.2   (*continued*)

- How have these persons helped you?

  _____

  _____

- What difference did/does that help make for you?

  _____

  _____

- Who knows the kind of person you are?

  _____

  _____

- Who does not know the kind of person you are but would not be surprised to learn about you?

  _____

  _____

- Who other than the people already named need to know the kind of person you are?

  _____

  _____

- What difference would it make for you to have others who are unaware to know more about the person you are?

  _____

  _____

- What is one thing you can do in the future to continue to grow as a person?

  _____

  _____

- What would be a first step toward making that growth happen?

  _____

  _____

- What would be the benefits of the continuing growth you named?

  _____

  _____

problems) and what they feel needs to happen for their lives or situations to improve (for example, nothing, new perspectives, new actions, change in interactions). This information assists in matching methods with the client's levels of motivation as a means to increase the chance of a successful outcome.

Evoking and amplifying client strengths and contributions to change does not mean downplaying real-life difficulties, pain, and suffering that people have experienced or are currently going through. Rather, doing so means acknowledging and attending to the hardships that clients face while focusing on the possibilities for change. Table 2.2 offers additional ideas for maximizing client contributions to change.

Therapeutic Relationship and Alliance

Numerous studies have indicated that client ratings of the therapeutic relationship and alliance are significantly related to therapeutic outcome and are possibly the best and most consistent predictors of improvement (Bachelor & Horvath, 1999; Baldwin, Wampold, & Imel, 2007; Horvath & Bedi, 2002; Martin, Garske, & Davis, 2000; Orlinsky, Grawe, & Parks, 1994; Orlinsky, Rønnestad, & Willutzki, 2004). Those who are engaged and connected with their therapists are likely to benefit most from therapy. Therapists who are attuned to the importance of clients' relational needs and monitor relationships are better able to ensure that clients feel heard, understood, and connected. Effective therapists monitor their relationships with clients and remain responsive to changes throughout the course of therapy.

Client ratings of therapists as empathic, trustworthy, and nonjudgmental are better predictors of positive outcome than are therapist ratings, diagnosis, approach, or any other variable (Horvath & Symonds, 1991; Lambert & Bergin, 1994). Said differently, it is not whether therapists believe they are connecting with clients but whether clients experience connection with their therapists. Connection, most frequently monitored through client self-report measures and feedback processes (to be discussed in Chapter 3), is consistently linked with high ratings of empathy, genuineness, and positive regard on the part of therapists. Therapists convey these core relational dynamics by listening and attending to, acknowledging, and validating clients' experience. This includes feelings, sense of self, bodily sensations, and sensory experience.

Client ratings of therapists are related to similarity in the client-therapist linguistic style. Therapists must pay close attention to the ways that clients use language and talk about their lives, situations, and concerns. Therapists strengthen relationships by accommodating and matching clients' use of language and nonverbal communication (Bedi, 2006).

Another noteworthy feature of the client-therapist relationship is time. The strength of the therapeutic bond is not highly correlated with the length of treatment (Horvath & Luborsky, 1993). Although therapists should be aware of influences (for example, belief systems, previous therapy experiences, expectations) of and threats to the client-therapist relationship, many clients experience a quick sense of connection with their respective helpers. In fact, studies indicate that client ratings of the therapeutic relationships can predict outcome prior to the application of specific therapy procedures (Lambert & Ogles, 2004; Martin, Garske, & Davis, 2000). The amount of time it takes for clients to feel comfortable in their relationships is contingent on their experiences and perceptions.

Table 2.2

Actions That Maximize Client Contributions

- Identify and explore client contributions to change.

- Recognize clients as competent and capable.

- Identify and encourage client qualities and characteristics including resiliency, coping skills, and protective factors to effect change.

- Elicit and evoke client traits and abilities to pursue possibilities and solutions.

- Identify qualities and abilities typically utilized in contexts other than the problem area(s) and link them to present concerns or problems.

- Identify and assist clients in developing supportive social systems, resources, and networks (for example, family, friends, educators, employers, religious/spiritual advisors, groups, and other outside helpers and community members).

- Attend to clients' motivations and interests.

- Learn what clients do to meet their everyday needs (i.e., whom the client seeks out for support, where the client goes for support).

- Identify what clients *already* have in their lives that they can use in the present.

- Identify exceptions and/or moments in the past or present—even if fleeting—when the client's problems were less present or absent altogether and the client's role in those exceptions.

- Explore moments in the past or present when clients have made beneficial decisions and/or exhibited the ability to lessen or avoid problems.

- Even when external influences factor into change (e.g., psychotherapy, medication) or clients assign change to other things (e.g., luck, chance), attribute the majority of change to clients' qualities and actions.

- Share the credit when others have made contributions to change.

- Assist clients in evaluating the benefits of positive change.

- Identify ways that clients can utilize abilities to face future challenges.

- Encourage personal agency and accountability.

- Acknowledge that caregivers are capable of keeping their children safe.

The concept of the therapeutic relationship has been expanded to include the *therapeutic alliance*. This broader term highlights the collaborative partnership between clients and therapists. In addition to the strength of the client-therapist bond, the degree to which clients collaborate with therapists regarding processes (e.g., how to meet, when to meet), therapy directions, and goal establishment as well as methods to achieve those goals is paramount (Bordin, 1979). Orlinsky, Grawe, and Parks (1994) noted that the quality of the client's participation in therapy is a crucial determinant of outcome. Negative outcome is often traced to therapists' excluding clients from decisions regarding the therapeutic processes. As Duncan, Hubble, and Miller (1997b) stated, "Impossibility, we decided, is at least partly a function of leaving clients out of the process, of not listening or of dismissing the importance of their perspective" (p. 30).

The exploration of directions, goals, and outcomes is the primary way in which clinicians learn about clients' preferences. *Directions* relate to a general sense of where clients would like their lives or situations to be headed in the future and specifically involve what clients would like to focus on and what they deem as meaningful conversational pathways. *Goals* are concrete representations of what clients want to see change from session to session. They are clearly defined, action-based descriptions of aspects of clients' futures. Finally, *outcomes* are clients' perceptions of the impact that services have on the major areas of their lives (for example, individually, interpersonally, socially).

Although subsequent chapters will explore directions, goals, and outcomes in detail, at this juncture it is important to note that therapists who are not clear about clients' concerns, what clients want to have change, and what will constitute successful outcomes risk providing therapy that is chaotic, confusing, and without any sense of structure (Bertolino, 2003). This point is evidenced by research suggesting that a lack of focus and structure is a predictor of *negative* outcomes (Mohr, 1995; Sachs, 1983). Consequently, both clients and therapists can experience frustration, anger, or other feelings or thoughts that may lead to a loss of hope and thoughts of giving up, resulting in increases of no shows and dropout rates. Moreover, these clinicians are at risk of viewing clients as resistant, unmotivated, and/or incapable of change.

The therapeutic alliance is founded on collaboration. Therapists work *with* clients as opposed to on them, reflecting a commitment by therapists to invite clients into conversations and processes. These are open invitations and allow clients to move in (and vary their degree of involvement) and out of therapeutic processes in ways that are right for them. As you will learn, collaborative partnerships begin prior to the start of "formal" therapy or services and continue throughout (Bertolino, 2003; Bertolino & O'Hanlon, 2002). Collaboration puts trust in clients and allows them to choose directions that fit them. The following story about psychiatrist Milton Erickson illustrates this:

> When Erickson was a young man a horse wandered into his yard. Although the horse had no identifying marks he offered to return it to its owners. To accomplish this, he mounted the horse, led it to the road, and let the horse decide which way it wanted to go. He intervened only when the horse left the road to graze or wander into a field. When the horse finally arrived at the yard of a neighbor several miles down the road, the neighbor asked the young Erickson, "How did you know that horse came from here and was our horse?" Erickson replied, "I didn't know— but the horse knew. All I did was keep him on the road" (Rosen, 1982, pp. 46–47).

Collaboration in this sense involves showing clients the road and letting them choose the direction. Therapists must also extend a collaborative stance to those helpers (for example, family members, social service workers, probation officers, teachers) who may be involved or have investment in the therapy. Being collaborative does not mean never being directive. Practitioners may need to become more or less directive depending on client preferences, context, and issues such as safety, which is important because therapists have ethical and legal responsibilities for client care, particularly when it comes to risk of harm to self or others. Even in cases that have risk, therapists can convey respect while being more direct.

Strengths-based practitioners facilitate change. They use language, questions, and other processes to promote change. As previously mentioned, therapists do not impose ideas and questions on clients but "offer" them in a nonauthoritarian way as possibilities for consideration. In this way, clients and others involved with therapy have the space to agree or disagree, modify, or correct what has been offered. Table 2.3 offers other possibilities for strengthening the therapeutic relationship and alliance.

Cultural Competence

The premise that binds all other propositions in SBE is *culture*. Identifying a gap in current practices, Wampold (2001) stated, "Because specific ingredients of most treatments . . . are designed and implemented without consideration of race, ethnicity, or culture, these treatments are recommended for a disorder, problem, or complaint blind to the client's cultural values" (p. 221–222). Without cultural influences, therapists cannot adequately understand clients, their lives, situations, and problems.

Culture specifically refers to a system of shared beliefs, values, customs, behaviors, and artifacts among various groups within a community, institution, organization, or nation.

From generation to generation, members of society use their cultural references to cope with their world and with one another.

Culture is reflected though diversity. Arredondo and D'Andrea's (1995) stated:

> Diversity refers to other characteristics by which persons may prefer to self-define. This includes, but is not limited to, an individual's age, gender, sexual identity, religious/spiritual identification, social and economic class background and residential location (i.e., urban suburban, rural). (p. 28)

Hays (2007) has suggested the acronym ADDRESSING as a way to identify different aspects of diversity: age, developmental and acquired disability, religion, ethnicity, social class, sexual orientation, indigenous heritage, national origin, and gender/sex. Brown (2008) has expanded Hays' foundational but not inclusive list to include factors such as other social locations as vocational and recreational choices, partnership status, parenthood (or not), attractiveness, body size and shape, and state of physical health.

Culture also includes *context*, which relates to other factors that can influence thinking and behavior. These include but are not limited to family history, social relationships, development (physical, cognitive, emotional), genetics and biology, politics, and economics. Context also includes time and space (when, where, duration, intensity) and conditions and settings (cultural, philosophical, physical, psychological, and social). Concerns, problems, possibilities, and solutions do not exist in a vacuum. They are situated in and influenced by context.

Context has at least two connotations. First, it refers to the healing environment and relationship and the meanings attributed to it by participants (Frank & Frank 1991). Second, context refers to individual differences and

Table 2.3

Possibilities for Strengthening the Therapeutic Relationship and Alliance

- Accept clients for who they are as persons and convey this through acknowledgement and validation.

- View clients as cooperative.

- Demonstrate respect for clients.

- Use active listening, attending skills (for example, genuineness, positive regard), and engagement processes while recognizing that clients' caution toward professionals may be an appropriate response to past experiences.

- Create multiple pathways for developing supportive, stable relationships with family, staff, peers, and other caring participants in clients' lives.

- Acknowledge clients while inviting accountability for their actions.

- Use respectful, nondepersonalizing language and descriptions of problems and avoid unnecessary professional jargon. Recognize that such terminology may be useful in some professional contexts (for example, for securing services, making differential diagnosis) but can be disrespectful and stigmatizing and threaten relationships with clients.

- Collaborate with clients in determining goals.

- Collaborate with clients on tasks to accomplish goals.

- Attend to therapists' personal contributions to the alliance including possible positive and negative effects.

- Incorporate an outcome orientation as a means to monitor the impact of services from clients' points of view.

- Collaborate with family members, outside helpers, and community resources to create strong social networks and systems of support.

- Incorporate the views of involved helpers (for example, extended family, social service workers, medical personnel, educators, law enforcement, educators) in setting goals and determining directions.

- Learn clients' expectations.

- Offer options and choices in services and processes.

- Accommodate therapy and services to clients' views.

- Discuss with clients possible benefits and side effects of services.

- Discuss with clients parameters of confidentiality.

- Provide rationale for services.

- Incorporate processes for learning clients' views of service-oriented relationships and integrate feedback into all aspects of services.

- Respond to potential threats to and ruptures in the client–therapist alliance.

Table 2.3 (*continued*)

- Learn and adapt to the ways in which clients' use language.

- Demonstrate concern for the well-being, feelings, and interests of clients.

- Complement clients for positive intentions and actions.

- Practice directness without being confrontational.

- Consider clients as experts on their lives, learning about and respecting their ideas.

- Respect and elicit the contributions and talents of others who may be involved with clients.

- Serve as positive role models to others.

- Develop and increase awareness regarding personal biases and viewpoints and how they can affect relationships and services.

- Attend supervision or seek consultation on a consistent basis.

factors that may influence problems, possibilities, and solutions.

Identifying any one aspect of context as being the true *cause* of a problem is difficult, it is therefore more helpful to view contextual factors as *influences*. Because any one problem can have multiple influences, what is most important during therapy are the meanings that clients attribute to aspects of context. Clients continue to demonstrate that they are motivated by what they believe to be influences on their problems more than any other factor. It is not that clients always enter therapy with clear-cut theories of causation, yet they do often have ideas about the nature of or influences on their concerns (Bertolino, 2003; Brickman et al., 1982; Wile, 1977). Client ideas are often embedded in their language and can be cultivated through careful listening. More powerful than therapist explanations are clients' perceptions and attributions regarding the influences of culture and context on their problems.

Culture is a powerful filter through which behavior can be understood; however, no one aspect provides a comprehensive explanation of it (Sue, Arredondo, & McDavis, 1992). Multiple factors vary in their degree of influence. For example, a client experiencing insomnia may identify stress from work as its cause, but there are likely to be other influences as well (for example, not establishing a consistent time to retire to each night, working odd hours, ingesting too much caffeine). Most important is the meaning the client attaches to his or her situation and the various influences on it. A client who *believes* that work stress is to blame is more likely to be motivated to make changes that are consistent with that viewpoint.

Strengths-based practitioners attend to clients' ideas and collaborate with clients to develop mutually acceptable ways to approach concerns. Attending to client motivation is not only a respectful stance but also can strengthen relationships; that, in turn, allows therapists to have more influence when needed. In the insomnia example, by honoring the client's viewpoint and then offering an alternative perspective, the therapist increases the likelihood that the client will be open to a new perspective.

Cultural competence is a cornerstone of a strengths-based philosophy. It translates to having the capacity to function effectively in other cultural contexts. It is reflected through awareness and practices that involve learning new patterns of behavior and effectively applying them in the appropriate settings. This requires valuing diversity, which means accepting and respecting differences. People come from different backgrounds, and their customs, thoughts, ways of communicating, values, traditions, and institutions vary accordingly.

Cultural competence is also a developmental process and is demonstrated in many ways, the most influential of which are language and interaction. Practitioners who have diverse backgrounds can draw on those backgrounds and their general cultural knowledge to match clients' ideas about problems, possibilities, and potential solutions. Therapists engage in conversations with clients through which a multitude of possibilities can be generated and explored. Practitioners encourage dialogues that allow new perspectives to emerge. Thus, knowledge of different cultures and perspectives is beneficial by allowing therapists to view situations differently without having to align with any one viewpoint. This knowledge also brings with it an expanded repertoire of methods to use that may be helpful in services.

Strengths-based practitioners complete ongoing cultural assessments, create consciousness about the dynamics inherent in cultural interaction, institutionalize cultural knowledge, and develop adaptations to service delivery reflecting an understanding of diversity between and within cultures. These elements are reflected in attitudes, structures, and policies and are manifested in every level of service delivery systems.

Ongoing efforts that ensure positive growth and development in the various settings and programs serving clients create *cultural safety*. These include program accessibility, physical settings, procedures, and level systems. All aspects of environment and programming are monitored to maintain a culture of care and respect (see Chapter 1) and are responsive to issues of race, culture, gender, development, and social and economic status (Bertolino, 2003). Cultural safety is achieved primarily through language and interaction. As discussed previously, however, we speak and act in ways that are consistent with our beliefs, which represent the familial, cultural, and societal experiences in which we have been immersed. Because society tends to be seeped in problem-saturated discourses, the tones of language frequently ring of deficit, negativity, marginalization, and depersonalization. A strengths-based perspective provides a respectful response to these threats by emphasizing abilities and capacities.

Developing our awareness about the impact of language is a crucial first step toward increasing cultural sensitivity. We can then work to make changes in our basic language and refine our communication in ways that convey respect, inspire results, create hope, highlight strengths, and promote change. Refer to Table 2.4 for examples of words and phrases that move from being deficit-based to competency-based terminology.

Maintaining an awareness of "off-the-cuff" labels that are used indiscriminately can further ensure cultural sensitivity. The depersonalizing effect that can result from the use of such labeling is of particular concern. Sensitivity to these

Table 2.4

Competency-Based Vocabulary

Deficit-Based Words		Strengths-Based Words
Fix	→	Empower
Weakness	→	Strength
Limitation	→	Possibility
Pathology	→	Health
Problem	→	Solution
Insist	→	Invite
Closed	→	Open
Shrink	→	Expand
Defense	→	Access
Expert	→	Partner
Control	→	Nurture
Backward	→	Forward
Manipulate	→	Collaborate
Fear	→	Hope
Cure	→	Growth
Stuck	→	Change
Missing	→	Latent
Resist	→	Utilize
Past	→	Future
Hierarchical	→	Horizontal
Diagnose	→	Appreciate
Treat	→	Facilitate
End	→	Beginning
Judge	→	Respect
Never	→	Not yet
Limit	→	Expand
Defect	→	Asset
Rule	→	Exception

labels can prevent seeing a client as or becoming the label without recognizing his or her actual self. In essence, the person is seen as—or in some cases, *becomes*—the condition or label, depersonalizing him or her. For example, one might say, "He's the picture of ADD" or "She's borderline." In other instances, clients may even use depersonalizing language when referring to themselves by saying things such as, "I'm bipolar" or "Didn't you know that I'm hyperactive?" What seems to happen in these cases is that people lose their sense of self and develop identities consistent with the label. In turn, other people look though diagnostic lenses at people who have been labeled and see only the symptoms associated with the label, not the individual person.

Although diagnostic applications are appropriate in certain circumstances, use of labels can unnecessarily depersonalize, stigmatize, and harm. *People are people, not disabilities.* Our language needs to reflect this fact. The respectful way to describe any person is to use person-first language (see Table 2.5). A disability may be an aspect of a person's life but certainly does not identify who the person is. To learn about our clients and who they are as people, it is imperative that we attend closely to how we see others and the words we use to describe their situations.

Person-first language is consistent with the view of *disability* along a continuum of health (Olkin, 1999). Some disabilities interfere with a person's functioning in some but not all circumstances. Other disabilities have few or no effects on general health making it important to look at the effects of each condition on the range of functions faced by persons with disabilities. Olkin (1999) has recommended that culturally competent practitioners practice from a "minority" base as opposed to a "deficit" model in therapy with individuals with disabilities. Brown (2008) developed this point:

What is true is that people with disabilities have some (or several) aspects of their bodies that function differently than those of a majority of other humans. Frequently, however, the challenges for these individuals

Table 2.5

Person-First Language: Using Words with Respect and Dignity

Words/Phrases to Avoid	Words/Phrases to Use
This person . . .	
is crazy; insane; sick; a mental patient; a borderline; a schizophrenic.	has been diagnosed with_____ (fill in the blank) psychiatric disability; emotional disorder; mental illness.
is slow; retarded; stupid; an underachiever.	has a learning disability; developmental delay; intellectual disability.
is a cripple; handicapped; invalid.	is a person with a disability.
victim; is afflicted with _____ (state affliction).	is a person who has; person with _____ (state diagnosis, disability).
is restricted, confined to a wheelchair; wheelchair-bound.	uses a wheelchair.
is normal.	is nondisabled.
is a deaf mute; deaf and dumb.	is deaf; nonvocal; does not voice himself/herself.
has a birth defect.	has had a disability since birth; was born with _____.
fits.	has epilepsy; seizures.

lie not in those physical differences but in the barriers created to fullest possible function by cultural institutions and practice. (p. 29)

This idea epitomizes the importance of viewing individuals as persons with disabilities instead of *being* disabilities. It also counteracts generalizations and biases that can contribute to oppression and marginalization. Remembering the importance of learning from clients about cultural influences is essential to help them. In addition, as practitioners, we continue to our expand knowledge of different cultural backgrounds through education and experiential activities.

To summarize, Sue and Sue (2007) outlined characteristics of culturally competent counselors across three dimensions. They stated that culturally competent practitioners:

1. are actively in the process of becoming aware of their own assumptions about human behavior, values, biases, preconceived notions, personal limitations, and so forth

2. actively attempt to understand the worldviews of their culturally different clients without negative judgment

3. are in the process of actively developing and practicing appropriate, relevant, and sensitive intervention strategies and skills in working with their culturally different clients

Table 2.6 provides ideas for ensuring cultural and contextual sensitivity.

Table 2.6

Actions That Ensure Cultural and Contextual Sensitivity

- Maintain cultural self-awareness and sensitivity to one's own cultural heritage, background, and experiences and their influence on one's attitudes, values, and biases.

- Recognize limits of multicultural competency and expertise.

- Recognize sources of personal discomfort with differences that may exist between therapists and their clients in terms of race, ethnicity, culture, gender, and other influences.

- Acknowledge that specific racial and cultural factors influence service and therapeutic processes—understand and respect each client's cultural heritage and practices.

- Emphasize a multilevel understanding that encompasses the client, family, community, helping systems, culture, and other influences.

- Consult others who share cultural similarities and expertise with clients being served.

- Create safe and nurturing cultural, physical, psychological, and social environments and settings.

- Use assessment processes that identify concerns, risks, and threats to safety and well-being.

- Acknowledge and address risks and issues related to cultural safety.

- Create culturally meaningful experiences.

- Individualize services (avoid "one-size-fits-all" approaches).

- Acknowledge clients as teachers and experts on their own lives and experiences.

- Emphasize clients' capacities to adapt, change, and grow.

- Empower clients and others by using practices that identify and employ their unique capabilities.

- Use a "minority-" rather than "deficit-" based approach in therapy with individuals with disabilities.

- Identify, assess, address, and monitor barriers to services.

- Create plans of action that are culturally sensitive.

- Exercise care in matching methods with clients.

- Utilize strategies that are respectful and reflective of differences.

- Employ proactive (as opposed to reactive) systems of response.

- Approach services as opportunities to educate and prevent.

- Use culturally sensitive methods of research and evaluation.

- Conduct ongoing cultural self-assessments.

- Conduct program and organizational assessments to explore cultural practices.

(Continued)

Table 2.6   (*continued*)
Actions That Ensure Cultural and Contextual Sensitivity

- Manage the dynamics of difference.

- Acquire and institutionalize cultural knowledge.

- Adapt to the diversity and cultural contexts of the individuals, families, and communities served.

Change as a Process

Three points characterize the premise of change as a process. First, emphasis is on enhancing change as opposed to searching for explanations about the nature of problems. Second, change is constant; people, situations, and problems are not static. Third, change is predictable. These points are key considerations for all practitioners working to promote growth in the form of possibilities and solutions.

Change Can Be Enhanced

With a lineage that can be traced back to the first wave (see the Appendix), psychotherapy is grounded in explanatory-based theories. Although this provided a starting point for talk therapies, evidence has not supported the belief that having therapists provide explanations regarding the cause(s) of problems leads to change. Instead, research suggests that therapists should concentrate efforts on identifying and mobilizing factors responsible for change. Doing so means focusing more on change as a process and less on providing explanations or theories of causality. Miller, Duncan, and Hubble (1997) echoed this sentiment, stating that a growing body of literature suggests that:

> Therapeutic time is spent more productively when the therapist and client focus on and enhance the factors responsible for change-in-general rather than on identifying and then changing the factors a theory suggests

are responsible or causing problems-in-particular. . . . Indoctrinating clients into a particular model of problem causation might actually . . . [undermine] the very factors responsible for the occurrence of change by drawing clients' attention to whatever a particular theory suggests is causing their suffering (p. 127).

Therapists must contend with personal theoretical maps and constructions that can greatly alter the course of therapy. Explanatory-only approaches grant a privilege to therapists' theories and can be counterproductive by obscuring client abilities and unnecessarily stigmatizing and blaming them for problems. An emphasis on therapist-derived explanations is indicated only when clients communicate that they prefer such a focus or agree with therapists as to the possible benefits of the focus (Bertolino, 2003; Bertolino & O'Hanlon, 2002). The key consideration in therapy is the client's search for explanations as opposed to the therapist's imposing them because he or she believes that explanations are necessary for problem resolution and positive change.

Change Is Constant

Clients' problems fluctuate in frequency, intensity, and duration. Recognizing this variability, therapists engage clients in conversations to learn more about times when problems are more or less manageable or absent altogether.

This includes finding out about the influence that clients have over problems and factors that can increase this influence. Explorations of differences and influences help therapists understand how change occurs in clients' lives and how they are able to mobilize their resources in problematic situations.

Central to change as a constant is *spontaneous change*. The significant portion of change occurs outside therapy sessions. A strengths-based therapist takes care to notice moments of change regardless of where or when they happen and to incorporate those changes into services. The key to doing this is to identify change and determine its role and/or effect on the problem area.

A *future focus* is also an aspect of change as a constant. Therapists work to understand their clients' concerns and how they affect their lives. In addition, therapists help clients determine what kind of change they are seeking and how the change will make their lives different. Having a future focus means concentrating on client futures when problems will be absent or at least more manageable. Maintaining a future focus does not mean dismissing past events. As it is with a preference for an explanatory focus, attending to client preferences, even if they are past oriented, is the respectful path. Alternatively, therapists do not assume that clients must explore the past and go through cathartic experiences to resolve conflicts.

Inherent to a future focus is emphasizing client needs as conditions that all human beings require to function, at least minimally (Maslow, 1943). *Needs* include (but are not limited to) food, water, sleep, and safety. Although needs have different weights in their relationship to survival, it is essential that helpers, no matter what their roles, assume responsibility for helping clients to have their needs met. Helpers can

do this by offering direct assistance or identifying indirect pathways. *Direct assistance* would be taking a client to a food pantry. *Indirect assistance* could be referring clients to services that would help them meet their needs. For practitioners to focus only on higher-level needs or problems when clients are struggling with life necessities is irresponsible. In addition, it is unrealistic to expect clients whose basic needs are not being met to focus their attention and energy on making and maintaining change in other areas.

Change Is Predictable

Miller, Duncan, and Hubble (1997) found that "all large-scale meta-analytic studies of client change indicate that the most frequent improvement occurs early in treatment" (p. 194). Most of the major positive impact in therapy happens during the first six to eight sessions (Fennell & Teasdale, 1987; Howard et al., 1986; Howard et al. 1993; Ilardi & Craighead, 1994; Smith, Glass, & Miller, 1980). Furthermore, studies have demonstrated that 60–65% of clients experience significant symptomatic relief within seven sessions (Brown, Dreis, & Nace, 1999; Howard et al., 1986; Howard et al., 1996; Lambert, Okiishi, Finch, & Johnson, 1998; Smith, Glass, & Miller, 1980; Steenbarger, 1992; Talmon, 1990; Talmon, Hoyt, & Rosenbaum, 1990).

Findings regarding the concept of change indicate that it occurs early on in therapy. Regardless of the model employed, the average number of sessions that clients attend is 6 to 10 (Garfield, 1989; Koss & Butcher, 1986). Indeed, in most outpatient/outclient settings, the modal number (that is, the most frequently appearing number in a distribution) of therapy sessions that clients attend is one. Although clients end therapy for a variety of reasons (with many achieving the results they expected in a single session), these findings indicate that not only does the majority of change happen early on but also *clients expect at least some degree of change to happen early* and, more often than not, before 10 sessions. Clients who do not experience sufficient change are likely to move on. These findings underscore the importance for therapists to seek to be as effective as possible by learning from clients what minimally needs to happen in each interaction or session to bring about meaningful and noticeable improvement.

Clients can benefit from therapy that extends beyond eight session. This most frequently depends on factors such as the severity of clients' symptoms and personality characteristics as well as the strength of their social systems. Therefore, some clients may respond and make appreciable gains more slowly than others; as a result, the most significant portion of change will be demonstrated over the long term, but this appears to be more the exception than the norm. Research suggests that as treatment progresses, a reliable course of diminishing returns occurs with more and more effort required to obtain barely noticeable differences in client improvement (Howard et al., 1986). Even though the amount of change decreases over time, as long as progress is being made, therapy can remain beneficial. Furthermore, if clients are "early responders" and experience meaningful change in the first handful of sessions, the probability of positive outcome significantly increases (Haas et al. 2002; Percevic, Lambert, & Kordy, 2006; Whipple et al., 2003). In contrast, when clients show little or no improvement or experience a worsening of symptoms early on in treatment, they are at significant risk for negative outcome (Lebow, 1997).

It is not the number of sessions that is most important but practitioners' collaboration with clients to determine where they want to go, when things are better, and when needs, goals, and outcomes have been achieved. This cooperation by nature makes therapy generally briefer and more client informed. Therapists should consider that clients will vary in their use of therapeutic services; some will move in and out very quickly. Others will attend therapy over extended periods of time or in "rounds" (i.e., intermittently, a few sessions at a time). Thus, flexibility in terms of allowing for clients' entry, termination, and reentry is needed. The next chapter will describe this "open door" perspective, and this will also be discussed further in later chapters. (See Table 2.7 for actions therapists can take to tap into change.)

Expectancy and Hope

Of the core premises of SBE that contribute to positive change and outcome, none may be as difficult to grasp as expectancy and hope. These factors refer to the portion of improvement derived from clients' expectations for treatment, their development of hope, and the credibility they place on the rationale for the specific techniques used in therapy (Duncan, Miller, & Sparks, 2004). Researchers estimate that this combination of premises contributes a minimum of 15% to the variance in outcome (Asay & Lambert, 1999; Lambert, 1992). Despite the wide variance, the influence of these aspects is clear. Effective therapists not only maintain an awareness of expectancy and hope but also focus on ways to increase the two in all aspects of services.

Clients' and therapists' expectations about therapy are crucial, especially at the beginning. People would not bother with therapy if they did not believe it could be beneficial in some way. This factor is commonly referred to as *pretreatment* or *preservices expectancy*

Table 2.7
Actions That Tap into Change Processes

- Focus on meeting clients' basic needs (for example, food, water, sleep, safety).

- Listen for and honor clients' ideas about directions for therapy/services.

- Incorporate a sense of structure in sessions to assist with direction and to focus attempts at helping.

- View meaningful change as attainable problems as barriers to progress, not fixed pathology.

- View growth, development, and maturation as part of the change processes.

- Focus on maximizing the impact of each interaction and/or session.

- Monitor change from the outset of services, recalling that change tends to occur early in service provision.

- In lieu of positive change, engage clients in conversations earlier rather than later to make adjustments in services.

- Emphasize possibilities for change through a future focus.

- Explore exceptions to problems and how change is already happening in clients' lives.

- Focus on creating small changes, which can lead to bigger ones.

- Scan clients' lives for spontaneous change and build on those changes.

- Approach assessment processes as opportunities to initiate positive change.

- Allow reentry or easy access to future services as needed.

- Create opportunities for clients to acquire and develop new skills.

- Explore ways that clients can extend change into other areas of life in the future.

(Mueller & Pekarik, 2000; Safren, Heimberg, & Juster, 1997; Schneider & Klauer, 2001). The expectation that therapy can lead to positive change is one that counteracts demoralization and increases hope. Pretreatment expectancy is important for therapists as well as clients.

Therapists' attitudes can promote or dampen hope. For example, an attitude of pessimism or an emphasis on psychopathology or the long-term process of change can negatively affect hope. In contrast, therapists' attitudes that positive change can and does occur even in difficult situations coupled with an emphasis on possibilities and improvement can instill and promote hope. Processes and practices that are respectful, collaborative, honor clients' ideas about change, and, ultimately, build on, create, and/or rehabilitate hope increase the prospects of change. Therapists using such processes and practices expect and anticipate positive change and continuously monitor for it.

Expectancy is multifaceted. First, both the client and therapist must believe in the procedures and restorative power of therapy. Clients' expectations that therapy can help serves as a placebo and can counteract demoralization, activate hope, and advance improvement (Frank & Frank, 1991; Miller, Duncan, & Hubble, 1997). In most cases, what accounts for a significant part of a specific change is the client's *belief* in the technique or method being used and in the therapist (the feeling of being in "good hands") rather than the specific technique or method used.

Although specific methods and techniques contribute little to the variance in outcomes, all therapeutic processes involve techniques or rituals (Frank & Frank, 1991). As discussed, the important aspects in bringing about change are (1) the processes and practices therapists use that contribute to the expectancy for change and increase in hope, (2) clients' and practitioners' belief in the treatments and the rationales behind them, and (3) the fit between methods and clients' perspectives about their problems and possibilities for solution. This third aspect will be discussed in the next section.

Expectancy and hope offer a remedy to impossibility. When things are going poorly, most people would like their lives, at some level, to improve, at least minimally. Hope for this improvement is not about people looking at the world through rose-colored glasses but recognizing that if people have choices, most prefer things to be better. An underlying pessimism or negativity—unless to emphasize with the client—can dampen hope and represent the difference between clients having a positive experience and continuing services (see Table 2.8).

Table 2.8
Actions That Increase Expectancy and Hope

- Demonstrate faith in clients.
- Maintain the belief that change is possible.
- Demonstrate faith in the restorative effects of therapy.
- Build on preservice expectancy.
- Create expectancy for change by focusing on what is possible and changeable.
- Create expectancy for change by using language that is respectful and emanates hope.
- Enhance placebo effects by building on the client's belief in therapeutic processes.
- Believe and demonstrate faith in the procedures and practices utilized.
- Show interest in the results of the therapeutic procedure or orientation.
- Ensure that the procedure or orientation is credible from the client's frame of reference.
- Ensure that the procedure or orientation is connected with or elicits the client's previously successful experiences.
- Work in ways that enhance or highlight clients' feelings of personal control.
- View clients as people, not as their problems or difficulties or in ways that depersonalize them.

Method and Factor of Fit

All therapeutic approaches assist clients with making changes in one or more aspects or domains in their lives (see Table 2.9). Therapy uses technique to facilitate change, at least to some degree. Methods can be general as with using listening and attending skills or open and closed questions, or they can be specific such as assigning tasks, suggesting interpretations, and teaching skills. Most procedures are designed to have clients experience emotion, change sensory sensations (i.e., visual, auditory, kinesthetic), change thinking, develop new understandings or meanings, and/or change patterns of behavior.

It has been suggested that a primary aim of these procedures and, in fact, of all effective approaches and methods is to create shifts in systems caused by developing new perspectives, thereby leading to *second-order change* (Fraser & Solovey, 2007). In contrast to first-order change, which relates to change that involves systems that remain the same, second-order change moves beyond temporary or short-term solutions. It involves the creation of new perspectives that counter the previous problematic ones that have maintained and governed social and relational systems.

Empirical findings that indicate that methods, models, and techniques account for little of the variance in therapy outcome are supported anecdotally: Clients rarely mention therapeutic interventions or techniques but typically identify helpful aspects of services with statements such as, "I was finally able to see things differently," "My therapist listened to me," and "I felt the therapist understood me." Such statements tend to correlate with client contributions and relational factors.

Although research indicates that nontheory-specific effects account for the majority of the variance in outcome, methods are not irrelevant. Instead, how methods are used is crucial. Methods result from therapists' having collaborative conversations with clients, matching their orientations (in other words, ideas about problems and possibilities for solution) with clients, and activating and enhancing the contribution of general effects (in other words, the factors described in the first five premises). Jerome Frank stated:

> My position is not that technique is irrelevant to outcome. Rather, I maintain that . . . the success of all techniques depends on the patient's sense of alliance with an actual or symbolic healer. This position implies that

Table 2.9		
Domains of Change		
Experiential/Affective	**Cognition/Views**	**Action/Interaction**
• Feelings	• Cognitions	• Action patterns
• Sense of self	• Points of view	• Interactional patterns
• Bodily sensations	• Attentional patterns	• Language patterns
• Sensory experience	• Interpretations	• Nonverbal patterns
• Automatic fantasies and thoughts	• Explanations	• Time patterns
	• Evaluations	• Spatial patterns
	• Assumptions	
	• Beliefs	
	• Identity stories	

ideally therapists should select for each patient the therapy that accords, or can be brought to accord, with the patient's personal characteristics and view of the problem (Frank & Frank, 1991, p. xv).

Frank's statement illustrates the importance of therapists' selection of methods that emerge from the therapeutic relationship, alliance, and client factors, as opposed to entering therapy with a preset model. When clients experience therapists who work with them in ways that are consistent with clients' views of concerns and problems and the resolution of those concerns and problems, an increased "factor of fit" occurs.

Therapists can increase factor of fit by checking with clients to determine the validity of methods. Although most clients will not know whether a "technique" is being used, how they respond to therapists' use of questions, for example, can make a difference. Furthermore, as discussed previously, clients' beliefs about particular focuses (for example, emphasizing thoughts, behaviors, interactions) in therapy weigh heavily on the fit of the approach. A lack of fit (for example, when the therapist focuses on cognitions and insight but the client sees the problem as relational) can have detrimental effects by negatively affecting the therapeutic relationship, dampening hope, and curbing expectancy for positive change (Bertolino, 2003).

Although clients' orientations drive therapy and are pivotal to increasing the factor of fit, therapists can draw on their knowledge of theories to match clients' ideas about their problems, possibilities, and potential solutions. This knowledge can help engage clients in conversations that may allow new perspectives to emerge. It also allows therapists to view situations from varying perspectives without having to align with any one model or viewpoint.

Methods are rituals—practices that therapists use as part of personal therapeutic traditions. They are particularly important in mobilizing the first five principles of SBE discussed in this chapter. However, methods are not the causal agents of change. Wampold (2001) remarked that treatment procedures "are beneficial to the client because of the meaning attributed to those procedures rather than because of their specific psychological effects" (p. 27). In the best sense, practitioners use methods to promote hope and facilitate change.

Using methods—like establishing directions and setting goals—provides a means to incorporate structure into therapy sessions. This structure can be especially helpful to students and newer therapists. It is necessary however, to not let methods become the driving force in the therapeutic milieu.

The primary issue is the selection of methods and techniques. Training and education expose therapists to numerous methods and techniques; others emerge from client interactions or originate from creative thinking. It is essential that methods not be chosen and implemented randomly. Their selection must be based on client interactions and sound rationale. Factor of fit can be enhanced through general frameworks that incorporate client characteristics and systems of structure that assist with the selection of research-based methods to increase the likelihood of success. Frameworks that will be explored in upcoming chapters include *systematic treatment selection* (STS) and the *transtheoretical approach* (TA).

STS is based on identifying the effective parts of therapy and their systematic application in therapy. Client characteristics such as severity/functionality, problem complexity, distress, level resistance, and coping style (externalizing, internalizing) determine which methods to select (Beutler & Harwood, 2000). Stricker (2002) described STS as "an approach that draws from efficacy research and manualization of treatment, but transcends it and moves into effectiveness by allowing the practitioner far more flexibility to combine approaches and deviate from strict adherence to a manual" (p. 1279). A second framework, TA, is founded on *stages of change* and is based on selecting and matching methods of therapy that are complementary to clients' states of readiness to change (Prochaska & DiClemente, 2005). It is believed that within each stage are processes common to multiple therapies that can be used to facilitate change.

Both STS and TA provide conceptual maps for selecting therapy approaches that are likely to provide a higher degree of fit for clients. The two also offer latitude by allowing therapists to use their experience and intuition in making decisions and represent general frameworks for selecting methods that are respectful, culturally sensitive, and allow space for clients to give feedback. By monitoring the factor of fit, clients continue to be in charge of change processes and increase their chances for reaching their goals and achieving positive outcomes (see Table 2.10).

Table 2.10

Actions That Increase Factor of Fit

- Use methods as vehicles for activating and enhancing the other core premises of SBE.
- Use methods that fit with, support, or complement the client's worldview.
- Use methods that fit with or complement the client's expectations for treatment.
- Use methods that capitalize on client strengths, abilities, and resources.
- Engage clients in conversations and feedback processes to learn their thoughts about methods being considered.
- Use methods that fit clients' coping styles (internalized or externalized).
- Use methods to incorporate structure to sessions/interactions.
- Use methods to target change in specific areas of clients' lives (for example, thinking, action).
- Employ client strengths in strategies to assist in making change.
- Utilize the client's environment and existing support network.
- Use methods that positively reinforce healthy behaviors and functioning.
- Use a model to help think differently about a problem or situation when positive change is not occurring to assist in viewing concerns from different frames of reference.
- Use a method that the client considers empathic, respectful, and genuine.
- Use methods that increase the client's sense of sense of hope, expectancy, or personal control.
- Use methods that contribute to the client's sense of self-esteem, self-efficacy, and self-mastery.

Exercise 2.3

Reflections on SBE Core Premises

- In learning about the core premises of SBE, what stood out for you?

  _____

  _____

- With what premises of SBE do you agree? Why?

  _____

  _____

  _____

- With what premises of SBE do you disagree? Why?

  _____

  _____

  _____

- What, if any, revisions would you make to the four to six general ideas you listed in Exercise 2.1?

  _____

  _____

  _____

- What one thing about SBE stands out for you most?

  _____

  _____

  _____

- How might this one thing positively affect you?

  _____

  _____

  _____

You have thus far learned about a series of principles that emerge from the primary research agendas associated with psychotherapy and form the foundation of SBE. Please take a moment to reflect on these principles by completing Exercise 2.3, Reflections on SBE Core Premises. It is important to note that the strengths-based principles described are highlighted throughout psychotherapy literature but typically as independent entities. For example, the therapeutic relationship is highlighted in various models but little or no attention is given to client factors, such as internal strengths and external resources. Other models emphasize client factors yet largely ignore the role of expectancy and hope. The principles of SBE outlined are not independent ingredients that act in isolation from one another. Conceptualizing each principle as a distinct, independent entity would minimize the relative effectiveness of their interrelatedness. When used in concert with one another, these principles create a foundation based on the five C's listed in Chapter 1: culturally sensitive, collaborative, client informed, competency based, and change oriented. Later chapters will examine ways in which strengths-based principles inform practice and contribute to successful services.

SUMMARY POINTS

- Research has contributed to a significant expansion of knowledge regarding "what works" in therapy and *how* therapists can increase their effectiveness.
- Eclectic and integrative hybrids developed as alternatives to single models have gained great popularity by offering flexibility to therapists and clients, but not without raising questions about the models' validity and viability.
- Four primary agendas in research and practice have paved the landscape of therapy: *empirically supported treatments* (ESTs), *common factors* (CF), *empirically supported relationships* (ESRs), and *outcomes management* (OM)—each with its strengths and shortcomings.

  - *ESTs* (based on model-based research, which is also used to identify *evidence-based practices* and *treatments that work*) involve identifying treatment methodologies for which scientifically collected evidence has been gathered through randomized clinical trials (RCTs) in which treatments must show efficacy over the placebo condition or no-treatment alternatives.
- *CF* is based on meta-analytic studies suggesting that successful therapy outcome is contingent more on general effects or common factors including client contributions, therapeutic relationship, and expectancy than on specific effects of ingredients such as methods, models, and techniques.
- *ESRs* relate to the identification of elements of effective therapy relationships that affect treatment outcomes and determine efficacious methods of customizing therapy for individuals based on their particular characteristics.
- *OM* introduced the concept of client-based, ongoing, real-time feedback systems, including *alliance* (to track clients' ratings of the therapeutic relationship) and *outcome* (to track clients' ratings of the impact of services on major dimensions of life functioning) as measures to

monitor progress and provide therapists information they can use to make adjustments in therapy.

- Although the major agendas in research and practice approach the question of "what works" from different angles, they have significant intersections, common ground, and points of convergence.
- The most recent definition of EBP by the APA task force in evidence-based practice in psychology (EBPP) represents the broadest characterization of the practice to date and acknowledges previous factors including client characteristics and elements that have been noticeably absent in past definitions. It also underscores the importance of convergence among adjoining disciplines.
- The six core principles of SBE emerge from an intersection and convergence of major research and practice agendas.

  - *Client contributions* include clients' internal strengths and external resources, providing the largest percentage of variance to outcome.
  - *Therapeutic relationship and alliance* are based on collaborative client-therapist partnerships that accommodate clients' views about therapy processes and goals and the tasks to accomplish those goals.

- *Cultural competence* focuses on the importance of the various influences that affect all aspects of therapy including but not limited to creating safe, nurturing, and respectful contexts that encourage and facilitate growth and change.
- *Change as a process* emphasizes present and future change and the constancy of change as opposed to the determination of the causes or explanations for problems except when this focus does not fit with or invalidates clients.
- Both clients' and therapists' *expectancy and hope* about therapy affect change. Therapy must honor, respect, and accommodate clients' expectations, beliefs, and ideas. Therapists tap into expectancy by using processes and practices that encourage, empower, and create hope.
- *Method and factor of fit* refer to the fact that therapists must select methods that are respectful, culturally sensitive, and fit with clients' beliefs about problems and about how change might occur.

- The principles of SBE are interrelated. Each is part of a matrix that creates a foundation characterized by five C's: culturally sensitive, collaborative, client informed, competency based, and change oriented.

DISCUSSION QUESTIONS

1. What disciplines do you consider influential in understanding human experience and in helping people to change both psychologically and relationally? How do the disciplines you identified intersect, interconnect, and interact to form points of convergence?

2. What are potential strengths and limitations of eclecticism and integrative approaches to therapy?

3. What is the basis for each of the primary research and practice agendas discussed in

the chapter? What are arguments for and against each?

4. What are some points of intersection among the agendas? How might this intersection benefit clients?

5. What does this statement mean? "Clients are what make therapy work and the single most important contributors to outcome." What are ways that therapists can tap into client contributions?

6. What does the term *therapeutic alliance* mean? How can therapists work to strengthen the therapeutic relationship and alliance?

7. In what ways do culture and context factor into therapy processes? How can therapists actively attend to influences of culture and context?

8. What does the term *change as a process* mean? What are ways that therapists can enhance change?

9. How do expectancy and hope facilitate change? In what ways can therapists promote these premises in what ways?

10. What is the role of therapeutic method and technique? What does the term *factor of fit* mean? How can therapists use methods to enhance the factor of fit?

PART TWO

Chapter 3

Keys to Collaborative Partnerships

First Steps in Client-Therapist Engagement

■ Numerous variables affect and shape the therapeutic relationship and alliance. As noted in Chapters 1 and 2, the strength of the therapist-client bond largely determines positive change, and it has been demonstrated that high client ratings of the therapeutic alliance predict positive outcomes (Duncan, Miller, & Sparks, 2004). This chapter explores the weaving of the threads of the therapist-client partnership during therapeutic engagement. The chapter discusses ways to strengthen relationships by engaging clients prior to face-to-face contact, during initial interactions, and throughout therapy. By using collaborative engagement processes, therapists can increase the probability of a successful outcome. Although funding stipulations, organizational and/or program parameters, third-party reimbursement guidelines, and other constraints may not always make it possible to accommodate clients' preferences, collaborative efforts can promote client participation in services, strengthen the relationship and alliance, and increase hope and expectancy for future change.

Keys to Collaboration in Initial Client-Therapist Engagement

Therapeutic engagement, or alliance formation, refers to the collaborative partnership that honors and respects clients' voices, including their experiences and preferences. Engagement encompasses all aspects of therapy, which begin with *any* initial contact with an individual or organization that provides services. Bedi (2006) stated, "Alliance formation, as understood by clients, actually begins before the counselor fully engages the client" (p. 33). Therapists must be aware of the impact of engagement processes throughout the experience, even during the first contacts whether by telephone, in writing, or in person. These initial contacts significantly affect the therapeutic relationship and serve as the foundation from which possibilities for change emerge.

Initial contacts also convey the "transparency" of therapy practices (Madsen, 2007). Therapists openly share their experiences, ideas, and intentions through comments, questions, and suggestions in collaborative practices that invite clients to participate in the therapy process on as equal footing as possible. Providers recognize that the quality of the client's participation is a critical factor in outcome (Orlinsky, Grawe, & Parks, 1994).

Transparency begins prior to formal therapy and initial interactions and continues throughout providers' involvement with clients. *Transparency* refers to providers involving clients in all facets of services by (1) inviting them to express their preferences and orientations (in other words, ideas and perspectives), (2) valuing and respecting clients and their perspectives and communicating this acceptance through language and interaction, (3) including clients in the development of goals and ways to achieve those goals, and (4) using continuous feedback mechanisms to learn about and incorporate clients' experiences of therapeutic processes. These participatory processes help therapists to better accommodate therapy to clients' needs. By creating collaborative partnerships from the outset, and maintaining them throughout services, practitioners can tap into client contributions, attend to cultural influences, increase expectancy and hope, and enhance the change-affecting factors discussed in Chapter 2.

The processes that assist in gaining information as a means of better matching therapeutic methods with client preferences are *collaboration keys* (Bertolino, 2003; Bertolino & O'Hanlon, 2002). Although the ideas discussed in this chapter offer possibilities for client engagement and strengthening relationships, it is important to note that in some circumstances, one or more ideas offered will not be applicable in a particular context. For example, a therapist in a given context may not be able to offer variations in meeting times, and another may be required to maintain one-hour sessions. In such instances, therapists should not offer a particular collaboration means that is not possible given the preestablished rules or parameters of a program or service. If it is possible to expand or negotiate the rules of a program or service, however, practitioners should think creatively, consult with others, seek supervision, and always advocate for the best interests of clients.

Collaboration Key 1: Addressing Service Expectations

Clients begin services with beliefs created by media exposure (television, radio, magazines), social relationships (family, friends), and any previous therapy experiences. Although clients may express some of these to therapists, many will not. These beliefs will, however, influence clients' expectations of services and can affect how services progress and the degree to which they can be beneficial (Frank & Frank, 1991). These preconceptions make it important for therapists to invite clients to share their beliefs and expectations as they relate to the services being offered.

Creating "Space" during Initial Contacts

Making contact with a therapist is often a big step for a client. A host of feelings about seeking help can come to the forefront, and they may be intensified by and contribute to a sense of being "one-down" in relation to the therapist, resulting in clients' distrust and suspicion.

One way to neutralize this sense as well as myths about services and ambiguity during initial phone contacts, information-gathering processes, meetings, and sessions, is to ensure that clients are able to ask questions about services, processes, and what to expect. It is important, however, that therapists not feel pressured to respond to questions they are not prepared to answer. Few questions require immediate responses. Premature answers or responses can create problems and distance in client-therapist relationships. Be respectful, acknowledge clients' interest in gathering information, and assure them that their questions will be answered in a timely manner. Be sure to follow through. See the following examples of approaching these elements during initial phone conversations.

Therapist: We can talk in depth when you come in for your appointment, but is there anything that you'd like to know about how I work with people before then?

Caller: Now that you mention it, I've never been to therapy before and I'm a little worried that are you going to analyze me and well, tell me what's wrong with me. I mean, if that's what you do . . . but I don't think that's what I need.

Therapist: My aim is understand what you want from therapy and how I can best help you. We'll work together in deciding what is right for you. How does that sound?

Caller: That sounds good. It's a relief. I'm looking forward to our appointment.

Therapist: Great. See you then.

Caller: I'm not sure about all of this. What do you do when people come to see you?

Therapist: That's a very good question. First, I'd like you to know that should you decide to set an appointment I'll provide specific details about my approach and what you can expect.

For now, let me say in general that I work collaboratively with my clients to determine what they are concerned about, how they want things to be different, and how best to achieve those changes. I approach each client and session individually. Does that answer your question?

Caller: Yeah.

Conducting Client "Preinterviews"

When someone other than the potential client (for example, when several clients are involved) has made an appointment for another person (for example, adolescents, court/social service–referred individuals), an option is to suggest that the caller/contact person (for example, parent, member of a couple) have potential client(s) or other(s) call the provider to do a "preinterview." Doing so provides an opportunity for the person(s) who did not schedule appointments or were not involved in the decision to initiate services to ask questions about what to expect. The aim of these conversations is not to get another "side" of the story or engage in "problem talk" but to answer questions about therapy processes. As noted, this can help dispel myths, build hope, and strengthen relationships.

Preinterviews can help in the selection process for prospective clients, particularly adolescents. Sometimes people have a list of qualified therapists and are encouraged to contact each one on the list and interview them (Loar, 2001). The caller can identify the ones with whom he feels comfortable and schedule an appointment with the one who might provide the "best fit." Those who are involved in therapist selection are likely to be more invested in the success of therapy.

Preinterviews provide an early opportunity for therapists to answer general questions, describe what sessions are like, and/or dispel any misconceptions or myths (Bertolino, 2003). In addition, the process can serve as an "illusion of alternatives" (Cade & O'Hanlon, 1993; O'Hanlon, 1987) for potential clients who may not have been given a choice about attending therapy. Even if a therapist has already been selected or no other options are available, potential clients can still be offered the opportunity to "check out" or interview the therapist prior to the initial face-to-face session. The preinterview allows clients to reach out and encourages involvement from the start.

It is important to note that for some (more so for therapists than clients), the word *interviewing* seems antithetical to a collaborative stance, suggesting an asymmetrical relationship. Interviewing in this context refers to the therapist being open, flexible, and genuine as in face-to-face sessions. It also refers to encouraging clients to take the lead and become involved early in decisions (for example, whom to see, when to schedule the first appointment, what time to schedule it). The following examples provide ideas about approaching preinterviews:

Caller: My wife told me to call you or she'd leave me.

Therapist: I'm glad you called. How can I help you?

Caller: She told me to call some places and that's how I got you. I'm calling to figure out who I should see.

Therapist: What would you like to know to help you with your decision?

Caller: What should I expect?

Therapist: Do you mean if you were to come and see me?

Caller: That's right.

Therapist: I'll talk with you about what brought you to see me and how we could best approach those concerns.

Caller: Well, I don't think I really have a problem, but my wife does.

Therapist: If you decide to come to see me, we could talk about that further. What I want you to know is that I work with people on what they want to work on to improve their lives in ways that seem to fit. It's a partnership.

Caller: Okay. That makes sense.

Caller (Adolescent): Yeah, my mom told me to call you. I have to see a therapist.

Therapist: Thanks for calling. So, your mom told you to call?

Adolescent: Yeah. I don't have a choice.

Therapist: You mean you don't have a choice about seeing a therapist?

Adolescent: Yeah.

Therapist: It must have taken a lot on your part to call. I admire that. How I can help you with this?

Adolescent: I guess . . . well, what do you do when you meet with people?

Therapist: Well, the main thing is I want each person to know that I respect him or her. I also want to take the time to make sure that I understand where each person is coming from. After that, I find out what people who choose to continue working with me want and how we can get that to happen.

Adolescent: Would you take their side?

Therapist: You mean your parents?

Adolescent: Yeah.

Therapist: I respect each person's opinion. Because your parents are your parents and they care about you and are responsible for you, they're going to have opinions about what is best for you. I'll support them. I'll also support you because you're entitled to your opinion. You don't have to agree with what your parents want for you, you just have to accept that that's how they see it. Do you know what I mean?

Adolescent: Yeah. That's cool. Well, what if I don't like therapy? Will you tell them I don't have to come any more?

Therapist: If you were to choose to see me and you found that you didn't like it, I'd certainly want to know. Knowing what's going on helps me to learn what's working and what's not and make adjustments so you feel better about coming to therapy. So, if you felt it wasn't working out, I'd want to talk about it. As far as not having to come back, I wouldn't claim to know what's best for you and your family. I can only say that I would want things to work out for all of you. If you didn't like therapy, I'd support you the same way that I would support your parents. I would help you and your family to arrive at a decision that makes sense for all of you.

Adolescent: Okay . . . do I have to tell you everything?

Therapist: You have to tell me only what you feel comfortable with. So that's for you to decide.

Adolescent: Okay, I'll give it a try.

Exploring Preexisting Beliefs

A final aspect of service expectations relates to what people know about therapists and/or the contexts (i.e., the organizations, agencies, or programs) they work in or are associated with. Moreover, prospective clients' past experiences with these entities can influence the effectiveness of services rendered. Said differently, reputation matters. One way to start services off on the "right foot" is to ask clients what they know about you and/or your setting/organization/agency/practice, and so on. Another is to ask people about any previous experiences with services. Answers to these questions offer therapists the opportunity to dispel any myths that clients may have and clarify what actually happens during service delivery.

It is important to keep in mind that clients' preexisting beliefs can have effects beyond the immediate practitioner and/or her practice. Clients whose experiences with therapists and/or their practices have been positive are more likely to be involved with and benefit from services. Conversely, negative experiences (for example, feeling devalued, invalidated, being left out of discussions about services) can affect the degree to which clients benefit from current *and* future services (both within a practice/organization and with current or future outside helpers).

These questions can help learn about clients' expectations of service expectations:

- Do you have any questions about what our [therapy/services] are or are not?
- Do you have any questions about how [I/we] work with people?
- Do you have any questions about what we do here?
- What do you know about [us/me]?
- Do you have any concerns about seeing [us/me]?
- Although [name of another person] made the appointment, I'd like to know whether you have any questions you'd like to ask about our services.
- Although I'll talk more about this when you come in for your first meeting, at this point, is there anything you would like to know about our services or what we do here and the possible benefits or drawbacks?
- Is there anything I can do to increase your level of comfort in starting services?
- (If clients have received services previously) What has been your experience with services in the past?
- (If clients experienced previous services as negative) What can we do differently here to ensure that things go better for you this time?

Introducing other factors that may influence how clients expect therapy to proceed can also be helpful. These can include but are not limited to intake processes, paperwork and documentation, payment processes, phone calls after hours, crises and emergencies, referrals, clinical supervision, staff meetings, and so on. Clients may have more or fewer questions about specific procedures and processes, but providing information in written form that can be followed up on during meetings is generally good practice. Informational materials should reflect the philosophy and language of the staff and the overall organization or practice and include how those who seek services will be referred to (for example, as patients, clients, consumers), how staff refer to themselves (counselors, therapists, social workers), and the general language that will be used with clients, in conversations with staff and other professionals outside the setting, in reports and publications, and in community relations (for example, fund-raisers and interviews).

Collaboration Key 2: Determining Who Should Attend and the Format of Meetings/Sessions

Different paradigms and models within those paradigms carry protocols about how therapy should be conducted (see the Appendix). For example, models that are consistent with the psychological paradigm (in other words, first wave) traditionally view problems as existing within the mind or psyche of individuals. It is believed that people are essentially held captive by internal cognitive processes or are shaped or conditioned by external factors. This makes the individual client the target of treatment. Even when family therapy is indicated, adherence to the psychological paradigm means helping individuals to change intrapsychic processes, therefore benefiting interpersonal relationships.

The systemic-relational paradigm (in other words, second wave) provides a contrast. From this point of view, problems are considered interpersonal in nature, originating from dysfunctional patterns of interaction. The target of therapy is relationships with emphasis on having all or as many family members as possible present for treatment.

Positive change can be inhibited when therapists' rules or preferences regarding therapy run counter to or do not match those of clients. One way to learn of clients' concerns and problems is to invite them to bring to therapy (or have present) whoever they think will be helpful in resolving the concern. Including others prior to the start of formal therapy acknowledges and respects clients' ideas about how to begin and how positive change might occur.

The following examples show how therapists might talk with callers about their preferences for meeting arrangements:

Caller: I'd like to go ahead and make an appointment to talk with you about my marriage.

Therapist: Okay, will you be coming by yourself, or will there be anyone with you?

Caller: Just me to start. Is that okay? Is it weird that I want to talk about my relationship but don't want my husband there?

Therapist: It's not weird at all. I'd prefer that we start where you're most comfortable, and if we have other ideas when we meet, we can weigh those.

Caller: That's good. It's just that I think it will make things worse if he comes. This is really for me.

Therapist: That's fine. Let's go ahead and set a date and time to meet.

Caller: My daughter is causing problems. Should I bring just her? Or should I bring the whole family? I've never done this before.

Therapist: We can approach this in different ways. Because I can never know you or your family the way you do, I'd first like to find out whether you or anyone else in your family has a preference about who should come to the first session.

Caller: I know my daughter needs to come; she's the one who started all of this. But I know she'll go only if I make her because she already told me, "I don't need a shrink!"

Therapist: Okay. One possibility is to invite those you think can help with the concerns that you or your family are having. Another is to ask each person involved if he or she would like to come. You could also just make a decision yourself as to who should come in. We can always make adjustments later by including more or fewer people.

Caller: I really don't know. What do you recommend?

Therapist: From what you've described, it sounds like what's been happening with your daughter has had an affect everyone in your family to some degree, so my inclination would be to see your whole family. This way I'll be able to hear different points of view and then we can go from there. How does that sound?

Caller: That sounds good. I'd like for both of my kids and my husband to come. But I do have another question. Can this still work even if everyone doesn't come? I mean, I don't know if my husband will come. He thinks there's a problem but he just thinks our daughter needs to change her attitude. So he may or may not be willing to come.

Therapist: There are going to be times when people might not be able to make it. Some might not be able to because of a scheduling conflict or, like your husband, may just not want to be involved. It's your call as to whether or not you push the issue or if you want me to talk with someone. Even if we start with certain people, we can always make

changes in future sessions. Therapy can work without every family member being present. I'm confident that we can move toward the change you want with those who do come in.

Caller: That sounds good. I think we should start with all of us, and if my husband refuses to come, so be it. That makes the most sense to me. Let's set an appointment.

Practitioners may at times suggest that expanding sessions to include other persons (for example, family members, friends, outside helpers) could be helpful. Adding people might generate more ideas that can help overcome client hurdles or impasses in services. It is important to let clients determine whether such suggestions are acceptable. In approaching these situations, therapists offer ideas about expanding the system rather than imposing them. Bertolino and O'Hanlon (2002) stated:

> The difference here is that a collaborative therapist would not hold or present the idea that this must occur or that this is the only way that positive change will take place. Instead, the therapist might suggest that bringing in another voice might offer a new perspective or lead to the generation of some new ideas. Ultimately, clients decide whether such ideas are acceptable to them and whether they are within their personal theories about how change will come about (p. 32).

"Family" therapy can involve part of a family just as "couples" therapy can occur with just one member of a couple. Positive change is possible whether the therapist is working with an individual, one member of a couple, three members of a five-person family, or some other "nontraditional" configuration. Because client preferences, situations, and problems change, who attends therapy can change from session to session, calling for ongoing dialogue between the therapist and clients to determine best procedures. By inviting clients into conversations that honor their preferences, therapists continue to strengthen the therapeutic relationship and alliance.

Extenuating circumstances at times necessitate that therapists take more directive approaches. When clearly delineating what each person in a group is concerned about and wants to see change is too difficult, it may be helpful to separate clients to give each person time to voice his or her concerns and expectations.

In addition, meeting preferences of adolescents, young adults, and others could create a risk of harm (Bertolino & O'Hanlon, 2002). Volatility, hostility, or other interactions between clients may cause therapists to see them individually. For example, if a client uses verbally abusive statements about another and the therapist's immediate efforts do not end such behavior, it may be necessary to dismiss one or more persons from the group. Even if the behavior indicates what occurs elsewhere, it is not acceptable during the session. In such cases, clients may be brought back together when they agree to treat others more respectfully. Client safety and well-being are always therapists' primary considerations.

Some other questions to ask to determine who attends the sessions follow.

- Do you have a preference about who should attend sessions/meetings?
- (If clients have had previous experiences with social/psychological/health services) In the past, what groupings have worked best for you?
- (If a couple or family) What do you think about meeting together like this? Or: How would it be for each of you if we were to split up and I was to meet with each of you separately at times?

- Would it be okay with you if we occasionally vary who meets? For example, sometimes we might all meet together and at other times we might split up with two of you meeting with me at a time. How would that or some other variation be for you?
- Would you let me know if, at any point, you have any ideas—new or old ones—about how we should meet?

Mandated Meetings/Sessions

Some conditions necessitate that therapists take different courses of action. One of these relates to working with clients who are mandated to therapy by officials from outside entities (for example, judicial court systems, social service agencies). In some cases, certain family members or an entire family will be required to attend therapy. In these situations, the outside entity frequently sets specific goals for sessions. Recommendations regarding who should attend therapy and particular forms of intervention (for example, family therapy, anger management groups) often represent what referring persons are most familiar with, have the most faith in, or have been told is most effective. In most cases, the referring entity is seeking resolution to some problem that led to the referral in the first place. In other words, it is not so much the method of intervention that is important to referrers as the overall outcome.

Therapists can respond to referrers by inviting them into conversations to clarify the outcomes sought and service alternatives for achieving those results. Some referrers will negotiate and perhaps even leave the decision about who attends sessions and how to achieve change up to therapists as long as outcomes are reached.

Questions and comments to help learn about who should attend mandated meetings/sessions follow.

- Whom would you like to invite to the first session/meeting?
- Whom do you think ought to be present?
- (If a client is unsure about whom to invite or who ought to attend) I'd like to recommend that you invite the people to attend who you think will be most helpful in resolving the concern/problem.
- (If someone cannot/will not attend) For a variety of reasons, one or more persons may not be able or will not want to attend sessions/meetings. Change is constant and is possible even in very difficult situations. Having said that, I'll work with whoever is present to achieve positive change.
- I want to be sure that we explore avenues that might help to improve things with you [your situation]. If it's okay with you, I'd like to offer an idea. What do you think about the idea of inviting [name(s) of person(s)] to attend a session sometime in the future?
- What conditions would make it comfortable with you to have [name(s) of person(s)] present at a meeting/session?
- (If client does not wish to include another person or expand the system) That's okay. I respect your decision not to include [name(s) of person(s)]. Please let me know in the future if you think bringing in another person might help move things along for you or your situation.

In addition to who should attend sessions, questions arise about whether clients should be seen together (a unit or family), separately, and so on. Because therapists' theoretical approaches and training vary, they could have preconceived ideas and preferences about such questions. Clients, however, often have their own ideas and preferences that may differ from those of the therapist. When several clients work as a group, there may be a number of ideas about how to proceed. Moreover, in particular situations, such as working with adolescents, caregivers will not only have opinions but also firm expectations about "what needs to happen." For example, it is not uncommon for caregivers to identify adolescents as "the problem" and expect that them to be seen separately, but this can also change from session to session.

When asked how they would like to meet, clients commonly respond in one of three ways. As previously mentioned, they first identify the person(s) they feel is(are) most responsible for problems and should be the focus of attention, either in individual meetings or as part of family sessions, but including them can lead to finger pointing. The second way clients respond is by sharing responsibility for problems among those present. This often suggests a focus on all persons involved in the therapy. The third common response is clients will say, "We're not sure. What do you think we should do?" or "What do you usually do?" This can offer more latitude about how to proceed and perhaps indicate that clients are placing value on the therapist's knowledge and expertise. Although there will be contrasting viewpoints as well as benefits and drawbacks of meeting arrangements, acknowledging the perspectives of those present is a respectful way to begin.

Using the word *and* to link different perspectives, the therapist might say, "You would like to meet with [name(s) of person(s)] *and* you would like to meet with [name(s) of person(s)]. Is that right?" The therapist would then work to negotiate a resolution that is acceptable to those present. Sometimes this means beginning one way and shifting to another. At times those who initiated therapy or have the power to end it will insist on certain meeting configurations. It is important to understand the various positions and at least acknowledge each even if a consensus is not reached.

The following examples illustrate how to talk with clients about the format of sessions.

Therapist: We can meet in different ways. Some people prefer to keep everyone together. Others are more in favor of having each person have some individual meeting time. Some like a combination of both. And that can change each time. Does anyone here have a preference about how we should start?

Client: This is new for us. So, whatever you think is best.

Therapist: Okay that's fine. Would anyone else like to share his or her thoughts about it?

(No response from the other family members)

Therapist: Okay. Would it be okay with each of you if we continued meeting just like we are now?

(Nods around the room indicate consent.)

Therapist: What about if we split up on occasion and I met with some or all of you separately from time to time—would that be okay with each of you?

(Nods around the room indicate consent.)

Therapist: Great. If you continue to meet with me, we can make changes from session to session. All you need to do is voice your opinion.

Therapist: There aren't any right or wrong ways about how we approach your concerns. We could keep everyone together or I could spend some individual time with each of you, or we could do a combination of both. Whatever we decide, we can also change. Does anyone here have an opinion about how we should start?

Parent: Well, we tried therapy before and it didn't work. I think it's because we argued so much and talked over each other that we really couldn't get anywhere. So my vote is that we do something else.

Therapist: What might be a good way start?

Parent: I think we should try meeting like this, but if we start arguing, maybe we should talk with you separately. That might be a good idea anyway—to talk to us separately once in a while.

Therapist: Okay. Who else agrees or has another idea?

(Two of the family members agree, and one does not give a verbal response.)

Therapist: Okay, so two of you agree. Reggie, you didn't say anything, but I saw your shoulders drop. What do you think?

Reggie: I don't care. This is stupid. I don't have anything to say anyway.

Therapist: That's fine. I just want to be sure that if you have an opinion you are able to share it. Will it be okay with you if you and I spend a few minutes together once in a while?

Reggie: I guess.

Therapists have no reason to be bashful about sharing their thoughts. They should not impose a format that is disrespectful or incongruent with clients' expectations (Bertolino & O'Hanlon, 2002) but instead invite clients to share their preferences. Although therapists could suggest ideas, addressing clients' spoken or unspoken preferences will improve the chances of achieving successful outcomes. As with other processes, therapists offer ideas in conversations, noting clients' responses to them. The following example illustrates the process.

Client: I'd really like to know what you think we should do. I mean, you see people everyday. What do you think?

Therapist: Yes, I do. What I've learned is that what fits and works for one may not necessarily fit and work for another. Now, I've got some ideas that I think make sense given what I've heard. What I'm going to ask of you is to let me know if makes sense for all of you. I want to be sure that you feel comfortable in letting me know, at any point in time, if something doesn't fit. Okay?

(Nods around the room indicate consent.)

Collaboration Key 3: Determining the Physical Space and Setting of Sessions

The physical space and setting of the counseling sessions may at first seem to be a minor factor but can be important to some clients and contribute to the strength of the therapeutic relationship. Physical space includes the design, setup, and accessibility of areas that clients and others may utilize (e.g., reception areas, hallways, stairs, ramps, elevators, waiting rooms, therapy offices, restrooms, parking). Setting also involves pictures and wall fixtures, reading materials (both leisure and educational), toys, and other physical elements that create a culture of care and respect.

Although the most common physical setting for therapy is an office, other options include schools, homes, and prisons, where more and more services are being provided. Because of funding or other guidelines, clients may not have choices about where sessions are held. They will be seen in whatever context the particular service or program designates. Other situations offer more flexibility. For example, some providers offer the choice of holding sessions in clients' homes. This option can allow people who have transportation concerns or physical disabilities to have access to services. Such flexibility can also contribute to a better fit between clients and providers. Physical setting options can be discussed during initial contacts. The following examples are brief dialogues that offer such options.

Therapist: Our services are set up so that we have a few choices in terms of where we can meet— in our office or your home or . . .

Caller: . . . That's actually why I chose to call you. We don't have transportation, but we really need help. I heard from a friend you guys can come out and see us.

Therapist: That's true. There are two days a week that I go to people's homes. I can arrange to see you on either a Monday or Thursday— which are the days I'm in your area.

Caller: You don't do Fridays?

Therapist: I'm sorry, I only have office appointments on Fridays.

Caller: That's okay. We can work with that. This is really important.

Therapist: That's great. For what day would you like to schedule an appointment?

Therapist: We have a few choices in terms of offices where we can meet.

Parent: Really?

Therapist: Yes, we could meet at the main office, which is in the county. I'm there on Mondays and Wednesdays. A second possibility would be to meet at one of our two satellite offices. I'm at the south office on Tuesdays, and we have another therapist who works out of the north office. She's there Tuesday through Friday.

Parent: Wow. I had no idea that I would have a choice. Let's try for a Monday appointment at your county office. My work is nearby and I can come straight over if we can find a time between 4:30 pm and 7:00 pm.

Therapist: Great. I've got a 5:00 pm available next Monday. Will that work?

Parent: Yes, that's fine.

Offering a choice of setting has both benefits and drawbacks. One benefit is that clients have a choice of context in which they are most comfortable. It can provide therapists the opportunity to observe and learn about clients in a different setting, such as the home environment. Indeed, some contend that unless clients, particularly families, are seen in their homes, therapists cannot accurately understand their situations. One drawback to having sessions outside a practitioner's office is safety. Although threats to well-being certainly exist in offices, ensuring safety and monitoring variables in external environments can be much more difficult. Any therapist doing out-of-office work should be trained in measures that ensure safety and have support systems in place to respond to potential dangers.

Session-setting choices offer clients flexibility, possibly reducing premature dropout. In addition, studies have demonstrated that explaining processes and rationale to clients prior to formal therapy decreases dropout rates (Garfield, 1994). However, people must be accountable for their choices and actions (for example, missing or being late for appointments, not being present for in-home sessions). Case Examples 3.1 and 3.2 are conversations regarding client preferences.

CASE EXAMPLE 3.1

Mariah sought therapy after experiencing several panic attacks while out socially. Near the end of the initial phone call, she nervously inquired, "Would it be possible to meet in a room where it isn't too loud? I don't mean just loud with sound. I mean a room where there aren't many things on the walls . . . it's not cluttered. It's quiet. Is that possible?"

"Sure," I replied. "We have an office that has a couch and two chairs, a bookcase, and a desk, but there are very few others things in it—just one picture. I can show it to you when you come for your appointment. And if you don't find it comfortable, I have another in mind as well."

Mariah sighed in relief, "Thank you. I don't want to be a pain but I've been feeling really overwhelmed in rooms that are cluttered and loud these days, and that would help me to relax."

CASE EXAMPLE 3.2

Brian, a 15-year-old, was placed in an emergency shelter where I was a therapist. Prior to meeting with him, his mother informed me, "Therapy won't work with Brian. We've already tried it." When asked to elaborate, the mother would only say, "He hates to sit and talk. And even if he does sit down with you, he won't say anything more than 'yes' or 'no' to your questions."

Before my first meeting with Brian for therapy, I asked him if he preferred to talk inside the house or in an office, outside in the yard, or on a walk around the neighborhood. With a surprised look, Brian responded, "Can we really go outside and talk?" "Sure," I responded.

Brian and I ended up talking outside on the stairs of the emergency shelter. During that time, he openly expressed what he had been experiencing. In future meetings we shot baskets, walked down to the local waterfront, and even talked inside in an office.

Working with clients in settings that increase their comfort improves the chances for present and future change.[1] That having been said, space restrictions and the timing of sessions (for example, certain days and times therapists are at certain locales, a limited number of available appointment times, driving distances to client homes, time of travel between appointments) can provide barriers to some setting options. Bertolino and O'Hanlon (2002) stated, "Although it may not always be possible to change the meeting place, consulting with clients about their comfort level with regard to different contexts can let them know that you are sensitive to their needs" (p. 34). The idea is to include clients in therapy processes and accommodate, whenever possible, their preferences about meeting arrangements. Additional questions related to choosing a setting follow.

- Where would you feel most comfortable meeting?
- (If clients have had previous experiences with social/psychological/health services) In the past, in what type of setting have you been most comfortable in discussing [yourself/family/situation/concerns/problems, etc.]?

Studies suggest that setting variables, often referred to as an aspect of *site effects*, consistently affect the variance in client outcomes and contribute to them more than technique does (Greenberg, 1999). These setting variables remain a largely unexplored area, however, and provide fertile ground for future research in helping relationships.

Collaboration Key 4: Determining the Timing, Length, and Frequency of Meetings/Sessions

Most practitioners are familiar with the complexities of client scheduling. Clients must contend with school and employment schedules, child care issues, and other commitments and responsibilities. Although adult clients generally have more flexibility in their schedules (for example, they can see therapists before or after work, schedule sessions over lunch breaks, take time off), adding children, adolescents, and families to the equation can narrow the options. For example, appointments with children typically are scheduled after school, and involving a number of family members in therapy requires coordinating multiple schedules.

Scheduling may be less complicated in some settings such as residential treatment programs because clients will be present for extended periods, providing more options for meeting times. However, some clients may prefer to be seen at specific times during the day. For example, certain adults are "morning" people and prefer early sessions. Some youth may respond better in sessions held right after school, and others will do better with evening meetings. Therapist and program flexibility in terms of the timing of sessions can make a difference in meeting clients' needs.

---

[1]When meeting with clients outside of an office-based setting, practitioners must be sure to get proper consent and discuss any issues related to confidentiality. (For example, if going for a walk with a person under the age of consent, providers must first gain permission from the legal guardian to do so. Practitioners should also discuss with those involved the possible threats to confidentiality—such as being seen by others—and how to handle these issues. This may also be an issue for accrediting bodies.)

Funding and reimbursement can affect scheduling as well as length and frequency of sessions. Multiple constraints (e.g., having to see a minimum number of clients per week, keeping sessions to one hour) that are rooted in economics can affect how therapists offer services. These constraints can cause clients to be left out of decision making, thus preventing them from being able to fully participate in therapy. These factors can negatively affect clients' expectancy and hope that often accompanies the start of therapy. Even when it is not possible to change the time or length of meetings due to organizational, funding, or other constraints, therapists should explain this to clients and express their determination to accommodate their needs whenever possible. The following example illustrates one way that a therapist might address these concerns.

> One of my hopes is that you'll share with me any thoughts you might have about scheduling our meetings. Whether it's the time or length of our meetings, how often we meet, or any other ideas you may have, I'd like to hear your thoughts. Because there are many ways to approach therapy, this information can help me better understand your needs and expectations. Although I can't make promises that I'll be able to accommodate every request, I want you to know that I'm committed to doing whatever I can to ensure that therapy is a positive experience for you.

An aspect associated with scheduling and timing is the length of sessions. The idea of hour-long sessions is especially worthy of discussion because of the North American managed-care climate in which session length in addition to frequency are mandated.

Most clients adapt well to one-hour (or perhaps 50-minute "hourly") sessions. Others may need longer sessions or perhaps multiple meetings each week. If clients travel long distances to see therapists or therapists do the traveling to see clients in home settings, longer sessions can make better economic sense. In addition, large families and clients who are exploring intense, painful issues could need longer sessions. Alternately, shorter sessions (for example, 20 minutes two to three times per week) may provide a better fit for children. Such varying needs make it important for therapists to consider how they might negotiate with funding sources to best meet their clients' needs and provide services with sensitivity. Attention must also be given to the influence of culture and family background regarding length and frequency of sessions.

Meeting frequency is contingent on clients' and therapists' availability, mandates from referral (funding) sources, or organizational or program philosophies and guidelines, for example. Although clients often opt for once-a-week visits, some want more frequent sessions, and others find that every-other-week visits will suffice. As therapy progresses, sessions may become more or less frequent. When positive change has occurred and goals are being reached, it is not unusual for clients to see practitioners less often. Flexibility on the part of practitioners can allow clients to schedule sessions in ways that fit them and their lifestyles, thereby increasing the chances of successful outcomes.

Talk with clients about their preferences regarding which dates, days, and times of day are best for meetings/sessions. If one or more of these is limited, demonstrate sensitivity to their scheduling concerns by trying to offer at least two options. The following are some questions to assist in this process.

- Do you have a preference about when we should meet? (for example, day of the week, time of day)
- Do you have a preference as to how long our meetings/sessions should be? (for example, 30 minutes, 1 hour, 2 hours)
- What might work best for you?
- (If options are limited or client has trouble making a decision) Would you prefer to schedule our next meeting for [specific day or date] or [specific day or date]?
- What ideas to you have about how often we should meet? (for example, once a week, twice a week, once every two weeks, once a month)
- (If clients have had previous experiences with social/psychological/health services) In the past, has worked best for you?
- (If the worker has flexibility in scheduling) Generally, do you or your family prefer to set a standing meeting time or to remain flexible and see what schedule works for you from meeting/session to meeting/session?
- Would it be okay with you if we revisited our meeting/session arrangements each time?

Collaboration Key 5: Utilizing an Open-Door Perspective

Gaining access to counseling and therapy can be a challenging endeavor. Unless they can afford to pay for services out of pocket, many clients need to receive authorization to find local providers and initiate services. Access to programs that offer services at little or no cost (or may require copayments) can be difficult because of long waiting lists and limited choice in providers. These factors can intensify pain and suffering for people in crisis. Another factor to be considered is clients' reluctance to make the transition out of therapy for fear that if they need to restart, they will face the same access challenges.

By and large, organizations and agencies rather than clients' needs determine the access to as well as length and frequency of session. As a result, a mismatch between organization, program, provider designs, and client needs can occur.

One way to address this access problem is to employ an *open door* in service provision (Bertolino, 2003) that offers reasonable access to people who are in immediate need. For example, physicians use a general practitioner open-door model that allows people to set appointments with their doctors as needed. In other words, physicians *expect* to see their patients for preventative services, checkups, and future concerns, but the same cannot be said about psychotherapy. Clients who return to counseling for recurrence of original concerns or new ones are frequently viewed negatively, as having *deeper, unresolved* "issues."

An open-door service provision in psychotherapy would offer a fit for clients as they move through life stages and transitions. More and more people now are coming to therapy to straighten a few things out and then move on, returning in the future if necessary. Case Examples 3.3 and 3.4 illustrate this concept.

This family's approach to therapy was consistent with the general practitioner, or open-door, model referred to earlier. Clients experience different concerns and problems at different times. Therapy is not about trying to help clients to live problem-free lives. The late John Weakland of the Mental Research Institute used to say that we thought we could make people's lives problem free if we just provided good enough and long enough therapy.

CASE EXAMPLE 3.3

Joy, a 37-year-old mother of three, initiated therapy as a result of feeling "overwhelmed" by her recent divorce. At the end of the initial session, she told her therapist that she felt "considerably better" and relieved that what she was experiencing wasn't "crazy." Joy attended a second session and then told her therapist that she knew what she needed to do and would be in touch if necessary. About two months later, Joy called and asked if she could come back to therapy for a "refresher" session. After the session, she again told the therapist that she would call if she needed further help. Joy phoned several months later, not to make an appointment, but to check in and to let her therapist know that she was doing well.

CASE EXAMPLE 3.4

Cory, a 14-year-old boy, was referred to therapy after firing a BB gun at another teenager. A family court official strongly suggested but did not mandate that Cory attend therapy. In response, his mother brought him to see me. As I did in each session, at the end of the fourth session, I asked Cory and his mother how they would like to proceed. Because Cory had been doing well, his mother suggested that we meet again in two weeks. We all agreed and set an appointment for two weeks later.

To my surprise (they had been consistent), Cory and his mother did not show up for their scheduled appointment. I attempted to contact the family by telephone but my calls were not returned. I followed this by sending a series of three letters to the family. Once again there was no response. After a few weeks passed without any contact from the family, I closed the case file.

About six months later, I received a telephone call from Cory's mother. She asked if she could bring him back to therapy. I agreed. At the appointment, I began by asking both Cory and his mother about the concern that had brought them to therapy previously (the incident with the BB gun). Both Cory and his mother reported that he had been doing well and that he had not been in trouble of any kind. I was curious as to why they had chosen to return. My suspense was quickly abated when Cory's mother stated that recently he had met his biological father for the first time. Because his biological father had only recently become involved in his life, Cory was angry with him for having shown no interest in him in the past.

For the next few weeks, Cory and his mother consistently attended their scheduled sessions. Following the third session, they scheduled a fourth for three weeks later. Then, just as with the first series of sessions, he and his mother did not show up for their next scheduled session. Once again, I attempted to contact them through telephone calls and letters. Again I obtained no response.

Nearly one year later, I was surprised when Cory's mother contacted me, seemingly out of the blue. She was to the point in telling me that Cory had been struggling with his grades and seemed disinterested in school. There was no mention of previous sessions or concerns. She simply asked to bring Cory back to therapy. I again agreed.

CASE EXAMPLE 3.4 (continued)

Going into the scheduled session, I was determined to find out what had led Cory and his mother to drop out of therapy on the previous two occasions. I said to Cory and his mother, "I have to tell you that I'm a bit confused here. This is the third round of sessions that we've had. After the first two, you disappeared. And I'm still wondering if I did something wrong or just what happened." To this the mother replied, "Oh no. You've been great. That's why we keep coming back. What happens is we come for a few sessions until we can handle things better. Then we come back if we need to." "OK. I would greatly appreciate it if you could do me a favor," I requested. "The next time you feel like things are where you think you can handle them, will you let me know so that I don't get a complex?" The mother laughed and replied, "Sure. I'll be sure to remember this time."

Over the course of two months, I met with Cory and his mother for six sessions. We focused primarily on school-related concerns although we did delve into a few other areas that came up from session to session. Then, what seemed unthinkable to me happened again. The family did not show up for a scheduled seventh session.

As time passed, I periodically wondered about Cory and how he had been doing. I was also puzzled because of the therapy pattern with them. Nearly a year later I was again surprised, although less so than previously, when Cory's mother called for an appointment. He was now 17 years old. In fact, it was Cory who did most of the talking, seemingly taking the reigns of therapy. He explained that his girlfriend had broken up with him and that he was "bummed out" because he had to decide what to do after graduating. As in the past, I asked Cory and his mother to please let me know when they feel that they had a better handle on things. I went on to meet with Cory for three sessions, with his mother sitting in on occasion. Following the third session, his mother said, "We're doing well. Thanks again and we'll see you down the road if we need to."

But after 100 years of therapy, that goal has been found to be too utopian because life, as the old saying goes, is just one damn thing after another. Just when we think we've got everything sorted out, we move into a different developmental stage and life hands us new dilemmas. But for the people who seek therapy, life has become the same damn thing over and over. Our job as therapists is to get them from the same damn thing over and over to only one damn thing after another and then get out of their lives. We want clients to know that we value our relationships with them and will do what we can to provide the services they need as they encounter the challenges of life.

Providing services in a timely manner when people need them echoes what was discussed in Chapter 1. The provision of therapeutic services can be cost effective because it can actually result in significant reductions in medical expenditures—especially for people with a history of overutilization. Therapy also offers benefits that extend beyond economics by offering services to people before they experience full-blown crises. Offering clients services when they first need them is proactive and respectful with an emphasis on *prevention* (Bertolino, 2003). An open-door perspective is part of creating a collaborative context that allows for entry, termination, and reentry, depending on client needs. This flexibility allows individuals, couples, and families to seek help whenever they feel it is necessary.

Practitioners and those who authorize services should not make promises that cannot be kept. For example, clients who have transitioned out of therapy should be welcome to return to a practice but not guaranteed that the same therapist will be available. Practices should let clients know they will be seen in a timely manner and offered as many choices about service parameters as possible; however, they should be advised in advance that therapists may have full case loads, may have left the practice, and so on. If scenarios involve a change in the type of and manner in which services can be provided, someone in the practice should discuss this with the client and explore alternatives. For example, offer a client who needs to be put on a waiting list a one-time consultation. Change can happen quickly, and a one-time meeting can be a good way to address problems in an otherwise stuck situation or system.

Some ideas for talking with clients about an open-door philosophy follow.

- We're here in much the same way that you might see your primary physician for check-ups. If you feel that at some point it would be a good idea to come in for a check-up session, give us a call.
- People encounter challenges at different times in their lives. I want you to know that if anything were to arise in the future that you would need to address, all you need to do is contact us. We'll do our best to provide what you need as soon as possible.
- We all experience ups and downs to some degree. If you were to feel that you are experiencing something that won't improve on its own, please know that we are here if you'd like to come back.

Collaboration Key 6: Emphasizing Premeeting/Session Change

Because people generally begin therapy when they face problems or significant life events, it is easy to engage them in conversations about such things. It is important to realize, however, that change is the only constant; people's problems fluctuate in frequency, intensity, and duration. Thus, clients can be helped to identify subtle differences that can occur prior to their first session. This concept has been referred to as *presession* (or pretreatment) *change* (Weiner-Davis, De Shazer, & Gingerich, 1987). The idea is to help clients to notice times when the problems they experience were absent or less intrusive. During initial therapy sessions, practitioners ask, "Many times, people notice that things seem different between the time they make the appointment for therapy and the first session. What have you noticed about your situation?" (p. 360). Estimates are that between 15 and 60% of clients experience some form of positive pretreatment change (Howard et al., 1986; Lambert, Shapiro, & Bergin, 1986; Lawson, 1994; Weiner-Davis, de Shazer, & Gingerich, 1987; Ness & Murphy, 2001).

From a strengths-based engagement perspective, focusing on presession change has these objectives:

- To learn more about what is happening during times that problems are better or worse and what clients are doing differently to cause this.
- To help clients notice more about the influence they have over problems.
- To build on or create an increased sense of hope.

It is easy to become entrenched in the view that situations and problems are unchangeable and are constant with little or no differences in intensity. Inviting clients to notice and then describe variations helps clients to indirectly challenge their assumptions.

Invitations to focus on presession change do not need to wait until the first session. During initial telephone contacts, therapists can invite clients to notice any differences regarding their concerns, emphasizing change in general, not just positive change. In fact, by emphasizing only one direction, therapists may be missing opportunities to learn about variations in the influence of problems. To introduce the concept of presession change, Bertolino (2003) offered the following example for initial contacts:

> Now that we've got a time set and we know where we'll be meeting, I was wondering if I might ask for your consideration in a matter. I'd like to invite you, in between now and our first meeting together, to notice any differences or variations with the situations, concerns, or problems that lead you to making this appointment. You might notice changes with the intensity of problems—when things are a little better or worse, with how long they last, what brings them to an end, who's around when they occur or don't occur, and so on. I'll leave that up to you. I'd just like to invite you to consider noticing any differences and then telling me about it when we meet. If you'd like you can ask others to do the same thing. If you or others want to write down these differences that's fine too, or you can just remember them. Just do what makes the most sense to you (p. 73).

Simply by paying attention to differences, some clients will make small shifts in their views, moving from "it's always that way" to "sometimes it's a little better" or "it's not always as bad as it seems." These shifts, however subtle, can lead clients to doubt their own perspectives, thus opening doorways to view their situations and problems differently. After asking clients during initial phone contacts to notice differences, therapists can follow up on this in the initial session. Information gained can help therapists learn both specifics about problems (in other words, who, what, when, where, and how) including their influence over clients, and the influence that clients have over their problems. Furthermore, when clients report a reduction in or elimination of problems, therapists can explore how those changes came about, what they mean, and how to continue those changes into the future. These are some questions to ask in introducing presession change:

- What did you notice happening with the concern you've been facing that you would like to have continue?
- What is noticeable about the times when you've had the upper hand with the problem you've been facing?
- What does this tell you about your situation?
- How might this be a step toward resolving your concern?
- What else might you do with this information?

Collaboration Key 7: Introducing Feedback Methods

Research conducted over the last several decades has found that a combination of a client's rating of the therapeutic alliance with the experience of meaningful change in the initial stages of treatment is a highly reliable predictor of eventual treatment outcome (Duncan, Miller, & Sparks 2004). In one study of 2,000 therapists and thousands of clients, for example, researchers found that therapeutic relationships in which no improvement occurred by the third visit did not on average result in improvement *over the entire course of treatment* (Brown, Dreis, & Nace, 1999). In terms of predicting outcome, the researchers note that variables such as diagnosis, severity, and type of therapy (including medication) were, "not . . . as important as knowing whether or not the treatment being provided is actually working" (p. 404).

Although much can be drawn from empirical evidence regarding factors of effective therapy, two points stand above the rest. First, clients are the most significant contributors to outcome; second, clients' ratings of the therapeutic relationship are the most consistent predictor of outcome. Therefore, it is imperative that therapists incorporate methods that encourage clients to voice their perceptions, ideas, perspectives, preferences, observations, and/or evaluations. Through collaboratations with clients, therapists learn what is and is not working, what clients need more or less of, what adjustments would be helpful, and so on.

Therefore, beginning with initial interactions, clients are involved in discussions about what therapy will entail and are introduced to therapeutic processes that are intended to magnify their voices.

Process-oriented feedback involves methods for eliciting and incorporating clients' perceptions of the therapeutic relationship and alliance. *Outcome-oriented* feedback relates to methods that monitor clients' perceptions of the impact of services. As described in Chapter 1, these two mechanisms are based on *real-time* feedback and create a system of outcome management.

Let's briefly explore each of these feedback methods.

Process-Oriented Feedback

Client satisfaction is not the same as process-oriented feedback, nor is it a consistent predictor of client improvement. Lunnen and Ogles (1998) found that clients "tend to report high levels of satisfaction regardless of outcome" (p. 406).

Being process informed means checking in with clients periodically to learn about their perceptions of the therapeutic relationship. Are clients feeling heard and understood? Are they satisfied with the direction of therapy? Do they feel the means used to achieve goals are a good fit? As meetings/sessions progress and end, practitioners check with clients to learn their perceptions of interactions, again learning what worked well, what did not, and make any necessary adjustments to accommodate clients' preferences. The following example is a way to introduce clients to this idea:

> I'd like to share with you a little about how we like to work at our [agency, clinic, practice]. We are dedicated to helping the people we work with achieve the results they want in therapy. From the start, I'll be talking with you about your experience with therapy. I'll check in with you to find out what's been helpful to you, what's not, what's working, and what's not. There are several ways that I can learn from you how you think things are going. For example, I might suggest a brief pencil and paper questionnaire. Or I might just ask you a few questions. Your ongoing feedback will let me know if any changes are necessary. Is this okay with you?

Therapists may also choose to use formal instrumentation such as the Revised Helping Alliance Questionnaire (HAq-II)(Luborsky et al., 1996), the Working Alliance Inventory (WAI)(Horvath & Greenberg, 1989), or the Session Rating Scale (SRS)(Duncan et al., 2003), and/or informal questioning as a means of acquiring feedback. In the next chapter we will explore specific examples of questions that can assist in learning clients' perceptions of the therapeutic relationship and alliance. What is important at this juncture is introducing the role of process feedback to clients.

Outcome-Informed Feedback

The second part of real-time feedback is to monitoring clients' reports of the subjective benefit of services provided. Commonly referred to as being "outcome-oriented," this includes the idiosyncratic meaning attached to the benefit of services by the client. Outcomes encompass clients' perspectives regarding the impact of the services on major areas their lives (for example, primarily personal distress, close interpersonal relationships, social role functioning). By monitoring outcomes, therapists are able to learn from clients whether and to what degree services provided are beneficial. Examples of outcome measures include the Outcome Questionnaire 45 (OQ-45.2)(Burlingame et al., 1995; Lambert & Burlingame, 1996; Lambert & Finch, 1999; Lambert et al., 1996), Youth Outcome Questionnaire (Y-OQ) (Burlingame, Wells, & Lambert, 1996; Burlingame et al., 2001; Burlingame et al., 2004; Dunn, et al., 2005), and the Outcome Rating Scale (ORS) (Miller & Duncan, 2000; Miller et al., 2003). Consistent with being process oriented, therapists introduce the importance of monitoring outcomes. An example of the introduction follows:

> In addition to talking with you about your experience in therapy, I'll also be curious to learn whether or not the work we've done together has been of benefit to you. To do this, I'd like to periodically ask you a few questions or have you complete a brief pencil and paper questionnaire to let me know if and how what we've been doing in therapy has been effective. So, I'll be able to learn from you if therapy has helped with the concerns you came in with, if anything

> needs to change in terms of the services we've provided, or whether a referral to another service would help you to get what you want.

It is essential that information gleaned from outcome-informed processes be incorporated into sessions as a way to ensure the fit with the client's preferences and the approach being employed. Upcoming chapters will provide ways to monitor outcomes. In being both process and outcome oriented, therapists help to create a context in which clients are the engineers of change. Clients' experiences, perceptions, and orientations drive therapy.

Collaboration is a necessary component of change. Clients often experience human and social services as being done *to* them as opposed to *with* them. By beginning services with a clear emphasis on creating collaborative partnerships with clients, practitioners increase the chances that clients will benefit positively from the process. Collaboration with clients in regard to the keys discussed here can enhance general effects, such as client and relational factors, expectancy, and hope. Collaboration keys also represent building blocks for future change. To experiment with these ideas, please refer to Exercise 3.1, Using Collaboration Keys.

The significance of engaging clients early in services is supported by empirical evidence:

- Clients only attend a handful of sessions regardless of therapists' orientations.
- The most significant change in therapy typically occurs in the first handful of sessions.

These findings underscore the importance of working with clients in the early stages of therapy to give voice to their perceptions. Leaving clients out of processes is both an unwise decision and a sign of disrespect.

Exercise 3.1

Using Collaboration Keys

The quality of the client's participation is a critical factor in outcome. This suggests a focus on involving clients in all facets of services to better accommodate therapy to their needs. By creating collaborative partnerships from the outset and maintaining them throughout services, therapists can tap into client contributions, attend to cultural influences, increase expectancy and hope, and enhance change-affecting variables. The purpose of this exercise to create questions that can be used in conjunction with the collaboration keys outlined in this chapter. To complete this exercise, please follow the directions and write your responses in the spaces provided.

1. Create two questions for each collaboration key listed.

Addressing Service Expectations

a. _____

b. _____

Determining Who Should Attend and the Format of Meetings/Sessions

a. _____

b. _____

Determining the Physical Space and Setting of Sessions

a. _____

b. _____

Determining the Timing, Length, and Frequency of Sessions

a. _____

b. _____

2. Create a brief narrative for introducing each of the following collaboration keys to clients.

Utilizing an Open-Door Perspective

_____

_____

_____

_____

_____

Emphasizing Premeeting/Session Change

_____

_____

_____

Exercise 3.1   *(continued)*

_____

_____

Using Process-Informed Feedback

_____

_____

_____

_____

_____

Using Outcome-Informed Feedback

_____

_____

_____

_____

_____

SUMMARY POINTS

- The quality of a client's participation in therapy is a critical factor in outcome.
- Therapeutic engagement encourages client participation by creating collaborative partnerships in which therapists elicit client experiences and preferences and integrate this information into all aspects of therapy.
- Therapists begin engagement processes prior to formal, face-to-face meetings and continue using them during initial interactions and throughout therapy.
- Seven *collaboration keys* can help to explore and learn clients' preferences, expectations, and ideas; strengthen the therapeutic alliance;

and better match therapeutic methods to their needs.

- *Addressing clients' service expectations* is important because they can affect how services progress and the degree to which they are beneficial. Therapists use strategies of *creating space, conducting preinterviews,* and *exploring setting expectations* to learn about and address clients' expectations.
- *Determining who attends and the format of current and future meetings/sessions* must occur in collaboration between clients. This includes clients' ideas and preferences about whether they should be seen

together (a unit or family), separately, and so on. Therapists partner with clients to determine which format provides the best fit.

- *Determining the physical space and setting of meetings/sessions* (in offices, schools, homes, prisons) can be meaningful to clients and creates a culture of care and respect.
- *Determining the timing, length, and frequency of sessions* can raise issues for both therapists and clients but should be accomplished collaboratively. Providers should be aware of individual preferences and make reasonable accommodation for them when possible.
- *Utilizing an open-door perspective* refers to programming that offers reasonable access to people who are in immediate need. It also allows people to move in and out of therapy as necessary and as their lives and needs change to provide a fit for clients as they move through life stages and transitions.

- *Emphasizing premeeting/session change* acknowledges the fact that problems fluctuate in frequency, intensity, and duration. Therapists therefore enable clients to help identify subtle differences in their problems prior to first sessions as a means to facilitate positive change.
- *Introducing Feedback Methods* results from the fact that clients' perceptions are the consistent predictors of therapy outcome. Therapists therefore explore ways to incorporate client feedback in all aspects of therapy. There are two ways of doing this 1) *Process-oriented* feedback involves methods for eliciting and incorporating clients' perceptions of the therapeutic relationship and alliance. 2) *Outcome-oriented* feedback relates to methods that monitor clients' perceptions of the impact of services. Therapists introduce and encourage both forms of client feedback and incorporate that feedback to strengthen the therapeutic alliance and increase the opportunities for successful outcome.

DISCUSSION QUESTIONS

1. Why is therapist-client collaboration integral to therapy? How might collaborative practices strengthen the therapeutic relationship?

2. What are specific ways that therapists can promote collaboration prior to the start of therapy and early in therapy?

3. In what ways can client service expectations influence therapy, particularly in early stages? What can therapists do to address client service expectations?

4. How can attention to attendance and format of sessions help therapists to increase the factor of fit with clients?

5. How might factors such as physical space and setting affect clients' perceptions and experiences in therapy? What can therapists do to address these factors?

6. How can attention to timing, length, and frequency of sessions benefit clients?

7. What is an "open-door perspective?"

8. What is the role of premeeting/session change?

9. How do *process-oriented* feedback and *outcome-oriented* feedback differ? What makes these forms of feedback important to therapy?

Chapter 4

Active Client Engagement

The Language of Change

■ By using the collaboration keys discussed in Chapter 3 and attending closely and being responsive to client preferences and expectancies in early interactions, therapists begin to create collaborative partnerships, which in turn strengthen the therapeutic relationship. Clients who are engaged and connected with their therapists are likely to benefit most from services. Collaboration assumes many forms that play vital roles in creating an atmosphere in which clients' experiences and views not only is valued but also serve as compasses throughout therapy.

Information employed in these interactive partnerships is gleaned from clients' expertise on their lives and experiences. Therapists have expertise in creating a context for and facilitating change, knowing what does and does not feel right, what has or has not worked, or what might work in the future. The doorway to learning about clients' experiences and ideas about how to accomplish the change they desire is the collaborative partnership. It also represents a respectful stance in opening possibilities for client change. By being attuned to client perspectives, therapists tap into a multitude of possibilities. Impossibility is often the result of attending only to therapists' own personal and theoretical perspectives or maps. Collaboration is an important key to unlocking possibilities, calling for therapists to work *with* clients in conversational, change-oriented processes.

This chapter discusses ways to use collaboration to create contexts in which clients feel secure and comfortable in sharing their stories and narratives. The first section identifies specific processes for actively engaging clients by accommodating their conversational and relational preferences and then explores a multitude of ways to use language as a vehicle for acknowledging clients' experience and opening possibilities for present and future change. Another section investigates the role of process feedback as therapy sessions progress, and the final section integrates all chapter concepts by analyzing a case example.

Creating Listening Space

Therapy involves careful attention to clients, their experiences, situations, concerns, and hopes for desired change. The primary doorways into clients' lives are their stories, which are social constructions of reality. It is therefore essential that therapists create "listening spaces," contexts in which clients feel comfortable about the details associated with their coming to therapy. The unfolding of clients' stories or narratives not only is essential for therapists but also will be the most important part of therapy for some clients. In creating listening space, therapists let clients dictate the direction of opening conversations. Practitioners invite clients to speak openly about only what they feel most comfortable, engaging them in dialogues that highlight both *what* they would like to talk about and *how* they would like to talk about it.

Creating listening space early in engagement results in process-informed therapy. As discussed in Chapter 3, real-time feedback is composed of both process- and outcome-oriented practices that elicit and incorporate clients' experiences in therapy. From a process standpoint, therapists want to build ways to glean clients' perceptions regarding the therapeutic relationship.

Although remaining completely neutral is not possible, therapists strive to do so. Therefore, they begin interactions with clients by asking general questions about their concerns. Doing so contributes to a flattened hierarchy between clients and therapists, which allows clients to begin where they feel most comfortable. Jenkins (1996) echoed this stance: "Respectful therapy involves a process of knocking on doors and waiting to be invited in, rather than breaking them down, barging in, and then expecting to be welcomed with open arms" (p. 122). Therefore, therapists create contexts in which clients can convey their stories, including any preferences, expectations, and hopes they may have, in as comfortable a way as possible.

As clients tell their stories, therapists listen for their conversational and relational preferences (Bertolino, 2003). *Conversational preferences* relate to what clients find meaningful to talk about in therapy. *Relational preferences* refer to the ways clients would like therapists to interact with them. Therapists incorporate information from both preferences into interactions to strengthen relationships. The following examples of opening and ongoing process-oriented questions invite clients' stories, including their conversational and relational preferences.

- Where would you like to start?
- What would you like to talk about?
- What is most important for me to know about you and/or your situation/concern?
- Are there certain things that you want to be sure we talk about?
- What do you want to be sure that we discuss during our time together?
- What ideas do you have about how therapy and/or coming to see me might be helpful?
- In what ways do you see me as helping you to reach your goals/achieve the change you desire?
- What do you feel/think you need from me right now?
- How can I be helpful to you right now?
- What do you see as my role in helping you with your concern?
- What, in your estimation, do therapists who are helpful do to help their clients?

As in-session dialogue progresses throughout the course of therapy, therapists track client conversational and relational preferences. This feedback is integral in monitoring the fit between clients, therapists, and the approach(es) utilized.

As clients' stories begin to unfold in early interactions, therapists pay close attention to clients' statements and responses, taking care not dismiss their internal experience(s) by pushing for change, trying to get them to move on, being too positive, or using other methods that clients may experience as being insensitive or disrespectful. As outlined in the "experiential/affective" domain of change provided in Chapter 2 (see Table 2.9), therapists acknowledge, validate, and show compassion by creating contexts in which clients can experience their pain and suffering void of others' attempts to fix things or give advice or suggestions.

Practitioners must remain aware of the inherent cultural bias that they may have toward redemptive stories and try not to change, reframe, or invalidate clients' nonredemptive, unhappy-ending stories too quickly and without properly attending to clients' emotional experience. Doing so requires avoiding the use of glib explanations (for example, "I wonder what you are meant to learn from this?" or "What part of you needs or benefits from this pain?") and platitudes (for example, "Everything will work out"; "God doesn't give you more than you can handle"; and "You are going to be all right.").

It is not uncommon for therapists' explanations to unintentionally run counter to clients' viewpoints. The use of metaphors based on therapists' personal assumptions and biases can alienate clients and close avenues to change. To address this, adopting a position of cultural curiosity can be helpful; therapists allow themselves to be taught by clients and their families about their cultures, contributing to a cross-cultural interaction in a mutually influencing relationship (Madsen, 2007). This moves therapy from a macro- to microlevel of understanding that views every family as its own distinct culture.

Cultural curiosity involves the elicitation instead of assignment of meaning. Therapists evoke from clients the meanings they have attached to events, situations, and relationships as opposed to ascribing some professional explanation or meaning. Assuming a position of "not knowing" can be helpful (Anderson & Goolishian, 1988, 1992). Harlene Anderson (1995) described a *not-knowing* stance as an attitude in which:

> a therapist does not have access to privileged information, can never fully understand another person, always needs to be in a state of being informed by the other, and always needs to learn more about what has been said or may not have been said (p. 134).

Adoption of a not-knowing stance does not mean that the practitioner forgoes or dismisses professional knowledge (Anderson, 2005). It suggests instead that therapists invite clients into relationships in which their constructed meanings are offered in conversations void of therapist-ascribed meanings. Furthermore, this stance encourages therapists to learn more about what they do not know and to clarify what they believe they know; this translates to dialogical interchanges that lead to the continuous renegotiation and construction of new meanings.

As clients' stories begin to evolve and take shape early in therapy, practitioners listen for and attend to subtle nuances that accompany both verbal and nonverbal communication. Therapists learn clients' preferred ways to communicate and search for ways that both acknowledge and encourage change.

Attending, Listening, and Changing

Therapists have two primary vehicles for facilitating change: language and interaction. *Language* is more than words. It is made up of two levels of communication. The first refers to what is verbally conveyed. The second level is based on what is nonverbally transmitted (for example, voice tone, rate of speech, intonation of words). It is imperative that therapists be attuned to both levels of communication as a way to increase their understanding of clients' experiences. *Interaction* includes both verbal and nonverbal communication but is more expansive, relating to the specific ways that therapists engage clients. Recall that therapists' contributions to change represent 6 to 9% of the variance in outcome (Wampold, 2001). For example, therapists may be more or less direct or use humor, storytelling, self-disclosure, and so on to interact in order to strengthen their connections with clients. Therapists maintain a posture of flexibility in adapting to client interactional styles, making adjustments based on what is communicated.

Both language and interaction are central in developing rapport and strengthening connections with clients. As clients convey their stories, therapists use language as a conduit for acknowledging clients, gathering information, and promoting change. But how exactly do therapists use these modes of communication as vehicles for change? The answer to this question is twofold.

Effects of Language on Psychology and Physiology

Words affect people on at least two levels. The first is the psychological level; most therapists, through training and/or personal experience, are aware of the psychological effects of language. Throughout this book, you will learn about ways that meaning is created through language and interaction and how therapists can use collaborative conversations to open possibilities for change. The second level is physiological. Before delving more deeply into this matter, please take a moment to complete both parts of Exercise 4.1, The Dual Impact of Words.

What did you notice about what you thought and experienced emotionally or in your body after reading the first group of words? How about after the second? Did you notice any differences between what you experienced with the first as compared to the second? The effects of language on thinking and emotion are well known. What people often do not fully recognize the impact that words have on their physiological states. Some words can bring about negative physical experiences, such as heaviness in the body, tiredness, and even somatic sensations (for example, upset stomach, body tension). Others can lead to feeling physically stronger and having an increase in energy.

Prominent researchers including Bessel van der Kolk (1994; van der Kolk, McFarlane, & Weisaeth, 1996) and John Gottman (1999) have studied the effects of language, interaction, and significant events on psychology and physiology from divergent perspectives. Van der Kolk's research, primarily on the effects of trauma, suggest that under certain conditions (for example, stress, threats, catastrophic events), the frontal cortex of the brain, which is responsible for thinking, speech, and language, becomes inhibited, thereby limiting a person's ability to reason and articulate thoughts. At the same time, portions of the area around the brain stem, including the amygdala and hypothalamus that are responsible for physiological

Exercise 4.1

The Dual Impact of Words

Part 1

1. Slowly repeat the following words aloud:
   sad, helpless, inconvenienced, bored, defeated, tired, lonely, doubtful, uninterested

2. Read aloud the following statement:
   Life is so hard. Nothing seems to go my way. There is no one to turn to or count on. It feels like I've been forgotten. Times are tough. Nothing seems to help. Things will not get better. In fact, they will probably get worse. There is no hope.

3. Take a moment to write down what you think, feel, and physically sense while reading the preceding statement. *About How I Have Felt All those Emotions And it hurts, Like No One Could possibly understand*

Part 2

1. Slowly repeat the following words aloud:
   exciting, fun, laughter, joy, anticipation, attractive, possibility, aliveness, peace, love

2. Read aloud the following statement:
   When I think about the future, I become excited. I'm energized. There is so much I can accomplish. Life is wonderful, and there are so many possibilities in the world.

3. Take a moment to write down what you think, feel, and physically sense while reading the preceding statement. *Things Will be better, I just have to be patient. God Will take care of us. Keep My Faith*

reactions, become increasingly active. This combination contributes to hyperarousal, affecting a person's ability to regulate emotion and think clearly.

A renowned authority on relationships, Gottman (1999) explored the triggering effects of interactions between couples and had similar findings. The researcher suggested that under perceived stress in relationships, people can experience both physiological arousal and psychological shutdown. The result is that people may experience difficulty to self-soothe, regulate emotion, and respond in calm ways when under distress.

From another perspective, Emoto (2004, 2007) found that language and different forms of vibration affect the molecular composition of water crystals. His studies exposed cylinders of water to harsh, loud sounds and then to soft, soothing sounds. He then used a high-power microscope to photograph the crystals under both conditions. Emoto found that water crystals exposed to the "negative energy" of harsh, loud sounds exhibited fragmentation and what appeared to be disease-like qualities. In contrast, the water that had been exposed to "positive energy" of soft, soothing sounds often revealed crystals that appeared to be growing and expanding.

It has been estimated that human bodies are 70% water. If vibration, tone, volume, and so on affect water, the implications of their impact on the human body are vast. It seems that words have the capability to directly influence our physiological states beyond what might be expected through cognitive processes (in other words, something said to us that we perceive as negative in turn affects our physiology). Subtleties communicated through tone of voice, rate of speech, pitch, and body posture can trigger increases or decreases in blood flow, heart rate, perspiration, and so on.

Although more detailed discussions exceed the scope of this book, an elementary point arises from these findings. Language and interaction at both verbal and nonverbal levels can affect psychological *and* physiological states.

Attending and Listening as Core Conditions of Client Engagement

Therapists use language and interaction as vehicles for change is by employing specific forms of attending and listening. Rogers (1951) identified *empathy, positive regard,* and *congruence* as necessary and sufficient conditions for therapeutic change. Although much has been written about each of these concepts,

there is little agreement as to their meanings. *Empathy* is generally understood as a person's ability to understand another's perspective or way to experience the world. Meta-analyses by Bohart et al. (2002) and Orlinksy, Grawe, and Parks (1994) have found a positive correlation between empathy and outcome. *Positive regard* is usually described as a person's warmth and acceptance toward the self or another. Using the Division 29 Task Force (Steering Committee, 2001) standard of 50% or more in a study demonstrating an element as positively correlated with outcome, it can be said that positive regard contributes positively to outcome. Furthermore, it has been suggested that high degrees of positive regard in therapy may contribute to clients continuing, also known as *treatment retention* (Farber & Lane, 2002). *Congruence,* sometimes referred to as *genuineness,* has been characterized by a person's personal involvement in a relationship and willingness to share this awareness through open and honest communication. According to the Division 29 Task Force standard, a preponderance of evidence has indicated a significant positive relationship between congruence and outcome (Klein, et al., 2002; Lafferty, Beutler, & Crago, 1989; Orlinsky & Howard, 1986; Orlinsky, Grawe, & Parks, 1994).

Viewed separately, *empathy* can be said to be "demonstratively effective" whereas *positive regard* and *congruence* are "promising and probably effective elements of the therapeutic relationship" (Steering Committee, 2001, p. 495). An important consideration with these core elements is their convergence and collective interplay. Said differently, each contributes to strengthening the therapeutic relationship; however, when therapists fully engage in processes so that clients experience empathy, positive regard, and congruence, the likelihood of successful outcome increases.

Language and interaction represent the gateway through which empathy, positive regard, and congruence flow. As clients share their stories, therapists use language to attend to clients' experiences. Essential ways to do this are by using acknowledgment, validation, paraphrasing, and summarizing.

Acknowledgment and Validation

The use of *acknowledgment* involves attending to what clients have communicated both verbally and nonverbally. It lets clients know that their experience, points of view, and actions have been heard and noted. It also serves as a prompt by encouraging clients to continue communicating. A basic way to acknowledging is to say, "Uh huh" or "I see." Another way is to reflect back, without interpretation, what clients have said. For example, a clinician might say, "You're sad" or "I heard you say you're angry." This can also be conveyed by attending to and acknowledging nonverbal behaviors. For example, a therapist might say, "You shuddered as you spoke" or "I can see the tears."

Validation is an extension of and is most often used in conjunction with acknowledgment. It involves letting clients know that whatever they are experiencing is valid. People are not bad, crazy, sick, or weird for being who they are and experiencing what they may. Therapists can use validation to *normalize* or convey to clients that others have experienced the same or similar things. Validation usually involves using statements such as "It's/That's okay" or "It's/That's all right." To combine acknowledgment with validation, add words or statements such as "It's/That's okay" or "It's all right" to what is being acknowledged. A clinician using acknowledgement and validation might say, "It's okay to be angry," or "It's all right if you're angry," or "I heard you

say that you're sad, and you can just let that be there." Acknowledgement and validation are responses that should be used throughout therapy. See the following example for a way to combine the two.

Client: I'm really not sure where to start. It's been a bad week all around.

Therapist: Can you say more about what you mean by that?

Client: Well, I started a new job, and my boss is on my case constantly. It's like I can't do anything right.

Therapist: Okay, I see.

Client: After a few hours each day, I've pretty much taken all I can take. It's so stressful and I get pissed off. I know it's stupid to let it get to me, but it does.

Therapist: Hmm. I can see how that could be stressful.

Client: It definitely is, and I don't know what to do about it.

Therapist: Sure. It does sound like a conundrum. I want you to know that it's okay to feel pissed off. It's not stupid; it just happens to be what you feel.

Client: That makes me feel better.

Paraphrasing/Summarizing and Highlighting (Aspects of Client Statements)

Paraphrasing can be used as a way to confirm what has been said by using a condensed, non-judgmental version of the client's words. See the following examples.

Client: I'm really feeling pressure at work and at home. I mean, at work it's just one thing after another, and then when I get home, I'm bombarded with the kids. It never stops.

Therapist: It sounds like with both work and kids you really have a lot going on and are feeling pressure as a result.

Client: My dad thinks his way is the only way. "Do this, do that." "Look at me when I'm talking." He's like a drill sergeant. I just wish he would cut me some slack. I'm sick of it.

Therapist: You've grown tired of your dad's way of approaching you—it isn't working for you and you wish he would cut you some slack.

Summarizing can be used as a way to check out what has been said by pulling together what a client has stated over a period of time. It provides a brief synopsis to acknowledge, clarify, and gain focus. See the following examples.

Client: . . . so that's about it. That's my world in a nutshell.

Therapist: Let me see if I follow you. You mentioned several things that seem to be in the forefront in your mind. One is the struggle you've been having with your son. Another is your sense that your life hasn't turned out the way you'd like and this particular feeling has become more intense since your class reunion. Is that right?

Client: . . . I feel like I could just keep talking about it but it wouldn't get me anywhere. It just feels like my life is going down the drain and there isn't anything I can do about it.

Therapist: You've had a lot happen recently. Perhaps most important is that two people who you've been close to for years moved away. And on top of that, you didn't expect your grades to take a dip like they did. Would you say those or other things are most pressing for you right now?

Therapists attend to clients at multiple levels, first by creating listening space so clients' stories can unfold. As they listen and attend to clients' narratives, therapists monitor their conversational and relational preferences, acknowledging and validating clients' experiences to ensure that they feel heard and understood. Doing so ensures that therapists are on track during initial conversations. As conversations continue, practitioners keep in mind that although client stories offer glimpses into their worldviews, they remain social constructions. One task of therapists, therefore, is to identify aspects of clients' stories that may contribute to their current problems and inhibit future change.

To avoid being drawn into conversations of impossibility, it is essential that therapists go beyond pure acknowledgment and validation and use language to cast doubt on clients' problem-saturated stories.

Using Acknowledgment as a Path to Possibility

Acknowledging and validating clients while making subtle changes in their language can help them move from impossibility to possibility. These methods are referred to as *dissolving impossibility talk* and *future talk* (Bertolino & O'Hanlon, 2002). Both methods offer ways to use language as a vehicle for creating change. See the Clinical Vignette on page 95.

Carl Rogers expounded on the importance of acknowledging and validating clients' internal experience. At the same time, if practitioners only reflect back these experiences and views, many clients will continue to use words that close down possibilities for change. In essence, they will paint themselves into corners through words and phrases by describing their views of themselves, others, and situations that imply impossibility. Not becoming drawn into problem-saturated descriptions can be difficult for therapists, but it is important to do more than acknowledge and validate. The therapist must combine these forms of attending with language that injects the element of possibility.

CLINICAL VIGNETTE

My first job in the helping professions was as a youth-care worker in an emergency shelter for runaway and homeless youth. Many of these youth had experienced at least one form of abuse (for example, physical, sexual, or emotional) or neglect, family crisis, substance abuse, and/or other debilitating circumstances. One of my responsibilities was to answer a 24-hour-a-day crisis hotline. I quickly learned the importance of establishing a connection with callers, who were frequently in crisis, and working toward problem resolution. If this did not happen relatively fast, callers might hang up and hurt themselves or someone else.

The dilemma with these crisis calls was finding a way to balance acknowledgment with directive questions. I needed to acknowledge people and their experiences and ask straightforward questions about their situations, what they needed, and what they wanted to change. I worked toward this by combining acknowledgment with direction as a way to opening up immediate possibilities. This seemed to provide the internal validation that clients were seeking while allowing me to intervene in some way to alleviate the crisis.

Although I had learned an effective way of working with people in crisis over the telephone, in my face-to-face interactions I was doing something different. I was relying primarily on pure listening and reflecting. I acknowledged but did not direct. The youth and adults I worked with seemed to respond well to this process, yet few experienced the change they desired. It was clear that most needed something more to facilitate positive change (Bertolino & Thompson, 1999).

Dissolving Impossibility Talk

The use of *dissolving impossibility talk* can add a twist to pure reflection in three ways (Bertolino & O'Hanlon, 2002). These methods combine acknowledgment with various forms of subtle changes in language, each of which provides a doorway to a different or new view of a potentially closed-down client account.

1. *Use the past tense.* Repeat clients' statements or problem reports in the past tense to create subtle openings in their perspectives. If only acknowledgement is used, clients may remain stuck. If only a search for possibilities occurs, some clients will feel invalidated. Using the past tense helps clients to feel understood but suggests that things can be different now or in the future.

Client: My situation isn't getting any better.

Therapist: You're situation *hasn't gotten* any better.

Client: He's always that way.

Therapist: He's *been* that way.

Client: Our problems are constant.

Therapist: The problems you've experienced *have been* constant.

Using the past tense to reflect the problem when the client uses the present tense can offer the possibility of a different present or future. This subtle linguistic shift both acknowledges/validates and introduces possibility into the conversation. When therapists only acknowledge and validate, some clients will move on, but most will not.

They will continue to describe situations as impossible and or unchangeable. Furthermore, some clients may experience service providers' simply stressing that people *should* move on as invalidation. The combination of acknowledgement and possibility suggested by using the past tense offers a way to dissolve present tense problem talk by introducing possibilities into otherwise closed-down statements and conversations.

2. *Translate client statements into partial statements.* Translate clients' statements using words such as *everything, everybody, always,* and *never* into qualifiers related to time (for example, *some things, somebody, sometimes,* and *much of the time*), intensity (for example, *a lot, a bit less, somewhat more*), or partiality (*a lot, some, most, many*). Therapists should take care not to minimize or invalidate clients' experiences. See the following examples.

Client: I'm always in some kind of trouble.

Therapist: You've been in trouble a lot.

Client: Nothing ever goes right in my life.

Therapist: Much of the time things just haven't gone right in your life.

Client: It just gets worse day after day.

Therapist: Lately it seems like it's been getting worse.

All-or-nothing statements can impede change, but combining qualifiers with acknowledgment—going from global to partial—can help to introduce the element of possibility into otherwise closed-down statements. This can create little openings in which change is possible.

3. *Translate into perceptual statements.* Translate clients' statements of truth or reality—the way they explain things for themselves—into perceptual statements or subjective realities (for example, *in your eyes . . . , your sense is . . . , from where you stand . . . , you've gotten the idea . . .*). See the following examples.

Client: Things will never change.

Therapist: Your sense is that things will never change.

Client: I'm a terrible parent.

Therapist: You've gotten the idea that you've been a terrible parent.

Client: My life is bleak.

Therapist: From where you're standing, your life seems bleak.

Clients' statements reflecting their perceptions of events, situations, or themselves, as discussed previously, are stories—powerful and influential—but they are social constructions, not the way things are. When reflecting back clients' statements as their perceptions, therapists acknowledge those points of view without subscribing to such stories of impossibility.

Several of the previous examples used a combination of different methods of changing language, for example, "You've been in trouble a lot" (past tense/partial statement) and "You've gotten the idea that you're a terrible parent" (perceptual statement/past tense). The more therapists practice with such changes in language, the more comfortable and consistent they become in identifying and attending to words, phrases, and statements that suggest impossibility. To practice these subtle changes in language, please complete Exercise 4.2, Dissolving Impossibility Talk.

Not losing focus on the importance of acknowledging clients' experiences is crucial.

Exercise 4.2

Dissolving Impossibility Talk

Clients sometimes use words, phrases, or descriptions that can close down the possibilities for change. In response, therapists can use acknowledgment as a path to possibility, which serves two purposes. First, it helps clients to feel that they are heard and understood. Second, it adds the element of possibility to pure reflection. Complete this exercise in the spaces provided by using each corresponding method to acknowledge while offering possibilities for change. Then combine two or more of the methods offered to acknowledge and intersperse possibilities through language.

1. Reflect back clients' responses or problem reports in the past tense.

Examples:

Client: *My girlfriend always picks fights with me.*
Therapist: *Your girlfriend <u>has picked</u> fights with you.*
Client: *Nothing ever works out for me.*
Therapist: *Things haven't worked out for you.*
Client: He always forgets to call if he's going to be late.
Therapist: _____
Client: Nobody ever understands me.
Therapist: _____
Client: I'll never get the chance to prove what I can do.
Therapist: _____

Take clients' general statements and translate them into partial statements.

Examples:

Client: *He always criticizes me.*
Therapist: *He criticizes you <u>a lot</u>.*
Client: *No one understands me.*
Therapist: *<u>Most people</u> don't seem to understand you.*
Client: He's always out of control.
Therapist: _____
Client: She never thinks about anyone but himself.
Therapist: _____
Client: Every time I try, something goes wrong.
Therapist: _____

Translate clients' statements of truth or reality into perceptual statements or subjective realities.

Examples:

Client: *I can't do anything right.*
Therapist: *It <u>seems</u> like that you can't do anything right.*
Client: *I'll always be anxious—it's just the way it is.*
Therapist: *Your <u>sense</u> is that you'll always have some anxiety.*

Exercise 4.2 *(continued)*

Client: Everyone hates me.
Therapist: _____
Client: Nobody knows how hard it is to get along with her.
Therapist: _____
Client: It's always bad at work.
Therapist: _____

4. Combine two or more of the methods to acknowledge clients and simultaneously offer possibilities for change.

Examples:

Client: *She'll always be a troublemaker. She'll never get any better.*
Therapist: *She's <u>been</u> in trouble, and it really <u>seems</u> to you that it won't get any better.*
Client: *I'm just a depressed person. It's who I am.*
Therapist: *So <u>you've been depressed,</u> and <u>your sense is</u> that's who you are.*
Client: He does whatever he wants whenever he wants.
Therapist: _____
Client: She's always nagging me about something and won't give up until she gets her way.
Therapist: _____
Client: Everybody thinks I'm stupid because I have bad grades.
Therapist: _____

Practitioners do not want to echo the voices of society that may suggest to clients that what they are experiencing is in someway wrong or that they must "move on" or "get over it" (Bertolino & O'Hanlon, 2002). Clients have often heard enough of such talk, which generally translates into invalidation and blame. If clients feel that their experiences are being minimized or they are being pushed to move on, they will likely respond with a statement such as, "Not *most* of the time—*all* of the time." If a client reacts in such a manner, the therapist must make sure the client feels heard and understood by validating further while keeping an eye on possibilities. For example, a therapist might respond to the previous client statement by saying, "Okay. *Your sense is* that things *have been* bad all the time."

Therapists who introduce possibility-laced language into conversations are *inviting* clients into different perspectives, not *coercing* them. Offering the idea that even though things have been difficult, painful, overwhelming, and so on lets clients know that their suffering, concerns, felt experiences, and points of view have been heard and understood. O'Hanlon and Bertolino (1998) commented on a hoped-for result of changing clients' basic language: "When acknowledgement and validation are combined with language of change and possibility in ongoing therapist reflections, clients begin to shift their self-perceptions. This process continues throughout the therapy. In time, clients can develop a more possibility-oriented sense of themselves" (p. 49).

Using Future-Talk: Acknowledgment and a Vision for the Future

Clients occasionally describe their situations in ways that offer little glimpses of the future and what might be possible. In these instances, they use language like the moving walkways in airports: They can maintain their same pace yet reach their destinations a little faster. Therapists can use language in a similar way to move clients in the direction of possibilities without their actually having to take steps toward those goals and preferred outcomes. Again, service providers who hear client stories that suggest impossibility can inject the element of possibility through language in three ways.

1. *Assume future change and/or solutions.* Assume the possibility that clients can find solutions by using words such as *yet* and *so far.* These words presuppose that even though things feel stuck or unchangeable in the present, they will change sometime in the future. A simple shift in language as in the following examples can help to create a "light at the end of the tunnel."

   Client: Things will never go right for me.
   Therapist: So far things haven't gone right for you.

   Client: My life is going downhill.
   Therapist: You're life hasn't headed in a direction you'd like yet.

   Client: I'll never have the life I really want.
   Therapist: The life you want hasn't happened the way you've hoped so far.

   By making only small changes in language, therapists are actually introducing the possibility that change can occur in the future. This seemingly simple shift gently challenges closed-down views and can open doorways to other, more significant changes.

2. *Turn problem statements into preferences or goals.* Take clients' problem statements such as those in the following examples and change them into statements or questions about a preference, preferred future, or goal.

   Client: It just seems like we argue all of the time.
   Therapist: Is finding alternatives to arguing one of the things you'd like to have happen?

   Client: I'm always in trouble.
   Therapist: Would you like to work on finding ways to change you relationship with trouble?

   Client: Work is driving me crazy.
   Therapist: Would it be helpful for you to spend some time on how work might be better for you?

Bertolino and O'Hanlon (2002) noted that this particular way to change language serves several purposes:

> First . . . it offers a way of acknowledging clients. A second purpose relates to situations that therapists often find themselves in. In the course of listening to the client's story it can become difficult to discern which problem concerns the client the most. Therapists must routinely make decisions regarding which client words, phrases, comments, and remarks should gain more or less attention. By turning problem statements into goals, therapists can acknowledge clients' statements and simultaneously clarify which problems are most important to them (p. 42).

It is not uncommon for clients to make statements, especially early in interactions when things are foremost in their minds, that are not intended as ongoing points of conversation. Some will just want to update therapists on recent events whereas others have things they want to get off their chests. Because therapists cannot know clients' reasons for making a given statement, it is important to use conversation as a way to clarification. Turning problem statements into goals can allow therapists to learn which points clients would like to focus on as in the following example.

Client: Everything is a mess. Work is awful. I don't have any friends—no social life at all. I also want to eat everything in sight. I do that when I'm bored.

Therapist: It sounds as if you've got a lot going on. And if I'm hearing you right, some of the things that we could focus on here are work, improving your social life and friendships, and the feeling of wanting to eat more than you would prefer.

Client: Yeah, I think so. Well, I mean, I do want a better social life. I also want to talk about eating less at some point. But really, the most important thing to me is work. It's a nightmare and what really made me decide to come here.

By turning problem statements into goals, practitioners not only clarify what clients are more or less concerned about but also provide a way to prioritize concerns (when multiple concerns exist). This helps to understand which issues clients view as most burdensome and what they want to be different in their lives and enables therapists to set aside personal biases and ideas about what should or should not be the focus.

3. *Presuppose changes and progress.* Assume changes and progress toward goals and preferred futures by using words such as when and will. See the following examples.

Client: No one wants to hang out or be friends with me.

Therapist: When you've started spending time with people you consider your friends, I'm curious about what other kinds of changes you'll notice.

Client: I'm always getting angry and then saying things I shouldn't say.

Therapist: When you're able to express your anger in ways that are better, how do you suppose your life will be different than the way it is now?

Client: If I could feel less anxious, my life would be so different.

Therapist: When you reach the point that your anxiety has been dialed down a notch or two, I wonder what positive turns your life will take.

The use of presupposition offers a way to orient clients toward future changes by linking one change with another. Its use helps to shift clients' attention toward change in general and to tap into the "ripple effect." Therapists work with clients to notice that like a stone landing in a pool of water, ripples or additional changes can result with the first splash. It is worth noting that Milton Erickson used presupposition in his hypnotic work with patients to link their specific movements with the suggestion of internal, automatic changes. For example, he might say, "When your hand begins to lift, I wonder what changes you'll make within yourself?" In a nonhypnotic manner, therapists can use the same concept to presuppose changes and progress toward goals and preferred futures.

Presupposition can be used in two ways. The first involves responding with a statement. Examples 1 and 3 (above) illustrate this. A second way is to frame the response as a question as in example 2. Adding the use of conjecture, wonderment, or speculation, whether in a statement or a question, can be helpful. Doing so offers speculation or inquiry concerning how future changes will make a difference for the client. To use conjecture, simply add *I wonder* or *I'm curious.*

Employing future-focused language can be especially valuable with clients experiencing hopelessness, pain, and fear because a lack of a vision for the future often exacerbates these forms of emotional reaction. If clients have the sense that the pain or suffering that they are experiencing now will somehow be alleviated or dissipated altogether, they are better able to keep moving. People who have a sense that their pain will end and that things will improve in the future have higher prospects for recovery from chronic illness. Presuppositional language provides a respectful response to clients' verbalization of problems or concerns without minimizing them and the suffering the clients are currently experiencing. To practice the ideas offered here, please take a moment to complete Exercise 4.3, Future Talk.

Dissolving impossibility talk or using future-talk independently offers ways to open initial pathways with possibilities. Collectively, their use can create a significant impact in combination with two or more other methods. In fact, many therapists do this automatically.

They make subtle changes in language without realizing it. For example, numerous accounts of Carl Rogers's changing language can be found throughout transcripts of his sessions with clients (Farber, Brink, & Raskin, 1996). Rogers himself, however, did not specifically address changing language. See the following examples.

Client: Day after day, it's the same thing . . . nothing goes my way even though I want things to be different.

Therapist: Day after day it seems that it's been the same thing . . . little seems to have gone your way so far . . . , and I'm curious as to what will be happening for you when things are a little different. [The words *been* and have *gone* shift the client's concerns to past tense, and the phrase *so far* emphasizes future solutions. The multiple use of the word *seems* changes the client's statement to a perceptual one. Finally, the future change in the statement *what will be happening for you when . . . ,* presupposes that things will be different down the road.]

Client: Things never go the way I want.

Therapist: So far things haven't gone the way you'd like them to go. [*So far* is used to suggest the possibility of future solutions, and *haven't* changes from the present to past tense.]

Client: All I ever do is obsess about the decisions I've made.

Therapist: It seems like you've obsessed a lot about the decisions you've made. When you're able to manage your obsessions a little better, what will be different? [*Seems* translates the client's statement into a perceptual one, and *you've obsessed* uses the past tense. *When* and *will* presuppose future change.]

Exercise 4.3

Future Talk

To complete this exercise, use the specified method of acknowledging while offering possibilities for future change and achieving goals and preferred outcomes.

1. Assume future solutions through future talk.

Examples:

Client:	Things will never go right for me.
Therapist:	<u>So far</u> things haven't gone right or you.
Client:	I'm always in some kind of trouble.
Therapist:	You haven't found a way to stay out of trouble <u>yet</u>.
Client:	Nobody will ever understand me.
Therapist:	_____
Client:	I'll never be good at anything.
Therapist:	_____
Client:	My life is going down hill.
Therapist:	_____

2. Turn problem statements into preferences or goals.

Examples:

Client:	I'll never have the kind of life that I want.
Therapist:	So <u>you'd like to be able to find a way</u> to have the kind of life that you want?
Client:	I'm worthless.
Therapist:	So <u>one of the things that we could do</u> is to help you to find some self-worth.
Client:	I'm just not good at school.
Therapist:	_____
Client:	I never have fun anymore.
Therapist:	_____
Client:	My mom is always on my case.
Therapist:	_____

3. Presuppose changes and progress

Examples:

Client:	All I do is get into trouble.
Therapist:	So <u>when</u> you've put trouble behind you, <u>you'll</u> feel as though things are heading in a better direction.
Client:	No one wants to be in a relationship with me.
Therapist:	So <u>when</u> you get the sense that you've found people who might be interested in having a relationship with you, <u>we'll</u> know that we've made some progress.
Client:	I'm always getting angry and saying things I shouldn't say.
Therapist:	_____
Client:	Nobody will ever want to hang out with me.
Therapist:	_____
Client:	I'll never be a good student.
Therapist:	_____

Creating Additional Possibilities of Change through Language

Clients are invited during therapy to share their stories. Practitioners attend to clients both verbally and nonverbally; their words and interactions acknowledge and validate clients and their experiences while therapists listen for words, phrases, and statements reflecting views or stories that suggest impossibility and may inhibit change. When they hear problematic or potentially problematic stories, therapists work to make subtle changes to create openings for possible future changes, moving to another level of introducing possibility into conversations. Because different clients need different things, it is important that therapists not impose their ideas but use language that fits with clients. This section explores six areas that can strengthen the therapeutic relationship and open up further possibilities for change. These areas are *giving permission, inclusion, normalizing, utilization, matching language,* and *incorporating process-oriented feedback.*

Giving Permission

Some clients feel stuck or believe that they are bad or terrible for having some experience or thought that they should have. In these instances, clients need to be given permission to experience whatever is going on with them internally to let them know that they are not bad, crazy, or weird and that others have felt the same way. It is important to note that giving permission for *internal experience* does not mean giving permission for *action.* Internal experiences are quite different from actions. Therapists do not give permission for actions or behaviors that are or potentially could pose risk to clients or others but let clients know that

whatever they are experiencing is acceptable and that they are also responsible for their actions. There are three kinds of permission:

- *Permission to:* "You can."
- *Permission not to have to:* "You don't have to."
- *Permission to and not to have to:* "You can and you don't have to."

1. *Give permission "to."* Give clients permission for experiences, feelings, thoughts, and fantasies as is done in the following examples.

   Client: I just feel like quitting my job. How could I possibly feel that way when my family needs to eat? I'm really a bad person.

   Therapist: It's okay to feel like quitting your job, and that doesn't make you a bad person.

   Client: I feel like I'm doing something wrong when I feel angry about what happened to me.

   Therapist: It's okay to feel angry about what happened to you.

   Client: Every time I get depressed, I start cutting on my arms with whatever I can get my hands on.

   Therapist: It's okay to feel so depressed that you feel like cutting on yourself, and it's not okay to cut on yourself.

2. *Give permission "not to have to."* Give clients permission not to have to have experience, think, or do things that do not fit with them. See the following examples.

   Client: People keep telling me that I need to be more open about myself but that's not the kind of person I am.

Therapist: You don't have to be any more open about yourself than you are comfortable with.

Client: I'm not really the kind of person who is emotionally expressive. I've been criticized for that.

Therapist: It's okay not to have to express yourself in ways that aren't right for you.

Client: In the support group I attend for parents who've lost their spouses, everyone keeps saying that I need to express anger at my loss because that's a stage of grieving. But I've never felt anger. Is something wrong with me?

Therapist: Each person goes through grief in his or her own way. It's okay if you don't go through someone else's stages and take your own path to healing.

3. *Give permission "to" and "not to have to."* Include both permissions at the same time. See the following examples.

Client: Sometimes I'm angry and sometimes I'm not. I must be crazy.

Therapist: You can be angry and not angry about it, and that doesn't make you crazy.

Therapist: I'm really sad sometimes but then it goes away and comes back.

Client: It's okay to be sad at times and not other times and for it to cycle.

Client: I'm really hurt about what that says about me but not about what actually happened. Do you think that's weird?

Therapist: It's okay to feel hurt about what you think it says about you and not about the event itself and that doesn't mean you're weird.

Although the concept of permission may appear elementary, it can be anything but that for clients who have gotten the message that there are certain ways to feel or be. At the same time, if therapists give only one type of permission, some clients may feel pressured to experience just one part of the equation or may find the other side emerging in a more compelling or disturbing way (O'Hanlon & Bertolino, 1998, 2002). For example, if a therapist says only, "It's okay to be angry," the client might say, "But I don't want to be angry!" The therapist can counter this response by giving permission "to" and "not to have to: "It's okay to be angry and you don't have to be angry." Finally, as discussed previously, practitioners need to be careful regarding the actions for which they extend permission. For example, a therapist would not say, "It's okay to cut yourself and you don't have to cut your self"—never giving permission for harmful, destructive behavior.

Inclusion

F. Scott Fitzgerald once said, "The test of a first rate intelligence is the ability to hold two opposed ideas in the mind at the same time and still retain the ability to function." At times clients feel as if they are in binds and experience opposite or contradictory experiences that seem to present conflict. In these situations, therapists should include any parts, objections, feelings, aspects of self, or clients' concerns that might have been left out or seen as barriers to the therapy or goals and preferred futures. Doing so means including anything that may have been left out, devalued, or seen as irreconcilable opposites. The method calls for using *and* to link client experiences. Five ways to do this follow.

1. *Include opposite or contradictory feelings and emotions.* As in the following

example, link seemingly opposite or contradictory feelings and emotions.

Client: Sometimes when I'm under pressure, I'm bombarded by emotion to the point that I don't know what to feel. It's like I get frustrated and scared and nervous . . . it's hard to know which one is my true feeling.

Therapist: At times when you're under pressure, you feel frustrated, scared, nervous . . . and maybe others as well, and there's enough room within you for all of those emotions.

Client: I feel like I'm being pulled in two different directions. I love her but I can get so angry with her at times.

Therapist: You can love her and be angry with her at times.

Client: I really can't stand my job.

Therapist: You really can't stand your job and, as you've mentioned before, it can be very rewarding.

2. *Include opposite or contradictory aspects of self or others.* Link seemingly opposite or contradictory aspects of self or others. See the following examples.

Client: I constantly procrastinate.

Therapist: Yes, and you told me that yesterday you completed your page-long "to do" list on time. It seems you both procrastinate and get things done.

Client: It feels awkward to ask for help when I should already know the answers.

Therapist: It's okay to feel awkward asking for help and not to know the answers already.

Client: I feel anxious whenever I start new classes.

Therapist: You've experienced anxiety at the start of your classes and have somehow managed to get straight A's your first three semesters. It seems you have found a way to allow anxiety to exist in the just the right amount so you can excel in school.

3. *Use oxymorons.* Include the opposite side of a situation or experience in a phrase to create an oxymoron (a combination of contradictory or incongruous words or phrases) to include different feelings and aspects. See the following examples.

Client: I get so nervous that I feel like I need to get through things quickly but I also know it's better for me to slow down.

Therapist: You *slowly run* through things in a way that is right for you.

Client: My friends told me I did well, but I think my performance was awful.

Therapist: You can be *awfully pleased* with your performance.

Client: It's really unclear to me what I should do.

Therapist: You're *clearly foggy* about what to do.

4. *Use apposition of opposite.* Include the opposite side of a situation or experience but extend the tension throughout the sentence as in the following examples.

Client: I just feel like it's time to put an end to that part of my life, but I don't where to start.

Therapist: Perhaps by talking about it you are *beginning* to put an *end* to that part of your life.

Client: I'm ready to put that part of my life behind me.

Therapist: It sounds like you're *open* to *closing* the door on that part of your life.

Client: I know I've changed, but most people say I'm the same person I used to be.

Therapist: You might find that you *change* by staying the *same*.

5. *Use the opposite possibility.* Include the possibility of the opposite happening regarding a statement by highlighting the possibility that something positive can occur as well as drawing attention to an unrealistic expectation or goal. See the following examples.

Client: The next time I see him, I'm sure we'll argue as usual.

Therapist: That could happen, but perhaps it will go better than expected.

Client: I know I'll do just as poorly on the next exam as I did on the last one.

Therapist: That's a possibility, yet you might surprise yourself by getting better results.

Client: I'm sure everything will go just fine.

Therapist: I'm with you—and what if it doesn't go the way you'd hoped?

The use of inclusion allows therapists to pull together ideas and feelings that seem to be incompatible or in opposition and could be hindering the change process, perhaps freeing clients to experience all aspects of a situation.

Normalizing

Perhaps one of the least recognized ways of acknowledgment is *normalizing*. When clients know that they are not crazy or weird for feeling the way they do, they may experience deeper degrees of empathy and self-acceptance. To normalize clients' experiences, practi-

tioners acknowledge clients and give them permission. Just knowing that others have had similar experiences can be liberating for clients and open them to new perspectives. Three different ways to normalize clients' experiences follow.

1. *Use everyday examples.* Note in the following examples that the concern or problem is within the realm of human experience and is not bad, terrible, weird, bizarre, or otherwise.

Client: How many people would let something like what happened to me at work weigh on them the way I am?

Therapist: Given what you've been through at work, especially in recent days, I think most people would expect it to weigh on you.

Client: When I'm depressed, I feel very alone.

Therapist: I've heard other people say that very thing—that when they've been depressed, they've felt very alone.

Client: Sometimes I just want to wring his neck. I know I'm his stepmother and we've been married for only three months, but he still needs to listen. It's so frustrating!

Therapist: I can certainly understand that that would be frustrating for you. One of the things I've heard from other stepparents is that sometimes it takes a little time before kids start to really listen the way you need them to. I'm wondering if that's a possibility here.

2. *Use self-disclosure.* Use personal experience to normalize others' concerns or problems. See the following examples.

Client: I hang on to things for a long time before letting them go.

Therapist: I've heard others say similar things, and I've had that experience as well . . . . we sometimes hang on to things until we're ready to let them go.

Client: I really struggle with math. I just don't think that way.

Therapist: I struggled with math as well. What specifically have you found challenging about it?

Client: I get down on myself when things don't go right—like when I fail to meet deadlines.

Therapist: I think I follow you. I used to get down on myself when I set goals for myself and then didn't reach them. I'd go and wallow. What have you done when things haven't gone right for you?

3. *Use metaphor. Metaphor* is an implied comparison between two dissimilar things. It can play multiple roles in therapy. It is important to recognize and respond to metaphors while attending and listening because it helps to acknowledge, match language, and promote hope. The following examples show how the use of metaphor can assist in normalizing clients' experiences.

Client: I don't like it when people talk about me when I walk by.

Therapist: You mentioned that you really love music and sometimes it's a matter of tuning in what you want and tuning out the rest.

Client: I feel like I'm treading in rough waters and the waves are splashing in my eyes.

Therapist: Sometimes the waves can be rough and choppy. And, if you're able

look just below the surface, you might notice that it's calmer and easier to see things more clearly.

Client: When I'm suspended from school, I can't play sports.

Therapist: Even though you've had some trouble in the classroom, I'm wondering how you've managed to play between the lines when you've been on the field.

When asked about their experiences in therapy, clients routinely report higher levels of connection with their therapists when they feel acknowledged and accepted. Normalizing provides an effective way to let clients know that they are not alone, are respected, and have experiences that are valid and that do not make them crazy, weird, or abnormal.

Utilization

As you have learned, therapists help create conditions in which clients are more likely to achieve positive change and success in the future. Therapists are also facilitators in employing processes to stimulate change in clients' perspectives or actions. Clients, however, are the ultimate engineers of their destinies; their strengths and resources provide the fodder for change. It is therefore important that therapists explore ways to use what clients bring to therapy—no matter how small, strange, or negative the behavior or idea seems—to open possibilities for change. This process directly contrasts with more traditional approaches that often view what clients bring as symptoms or liabilities. Some ways to utilize client behaviors and ideas as vehicles for change follow.

1. *Use what is brought to services as resources to initiate change.* No matter how small, strange, or negative an idea or behavior

may seem, use it to open possibilities for change as in the following examples.

Client: He spends hours tinkering with electronic gadgets. I have no idea why he does it.

Therapist: It sounds like he's found something that really grabs his attention . . . something that he's interested in.

Client: My family is dysfunctional and chaotic.

Therapist: So you've had experience dealing with dysfunction and chaos.

Client: I don't like sports. I'm terrible at them anyway.

Therapist: You've ruled out sports, at least for now, so what else might you focus your efforts on?

Utilization allows therapists to take behaviors and ideas that are typically seen as deficits, inabilities, symptoms, or negative in general and turn them into assets. It can be a helpful way to get clients moving in the direction of the change they are seeking if they are not already doing so. Therapists should not be dismissive of others' points of view, which might suggest that an idea or behavior is in some way negative. One way to avoid causing clients to feel invalidated is by first acknowledging their perspectives. As in example 1 (above), the therapist might say, "I can see why his interest in electronics might lead you to wonder what he gets out of it. How do you think we might help him to use that interest in a way that can help with what you're concerned about?" Acknowledgment of one perspective should not dismiss another.

Matching Language

A final but important area of attending and listening relates to clients' ways to communicate. As discussed, therapists need to remain aware of both verbal and nonverbal communication. Clients often communicate in patterns that can go unrecognized and unattended. Recall that higher ratings of client satisfaction are significantly related to similarity in client-therapist linguistic style. Matching clients' language through using words and phrases, speed, intonation, and patterns can help practitioners create inroads to strengthen connection and initiate change. The following Clinical Vignette regarding Milton Erickson (1965) illustrates this idea.

CLINICAL VIGNETTE

A 25-year-old man named George was picked up by the police for irrational behavior and committed to the state mental hospital. His only rational utterances were, "My name is George," "Good morning," and "Good night." All of his other verbal offerings were continuous word-salad—a mixture of made up sounds, syllables, words, and incomplete phrases. On any given day George might be heard saying, "Bucket of lard," "Didn't pay up," "Sand on the beach," or irrelevant, mixed-up words that did not make sense.

For a few years, George sat by himself and mumbled his word-salad. Psychiatrists, psychologists, social service workers, nurses, other personnel, and even other patients had tried engage him in intelligible conversation but to no avail. George would simply continue his word-salad, in conversation with himself. Over time, George began to greet people who

---

CLINICAL VIGNETTE   (*CONTINUED*)

---

entered the ward with an outburst of word-salad. In between, he sat by himself, seeming to be mildly depressed. When approached he would typically spit out a few minutes of anger-laced word-salad.

Erickson joined the hospital staff during the sixth year of George's stay. He quickly learned about George and found that both staff and patients could sit next to him without eliciting word-salad as long as they did not speak to him. Erickson tried on occasion to learn his name, but all he got was an outpouring of garbled language. So Erickson enlisted his secretary to transcribe, in shorthand, George's word-salad. Although no meaning could be discovered from the transcriptions, Erickson found that he could make use of them.

Erickson carefully studied and learned George's pattern of using word-salad. He then paraphrased the word-salads, but used words that were least likely to be found in George's rants. Erickson could then improvise a word-salad pattern that was similar to George's, but with a completely different vocabulary.

Erickson began to sit along side George on a hospital bench that the patient frequented. He did this in increasing amounts of time until he was able to sit with George for an hour. At that point, Erickson addressed the empty air and identified himself but gained no response from George. The next day, he again identified himself, but this time directly to George. To this, George responded with an angry offering of word-salad. In reply, Erickson voiced out an equal amount of carefully contrived word-salad. George seemed puzzled, and uttered a small amount of word-salad back with an inquiring

intonation. Erickson responded in word-salad as if to answer the inquiry. After a few more interchanges, George lapsed into silence.

At their next meeting, both exchanged greetings and then George launched into a long word-salad speech. Erickson replied. He continued to visit with George on a regular basis and had word-salad conversations each time. Some of the conversations were long and taxing on Erickson.

One morning, after their usual greetings, and a few sentences of nonsense, George said to Erickson, "Talk sense, Doctor." "Certainly, I'd be glad to. What's your name?" asked Erickson. "O'Donovan, and it's about time somebody who knows how to talk asked. Over five years in this lousy joint . . . " (to which a couple of sentences of word-salad were added) replied George. Erickson responded, "I'm glad to get your name, George. Five years is too long a time . . . " (adding an equal amount of word-salad at the end).

The conversation continued with Erickson gaining a complete history from George that was sprinkled with word-salad. Each time Erickson responded, he interspersed the same amount of word-salad back. Although George was never completely free of word-salad, he spoke clearly with only an occasional offering of unintelligible mumbles. This led him to be discharged from the hospital within a year and become gainfully employed. George eventually moved to a distant city where he informed Erickson of his satisfactory adjustments. He ended his last correspondence with Erickson by signing his name properly and adding a few jumbled syllables.

The previous Clinical Vignette draws on the significance of speaking the same language as clients and moving away from psychological jargon that often accompanies conversations. Although they often introduce subtle changes in language to open up possibilities, therapists continuously adjust to clients' ways of communicating rather than having clients make the adjustments. Changes occur at the nonverbal communication level, which can be particularly important when clients appear to be resistant, disagreeable, noncompliant, uncooperative, or overly quiet or are tuning the therapist out (Bertolino & O'Hanlon, 2002). Instead of attending to such communication as resistance or lack of cooperation, therapists should consider whether clients are not responding to what is being done or are pushing for change too quickly and not doing enough acknowledging. The remedy in such cases is to change processes and try to communicate better with clients so that they will feel heard and understood. The following are respectful ways to use matching language.

1. *Match clients' rate and pace of speech.* Match clients' rate and pace of speech as a way to join them. When in sync with the client, the therapist can change the rate and/or pace, if necessary, to promote relaxation, calmness, to neutralize anxiety, and so on. Take care to not come across as mocking or mimicking, which can be invalidating. See the following examples.

   Client: [Quickly] I sometimes struggle to find the words . . . . [pause] like now.

   Therapist: [Mirroring the client's pace] Sometimes it's hard to find the words . . . [pause] and that's okay.

   Client: I don't know . . . [silence] . . . I just don't know why this happened to me.

   Therapist: Yeah . . . [silence] . . . Sometimes the answers are hard to come by.

   Client: I can't . . . I can't believe . . . All of this is so confusing.

   Therapist: Right . . . It just seems so confusing.

2. *Match clients' general use of language.* Listen to the words clients use and use aspects of that language to strengthen the therapeutic relationship.

   Client: I just don't get it, man.

   Therapist: Yeah, man, it does seem confusing.

   Client: She just needs to chill. It doesn't help when she's all ballistic.

   Therapist: If she were to chill a bit, what difference would that make for you?

   Client: I'm really freaked, ya know. Like I just dunno what to do.

   Therapist: Yeah, I'm with ya. I can see why you'd be freaked.

3. *Match clients' use of sensory-based language.* Listen for and match clients' use of sensory-based (visual, auditory, kinesthetic/tactile, gustatory, olfactory) language as in the following examples.

   Client: No matter where I turn, the message is the same . . . "you'll never amount to anything."

   Therapist: It seems like you've been hearing the same message from different directions.

   Client: The way I see it, he'll never change.

   Therapist: I see . . . that's the vision you've had of him.

   Client: I can feel it all over. The tension is almost unbearable.

   Therapist: You can feel it all over, and sometimes the tension is nearly unbearable.

The methods offered for matching language can be used independently or in combination with any of the others discussed throughout this chapter.

Incorporating Process-Oriented Feedback

The issue of effectiveness, as demonstrated using practices that stress accountability, continues to become an increasingly important aspect of the ever-changing therapeutic climate. As discussed at the beginning of this chapter and in the last chapter as a collaboration key, process-oriented feedback and outcome-oriented feedback are the two integral parts of outcome management, a cornerstone for monitoring clients' perceptions of the therapeutic relationship.

Process-oriented methods are often referred to as "bedside manner" in health care. For example, when physicians, nurses, dentists, and masseuses, for example, are applying treatments, they commonly say something like, "Let me know if you have any discomfort or feel any pain." They do this because they want their patients to be as comfortable as possible. Ascertaining the degree of comfort another person is experiencing is difficult—if not impossible—without patient feedback. In addition, patients who are more comfortable (in other words, experience lower levels of pain) typically recover faster. This concept not only applies to but also can be more crucial for psychotherapy. Beutler and Castonguay (2006) stated, "Improvement is best conceptualized as a product of the qualities that patient and therapist bring to the treatment and the relationship that is developed between them" (p. 5).

Research studies have demonstrated that the quality of the therapeutic relationship and working alliance is correlated consistently and positively with client improvement (Constantino, Castonguay, & Schut, 2002; Orlinsky, Rønnestad, & Willutzki, 2004). In addition, certain therapist factors are positively (for example, warmth, flexibility) or negatively (for example, rigidity, self-directed hostility) correlated with the quality of the therapeutic alliance. Constantino, Castonguay, and Schut (2002) found that early alliance is predictive of outcome and that poor client ratings predict premature service termination. Moreover, client ratings of providers as being empathic, trustworthy, and nonjudgmental are better predictors of positive outcomes than are provider ratings of relationships, diagnosis, approach, or any other single variable and are consistent predictors of client improvement (Bachelor & Horvath, 1999; Baldwin, Wampold, & Imel, 2007; Horvath & Bedi, 2002; Martin, Garske, & Davis, 2000; Orlinsky, Grawe, & Parks, 1994; Orlinsky, Rønnestad, & Willutzki, 2004).

Numerous alliance measures have been demonstrated to be psychometrically sound and can assist in gaining therapist, client, and observer feedback (Horvath & Greenberg, 1994). Most measurement instruments are relatively brief (taking three to five minutes) or "ultra brief" (taking less than one minute) (Duncan et al., 2003; Duncan, Miller, & Sparks, 2004). Client-based process instruments are typically implemented at the end of sessions as ways to gain feedback on the interaction that just occurred. It is worth noting that clients are not asked to rate the character or personal qualities of their therapists but perceptions of the processes employed, which consider *how* therapists come across in the therapeutic milieu. In other words, therapists use these instruments to determine whether they are being perceived as warm or flexible. In terms of the therapeutic alliance, the instruments focus on whether clients feel therapists respected and incorporated their views and preferences regarding goals and tasks to accomplish those goals into therapy. Case Example 4.1 supports this idea.

CASE EXAMPLE 4.1

An 18-year-old female came to see me because she had been experiencing problems with substance abuse. During our initial session, she stated that she had recently seen a "social worker" at a local community mental health center. When I inquired as to what her experience had been like in therapy, she stated, "The social worker I saw was very nice. She listened really well." When I asked the young woman how she knew the social worker had been listening to her, she responded, "She would say 'uh huh' and nod her head." I followed, "Is that what you feel you need from a therapist?" To this she replied, "That's not all I need. I didn't go back after a few sessions because I didn't think we were getting anywhere. I need someone to help me come up with some answers." After hearing this, I said, "Let me see if I follow you. Are you saying that what you need is someone who listens really well and also works with you to come up with answers?" "That's right. I need both," she replied. Although I had a good idea what would indicate to her that I was listening well, following her response, I spent time learning more from the young woman about how she thought I might help her in coming up with answers. Through the remainder of the therapy, I continued to check in with her to ensure that she was getting what she needed, to determine whether any changes or modifications were necessary, and if the ways in which we were approaching her situation were right for her.

The client's feedback in Case Example 4.1 influenced how future interactions evolved. Although using instruments is important for obtaining feedback, therapists are also encouraged to use questions to "check in" with clients to gauge their experiences of the therapeutic relationship. The following questions can be used during client-therapist meetings/sessions to check in with clients.

- Have you felt heard and understood?
- Do you feel/think we're talking about what you want to talk about?
- Have we been working on what you want to work on?
- How has the session been for you so far?
- Are we moving in a direction that seems right for you?
- What has the conversation we've been having been like for you?
- What has been helpful or not helpful?

- Are there other things that you feel/think we should be discussing instead?
- Is there anything I should have asked that I haven't asked?
- How satisfied are you with how things are going so far on a scale from 1 to 10, 10 meaning you are completely satisfied with things?
- Are there any changes we should make at this point?
- At this point, how has the way we've been approaching your situation/concern been for you?
- Is there anything I should be doing differently?
- To what degree has what we've been doing met your expectations for therapy so far?

Feedback from these questions allows therapists to learn from clients' perspectives whether therapy is on track or adjustments need to be made.

Therapists also need to keep in mind that even in strong alliances, some "trouble spots" and strains can occur from time to time. In fact, evidence suggests that alliances with "tears and repairs" were better predictors of subsequent client improvement than those that were stable and grew linearly (Kivlighan, 2001). The point is that therapists must respond to integrate client feedback and continue to monitor the alliance throughout the course of therapy. At the end of a session, therapists can ask questions such as these in addition to those previously listed.

- How was the session/meeting for you?
- How was the pace of our conversation/ session/meeting?
- Was there anything missing from our session?
- Is the way we approached your concern/ situation fitting with the way you expect change to occur?
- Are there any changes you would recommend if we were to meet again?
- Is there anything you would need me to do differently if/when we to meet again?
- How would explain your experience in therapy today to others who may be curious?

It is important that therapists be aware of and sensitive to cultural differences that could influence how clients respond to these types of questions. The aim is to invite feedback and if that is inconsistent with clients' cultural backgrounds, then providers want to respond accordingly. In addition, it has been argued that clients may be dishonest about when asked questions such as those listed. When clients are not asked about their experiences with therapy, however, they typically do not voluntarily offer feedback. A poor alliance is a primary reason for clients to end therapy. Elic-

iting and incorporating client feedback can reduce the risk of premature dropout. Accordingly, therapists would be wise to begin attending to the therapeutic relationship when meetings/sessions begin. Alliance problems can often be solved when the therapists deal with them directly, openly, and nondefensively. Doing so may allow relationships to get back on track or promote positive relational experiences for clients (Safran, Muran, Samstag, & Stevens, 2002). It is therefore imperative to incorporate any form of process feedback, whether from pencil and paper measures, questions, or both, into therapy.

The therapeutic alliance is not a symmetrical relationship. Clients and therapists have different responsibilities; theory, professional experiences, and perhaps past personal relational experiences determine the therapist's understanding of the alliance whereas in-session interactions and past relational experiences affect the client's experience more. As Horvath and Bedi (2002) remarked, "Each of these perspectives throws light on a qualitatively different aspect of the phenomenon" (p. 91). From the therapist's perspective, process-oriented feedback strengthens and promotes the alliance and should be used as a way to:

- accommodate services to the client's motivational level
- accommodate services to the client's view of the relationship
- collaborate with clients in establishing directions and goals for services
- collaborate with clients to determine tasks to accomplish those goals
- match clients' use of language

The use of process-oriented feedback is essential to the integrity of therapy. It helps therapists to maintain accountability to clients. It is imperative that therapists continuously reflect on how clients may be experiencing interactions with them. By encouraging client feedback and integrating what is learned, they are engaging in processes that assist in creating the best possible fit between their approaches and clients' ideas about how therapy should take place. In a more general sense, therapists should ask themselves questions to ensure that they are considering their clients' experiences (Madsen, 2007). For example, they might ask themselves, "How might this client be experiencing our interaction right now?" or "Would this client say our interaction is more or less in sync with his needs, expectations, or ideas?" Such questions can serve as a reminder for understanding how clients experience the therapeutic interactions and the impact they can have over the course of therapy.

Putting It All Together: Constructing Conversations for Change

Language can be used in various ways to strengthen the client-therapist relationship and create pathways for present and future change. This final section uses Case Example 4.2 to pull together all of the information in the chapter that a therapist might use to interact with a client during a first session. See whether you can identify which method(s) is (are) employed in each numbered part of the exercise.

CASE EXAMPLE 4.2

Therapist (1): What would be a good starting point for you?

Client (1): Well, I've just got a lot on my mind. I thought it would be good to talk with someone about it.

Therapist (2): I'm glad you did.

Client (2): Nothing's going right. I feel like the world is just collapsing around me and there's no way out.

Therapist (3): You've felt as if the world were closing in on you. Things haven't been going right, and your sense is that there's no way out.

Client (3): That's right.

Therapist (4): Can you tell me a little more about what's specifically been happening?

Client (4): It's kind of hard . . . but I guess what I've noticed lately is that I can't get my work done. My school work. I don't feel motivated at all. And worse, I'm flunking out of college.

Therapist (5): It's been a bit hard . . . and you've haven't been getting your work done the way you'd like to lately. And that's shown up in your grades. Is that right?

Client (5): Yeah. I don't want to flunk out of school. If I do, I'll have to go back home and live with my folks again. That would be rock bottom. I definitely don't want to do that!

Therapist (6): I see. So let me see if I'm following you. One concern is how you've been doing in school lately and that if this were to continue, you might return to live with your folks. Are there other things that have happened with you that you think are important for me to know about?

Client (6): Really, the only other thing is my girlfriend. She's really smart. I'm not doing as well as her and that's really hard. And she doesn't know how bad I'm doing. If she found out, she

CASE EXAMPLE 4.2   *(continued)*

might think that I'm stupid. I know it's dumb to feel that way. . . . She really wouldn't think that. I'm not dumb; I just haven't put in the effort.

Therapist (7): It's okay to feel that way, and I gather from what you've said that you know that it's not about your ability but how you've applied yourself so far. It also sounds like while you really value your girlfriend's views at some level, you seem to know it's your view of yourself that is most likely to get in the way.

Client (7): Exactly.

Therapist (8): Anything else?

Client (8): No, that's how I see it.

Therapist (9): So there are a few things that we could focus on here—getting your work done and doing better in school . . . .

Client (9): That's really the key for me. I need to get my grades up, but it seems like such a long haul. I mean, I don't really feel like I can turn the corner. It's so overwhelming.

Therapist (10): I can see why it would feel that way. It can seem like turning the corner is overwhelming and you still can make that turn. What is the most overwhelming part of it?

Client (10): Well, just figuring out the first step. It's not impossible, but it sure seems like it.

Therapist (11): Right. The first step can be a challenge, and you haven't quite figured it out yet, which can make it overwhelming.

Client (11): Yeah, that's it exactly.

Therapist (12): And so when you do begin to turn the corner, what will be different for you?

Client (12): Well, my grades will be up and I'll feel better about myself for starters.

Therapist (13): So your grades will be up . . . to what?

Client (13): Passing, for starters.

Therapist (14): Do you mean C's?

Client (14): Yeah . . . hopefully C's and B's, then eventually all B's.

Therapist (15): And you mentioned feeling better about yourself. Is that something you'd like to work on in here?

Client (15): Definitely. My self-esteem needs to be higher.

Therapist (16): And what will higher self-esteem allow you to do differently than what you are doing now?

Client (16): It will help me to stay the course of making sure I'm studying and going to class to get my grades up.

Therapist (17): I see. So what then might be a very small step that might help you to take a step toward that corner that you would like to turn?

Client (17): I just need to start going to each class.

Therapist (18): What would it take for that to happen a little more often than it does now?

Client (18): I have to make sure I go and not make up any excuses.

Therapist (19): Okay. Before we explore this further, I'd just like to check in with you to see how you're doing. Is that okay with you?

Client (19): Sure.

Therapist (20): How has our meeting been for you so far?

Client (20): It's gone good.

Therapist (21): Have we talked about what you want to talk about?

Client (21): Yeah. We're right on it.

Therapist (22): Ok. Is there anything you want to be sure that we discussed that we haven't yet?

Client (22): Not that I can think of. I want to talk about getting on track with my grades and that's what we've been doing.

(continued)

CASE EXAMPLE 4.2 *(continued)*

Therapist (23): Okay. Please let me know if at any point we need to make any adjustments to our sessions. I want to ensure that you're getting what you need.

Client (23): Great. I will, but it's fine now.

What did you notice about the conversation between the client and the therapist? In the author's experience, when attending to and introducing possibilities through language, clients, colleagues, and students do not notice anything out of the ordinary. It just seems like a conversation between people. Now, which of the ways to work with clients' language did you identify? The therapist responses and respective methods used follow.

Therapist (1): Process-oriented opening question

Therapist (2): Acknowledgment

Therapist (3): Paraphrasing; using the past tense; translating into perceptual statement

Therapist (4): Using the past tense

Therapist (5): Matching language; using the past tense; matching language

Therapist (6): Summarizing; matching language; using the past tense

Therapist (7): Permission; presupposing change and progress

Therapist (9): Matching language; recasting problem statements

Therapist (10): Acknowledgment; inclusion

Therapist (11): Acknowledgment; assuming future changes

Therapist (12): Presupposing changes and progress

Therapist (15): Recasting problem statement into preferences or goals

Therapist (16): Presupposing change and progress

Therapist (17): Acknowledgment; future focus

Therapist (18): Future focus

Therapist (19): Acknowledgment; incorporating process-oriented feedback

Therapist (20): Attending to client's view of alliance; assuming future change or progress

Therapist (21): Process-oriented feedback

Therapist (22): Process-oriented feedback

Therapist (23): Incorporating process-oriented feedback

As therapists attend and listen to client narratives, they must take care to acknowledge and validate clients' experience and views while listening for statements that reflect stories of impossibility and then work to introduce possibilities into these otherwise closed-down views. Because clients' problems are often embedded, at least to some degree, in "problem-talk," the role of language in change cannot be overstated. In addition to letting clients know therapists are "with" them, language assists with creating small openings in otherwise closed-down situations. Although it is possible for significant spontaneous change to occur, these methods work to create small movements as opposed to dramatic ones. Finally, incorporating some form of client-therapist process-feedback mechanism is necessary to learn of clients' perceptions of therapeutic processes and then to make any changes that could benefit clients. To become more familiar with using language as a vehicle for change, try combining the methods offered in this chapter.

SUMMARY POINTS

- Client engagement is an active process that involves eliciting clients' experiences and views and using those as guides to therapy.
- Therapists create listening space so that clients can share their stories; for some, this can be the most powerful part of therapy.
- Clients' stories reveal their *relational* and *conversational preferences*: what clients find meaningful to talk about and the ways that they would like therapists to interact with them.
- Language and interaction are the primary ways that therapists promote change on both having an effect on both psychological and physical states.
- Use language to convey empathy, positive regard, and congruence, which have been correlated with outcome.
- Therapists use *acknowledgement* and *validation* as gateways to increase levels of empathy, positive regard, and congruence.
- Encouragers including *paraphrasing, summarizing,* and *highlighting* are used to acknowledge, validate, confirm, and capture the essence of clients' experience.

- *Dissolving impossibility talk* uses language that combines acknowledgement and possibility as a way to capture the essence of clients' experience and create openings in otherwise closed-down statements.
- *Future-talk* is a way to use language to combine acknowledgement and methods for introducing the element of future possibility and change.
- Therapists can strengthen the therapeutic relationship and inject possibility by employing methods such as *giving permission, inclusion, normalization, utilization, matching language,* and *process-oriented feedback*.
- *Process-oriented feedback* is used to identify and understand clients' perceptions of the therapeutic relationship and alliance. Therapists check in with clients throughout sessions and incorporate feedback on a real-time basis to accommodate clients' motivational levels and views of the relationship. Client feedback also guides goal setting and determining tasks to accomplish goals.

DISCUSSION QUESTIONS

1. What are client's relational and conversational preferences? What role do they play in therapy?

2. What are possible ways that language can affect people and relationships?

3. What are the differences between empathy, positive regard, and congruence? In what ways can each enhance the therapeutic relationship?

4. In what specific ways can therapists both acknowledge clients' otherwise closed-down statements and inject the element of possibility into them?

5. What are specific ways that therapists can both acknowledge client statements and simultaneously offer a glimpse of the future in response to them?

6. In what other subtle ways can therapists use language as a vehicle for change?

7. At what points in therapy should therapists use process-oriented questions to obtain feedback? What are three process-oriented questions?

PART THREE

Chapter 5

Establishing Structure and Direction

Using Information-Gathering Processes

■ A distinguishing feature of therapy, and one that separates it from other forms of helping relationships and those that focus primarily on providing support, is a focus on specific concerns and problems. A percentage of clients enter therapy wanting to deepen their understandings of themselves through increased awareness, for example; however, most seek some form of immediate change, typically originating from some source of current conflict. This goal requires that therapists work with clients and others who may be involved to establish agreed-upon directions in therapy. Absence of direction or ambiguity, as you have learned, can lead to confusion and frustration and contribute to a lack of structure linked with negative outcome (Mohr, 1995). In addition, not continuously monitoring for improvement and changes in direction can cause clients to remain in therapy beyond points of maximum benefit.

This chapter discusses ways to establish structure and direction in therapy. These processes give shape and focus to therapy, provide pathways to strengthen the therapeutic alliance, and elicit crucial information to select therapeutic methods and techniques. The chapter first explores formal information-gathering processes that involve the use of instrumentation including strategies and methods for conducting screenings and evaluations. The second part of the chapter explores informal information-gathering processes that are integral to change processes because they represent the client-therapist agreed-upon goals and directions for therapy and preliminary conversations about ways to accomplish those goals.

Generative Conversations: Information-Gathering Practices as Gateways to Change

Therapists often use information-gathering processes to assess client mental status (pathology and patterns of relational dysfunction) and determine diagnosis. They then use this information to match service or treatment planning and guide therapy. As previously discussed, information can be gathered from standardized assessment measures that require clients to fill out questionnaires and forms and/or structured interviewing that asks clients a series of questions. In either case, therapists must ultimately make sense of the information obtained and determine how to use it, if at all—putting conversation, language, and interaction at the forefront.

Because of the emphasis on collaboration—processes that are respectful of and include clients—the term *information gathering* is used as opposed to *assessment*, and *conversation* is used instead of *interviewing*. The overarching idea is to use language that encourages collaborative partnerships in which clients' preferences and feedback are encouraged. In accord with the use of the collaboration keys discussed in Chapter 3, therapists should remain as collaborative as possible even when situations require them to be more deliberate or directive.

Strengths-based engagement (SBE) uses formal and informal information gathering (Bertolino & O'Hanlon, 2002). *Formal informational gathering* refers to those methods that involve standardized instrumentation (for example, inventories and tests) and procedures (for example, assessment forms required by hospitals, residential facilities, and HMOs). Many forms of instrumentation emphasize identifying problems, pathology, and deficit. Formal informational-gathering methods can help therapists understand how and to what degree clients experience problems and to elicit clients' strengths and resources. Being strengths-based means attending to the difficulties clients face while exploring internal and external resources that may assist in resolving concerns and complaints. It also translates to incorporat-

ing standardized measures that track outcome from clients' perspectives. That is, practitioners want to know whether or not and to what degree clients experience improvement. This information helps to determine the next steps in therapy.

Informal or *ongoing information gathering* refers to processes that focus on goal setting and clients' views of their concerns and problems including their ideas about change. Conversations assist therapists in gaining valuable information to use to determine which methods will create the best fit for clients. Informal information gathering begins with the first session and ends when clients have made the transition out of therapy or the service being provided. As therapy progresses, as goals are met, and as clients' perspectives change, information gathered through these conversations gives shape to future directions.

In review, as practitioners approach information gathering they engage in the following processes that inform strengths-based therapy.

- *Invite clients into collaborative relationships prior to the start of therapy.*
- *Listen and attend to clients' stories.*
- *Begin to create small, subtle changes in clients' language to open possibilities for change.*

These processes help establish collaborative partnerships, learn clients' views, match linguistic styles, and open possibilities for change through language.

Strengths-Based Information Gathering: Formal Processes

Formal information-gathering procedures are commonly used to identify pathology, create or corroborate diagnostic impressions, and provide direction for treatment. Some forms of instrumentation (for example, Beck Depression Inventory) are screening devices for specific conditions; others (for example, Minnesota Multiphasic Personality Inventory [MMPI]) identify multiple symptoms. Instrumentation can be objective in format (for example, California Psychological Inventory [CPI]; Millon Clinical Multi-axial Inventory-III) by using true/false responses or ordinal scales. Objective testing should result in less interpretation, whereas projective testing (for example, Rorschach Ink Blot Test, Thematic Apperception Test) relies heavily on subjectivity.

Formal information gathering also is conducted by using protocols that ask clients a sequence or series of questions although practitioners often have flexibility in how to ask them. Flexibility allows for a "flow" during these interactions. No matter the method employed, the central focus is on gathering information about the problems clients are experiencing, whether individually or interpersonally.

Therapists must acknowledge and recognize that their expectations can unconsciously and often inadvertently influence clients in all aspects of therapy, particularly when using formalized processes. In research, this is known as the *observer-expectancy effect,* which is associated with the allegiance effect. These concepts underscore the notion that therapists' expectancy biases, whether positive or negative, will influence the course and outcome of therapy. Thus, therapists could fall prey to "theory countertransference" (Hubble & O'Hanlon, 1992) by which their theoretical biases and unrecognized assumptions can influence the content, process, and direction of therapy. The concern is that therapists may believe that what they are observing and simultaneously influencing is "real" and objective. They become certain they are discovering *real* problems.

It is important that therapists learn from clients how their problems have evolved and affected their lives without becoming overly entrenched in theoretical biases that may result in "problem talk." Recall that clients are the most significant influences on outcome and conversations that emphasize pathology can cloud client strengths and contributions to change. In addition, the more clients talk about their problems and the more therapists emphasize with what is wrong through their questions and methods, the higher is the likelihood that both individuals will become subject to the idea that things are actually worse than first imagined.

Learning about client concerns and problems is only one part of understanding a therapist needs to gain. An equal if not more essential way is to use formal information-gathering processes as opportunities to explore clients' strengths and resources, which can be used to address problems and bring about present and future change. This means learning how clients have faced problems in the past and identifying how they might use these methods more actively to improve their lives and situations. Focusing on clients' strengths can counter invalidation and blame that can accompany a problem-only focus.

A strengths-based philosophy relies on using a balance of problem/pathology-based and possibility-oriented questions. It not only allows therapists to gain perspective regarding client abilities and resources but also helps identify mitigating factors that could put both the client and institution at risk for unnecessary hospitalizations, increased length of stay, and ineffective treatment. Therefore, information gathering involves an interplay between problems, strengths, and exceptions. *Exceptions* relate to times when things are or have gone differently in regard to a client's problem (de Shazer, 1988, 1991; O'Hanlon &

Weiner-Davis, 2003). Exception-oriented questions ask for information about when the concern or problem was less dominating, occurred less frequently, or was absent altogether. Essential in this process is to identify what the client did differently in such instances. Doing so helps identify a client's internal strengths and external resources and serves to intervene in the present while providing building blocks for future change.

Introduction of Formal Information-Gathering Processes

Achieving a balance between determining the influence of problems and strengths begins with the approach the therapist uses to introduce clients to formal information gathering. One approach is to let clients know that every client goes through the same or similar procedure. In the event that different forms of information gathering are used for specific purposes and not universally with every client it is important to provide rationale and create space for the client to ask questions. This can normalize the process of using instrumentation and can help clients understand the purpose of conversations they are about to engage in and how the information gathered from these conversations will be used. When the manner and order in which questions are asked are flexible, as in the following example, therapists have options for putting clients at ease.

> I'd like to ask you some questions that we ask everyone who comes to see us. The information you give will help us to understand what you're concerned about and how that's affected you, what you'd like to see change, what has and hasn't worked for you in trying to manage your concerns, and how we can be of help to you. And as we proceed, if you feel like or think we've missed something, please

be sure to let us know. We want to make sure that we fully understand what you need. How does that sound?

Some procedures are more "front loaded" with problem-focused questions, and the therapist must find ways to intersperse the procedures with strengths-based questioning. Even the most pathology-oriented procedures offer opportunities for therapists to explore client strengths. See the following example for a way to open conversations with clients when processes may be slanted more toward problems.

> I'd like to ask you to answer some questions (and fill out some forms) that we ask of everyone who comes here. The questions will help me to understand what's happening with you or in you life that's of concern. Although we will ask you to describe more of the specifics about what's troublesome, I want you to know that once we finish with those questions, we'll move on to some others that will tell us more about what you do well and what has worked or might work for you in the future regarding your concerns. How does that sound?

The idea is to view clients' concerns as existing on a continuum with better and worse times. Practitioners want to know about each end of the continuum as well as what is happening between. Although traditional "assessment" procedures tend to focus almost exclusively on problems and pathology, they allow room for therapists to ask questions that elicit client strengths, abilities, and resources, thus introducing some balance to the information gathering process. For example, a therapist might focus on a concern by saying, "Tell me more about the trouble that you've experienced with your co-worker." The therapist might then explore another aspect by saying, "Tell me a little bit about a relationship that you have or had with another employee that went just a little better" or "What kinds of people do you tend to relate better to?" Rather than focusing solely on "trouble in the work environment" or "problems with relating to others," the therapist learns about differences in the client's work and other relationships.

At times problems will be more or less intrusive, situations better or worse, and solutions working or not working. Formal information-gathering processes help to learn about both problematic times (when problems seemed to be in control) and strengths (when clients seemed to be in control). Formal processes, whether via instrumentation and/or question-based interviewing, can enhance the client-therapist relationship and provide a way for the therapist to intervene and facilitate change early in therapy.

In addition to facilitating change, formal information-gathering processes maximize nontheory and method-related factors by:

- strengthening the therapeutic relationship and alliance
- building on or creating hope for the future
- creating space for clients to tell their stories
- identifying clients' use of language
- learning about clients' concerns and complaints
- eliciting and evoking clients' strengths, abilities, and resources
- learning clients' orientations to change.

It is important to keep in mind that formal information-gathering processes should always be culturally sensitive. Clients' experiences, preferences, and abilities determine whether a particular method is a good fit. Not all formalized instruments and forms of information gathering have been used consistently with culturally diverse populations. In addition,

intellectual capacities and other influences in client backgrounds will affect how and to what degree clients will be able or willing to complete various measures. By attending to these considerations in advance and incorporating feedback processes to check in with clients, therapists' practices will reflect an increased degree of sensitivity to clients and their needs.

General Information-Gathering Questions

To open pathways to strengths and resources when gathering information, therapists can use many general questions to search for exceptions and begin to understand the influence that clients have over concerns and problems. These questions can be interspersed at different junctures to obtain information useful in cultivating possibilities for solutions. These are some examples:

- It seems that when you experience the concern that brought you in, things are pretty difficult. When does the concern seem a little less noticeable to you?
- Tell me about a time recently when things went a little bit better for you in regard to the concern that brought you in.
- How did that happen?
- What did you do differently?
- What's different about those times?
- What's different about the times when you're able to get more of an upper hand with the problem?
- What persons, places, or things were helpful to you?
- How will you know when things are better?
- What will be different in your life?

These questions offer subtle efforts to help ferret out small as opposed to extreme differences. Therapists do not ask, "When don't you have the problem?" That is too big a leap for most clients and can prove invalidating for those who may get the sense that therapists are glossing over problems, moving too quickly, or perhaps focusing too extensively on solutions (Nylund & Corsiglia, 1994). It is important to let clients know that therapists understand their pain and not give short shrift to their concerns. Using questions that elicit small differences can do this and can be enough to help move clients in the direction of positive change.

Specific Content Area Questions

Many areas can be explored during formal information-gathering processes. These involve but are not limited to culture, education/school, work/employment, family/social relationships, hobbies/interests, and previous therapy experiences (Bertolino, 2003). In addition to gathering information about concerns, each area provides opportunities to inquire about strengths (for example, resilience and coping skills), abilities, and resources as well as exceptions and differences. Again, in searching for exceptions, practitioners are asking questions about times things have gone differently with regard to concerns and problems and what clients did differently. Information about exceptions and differences serve not only to intervene in the present but also act as stepping stones to future change. These are some questions that can assist therapists in each area.

Work/Employment

- How did you come to work at your current place of employment?
- How did you put yourself in position to get the job?
- What do you think your employer saw in you that might have contributed to hiring you?
- What have you found to be most challenging or difficult about your job?

- How have you met or worked toward meeting those difficulties/challenges?
- What keeps you there?
- What skills or qualities do you think you employer sees in you?
- What qualities do you think you possess that are assets on the job?
- (if self-employed) How did you have the wherewithal to start your own business?
- (if unemployed) What kind of employment would you like in the future?
- What would be a first step for you to make that happen?

Culture/Ethnicity/Religion-Spirituality

- How do you identify yourself culturally?
- How does your culture influence your everyday life?
- In what ways, in any, does your nationality influence your everyday life?
- What does spirituality or religion or higher power mean to you?
- How do you experience spirituality or religion or higher power?
- What is most meaningful to you about your [culture, ethnic background, nationality, spiritual beliefs, etc.]?
- How has your [culture, ethnic background, nationality, spiritual beliefs, etc.] been a resource for you?
- How do you maintain its presence in your life?

Education/School

- How did you manage to make it to/ through [9th grade, high school, trade school, junior college, a four-year university, two years of college, graduate school, etc.]?
- What qualities do you possess that made that happen?
- What did you like best about school?

- What did you find most challenging/difficult about school?
- How did you manage any difficulties that you may have encountered while in school? (for example, completing homework/assignments, taking tests, getting to school on time, moving from one grade to another, maintaining teacher/classmate relationships, participating in sports, etc.)
- In what ways did school prepare you for future challenges?

Family/Social Relationships

- Whom are you closest to in your [group, family, etc.]?
- What do you appreciate most about your relationship with [friend, husband/wife, father/mother, son/daughter, uncle/aunt, grandparent, colleague, etc]?
- What would he/she/they say are your best qualities as a [friend, husband/wife, father/mother, son/daughter, uncle/aunt, grandparent, colleague, etc]?
- How is that helpful for you to know that?
- What does it feel like to know that?
- Which relationships have been more challenging/difficult for you?
- How have you dealt with those challenges/difficulties?
- Whom can you go to for help?
- Who has made a positive difference in your life?
- How so?
- What difference has that made for you?
- When are others most helpful to you?

Hobbies/Interests

- What do you do for fun?
- What hobbies or interests do you have or have you had?
- To what kinds of activities are you drawn?

- With what kinds of activities would you rather not be involved?
- What would you rather do instead?

Previous Therapy Experiences

- What did you find helpful about previous [individual, couples, family, group, etc.] therapy?
- What did the therapist do that was helpful?
- How did that make a difference for you?
- What wasn't so helpful?
- (if currently or previously on psychotropic medication) How is/was the medication helpful to you?
- What, if anything, did/does the medication allow you to do that you wouldn't otherwise be (been) able to do?
- What qualities do you possess so that you were/are able to work with the medication to improve things for yourself?

Specific content area questions draw attention to the difficulties and strengths that clients experience. Using them can help therapists to learn from clients what has worked in the past (to any degree), what worked more recently, and what might work in the future. Efforts can then be made to apply or replicate what has worked at other times with current concerns. It is also important to find out about what has not worked so that therapists do not unknowingly use methods that clients have found either not helpful or disrespectful in the past. Although it is possible that a client could still benefit from something that was not previously helpful, it is best to begin with client feedback and then search for specific methods to provide a better fit.

Specific content area questions also help to identify clients' social support systems, which are integral in providing stability and connection. A way to identify these resources is

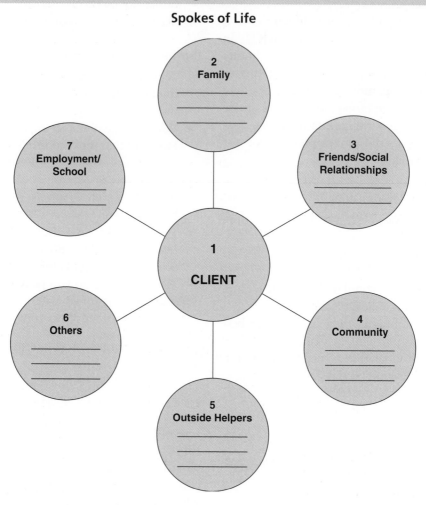

Figure 5.1

Spokes of Life

through the spokes of life outlined in Figure 5.1. This schematic provides a way for therapists to help clients list persons who make up their support systems and who might be helpful now or in the future. Therapists can help clients who have limited resources or have trouble identifying key persons use the schematic to identify new social supports as they emerge.

In addition, therapists often find themselves responding with "off-the-cuff" questions. These questions tend to occur spontaneously in dialogue and can be particularly useful in gathering information and creating a flow in conversation. Part of the challenge for therapists who prefer more free-form questioning is to maintain consistency in this less structured format. Therapists want to continue to gather and track information without losing the focus that structured questioning provides. This is an excellent example of how the art of therapy comes into play. Therapists must balance specific processes (most commonly in the form of questions on formalized tools) with intuition and creativity to formulate questions that elicit information about problems and/or needs, any risk or threat of harm to the client and/or other(s), and internal strengths and resources. To further illustrate this, you are invited to complete Exercise 5.1, There's More to See Than First Meets the Eye: Balancing Information Gathering.

Did you notice any similarities between what you identified in Part 1 versus Part 2 of Exercise 5.1? Exceptions (strengths and resources) to what we often identify as problems/concerns and potentially areas of risk can be used as agents of change. Therapists recognize that they rarely get two chances to view a specific interaction or session (although videotaping is useful, it does not provide the same experience as viewing one in real time). Each interaction requires practitioners to identify problem areas and strengths *at the same time*. Practicing activities similar to the one in Exercise 5.1 can hone practitioners' ability to gather information from multiple perspectives.

Diagnosis

Chapter 2 discussed the issue of diagnosis, including the DSM-IV-TR (the nosology at the time of this writing) at length. Many agencies, organizations, and practices recognize that a DSM-IV-TR diagnosis is required to gain authorization for service payment. How to approach this issue is complicated. The DSM-IV-TR offers a paradigm that is inconsistent and at best is of limited use with clients, particularly couples and families. Some clients find diagnoses meaningful; diagnoses can defuse blame that clients have placed on themselves or others have placed on clients regarding their conditions. For example, the author has had clients who expressed relief in knowing that others have been through similar situations

and that the diagnosis itself explained their concerns. Diagnoses have also led therapists to conduct research to find effective therapy approaches—perhaps the best result of assigning a diagnosis.

Concerns with diagnosis and the DSM are well established. Obviously, therapists should consider the labeling, depersonalizing, and stigmatizing effects that the identification of pathology can cause. Each diagnosis concern is linked to others: Diagnosis is based on identifying deficit and pathology; a pathology focus leads to labeling people as having "disorders"; and labeling can objectify people and depersonalize them. This can lead to considering those with the disorder as their diagnoses rather than as people. Labels can stigmatize individuals, possibly subjecting them to prejudices, biases, and in extreme cases, ostracizing them from every day activities. Professional literature clearly articulates these points. Further discussion is beyond the scope of this book except to note some actions therapists can take to avoid or lessen the potentially negative effects associated with diagnosis:

- Consider employment opportunities in which diagnosis is not required for the clientele served.
- If required to use a diagnosis in a specific context, talk with clients about its role and be sure to present them with choices (e.g., paying out of pocket rather than submitting a diagnosis to an third-party payer, referring then to agencies that do not require diagnosis) to avoid applying the diagnosis.
- If required to use diagnosis, talk with clients about it and factor in that feedback in decisions about how to proceed.
- If clients enter therapy with diagnoses already assigned, elicit the meaning(s) attributed to diagnoses during conversations

Exercise 5.1

There's More than First Meets the Eye: Balancing Information Gathering

Part 1

- Choose a movie that depicts an individual, couple, or family. Select a scene in the movie between 3 to 7 minutes in length that depicts a problem, situation, or event that could lead to the initiation of therapy.

- Watch the scene from the perspective of a therapist who is in the first session with a client. Identify any areas of concern, risk, or safety that you would include in your information-gathering processes. Once identified, these areas would be incorporated into service planning and addressed in therapy. (*Note:* Do not stop the scene while in progress or rereview it before completing Part 1.)

- In the spaces provided, write the areas of concern you have identified. If more space is needed, please use additional paper.

_____

_____

_____

_____

_____

_____

_____

_____

_____

_____

- Next consider the following questions: What did you learn? How might what you identified affect the way you approached this individual, couple, or family? What might you do as a result?

- Next discuss the areas identified with a colleague, peer, or supervisor. If the other person also completed the exercise, compare your findings with his or hers.

- When you have completed this part of the exercise, continue on to Part 2.

that are not dismissive of clients' views but open new opportunities to see themselves.

- In general, use diagnostic jargon as sparingly as possible and only when necessary.
- Use person-first language (see Chapter 2).
- Explain that assignment of a diagnosis means only that a client's symptoms fit a set of preestablished criteria and focus on clearly delineated behaviors and actions that clients have identified as troublesome.

- Work to help clients view themselves differently and make changes instead of trying to rid themselves of diagnoses. (See the section on informal information-gathering processes later in this chapter).

- Use outcome measurement systems to monitor change, which brings clients

Exercise 5.1 *(continued)*

Part 2

- Watch the same scene a second time, again from the perspective of a therapist who is in a first session.

- Identify any strengths and resources you would include in your information-gathering processes including exceptions to problems and individual or relational responses that once identified you would incorporate into service planning and use in the service of change. (*Note:* Do not stop or rereview the scene until you have completed the remainder of Part 2.)

- In the spaces provided, list the strengths and resources you have identified. If more space is needed, please use additional paper.

_____

_____

_____

_____

_____

_____

_____

_____

_____

_____

- When you have finished, consider the following questions: What do you notice when you review the list of strengths you identified? What might you do with this information? What do you notice when you compare the lists generated in Parts 1 and 2?

- Discuss the areas identified with a colleague, peer, or supervisor. If the other person also completed the exercise, compare your findings with his or hers.

- Consider what you learned, how what you identified could affect the way you approach this individual, couple, or family, and what you might do as a result.

more fully into the process of determining their goals for therapy and subsequent courses of action.

Each of these actions reflects the therapists' commitment to respectful, collaborative practices that informs clients, gives them choices, and acknowledges their voices. Therapists should recognize that diagnosis is just one form of story about clients and that focusing on other stories can move therapy in very different directions. Being supportive and progressive rather than invalidating and dehumanizing is most important.

Outcome Measurement

A final area central to formal information gathering is outcome measurement, which involves providing process- and outcome-oriented feedback in "real time." Chapter 3 suggested a way to introduce and discuss the role of both forms of measurement in therapy, and Chapter 4 described specific ways to elicit process-oriented feedback. This discussion focuses on how outcome-oriented feedback fits into formal information-gathering processes.

Recall that outcome-oriented feedback seeks to identify clients' interpretations of the impact of the course of therapy on major life dimensions (such as individual well-being, interpersonal relationships, and social role functioning). It provides a consistent and reliable indicator of client improvement. Most outcome measures are based on the presence or absence of symptoms associated with client distress (for example, depression, anxiety, relational conflict) and include "flag" questions that help identify high-risk concerns such as suicidal ideation and substance abuse.

Depending on the measure, lower or higher scores suggest different degrees of functioning and, over time, improvement or deterioration. Clients who are in the "functional" range are said to be "within the clinical cutoff," which indicates people who have high levels of symptoms or concerns. Those "outside the clinical cutoff" are not considered representative of those who typically seek therapy. Consider an example using the Outcome Questionnaire 45[1] (OQ-45.2) that has been researched rigorously for more than two decades (Burlingame et al., 1995; Lambert & Burlingame, 1996; Lambert & Finch, 1999; Lambert et al., 1996). The OQ-45.2 is a 120-point scale with a clinical cutoff of 44; lower scores indicate lower levels of distress and clients who are less likely to seek therapy. In contrast, clients with scores of 44 and above

are considered to be "within" the clinical population, indicating their higher degrees of distress. Clients at this level are consistent with "average" persons who seek therapy. During initial information-gathering sessions, therapists should note that clients with scores outside established clinical cutoffs may have ambiguous concerns because they are reporting fewer symptoms of distress and conflict.

Outcome measurement protocols are implemented just prior to or at the beginning of therapy sessions to determine how clients view their lives presently or in the very recent past (such as the previous week or since their last session). The practitioner then immediately incorporates this feedback (which is computed either through manual or automatic scoring) into sessions. Combining what clients verbalize in conversation with therapists' observations (and any other sources of information available) results in information triangulation and can help therapists create a more accurate picture of what is presently happening with clients during initial interactions. Chapters 11 and 12 discuss the role of outcome-oriented feedback in subsequent sessions.

Many instruments are available to measure different variables and range in length and estimated time to complete. Although an in-depth discussion of the intricacies and technicalities (including selection and implementation) of specific outcome management systems is beyond the scope of this book, it represents an area of research that can be accessed through psychology and health care-related databases. The important factor is that therapists show interest in and engage in processes to elicit and integrate client feedback as a way to improve the effectiveness of therapy.

---

[1] The remainder of this book uses the OQ-45.2 when discussing the application of an outcome measure.

Strengths-Based Information Gathering: Informal Processes

The ways in which therapy is carried out can differ significantly just as the contexts in which it is offered can. Many settings require that formal information-gathering processes be used; others do not. Moreover, some will allow for variation in required processes. For example, it is possible that certain formal inventories be administered initially and that as the interview progresses it becomes less formal, thus increasing clients' comfort in letting their stories emerge. Few settings require an "either/or" approach; a "both/and" mix of formal and informal processes is encouraged.

As discussed previously, an important part of therapy for many clients involves telling their stories. Thus, it is important for therapists to ask open-ended questions, such as those offered in Chapter 4 early in the therapeutic encounter. These questions help therapists to understand clients' conversational and relational preferences by inviting clients into conversations in which they can convey the details of their stories in ways in which they feel most comfortable. While attending to language, therapists use these conversations as opportunities to gain valuable information about what clients want to have different in their lives.

Effective therapeutic approaches encourage a focus on what needs to change. As discussed, a lack of focus and structure can not only bring about a negative outcome but also contribute to frustration on the part of both clients and therapists. It is also clear that lack of agreement and ambiguity regarding goals between client and therapist can lead to the selection of misguided methods that are poor fits for clients. It is therefore paramount that therapists work to clarify and translate general and sometimes ambiguous concerns into what clients do not want by outlining specific actions, desired changes, and clients' preferred futures.

Funneling: Creation of Direction and Increased Focus

At the heart of informal information gathering are processes that help move general conversations into ones that that increase direction and focus. Although it is understood that change often occurs as a by-product of ongoing conversations, lack of clarity about client expectations, what is most concerning them, and what they would like to have different can lead to dialogues that meander and may ultimately not be productive.

The ways in which therapists work with clients to foster direction and focus can vary. As a starting point, refer to the orienting questions offered in Chapter 4, which open space for clients to share their experiences through their stories. From these questions therapists lead into others that assist in narrowing conversations by what might be referred to as a "funneling effect." That is, broad conversations become focused as clients determine those aspects they would prefer to give more or less attention. The following questions may be useful in developing further focus:

- What would you like to see change?
- What would you like to have different with your situation/life?
- What did you hope would be different as a result of coming to therapy?
- What goals do you have for yourself?

Notice that these questions not only help therapists gain further focus but also emphasize clients' *preferred futures*. Viktor Frankl (1963, 1969) conveyed the importance of clients having a vision for the future and how that vision could have affect their actions in the present as well as their views of the past. Waters and Lawrence (1993) echoed this: "One of the great deficits of most therapy is the lack of a proactive vision of what people need to move towards instead of a sense of what they need to move away from" (p. 9). In a similar vein, therapists want to help clients to create well-articulated, preferred futures and then to turn those visions into realities. When clients already have a sense of a possibility-filled future, practitioners can help them rehabilitate and begin to move toward it. Some clients will need more encouragement to help them to imagine what is possible and how their futures can be different and better than the past.

The result of asking questions that begin to orient clients toward the future and a more concentrated sense of direction will lead most of them to respond in one of two ways. They could describe what they do not want, which is useful information because it can help therapists to understand more about clients' concerns and problems. The other way clients typically respond is by conveying what they do want, which represents their goals. Whether describing what they do or do not want, clients commonly respond with statements such as, "I want to be happy," "I just want some peace," "I want to get rid of anxiety," "I don't want to be depressed," or "I don't want him to be so impulsive." The problem with such statements is they are vague and nondescriptive.

Vague words and ambiguous statements can activate therapists' beliefs, biases, and theoretical opinions and lead them to assume that they know what clients' mean. Imagine, for example, that a client says he is experiencing "stress." By not taking time to find out what the client means by this, the therapist is at risk of relying on her experience and understandings of stress to guide change processes. Although experience working with clients who have reported "stress" in the past may be an asset, the problem is ambiguous without a description of the client's experience and could lead to the therapist's misguided attempts at problem resolution. To guard against doing this, it is important for the therapist to elicit clear descriptions of clients' concerns and complaints and their goals—what they want to have change. This can be accomplished through action-talk.

Action-Talk: Gaining Clarity with Problems and Goals

The quest for clarity is contingent on the use of questions that help clients to translate vague, ambiguous accounts into behaviorally based descriptions. To do this, practitioners use *action-talk* (Bertolino & O'Hanlon, 2002), which is a valuable method that they can and should use any time they need clarification. Three forms of action-talk that can be used for this purpose:

- *Action complaints* involve communicating to others what they have done or are doing that is disliked, undesirable, or problematic. The communication should be clear and descriptive (what can be seen or heard) and void of explanations or interpretations about other's motives, intentions, or character.
- *Action requests* involve telling others what actions are being requested of them in the present and future, again void of interpretations, characterizations, and vagueness.
- *Action praise* involves telling others what has or is being done that the person likes, appreciates, or values. It makes clear what

actions the persons describing them would like to see continue.

In therapy, action-talk involves determining how clients *do* their problem concerns and subsequently, what they will be *doing* when positive change has occurred and/or goals have been met. To use action-talk, when clients respond with vague, nonsenory-based words, phrases, or statements, therapists ask questions that require that the clients turn them into action- or interaction-based (that is, involving two or more people) descriptions.

For example, if a client says, "I'm depressed," the therapist might first say, "Could you please tell me what you mean by 'depressed?'" Although this may be a useful question and the kind that beginning therapists are trained to ask, it will not always help in understanding what depression looks like to the client in terms of behaviors and actions. So the therapist might ask, "Can you describe for me what you do or don't do when you are depressed?" or "What does depression look like in your life?" Does the person sleep late and not go to work or eat more or less, for example? The aim is to use action-talk to understand more about how the client *does (experiences)* depression. The better the description, the more information is available to understand what clients mean by their words and what they are experiencing when they convey concerns and problems. These three questions assist in clarifying understanding:

- When you are experiencing (concern/problem), what specifically is happening or not happening?
- What do you do or are you doing when you are in the throes of (concern/problem)?
- How do you do experience the (concern/problem)?

To practice using action-talk to clarify clients' vague statements and concerns, please complete Exercise 5.2, Problems in Action.

A specific variation of action-talk is *video-talk* (Bertolino & O'Hanlon, 2002), which involves using action-talk to have clients and others who may be involved describe the problem or goal as if it could be seen or heard on videotape. Ask, "If I were to videotape you being/experiencing (concern/problem), what would I see you doing that would indicate to me that you were being/experiencing (concern/problem)?"

In addition to hearing problem descriptions, practitioners learn what clients want different in their lives or situations and spend less time having them explain ambiguous descriptors (for example, anxiety, depression) and more on changing actions. For example, the practitioner can use action-talk with the client described earlier to find what she will be doing and what her situation or life will be like when the problem she came to therapy for has improved. The practitioner might say, "Tell me what will be happening when the problem that brought you here is no longer a problem." and "What will you be doing differently?" Other questions that can assist with this follow.

- How will you know when the problem is no longer a problem? What will be different?
- How will your life be different in the future you want and the (concern/problem) has gone away?
- What specifically will be better when you no longer need to come to therapy for the problem that brought you in?
- What will you be doing to maintain that kind of life?

Future-focused questions help to outline the goals of treatment, which vague and

Exercise 5.2

Problems in Action

The purpose of this exercise is to use "action-talk" to help elicit clear behavioral descriptions of complaints. It is a process that helps to determine the "doing" of problems. Action-talk can be used when problem descriptions, client requests for change, or focus in therapy lacks clarity. Let's first review a few examples of how action-talk can be used with vague problem descriptions:

Vague Problem Description	Action-Talk Question	Clear Problem Description
My son has a problem with his anger.	What has your son done that tells you that he's got a problem with his anger?	He's hit me and broken things in the house.
I lose control.	When you loses control, what do you do?	I yell at my boyfriend and call him bad names.
I'm self-destructive.	What do you do when you feel you are being self-destructive?	I cuts on my arms with glass or sharp objects.

Now it's your turn. In the left-hand column are examples of vague problem descriptions. Your task is to develop some possible questions for each by using action-talk.

Vague Problem Description	Action-Talk Question(s)
He's so irresponsible.	_____ .
My daughter is out of control.	_____ .
My life is anxiety ridden.	_____ .
I fly off the handle when things don't go right for me.	_____ .
I'm always in over my head.	_____ .

ambiguous language can veil. Goals represent clients' visions of the future—when their lives are more manageable and the concerns, complaints, or problems that brought them to therapy are less intrusive or absent altogether. Clients' goals are often simply the opposite of their problem descriptions.

Like action-talk, video-talk can offer an alternative for helping clients determine what they would like to have different in their lives. For example, we might say to a client, "Let's say we were to videotape you a few months down the road and the concern that you've been facing is gone and your life is going more the way you would like. If we watch that videotape now, what would we see happening?" Again, this approach has two goals: to clarify ambiguous language and to work with clients to articulate their visions of the future.

Consider two other points regarding goals. First, in learning what clients want, practitioners may find that what clients initially complain about is not their primary concern. They simply want their experience and

---

Exercise 5.2 *(continued)*

Next, partner with another person or a form group of three to five people for a 5–10 minute role-play. One person should be a client and another the therapist. Observers should write down any ambiguous problem statements the client makes in the left hand column of the following chart. Then list at least one corresponding action-talk question to help translate the vague description. If circumstances allow, ask the question(s) of the person role-playing the client until you elicit an action-talk description. List these responses in the right-hand column.

Vague Problem Description	Action-Talk Question(s)	Clear Problem Description
1. _____	_____	_____
_____	_____	_____
_____	_____	_____
2. _____	_____	_____
_____	_____	_____
_____	_____	_____
3. _____	_____	_____
_____	_____	_____
_____	_____	_____
4. _____	_____	_____
_____	_____	_____
_____	_____	_____
5. _____	_____	_____
_____	_____	_____
_____	_____	_____

---

views to be acknowledged and heard. For example, some mention numerous concerns so that it is unclear which ones take precedence and then move on to identify more significant ones. For this reason, therapists always check to be sure that they understand what clients want to see changed.

When clients have multiple complaints, therapists summarize and acknowledge all complaints and seek to learn which are most pressing (for an example of this, please refer to future talk in Chapter 4). If a client indicates that all complaints or concerns are of equal weight, the practitioner acknowledges this and then works to determine which concerns should be addressed first. One way to do this is to say, "It seems that you have several concerns, all of which are important. I want you to know that we'll address them all. To get us started, please tell me which one or two of the concerns you mentioned rise to the top and should be looked at first." This conveys to clients that all of their concerns are important and will be addressed but that the most troublesome ones should be identified and focused on initially. Research has indicated that giving clients choices regarding therapy goals is so crucial it can reduce rates of drop out (Rokke, 1999).

A second point to keep in mind is although the word *goal* is common to practitioners, funders, and many clients, some clients struggle to relate to it. Clients are interested in change and can describe their concerns, but the language of "goals" simply does not fit them. The therapist should remember gaining some sense of direction and clarity regarding how clients want their lives to be in the future is the important factor, not the word used. This means using language that makes sense for clients and with them to determine collaborating specifically what clients are concerned about and want to have different in their lives.

Case Example 5.1 illustrates the use of informal information gathering, including action-talk, to clarify concerns and develop a focus with a client.

As discussed previously, clients frequently give ambiguous descriptions (for example,

CASE EXAMPLE 5.1

Client: My life is out of control.

Therapist: Can you tell me about that?

Client: It seems like nothing is going right—it's just one thing after another.

Therapist: Things don't seem to be going well and it feels like things just keep happening—one after another . . . .

Client: . . . right—one thing after another.

Therapist: Do you mind if I ask you a little more about that?

Client: Fire away.

Therapist: OK. If I were to step into your life and really get a glimpse of it, what would I see that would make it clear to me that it was out control?

Client: You'd see me being mad.

Therapist: How would I know you were mad?

Client: Because I would be short with other people—sarcastic . . . everything would piss me off.

Therapist: I'd see you making sarcastic comments to others . . . and I can guess how that might cause some trouble . . . but how specifically has that been a problem for you?

Client: Well, I don't really have any friends . . . I'm alone because of it.

Therapist: So for you, being mad, and sarcastic as a result, has interfered with your friendships.

Client: Without a doubt.

Therapist: And is that what you mean by being out of control?

Client: Yeah, because it feels like I just fly off the handle and say things I shouldn't when I get the slightest bit mad.

Therapist: OK. So let me see if I can get a different kind of glimpse. Let's say we were able to take your life a few months into the future and you felt like things were going much better—more the way you'd like—and I could see that with you. What would I see happening that would let me know things were better?

Client: I wouldn't be ruining friendships.

Therapist: What would you be doing instead?

Client: I'd be making friends and not saying stupid stuff when I got mad.

Therapist: So you would be making friends and even though you might get upset once in a while, you would respond differently than you have in the past...

Client: . . . definitely.

CASE EXAMPLE 5.1   (continued)

Therapist: What might you do instead of flying off the handle and saying things you later regretted?

Client: I'm not too sure exactly what I would do, but something better than what I've been doing.

Therapist: Do you think that is something you'd like to spend time on in here? Finding ways of making friends and responding differently when you get mad so your relationships grow instead of splitting apart?

Client: Yeah . . . that's it.

Therapist: I see. And how will that help you when it's happening more often?

Client: I will be much happier?

Therapist: How so?

Client: In many ways. I'll feel better about myself and have a better social life.

Therapist: That sounds great.

"out of control," "fly off the handle"). It is important to ask clarifying questions and persist when answers include other ambiguous responses. Action-talk can assist with this. In addition, clients often report what is not wanted (for example, "I wouldn't be ruining relationships"). Action-talk conversations can aid in understanding concerns and their effects on clients. When clients describe what they do not want, the therapist should respect and follow their conversational processes rather than steering them toward immediate solutions. Clients choose to talk about their situations in ways that are most comfortable for them. These are invitations that allow practitioners to learn about clients' perspectives and problem descriptions and patterns associated with them. At the same time, practitioners not only want to be clear on what are client concerns but also to learn what their lives and/or situations will look like when they have improved and goals have been met. It is therefore important to get a clear description of what clients want *instead*. Doing so helps to increase effectiveness by clarifying vague, nondescriptive terms or labels for behaviors into clearly delineated ones that represent the goals for therapy.

Case Example 5.2 also illustrates the use of action-talk.

CASE EXAMPLE 5.2

Therapist: It seems that you've got a lot going on. I'd like to ask what's most concerning to you at this point.

Client: Things aren't going well for me.

Therapist: What's been happening?

Client: Well, I'm always feeling anxious. I mean . . . I used to go out a lot, now I don't. My friend says I need to just move on.

Therapist: Uh huh. So you haven't been going out like you used to. That's part of it. And when you're feeling anxious, what else happens?

Client: Well, I think a lot. I think about everything I've done wrong—my past decisions. I just dwell on things.

(continued)

CASE EXAMPLE 5.2 (continued)

Therapist: You tend to think a lot about your past decisions and dwell on what you think you've done wrong . . .

Client: . . . Yeah, and I also have trouble sleeping.

Therapist: Mm hmm, trouble sleeping. Tell me more about that.

Client: I can't get to sleep because I keep dwelling on things.

Therapist: So it's trouble getting to sleep. And when you finally do get to sleep, do you stay asleep?

Client: Yeah. Once I fall asleep I stay asleep but it takes three or four hour to get there. Then it's two or three in the morning and I have to get up at 5:30. Then I feel hungover at work and can't concentrate on what I need to do.

Therapist: I see. So not getting to sleep early enough really affects your work and how you feel the next day.

Client: Right.

Therapist: Are there other things that you do or don't do, when you feel anxious?

Client: It's really those things.

Therapist: OK. So if I were to see you being anxious, I'd see you staying at home and not going out, thinking about decisions you've made in the past, and not getting to sleep on time. Is that right?

Client: Exactly.

Therapist: Now I think I follow you, but for sake of clarity, I'd like to ask you another question if it's OK with you.

Client: Sure.

Therapist: You've mentioned a few things that seem to be troublesome to you. Which of the these—not going out, thinking about your past decisions, not getting to sleep, or something else—is most concerning for you right now?

Client: Definitely not getting to sleep.

Therapist: OK . . . and as you said, when you don't get enough sleep, it really affects you the next day at work.

Client: That's right.

Therapist: So am I right in thinking that you'd like to find a way to get to sleep quicker and feel more rested in the morning?

Client: No doubt.

Therapist: And so what's a reasonable amount of time for you to lie in bed before falling asleep?

Client: If I could get to sleep within a half hour of lying down, I'd be thrilled!

Therapist: So getting to sleep within a half hour would allow you to get a full night's sleep and perhaps be better rested for work.

Client: Uh huh . . . that's what I need.

Therapist: What will be different when you're getting to sleep earlier and getting a full night's sleep?

Client: My head will be clearer.

Therapist: How so?

Client: I'll be better rested and won't be obsessing so much.

Therapist: What difference will that make for you?

Client: If I'm not obsessing, then I'll be getting things done and going out more.

Vague words and statements such as "things just aren't going well for me," "I'm always feeling anxious," and "I think a lot" tend to activate therapists' personal and theoretical views and guide therapy in ways that may not be helpful. Just by hearing the word *anxious*, for example, some therapists immediately begin to ask questions about anxiety-provoking situations and consider that the client may have an anxiety disorder. Others may gravitate toward a sleep disorder. Although these may seem to be legitimate directions, they are based more on therapists', not clients', ideas about what to focus on and ask questions about. Therapists are encouraged to check with clients to see whether the conversation is in line with what they want and is helpful to them. The client's statements give little indication of what his concern(s) are. Although this person mentioned many, he ultimately wanted to find a way to go to sleep faster. Unless therapists orient toward clients' goals, they risk working in ways that are inconsistent with clients' preferences.

Case Example 5.3 also uses action-talk and video-talk to clarify concerns and goals.

CASE EXAMPLE 5.3

Client: The main thing for me is to get over my fear of failure, but that's easier said than done.

Therapist: Mm hmm. Tell me more about your fear of failure.

Client: Well, I keep finding myself going into situations and thinking the worst. Like everything is going to go bad.

Therapist: You've found yourself in situations where you've thought that the worst was going to happen...

Client: Right . . . . over and over again.

Therapist: So, if we were to catch you on videotape going into a situation where you were thinking the worst, what would we see happening on that tape?

Client: I'd be pacing around a lot . . . and probably not doing my work because I'd be obsessing about what might happen.

Therapist: Mm hmm, you would be pacing. And one of the ways that an outsider like myself would know that you were obsessing would be that you wouldn't be doing your work. Is that right?

Client: Yes.

Therapist: Is there anything else that you would be doing that might indicate to me or others that you were obsessing?

Client: I would go home and think about it more.

Therapist: I see. What would you be doing at home while you were thinking about it?

Client: Just sitting. Not eating or doing anything else that's important. Just obsessing.

Therapist: OK, just sitting and not doing other things that you sense are important. And if we were able to see inside your mind and videotape you obsessing, what might we see happening?

Client: That's easy. You'd see me thinking about the same thing over and over and thinking the worst. My only thoughts would be about failing.

Therapist: So let me see if I understand you. When you've experienced thoughts about failure, you've paced and sat around obsessing. And the way you typically obsess is to think about the same thing over and over again— usually about failing.

Client: That's right.

Therapist: And from what you've said, this has affected you because you haven't done the amount of work you'd liked to have at work or at home.

Client: Exactly.

(continued)

CASE EXAMPLE 5.3 *(continued)*

Therapist: Are there other ways that this has affected your life?

Client: I don't want to be so lazy and unproductive at home, but main thing is not getting my work done at my job. I don't want to get fired. I can't afford to. I've got to stop obsessing and get things done.

Therapist: OK. Let me see if I understand you. So you don't want to be what you call lazy and unproductive at home instead you'd like to get things done. Your main concern at this time is getting your work done on the job. Is that right?

Client: Yes.

Therapist: And if we were to videotape you in the future when things are going better for you, what would we see on that tape that

would indicate that things were better? What would you be doing?

Client: I would be turning my work in on schedule and keeping up on assignments . . . not falling behind.

Therapist: What kind of work?

Client: Documentation and billing.

Therapist: OK. So you'd like to find ways of getting your work done, specifically, documentation and billing, in a timely manner and keeping up on assignments.

Client: That's what I want.

Therapist: What difference will that make for you when that's happening?

Client: A ton! If I'm getting my work done, then my boss will be off my case and I can keep my job.

The vague, nondescriptive words and statements offered by the client could have led the therapist in any number of directions. The goal was to learn from the client what he does when he is experiencing a "fear of failure" and "obsessing." The therapist learned by focusing on actions and how they affect the person negatively that the client experiences the problem in specific ways. Thus, it is not the client's "fear of failure" that is of concern but actions such as not doing work that are results of viewing himself and situations the way he does. Many people experience feelings and thoughts that they would rather not experience. However, not everyone succumbs to fear of failure. It is ultimately what people do or do not do in their lives as a result

of their perspectives that affect their lives adversely.

The practitioner in Case Example 5.3 learned what the client wanted (as opposed to what he did not want). What he wanted turned out to be getting work completed. This specifically meant performing documentation and billing in a timely manner. This clear information gives direction to therapy and helps practitioners *and* clients to better understand when progress has been made and sufficient positive change has occurred.

It is also important that directions and goals be realistic, attainable, ethical, and legal. For example, it is not unreasonable for client who has lost someone close to want that person to return. Even though this is not possible, it may be possible for the person to experience a caring relationship with another person. Often what a client requests is a symbol for something else. By acknowledging clients' internal experiences and views, practitioners can cut through many unrealistic expectations and co-create solvable problems. See the following example.

Client: My dad died last year. I wish he were still here. I really miss him. That's really what I want . . . him to be back.

Therapist: I'm sorry about your loss. What do you miss most about him?

Client: He used to listen to me . . . really listen to me.

Therapist: How did you know when he was really listening to you?

Client: He would look me in the eyes and not judge me.

Therapist: What did he do to let you know that he wasn't judging you?

Client: Well, he didn't make comments like, "You should have..." or "That was stupid to do that."

Therapist: I see. And how did that help you?

Client: I knew he valued me and I haven't had that since.

Therapist: Is that something you would like to experience again in a relationship with someone—that sense of being listened to, not judged, and valued?

Client: I would love to have that again.

Therapist: What would be different for you as a result of having that again?

Client: I'd feel great. I'd feel better about going through each day knowing that I could talk with somebody who understood me.

Although it is not possible to bring back a deceased person, it is possible to provide a relationship in which the client feels listened to, not judged, and valued. So even when presented with impossible goals, the practitioner can help the client achieve what the goals symbolize. In addition to identifying direction by obtaining clear descriptions of clients' concerns, therapists can learn more about clients' orientations and potential ways to facilitate change. For example, if a client spoke about "feeling" a certain way, the practitioner would acknowledge and validate more of what she was feeling and focus on internal experience and affect. If a client talked about "seeing" or "doing" things in certain ways, the practitioner would focus more on views and behaviors, respectively. Subsequent chapters provide more detail about this. Descriptions provide a pathway for learning about clients' orientations of problem formation and resolution.

Please complete Exercise 5.3, From Problems to Solutions, to practice how to change clients' descriptions of problems into what they would like to have change. (*Note:* To complete this exercise in its entirety, you will need first to complete Exercise 5.2.)

Additional Techniques for Gaining a Focus Future

In addition to using action-talk and video-talk to learn what clients would like to have different in their lives and to gain, therapists employ methods such as the question, the crystal ball, the miracle question, and the time machine (Bertolino, 2003). This section briefly reviews these methods.

The Question

Alfred Adler (1956), the creator of individual psychology, maintained a "present-to-future"

Exercise 5.3

From Problems to Solutions

The purpose of this exercise is to use action-talk to move from obtaining clear problem descriptions (such as those you outlined in Exercise 5.2) to identifying what clients would like to have change in the future. These represent the goals or preferred futures clients have for themselves or others with whom they are close. Let's first review a few examples of how to move from clear problem descriptions to clear goal/future descriptions:

Clear Problem Description	Action-Talk Question(s)	Clear Goal Description
He hit me and broke things in the house.	What would you like to change or be different in the future with this concern?	When he gets angry, he chooses actions that are hurtful such as walking away or talking to others.
I yell at my boyfriend and call him names.	What would you like to have happen instead?	To be calm and tell him the way I feel when I'm hurt or am uneasy about things.
I cut on my arms with glass or sharp objects.	What will you be doing differently when this is no longer a problem for you?	I'll be going to school regularly and hanging out friends instead.

Keep in mind that even when clients have provided clear problem descriptions, they can slide back into ambiguity with responses such as, "I'll feel better," "I'll be less anxious," or "I won't say mean things." Such nondescriptive responses do not help determine what clients want instead of their problems or concerns or to state those goals or future preferences in clear ways.

To practice this, please complete the next section. Examples of clear problem descriptions are in the left-hand column. Your task is to develop some possible questions to determine goals for each by using action-talk.

focus in his work and originated what became known as *the question*. Rudolf Dreikurs (1954) further developed this often overlooked method. He would ask, "Let us imagine I gave you a pill and you would be completely well as soon as you left this office. What would be different in your life, what would you do differently than before?" (p. 132). This question is considered by some as a precursor to the miracle question, which will be discussed momentarily.

The Crystal Ball (Pseudo-Orientation in Time)

Milton Erickson's (1954b) "pseudo-orientation in time" is also viewed historically as a precursor to the miracle question. He used this concept hypnotically by having his patients positively hallucinate (that is, see something that is not really there) three crystal balls—one each for the past, present, and future. He would have his patients peer into the crystal ball that represented the future and suggest

Exercise 5.3 *(continued)*

Clear Problem Description	Goal-Oriented, Action-Talk Questions
I argue with others at work when I don't get my way. ▶	_____. _____.
He has failing grades in all of his classes. ▶	_____. _____.
I can't go into areas with more than five people because I feel like I'm going to pass out. ▶	_____. _____.
I have trouble sleeping at night. I sleep less than three hours total. ▶	_____. _____.
She doesn't call or notify me when she's going to be late. ▶	_____. _____.

Be sure that goals are realistic ("doable"), attainable, ethical, and legal. For example, it may not be realistic for an adolescent *never* to talk back to his or her parents. A realistic goal might be that 75% of the time, the adolescent responds in a way that is acceptable to his or her parents. An alternative might be that the adolescent can strongly and passionately debate issues as long as he or she uses acceptable language, which would be clearly outlined. Unrealistic and unattainable goals can lead to a sense of failure. Examples of unethical or illegal goals are stealing less, cutting oneself less, and being less abusive. Behaviors that are harmful or pose threats to the health and well-being of self or others should be addressed directly.

Also remember that some clients need assistance in determining which goals ought to take precedence. Help them to decide what needs to change first, second, and so on. It can also be helpful to remind clients that often only a small change is necessary. Little changes can lead to others much like a snowball gaining momentum as it rolls down a hill. In addition, it is common to have multiple goals in therapy, especially when there are multiple clients; in such cases, make sure all goals are clearly articulated and understood.

that they could see what their lives would be like without the problems that brought them to therapy. Erickson would then have them describe, in detail, how their problems were resolved. Later, he would essentially prescribe the remedies provided by his patients. Practitioners can use the same process without the use of hypnosis by having clients envision a crystal ball, look out a window, or look at a blank wall onto which they can imagine ("project") their future when their problems have been resolved (or at least alleviated enough that they no longer need to come to therapy) and describe it as clearly as possible by using action-talk. Questions that follow focus on having clients describe how problems were resolved. Finally, in "real" time, have clients identify steps to make their future visions reality and begin to take them.

The Miracle Question

Developed by Steve de Shazer (1988) and colleagues at the Brief Family Therapy Center (BFTC), in Milwaukee, Wisconsin, *the miracle question* has become synonymous with solution-focused therapy. This popular method is used to help clients envision their lives in futures when their problems have been solved. The miracle question is generally set up when the therapist encourages a client to use her imagination, then asking, "Suppose you were to go home tonight, and while you were asleep, a miracle happened and this problem was solved. How will you know the miracle happened? What will be different?" (p. 5). This question is followed up in detail with questions about the miracle scenario given.

A derivative for children and adolescents is *the dream method* (Bertolino, 2003). Using it, the therapist asks the client, "Let's suppose that tonight, while you are sleeping, you have a dream. In this dream the problem you have is resolved. Tell me about what might happen in that dream that would lead to your problem no longer being a problem. What might happen?" Another variation is to speculate about a past dream: "Suppose that you had a wonderful dream last night or sometime in the recent past. Up until now, however, you haven't been able to recall it. In that dream, you were able to see your future without the problem that brought you to me. What happened?" As with other methods in this category, the answer is then followed by asking other questions to further develop the future vision.

The Time Machine

Another method that involves some imagination and can be particularly useful for children and adolescents is *the time machine* (Bertolino, 1999). It is a way to help them to envision a future where things work out. You would introduce the time machine as follows:

> Let's say there is a time machine sitting here in the office. Let's say that you climb in and it propels you into the future, to a time when things are going the way you want them to go. After arriving at your future destination, the first thing you notice is that the problems that brought you to therapy have disappeared.

This pitch is followed by questions such as:

Where are you?
Who is with you?
What is happening?
What are you doing?
How is your life different than before?
Where did your problems go?
How did they go away?

Many variations of these methods can be used to create a future focus. They include pretending to peer through a View-Master (a child's toy similar to binoculars in which images are on a small reel and can be changed by clicking a switch) (Bertolino, 1999) and *future screening*, which asks clients to imagine that they are able to see their future on a movie screen (Bertolino, Kiener, & Patterson, 2009). Any of the methods described can be modified and used with physical props (such as pictures, drawings). For example, a client could be asked to create an image on paper of the future she would like by drawing a picture or using cutouts from magazines. The idea is to use what fits for the client. Whether using basic questions or creative methods, practitioners want to help clients to gain clarity and answer the rudimentary question, "How will you know when things are better?" Once what clients want is clear, practitioners can begin to collaborate with them on steps to make those positive changes occur.

Therapists must bear in mind that methods and techniques are merely means to learn what clients want but contribute little to the overall variance in outcome. It is not the method that matters, but what the methods help to achieve with clients. Too much reliance on methods can lead to therapy that is "one-size-fits-all." See Case Example 5.4 from the author's experience.

All practitioners have favorite techniques, and many of them benefit clients. The risk, however, occurs when methods overshadow clients. In the previous example, fortunately, I did not ask any scaling questions (although I frequently do, and they will be discussed later in this chapter) or the miracle question. Had I,

it is likely that the client would have felt invalidated and as if she were treated the same by all therapists among other things. This could have negatively affected the therapy in a variety of ways. It is therefore important use methods in ways that are respectful and fit clients.

The discussion of informal information-gathering processes has presented ways to clarify clients' concerns and problems and to have clients describe their goals by using a future focus.

Progress Toward Goals: Identifying Indicators of Change

At times considerable distance exists between clients' initial problem descriptions and the goals that they agreed on in therapy. These goals may be realistic and attainable, yet the amount of time needed to reach them will vary. In working toward those goals, some

CASE EXAMPLE 5.4

A father, mother, and stepmother came to see me because their 16-year-old daughter had been staying out after curfew, drinking, smoking marijuana, and failing two classes in school. The daughter did not accompany the parents during the initial session; they said she refused to attend. Curious, I inquired as to why the daughter had refused. The father replied, "She won't really say. But I think it's because we were in therapy before with another guy and it didn't go too well." At the end of the session, all three parents expressed their desire to have the daughter attend. I suggested that they ask her once more, letting her know that her view was very important.

At the next session, to my surprise, the daughter was in attendance. Over the next

three months, I met with her and her parents six more times. The situation had improved considerably, and during the last session I said to the teenager, "I had heard that you wouldn't come to see another therapist because you had a bad experience. I don't know if that's accurate or not, but I want to thank you for coming in and sticking it out." To this, the young woman replied, "This was much different than I expected. You acted like a real person. I think that other guy only knew two questions. He kept asking me about things 'on a scale of 1 to 10' and the other one was, 'If a miracle happened, what would your life be like?' I was, like, is that a question in a book or something? Everything was about miracles or on a scale of one to ten. I hated that."

clients may feel they are not improving and experience frustration, anxiety, and so on. When they get the sense that they are not making progress, they are at high risk of both giving up and dropping out of therapy. It is clear, however, that change is relative and will take different lengths of time to reach depending on clients, their problems, and the severity of those problems. Although clients remain focused on the end point of problem resolution, therapists can orient them to other aspects of movement. This includes identifying indicators or signs that progress is being made toward the established goals. These questions assist with this process:

- What will be the first sign or indication that things have begun to turn the corner with your problem?

- What will be the first sign or indication to you that you have taken a solid step on the road to improvement even though you might not yet be out of the woods?
- What's one thing that might indicate to you that things are on the upswing?
- What will you see happening when things are beginning to go more the way you'd like them to go?
- What would have to happen that would indicate to you that things are changing in the direction you'd like them to change?
- How will you know when the change you are looking for has started?
- What is happening right now with your situation that you would like to have continue?

Case Example 5.5 illustrates the importance of identifying progress.

CASE EXAMPLE 5.5

A mother brought her 15-year-old son, Stephen, to see me because according to her, he needed to "get his act together." Questioning for clarification led to the fact that the mother wanted her son to get to school on time, talk to her "nicely" when he became angry, and improve his grades. When asked what would be the smallest indicator to her that Stephen was beginning to turn the corner, she responded, "If he brought a book home from school I'd fall over!"

The next day, perhaps as a joke, Stephen brought a book home. He tossed it on the table and his mother laughed, "Oh, that's funny. I said if you brought a book home I'd fall over. You're funny." Following the brief interchange, the evening went well between Stephen and his mother.

Stephen later remarked that he liked the fact that his mother showed a sense of humor when he first brought a book home. He also stated that they had got along better. As a result, Stephen continued to bring at least one book home from school each day. Then, one evening, Stephen and his mother were watching television. When his mother began watching a program that Stephen didn't care for, he began thumbing through his world history book. Several days later he was shocked when he knew the answers to several questions on his history exam. Although he narrowly missed passing the exam, Stephen thrived on the feeling that he had when he realized he knew several of the answers. He enjoyed the feeling and wanted more of it. He also realized that had he done more than thumb through

CASE EXAMPLE 5.5 *(continued)*

the book, he might have known more and passed the exam.

Stephen continued to bring his world history book home and over time added others. He also began getting to school on time and reading at night. Over the course of a semester, he raised his grades to passing in all but one class. The following semester he passed all of them. In addition, the relationship between Stephen and his mother continued to improve, and he stopped yelling and began talking in a calmer voice. His mother recognized the efforts Stephen had made and regularly encouraged him.

By focusing on in-between change, therapists can help clients to identify progress toward goals. This can both counter frustration clients feel and help orient them toward exceptions and differences in regard to their described problems. In this way, clients notice what is happening that they want rather than what they do not.

Use of Scaling and Percentage-Based Questions

Therapists can ask questions in many ways. Some are straightforward and others are more indirect or require creative thinking on the part of therapists and clients. As a framework for determining concerns, goals, and progress, using questions that focus on quantitative or incremental change can be helpful. One way to do this is to use *scaling questions* (de Shazer, 1991). In using these questions, the therapist first establishes a continuum using a scale, most commonly from 1 to 10. Each number represents a rating of how the client views her life at different junctures (for example, the present and later points). The therapist introduces the idea of scaling by saying, "On a scale of 1 to 10, with 1 being the worst this problem has ever been, and 10 being the best things could be, how would you rate things today?" Once a number has been given, the therapist uses action-talk to ensure that what the number represents is clear. For example, if a client rates the situation at a 3, the therapist asks, "What specifically is happening to indicate to you that it is a 3?"

With a clear starting point, the next step is to ask the client what number would indicate that the goals of therapy have been met, that therapy has been successful, or that sufficient improvement has occurred. If the client described earlier stated that an 8 would indicate sufficient change, the therapist would then ask her to describe what specifically will be happening when she reaches an 8. Again, action-talk is used to clarify.

The final part is for the therapists to explore with the client what will indicate in-between change and progress. The therapist might ask, "You mentioned that things are at a 3 now and 8 is where you would like to be. What will it take for your situation to edge forward a little, from a 3 to a 3 1/2?" It is important for therapists not to strive for change that represents too big a leap for clients. Although it is possible for clients to make large gains very quickly, as discussed in previous chapters, it is usually a better idea to focus on movement that increases the likelihood of success for clients. This can create building blocks for future change and instill hope.

Another incremental questioning technique involves asking percentage-based questions. The therapist finds the percentage of the time that the problem interferes with the client's life, that would indicate progress toward goals and preferred outcomes, and that would indicate therapy has been successful. For example, "What percentage of the time do you think things are going more the way you like?" As an alternative, questions can focus on the percentage of time the client feels the situation is not going well or that the problem is present. The remaining percentage then makes up the starting point. For example, if a client reports that 75% of the time the problem he came to therapy for is interfering in his life, the therapist would make note that 25% of the time things are going well. Determining which method is the better fit depends on the therapist and client.

Once the therapist has a starting point, the client is asked, "What percentage of time would things need to be going well for you to feel like you no longer need to come to therapy?" Again, focus is on getting a clear image of what constitutes change from the client's perspective. Finally, the therapist inquires as to what will indicate progress or in-between change by asking, "What would it take to go from (X) percent to (Y) percent?" All percentages should be described in action-based language.

Determination of Concerns and Goals with Multiple Clients

When working with multiple clients (for example, families, couples), attending to each person's conversational preferences, and goals, and ideas about progress is important. Because various individuals will have different ideas about the way therapy should proceed, the concerns, the needs for change, and what will indicate success, practitioners commonly identify separate complaints and goals for each client. Despite the presence of differing preferences, most often there are common threads among the complaints and identified goals.

In searching for commonality, coordinating these complaints and goals by using three core processes—*acknowledgment, tracking,* and *linking*—can be helpful. The therapist acknowledges and restates each person's perspective in the least inflammatory way possible while acknowledging and imparting the intended feeling and meaning. Statements that do so are linked by the word *and* because doing so builds on a common concern. The following example illustrates one way to use acknowledgement, tracking, and linking:

Melanie (mother): I just want her to return to school. It's ridiculous for her to be out. And besides, if she doesn't go, she'll never get the kind of job she wants.

Therapist: You're concerned because your sense is there's really no reason for a 16-year-old to be out of school and that it could negatively affect her future.

Melanie: Right.

Carrie (daughter): What's the point? I can't stand school. Besides, if you're gonna continue to be on my case, then I'll never go back!

Melanie: See, that's what I get every day!

Therapist: I can see that it's been rough on both of you. And for you Carrie, you haven't found a reason to go to school and to tolerate it yet.

Carrie: Yeah. School is boring and if she doesn't back off . . . then, forget it.

Therapist: And what do you mean by your mom being "on your case"?

Carrie: She constantly says, "You better go. You better go. You can't miss another day!" It's like she thinks that I don't have a clue! I know that I need to graduate to get a good job. Duh!

Therapist: OK, and the ways that she's tried so far to get you to go haven't work so well for you?

Carrie: Nope.

Therapist: Let me see if I'm following the two of you. Melanie, you'd really like Carrie return to school, finish her education, and have a better chance of reaching her dreams. And Carrie, you seem to have some dreams for yourself, and even though I haven't heard about them yet, perhaps school is a part of that in some way. So you'd like to find a way to tolerate school so that you can graduate and work toward the career you want. And maybe there are other ways that your mom can be helpful to you with that—ways that don't involve her telling you to go, because you already know that—but ways that you see as being supportive with school.

Each part of this three-pronged approach is central to creating consensus among those involved. *Acknowledgment* assists by letting each client know her concern has been heard and is valid. *Tracking* allows the therapist to log and follow each concern, and *linking* via the word *and* provides the thread that weaves each together. Whether in couples, families, or other multiple-client variations, clients are free to clarify any misperceptions or areas of discomfort until mutually agreeable descriptions emerge. Therapists can then continue with clients to flesh out the directions and goals of therapy.

Collaboration with Outside Helpers

This final section considers the role of outside helpers (for example, those from mental health, juvenile and adult corrections, social service, educational, employment areas) in determining the weight of therapy issues and directions for services.

As in working with multiple clients, collaborating with others can be a challenging task when varying perspectives are represented. Although outside helpers can have different degrees of influence, it remains important to maintain a collaborative stance. This involves having conversations with outside helpers to learn about their expectations and goals. In doing so, the therapist realizes that those who have stakes in clients' lives often carry some level of responsibility and ability to alter the course of or end therapy. At the same time, they desire a positive outcome in order to resolve problems and change behaviors. *How* to achieve this is typically left up to therapists and will be discussed in future chapters. Collaboration at this juncture precedes the "how" of therapy in first agreeing on "what" needs to change or be different. Case Example 5.6 illustrates an approach with an outside entity.

As mentioned, especially when clients are being seen involuntarily (for example, adolescents, mandated clients), potential power differentials need to be acknowledged. Collaboration does not mean that everything is equal, but it speaks to the process of negotiating realistic and attainable change with all involved. Practitioners therefore collaborate with outside helpers and incorporate their feedback into therapy sessions.

Because practitioners do not always have direct access to them, an indirect way for involving outside helpers is to ask clients, "Did [name of outside helper] tell you what [he or she] expects us to focus on here?" If the client can answer this question (and it sounds reasonable),

CASE EXAMPLE 5.6

Therapist: I want to be sure that I'm clear here. Can you tell me what specifically you want to be addressed in therapy?

Probation Officer (PO): Ed's attitude. He seems to think that parole is a joke.

Therapist: What has happened that's given you that idea?

PO: He's stolen, and he keeps thinking that the next time he won't get caught even though he has [been caught] many times.

Therapist: You're concerned about Ed's history of stealing and that he might do it again.

PO: Right.

Therapist: What would you need to see happening with Ed to really believe that he had changed his ways?

PO: It's actually pretty simple. He'd have to quit stealing. Ed would also have to be more respectful to me.

Therapist: All right. And how would you know he was being more respectful to you?

PO: He would talk calmly and agree to do what I ask him to do.

Therapist: Ed, how does that sound to you?

Client (Ed): Same old song and dance.

PO: That's exactly what I'm talking about. He's always sarcastic . . . .

Therapist: You mean less sarcasm . . . and what would you see as a respectful way to responding to you?

PO: "Yes sir" would be great. Heck, I'd settle for "okay." But the flip attitude has to go before I'll budge.

Therapist: Ed?

Ed: Fine.

Therapist: So the one thing is how Ed responds to you. The other is for Ed to make positive choices and not steal anymore.

PO: Yes.

Therapist: What do think about that, Ed?

Ed: It's fine. I know that's what I'm supposed to do.

Therapist: OK, but does it sound reasonable to you?

Ed: Of course.

PO: There's the sarcasm again.

Therapist: How do you differentiate between what's Ed just being Ed and what's cutting, unacceptable sarcasm?

PO: I get your point. It just seems unnecessary to act like that.

Therapist: Sure. And I'll bet you hear your share of sarcasm.

PO: Yeah, and it wears on you after a while.

Therapist: I can see why.

PO: But as long as he doesn't swear at me and acknowledges what I expect of him, I can let the rest slide.

Therapist: How does that sound, Ed?

Ed: I can live with that.

Therapist (to PO): What, then, might you see Ed do that would at least make you wonder a little if he's turned the corner with stealing and is ready for a probation-free life?

PO: If he went six months with no further incidents of stealing—well, any violations, other than a parking ticket, for that matter. But I can't see that happening. He's never gone more than a month before.

Therapist: So you would be surprised?

PO: That's putting it mildly. I'd be shocked.

Ed: Now that's sarcastic.

CASE EXAMPLE 5.6   *(continued)*

Therapist: From what I can tell, you both have a flair for sarcasm!

PO: That's for sure.

Therapist: OK, well for the sake of clarity, when Ed has gone six months

without any major violations, what will that mean?

PO: I'll advocate for his release from probation.

Therapist: What do you think of that, Ed?

Ed: Wow. I didn't expect to hear that. That's great.

the practitioner proceeds by incorporating those goals or directions into the therapy. If the client does not know, speculation can be helpful: "What do you think [he/she] will say when I talk with [him/her]?" Therapists should invite all parties involved to share their perceptions and understandings of what others may have conveyed to them (Bertolino, 2003).

When clients truly do not know what outside helpers' concerns are or what is expected of them or when the perceptions they identify are inconsistent with what the therapist has been told, the therapist gently introduces understanding by saying, for example, "My understanding after talking with [person's name] is that [he/she] will have the sense that you're moving in the right direction when

you're [name of action(s)]." This is followed with, "How does that sound to you?" As with working with multiple clients, the therapist acknowledges each perspective and searches for continuity between the respective goals.

The involvement of outside helpers represents collaboration at its best. Welcoming multiple perspectives and expanding the system can generate new possibilities and potential solutions. When outside helpers join therapy sessions, it is important to remember that there are multiple ways to view situations with no one view being more correct than another. At the same time, perspectives that close down possibilities should be challenged and any that can facilitate change in directions and goals promoted.

SUMMARY POINTS

- Information gathering includes using both one-time and ongoing processes that help give direction, shape, structure, and focus to therapy.
- Information-gathering processes are collaborative and respectful and add more depth and dimension to clients' stories.
- *Formal information gathering* refers to processes that involve the use of instrumentation

including strategies and methods for conducting screenings and evaluations.
- Through the use of general and specific content-area questions, formal information gathering involves focusing on both concerns/problems and strengths. Therapists explore areas such as culture, work/employment, education/school, family/social relationships, hobbies/interests, and previous

therapy experiences to understand the client's world.

- Outcome measurement is implemented during formal information gathering as a way to learn clients' ratings of the impact of services on major life dimensions and to create baseline scores from which to measure future change and the impact of services.

- *Informal information-gathering* refers to ongoing processes aimed at identifying goals and directions in therapy and ways to achieve those goals.

- During informal information gathering, therapists focus on gaining clear descriptions of problems, goals, and indicators of progress or change in the direction of identified goals.

- *Action-talk* is used to translate vague, ambiguous descriptions into clear, behaviorally based ones.

- Various creative approaches can be used to help clients create or rehabilitate their visions of the future and what their lives will look like when the problems for which they have come to therapy have been alleviated or are less dominating in their lives. Core methods include *the question, the crystal ball, the miracle question,* and *the time machine.*

- When sessions involve multiple clients with different concerns and goals, therapists use *acknowledgment, tracking,* and *linking* both to help clients to feel understood and to find common ground among the concerns presented.

- Outside helpers' perspectives are acknowledged and integrated into therapy by using action-talk to ensure that concerns raised are being translated into clear descriptions so that all parties involved agree about the focus of therapy.

DISCUSSION QUESTIONS

1. What is formal information gathering? What are examples of it?

2. What is informal informational gathering? What are examples of it?

3. What are *exceptions,* and how might therapists learn about them? How can therapists use exception-oriented questions in therapy?

4. What do therapists learn about clients by using specific content area questions?

5. What is the purpose of *funneling?*

6. What is *action-talk?* What are the three forms?

7. What are some ways to help clients to create a vision of the future?

8. Why is it helpful to identify indicators of progress and change?

9. When working with multiple clients and/or outside helpers, what are some important things to keep in mind?

Chapter 6

Mapping the Topography of Change

Understanding Clients' Orientations

■ Previous chapters discussed various facets of therapy that help to create an overall context that increases the opportunities for positive client change. Remember that the processes or "how to's" outlined thus far are not random but are offered because of their association with effective therapeutic outcome and, more important, respectfulness of client contributions to change. Let's briefly review some of the key points discussed previously:

- Because client participation is essential, therapists invite clients into collaborative partnerships both prior to and throughout therapy.
- Because language is the primary vehicle through which therapists promote change, they therefore use language to acknowledge, validate, and strengthen relationships and open up possibilities.

- Formal information-gathering processes provide opportunities to explore the impact of clients' problems on their lives and to learn about clients' strengths and resources. Because clients are the most significant contributors to outcome, this information is used to create opportunities for present and future change.
- Informal information-gathering processes are essential in providing structure and direction to therapy. Therapists use methods to clarify concerns and establish goals, that is, what clients (and outside stakeholders) would like to have change as a result of therapy.

Each of these components is integral to and contingent on client participation and feedback. Because clients account for the largest portion of variance in outcome, it is imperative to include them in all processes. This chapter builds on the aforementioned processes by investigating specific ways to tune into clients' ideas about the development of their concerns and how they expect change to occur. This overarching idea is referred to as the *client's orientation*. The information gained from ongoing client conversations contributes to increasing the factor of fit between clients' ideas about the changes they desire and the methods therapists select to help bring about those changes. Many of these methods will be described in Chapters 7 through 10.

Therapy Theories and Factor of Fit

Among the many choices to be made in therapy, determining what approach creates the best fit for an individual, couple, or family is one of the most crucial. A poor fit between the client's perspective and the therapist and his or her approach can lead to ruptures in the therapeutic alliance and ultimately result in a negative outcome. At first glance, choosing an approach may appear to be a complex, daunting task. There are, however, various ways that therapists can collaborate with clients to improve the chances of a good fit. The following sections discuss ways of determining methods that provide the best opportunities for change.

From Philosophy to Theory

As you have learned, practitioners' personal philosophies, including ideas about the nature of problems and how change comes about, influence the ways they work with others. Let's also consider the influence of psycho-

logical and family therapy theories, which therapists must consider in increasing the factor of fit with clients. As therapists grow professionally, they are exposed to various "scientific" theories that often begin as general ideas then become more specific and technical (and sometimes more restrictive or narrow). This is particularly important given that of more than 500 existing therapy models, only about 20% appear well developed (although not necessary soundly researched and evaluated) and are routinely taught in educational and/or professional settings. It is difficult not to be drawn to the promise of new theories.

Most therapists use the theories with which they are most comfortable and/or have been trained. They commonly learn a few models in depth (or sufficiently in some cases) and implement whichever ones make the most sense in given situations. As a result, therapists favor some models over others, ultimately leaving fewer options for clients. Thus, as discussed in Chapter 2, many therapists have also experienced limitations with their theories and have chosen to refer to themselves as "eclectic," borrowing from approaches as they see fit. They do this partly because they have found using singular approaches to be constraining and ineffective with certain clients and problems. The limitations of models is supported by research suggesting that even some of the more celebrated therapies lack empirical evidence supporting their efficacy. For example, Lambert (2007) and colleagues (Hansen, Lambert, & Forman, 2002) found that in randomized clinical trials in which the treatments offered by therapists who have been carefully selected and closely supervised were provided to carefully screened patients with a specific disorder, about 35% to 40% of patients experienced no benefit. The researchers also noted that between 5% and 10% of patients deteriorate. A mitigating factor, which will be discussed later in this chapter, is whether a single, uncomplicated client concern (i.e., a specific problem such as "panic" that does not appear to have multiple contextual influences and can be separated from other problems) can be reasonably identified and isolated and whether the client agrees with the therapist's choice of approach to that concern.

There also is the risk of forgoing structure and being "theoryless." Although theoretical rigidity presents concerns (most notably leaving clients out of therapeutic processes), lack of theory is also an inadequate response to clients. Practitioners' aim, therefore, is twofold: (1) to elicit, respond to, and incorporate clients' ideas about change and (2) to utilize theoretical frameworks that provide structure while offering choice for and matching clients' ideas about change. Practitioners are not trying to achieve the perfect fit but are invested in using approaches that are both respectful of clients *and* provide the best possibilities for successful outcome. To determine the best fit, they turn to *client orientations*.

Inviting, Acknowledging, and Matching: Client Orientations as Compasses to Change

As noted throughout this text, therapists' theories are rarely the catalysts that jump-start positive change. In fact, no solid evidence exists to support the idea that therapist-derived explanations regarding the roots of dysfunction or focus on past events or pathology help clients to change (Beutler, 1989; Held, 1991, 1995). Conversely, *client orientations,* which represent their ideas about conditions that may increase the likelihood of change, are a form of *preliminary matching* and are instrumental in seeking charge. This section discusses ways

to tune into client orientations through inviting, acknowledging, and matching (*I-AM*).

Inviting involves creating a context that encourages clients' ideas. The therapist's aim is to collaborate with clients to establish conditions in which they feel safe and open enough to communicate the details of their lives and situations. Therapists demonstrate respect for clients' having the strength to let persons they do not know well into their lives to any degree. *Acknowledging* relates to an openness and commitment on the part of therapists to understand clients' views. It is important that clients feel respected and validated. Therapists do not have to agree with clients but instead strive to convey that clients' perspectives are valid. Further, therapists let clients know that they are not crazy, maimed, bizarre, or seen as having bad intentions. *Matching*, the final part of the I-AM process, refers to therapists' use of processes and practices that are respectful of and consistent with clients' ideas about their concerns and problems, possibilities for attaining solutions, and methods for achieving those desired changes. Practitioners learn through I-AM about two crucial aspects of client orientations: *influences of context* and *theories of change.*

Influences of Context

Client concerns and problems and exceptions to those concerns and problems are situated in and influenced by context. It is not possible for practitioners to fully comprehend clients' situations or be as helpful as possible without exploring the contexts surrounding their lives. In this sense, context has two connotations. First, *context* refers to the healing environment and relationship and the meanings attributed to them by participants (Frank & Frank 1991). Context also relates to the conditions created by therapists that demonstrate respect for clients' differences and create a climate in which to facilitate positive change. Second, as discussed in Chapter 2, *context* is a microcosm of culture and refers to variables that may influence problems, possibilities, and solutions including—but not limited to—family history and background, social relationships, genetics and biology, religion/ spirituality, gender, sexual orientation, nutrition, and economics.

We accept that because there are many possible influences on people's lives and ultimately, on their concerns, identifying any one aspect of a person's life or situation as being the true *cause* of a problem is difficult. Considering context as a collection of *influences* is more useful. Given that any one problem can have multiple influences, the emphasis clients place on aspects of context is crucial. Clients are motivated more by what they believe influences their problems than by the theoretical conceptualizations therapists use to address those problems. Clients do not necessarily enter therapy with clear-cut theories of causation, but they do often have general ideas about the nature of or influences on their concerns. Often these ideas are embedded in their language and can be cultivated through careful listening. It is the therapist's job to ferret out these influences through conversation.

This level of attention to possible influences on clients' lives is in contrast to psychotherapy as it was practiced in its first half century. During that time and since, our culture and the psychotherapy field have been subject to critiques and questions from various quarters. In the 1960s, a growing ecological awareness helped practitioners see that all people are connected within a context (in other words, a web of connectedness). Out of this ecological sensibility came the idea that the environment in which they occur influences psychological, emotional, and behavioral problems. One form that this environmental influence took was family therapy, particularly systemic therapy.

Other areas were critiqued. Biological psychiatry, which maintained that family background or psychology could affect psychiatric problems, was deemed to be wrong and result in a blaming environment. From this perspective, most disorders arose from some biochemical dysfunction, usually genetically based. The feminist critique (see the Appendix) argued that a male bias created many psychological and emotional problems for women. Psychotherapy pathologized women's desires to nurture and connect ("co-dependency"), meaning that many were not being heard, validated, or helped during therapy. Failure to recognize or include patriarchal and sexist influences on society led some women to be convinced that their problems stemmed solely from issues inside them. Other critiques addressed issues related to sexual preference and gender.

Strengths-based engagement (SBE) is not based on normative theories and models, nor does it look for evidence of deviation from some norm, so it involves inherently less inadvertent oppression. Therapists, however, remain subject to blind spots that reflect cultural and personal assumptions and values and counter these biases and blind spots by listening and attending to clients. Each person is a conglomeration of many different influences that separate her or him, however microscopically, from the next. Therefore, although everyone carries some general understandings and beliefs in relation to contextual influences, practitioners learn from clients what it is like to be them.

As this text stresses, clients and their stories play a vital role in both exploring and understanding the influences of both culture and context. Practitioners want to hear client's stories that answer questions such as "Who are you?" Practitioners explore the many influences in clients' lives by privileging their voices in order to learn how they have experienced the world and what they see as having shaped their lives. Practitioners can then explore the effects of such influences and how they can move clients forward and facilitate positive change and how they can restrain it.

To learn about context, therapists *invite* clients to share what they are most comfortable with and then listen to their stories and descriptions of their lives and situations. Madsen stated (2007), "Just as anthropologists (or more accurately ethnographers) immerse themselves in a foreign culture to learn about it, therapy from an anthropological stance can begin with immersing ourselves in a family's phenomenological reality in order to fully understand their experience" (p. 26). Clients' stories provide rich descriptions of their concerns, which are influenced by both internal and external factors. As described in Chapter 4, therapists practice "cultural curiosity." They continuously attempt to actively elicit clients' meanings rather than assuming prior knowledge or shared viewpoints and challenge their own values and beliefs and work with clients to do the same in ways that are respectful and open up possibilities. Clients are considered therapists' best teachers whose first-hand experiences help them to understand the influences of culture and context.

To promote disclosure, therapists use the I-AM approach by first *inviting* feedback from clients about what will help them to feel most comfortable and safe. As clients' stories unfold and evolve through conversation, therapists *acknowledge*, wanting clients to know that their perspectives have been heard. Again, therapists do not necessarily have to agree with these viewpoints. Therapists also ask questions to clarify, improve their knowledge, and to "fill in the blanks" regarding aspects of client stories

that are unclear or vague, seeking to learn what clients see as influences on their concerns as well as those that might positively affect change. With this information, therapists can *match* their methods and techniques to provide a better fit for clients. Case Example 6.1 illustrates the role of contextual influences.

Over the course of therapy, the therapist was able to explore what Elise had learned about being a mother that might pose challenges as well as benefit her with becoming the mother she wanted to be.

Like Elise, what some clients know or have heard about their families is negative. They make statements such as, "My mother was an alcoholic," "My father was a drug dealer," and "My family was full of crazy people." Clients may as a result have the idea that they are predisposed to or have inherited these negative qualities. Others know little or nothing at all about their families of origin. This, however, does not stop them from forming views about their parents and other family members. Many times, despite a lack of evidence, these views are negative.

Whether clients' generalizations about themselves or their families are based on personal experience or little or no information, practitioners can help them to identify qualities within themselves that are valuable or redeeming (such as resilience or coping skills) within their families or explore other influences (for example, culture, spirituality) that may counter negativity. A task of therapists is to delicately engage clients in conversations through which they can challenge and cast doubt on their own perceptions. As in Case Example 6.1, Elise was able to identify qualities from her biological mother as well as her adoptive mother that contributed to who she was as a person. The identification and amplification of such qualities can contribute to a

CASE EXAMPLE 6.1

As an infant, Elise had been adopted and was raised by a caring and loving family. Now, 19 years old and with two children of her own, Elise was feeling overwhelmed by raising her children, working, and trying to maintain her sobriety. Weighing on Elise was the story she had about her biological mother and how that might influence her ability to parent. The following dialogue took place in the second session:

Elise: I don't want to turn out like my mom. She was a bad mother. She was an alcoholic, she was promiscuous, and she died young. I mean, it was good that she gave up her children because she knew couldn't care for them, but she was bad otherwise.

Therapist: You don't want to be like your mom in that way—battling alcoholism and promiscuity—and yet there seemed to be this redeeming quality your mother had—she cared

about you and knew she needed to have someone else care for you when she couldn't. Do you think that you've inherited the quality of willing to do anything for your children?

Elise: Absolutely. I know I have. I would do anything for my children, so I guess I got that from my mom.

Therapist: And what else has contributed to you becoming the terrific mom that you are?

Elise: My [adoptive] mom has taught me a lot. She's had to deal with a lot and isn't perfect, but she's a great mom.

Therapist: So you've had the benefit of drawing on the qualities of two mothers.

Elise: I sure have.

Therapist: What does that say about the type of person you are?

Elise: I'd have to say that I've taken the best of both worlds and I left the rest behind.

change in perspective—one that increases hope and possibilities.

As a means to continue increasing practitioners' understanding of clients, their lives, and the nuances of their concerns and problems, therapists' use of one or more of the following areas and questions associated can be helpful. Information gained from these questions can assist therapists in understanding the cultural, contextual, relational, and other variables that may be influencing clients.

General Questions

- What do you see as being most significant (for example, family, cultural, religious, social relationships) influences in your life/concern/problem/situation?

- What do you see as contributing most/in any way to the concern/problem/situation you've been facing?
- How have those influences affected you?
- How have they been helpful to you? Not helpful?
- What would others say have been the most significant influences in your life/concern/problem/situation? Would you agree or disagree with them?

Family History/Background

- How has your family influenced your life?
- What have been the positive influences?
- In what ways has the influence of your family been challenging for you?

- What qualities do you think you (your son/daughter) have inherited from your family?
- What do those qualities say about the kind of person you are?
- How are they assets for you?
- [If the client or other does now know parent(s)]: Given the type of person that you are [caring/kind/honest, etc.], what do you think your (father/mother/parents) might have been like?
- What qualities do you think (father/mother/parents) have passed along to you that help you to move through life?
- What qualities would you like to pass on to your children? Why?
- How have you and/or other family members kept this problem from completely taking over your lives?
- How are you dealing with this problem differently than your (father/sister/mother, etc.) did?
- Who in your family has to any degree successfully dealt with this problem? How did (he/she/they) do that?
- What qualities do your family members possess so that they are/were able to stand up to the problems/adversity? What does that tell you about your family?
- What qualities or traits do you think that you've inherited from your family of origin that can help to make this problem fade from your life? What does that tell you about yourself?
- As changes occur, what will be different in your family from now?
- What do you think all of this might say about your family?

Culture/Ethnicity/Religion-Spirituality

- How has [person's name] influenced your life? What is most important for me to understand about that?

- What can you tell me about your (cultural/religious/other) background that will help me to better understand (yourself/ who you are/your concern/problem/situation)?
- What has it been like for you to grow up with your (cultural/religious/other) background?
- What has it been like to grow up _____?
- In what ways has your (culture/upbringing/background) been a strength for you? How could it be in the future?
- In what ways has your (cultural/religious/other) background presented a challenge for you? How have you dealt with that challenge thus far?
- What do people like me need to know about you to better understand the influence of _____ in your life?
- What has been your most profound _____ experience, if any?
- What kind of _____ activities would you like to do in the future, if any?

Social Relationships/Community

- How do you connect with other people?
- How have you typically met other people with whom you have felt a connection?
- Who is/has been helpful to you in your day-to-day life?
- How or what does (that/those person[s]) do to help you?
- Who has been helpful to you in the past in facing daily challenges? How has (he/she/they) been helpful to you?
- What did the assistance of these persons allow you to do that you might not have otherwise done?
- Whom have you met in your life who knew or knows exactly what you've been going through? How does (he/she/they) know that about you? How has knowing

that (he/ she/they) understood been help-ful to you?

- Whom do you look up to? Why?
- Who has helped you through tough times? How?
- Whom do you feel you can count on?
- When you're struggling, who knows just what to say/do to help you to get back on track?
- Who has the right idea about you?
- [To a client's family member] Who seems to be able to get through to (him or her)? How do they do that?
- Who seems to get through to or is able to have an impact on (him or her)? How so?

- Whom do you know that [name] responds to and would be willing to help out?

These questions seek a better understanding of how clients have constructed their worlds. The form in Exercise 6.1, Identifying Influences of Culture and Context, can be used to obtain information about which factors clients view as contributing to their concerns and could be possibilities for change. Because problems are always contextual, the more therapists understand the landscape of clients' lives, the more focused their attempts at promoting change can be. Case Example 6.2 demonstrates this.

Exercise 6.1

Ways to Identify Influences of Culture and Context

This exercise can help you to learn what clients view as influences on their concerns and problems as well as what might be considered areas of strength or resources. It is important to keep in mind that sometimes one influence can carry both a positive and negative connotation. The questions can be asked clients verbally or given to them to complete in a pencil and paper format.

- Which of the following influences do you feel have contributed to the problem you're facing and/or may be helpful and solving it? (Check as many boxes and/or write in what is applicable)

Biology _____   Genetics _____
Environment _____   Culture/Ethnicity _____
Community/Social _____   Gender _____
(work, school)   Religion/Spirituality _____
Family Relationships _____   General Relationships _____
Other _____   (friends, etc.)

- Next, transfer the influences checked in the first question into the following spaces. Then, for each influence, place a "–" next to those influences that have contributed to the problem and a "+" next to those that may be helpful in solving it. For those influences that fit both categories, use a "0." After assigning each influence a value, write how you think each particular influence has contributed to the problem, can assist with resolving it, or could influence both.

Influence _____   Value _____

_____

_____

_____

Exercise 6.1 (*continued*)

Influence _____   Value _____

_____

_____

_____

Influence _____   Value _____

_____

_____

_____

Influence _____   Value _____

_____

_____

_____

Influence _____   Value _____

_____

_____

_____

_____

Influence _____   Value _____

_____

_____

_____

_____

- Take a moment to review your responses for to the preceding question. Where did the idea come from that these influences are contributing to the problem, can help with resolving the problem, or both? What is most important for your therapist to know about these influences?

_____

_____

_____

_____

CASE EXAMPLE 6.2

A mother of two young children came to therapy with multiple concerns, one of which was the behavior of her son. She stated that her 5-year-old had been "having tantrums." This meant that he would "kick and scream" when he did not "get his way." When invited to share how she had addressed her son's behavior in the past, the woman remarked, "I never used to spank my children, but some people told me that I better get a hold of them or they would become terrors and end up in jail. I don't like spanking, but I got worried." When asked to clarify who the "people" were who offered their advice, she described two close friends whose advice she valued. The woman's experience was acknowledged. The therapist said, "It sounds like sometimes you really get frustrated." The woman was tearful.

When the client was ready, the therapist asked her several specific questions focusing on close relationships, which she had described as influential in decisions related to disciplining her children. These included "How often do you act on the opinions of others who are close to you?" "When people close to you share or give you their opinions, how do you figure out what fits with you and what doesn't?" and "How do you determine what to keep and use and how to cast aside what doesn't and say, 'That's just someone else's opinion and it's not right for me?'" After pondering the questions, the woman replied, "I never really thought about that. It makes sense though. I don't agree with everything that my friends tell me, but sometimes I don't think about it enough. This is certainly one of those times."

During the course of therapy the woman was able to develop and use alternatives to spanking in disciplining her children. She also created a plan for reflecting more deliberately on others' opinions and determining which ones did and not did fit for her.

In Case Example 6.2, the way the mother made decisions about disciplining her children was not random. Primary (but not the only) influences on those decisions were her close friends—not *all people* but *specific people*. The therapist's task, through the I-AM approach outlined earlier in the chapter, is to invite clients' perspectives, acknowledge them, and match them. By tuning into and attending to how clients make meaning and what they deem as influential on their concerns, therapists are matching clients' perspectives and creating opportunities for change.

Another way to map contextual influences that is deserving of mention here is the *genogram* (McGoldrick, Gerson & Petry, 2008).

Originating out of past-oriented approaches for gathering client/patient history as a means to trace pathology (primarily physical; for example, cancer and diabetes but later mental illness and interactional patterns) embedded in multiple generations, family therapists used genograms to identify and address the inter-generational aspects of problems. Traditionally, genograms have emphasized either pathology or problems (see the Appendix for a discussion about first and second waves in therapy) as a way to increase therapists' understandings of the level of dysfunction of individuals and in their relationships. Therapists have learned, however, that there are exceptions to what appear to be pervasive and repetitious problematic patterns.

Genograms provide a pathway for identifying exceptions, not explaining them. Once identified, clients' explanations and what they see as influencing patterns within their genograms can be explored. For example, even though alcoholism may have been repeated in three consecutive generations within a family, there are likely to have been members of each generation who did not develop an alcohol problem and/or who may have had the problem but were able to achieve momentary or ongoing sobriety at some point.

Although genograms provide a structured way to map strengths and exceptions, therapists can also utilize questions such as those offered previously to explore cultural and contextual influences and gently challenge any stories that diminish hope, suggest impossibility, blame, or deny accountability. See Case Example 6.3.

CASE EXAMPLE 6.3

Daniel, a colleague, was working with a family of three. The family included a single mother and two teenage sons. The mother, Stephanie, brought her two sons to see Daniel because both had been violent with schoolmates and each other. During the initial session, Daniel also learned that the boys had been physically aggressive toward their mother on multiple occasions, including shoving her against the wall, slapping her, and standing in her way so she could not pass by them. No police reports or charges had ever been filed because, the mother explained, she did not want her sons to "get in trouble with law." It was also learned during the initial session that Stephanie was herself a police officer, as were the boys' father, two uncles, and grandfather.

In the second session, Daniel was very disturbed by much of what he observed. The boys appeared more agitated and verbally aggressive. They argued with their mother, called her names, and denied responsibility for their actions. The oldest of the boys, Jordan, who was 14, said, "I warned her. She knew what was coming." He followed with, "She needs to shut her mouth and everything will be fine." On several occasions, because of their behavior, Daniel had to separate the boys from their mother and from each other. At the end of the session, Daniel asked each of the family members if he or she was open to another therapist joining the sessions to help come up with some new ideas. Stephanie stated that she thought it was a good idea. Brent, who was 13, said, "Whatever." Jordan shrugged his shoulders but did not respond verbally to the question.

Next, Daniel asked if I would assist him in working with the family of three. We agreed that I would join the next session to do co-therapy.

At the third session, the boys continued to berate their mother. When she would try to speak, one or both of the boys would say "Shut up" or "You don't know what you're talking about." Although Daniel had tried to establish ground rules about threats and verbal abuse and had separated the boys in the previous session, it had not worked. Therefore, the boys were both told that if they continued to make more threatening comments, they would not be allowed in sessions with their mother until they could treat her with respect.

I then asked Stephanie and the boys a series of brief questions. I started with what she had hoped to see happen as a result of coming to therapy. Stephanie stated that she wanted the boys to stop hitting her and to learn to be respectful of people. The boys were each asked

(continued)

CASE EXAMPLE 6.3 (continued)

the same question. Jordan stated, "I don't care. This sucks." Brent pointed at his mother and answered, "That lady needs to get a life and get out of mine." I then asked the Stephanie, "Where do you think the boys got the idea that violence and aggression are the way to handle things?" The following dialogue ensued between Stephanie, Jordan, Brent, Daniel (Therapist 1), and the author (Therapist 2).

Stephanie: I know where they got it. That's what they've been told for years by their father.

Therapist 2: What have they been told by their father?

Stephanie: To stand up to people. Don't let anyone walk over you. You have to be a real man.

Jordan: [raising his voice] Shut up!

Therapist 2: Jordan, you can be upset and you don't have to agree with your mom, but it's not okay to tell her to shut up or to be mean to her. This will be the final time that I will say this to you. The next time you will have to leave the session. Now, I'd like to ask you how you learned to deal with anger?

Jordan: [sighs] [is silent]

Therapist 2: It's okay if you don't feel like talking right now. I sometimes feel that way. [to Brent] Brent, do you have any ideas about that?

Brent: You've got to take care of yourself and don't let anybody walk on you.

Therapist 2: Anybody?

Brent: Yeah, but especially girls.

Therapist 1: Where did you learn that?

Brent: My dad always says that.

Therapist 2: What do you think he meant by that?

Brent: You have to be tough.

Therapist 2: What does that mean to you?

Brent: If people say stuff or make you mad, you have to stand up. You have to fight back.

Therapist 2: If you had to guess, where do you think your dad got the idea about having to be tough?

Brent: He's a cop. They have to be tough.

Therapist 1: He learned it through his training to be a cop?

Brent: Yeah, my uncles are cops too and my grandpa was one. I think they told him to be tough. My uncle Vic is a bad ass cop. He could kick anyone's ass.

Jordan: [interjects] Cops have to stand up.

Therapist 1: Sometimes they do.

Therapist 2: Brent, you mentioned that you've learned that it's really important to not let girls walk on you. What did you mean by that?

Brent: Men are in charge. Girls can't tell you what to do.

Therapist 2: Did you hear that from your dad too or somewhere else?

Brent: My dad, my uncle Vic, and my grandpa.

Therapist 2: So there are several men in your family who believe that to be true.

Brent: Yep.

Jordan: Yeah, they're right too because if you don't stand up, people will walk all over you.

Therapist 2: I'm curious about a few things. Can you tell me more about your family?

Brent: Like what?

Therapist 2: Well, you mentioned that you have two uncles who are police officers. One is your uncle Vic. Who's the other?

Brent: Wayne. He's cool.

Therapist 2: What does Wayne think about the idea that you have to be tough and stand up to people, especially women?

Brent: I don't know. He doesn't talk about it.

Jordan: I don't know either—but he's a cop and he's tough.

CASE EXAMPLE 6.3 *(continued)*

Stephanie: He's a very nice man.

Therapist 2: How so?

Stephanie: He treats Zoe, his wife, great and he's a terrific father too. He's got two girls.

Therapist 2: [to Jordan and Brent] What's the story with Uncle Wayne?

Jordan: He's nice to us, and we get to watch football with him.

Therapist 2: That sounds cool. And you have cousins who are Uncle Wayne's kids?

Jordan: Yeah, Elana and Missy. They're funny.

Therapist 1: So do you get along with your aunt Zoe and Elana and Missy?

Jordan: Yeah.

Therapist 1: What would you do if you didn't agree with them about something or didn't like what they were doing?

Brent: I don't know—probably just talk to them.

Therapist 2: Wouldn't you tell them to "shut up" or put them in their place? You know what I mean.

Jordan: No way.

Therapist 2: Why not? They're girls, right?

Jordan: Because Uncle Wayne would get mad at us if we did that.

Therapist 2: So your Uncle Wayne would step in. What do you think he would say?

Jordan: Don't fight. You don't need to fight.

Therapist 2: What else would he say?

Brent: One time I heard him say, "Everyone deserves respect."

Therapist 2: What do you think of what he said?

Brent: I don't know. I guess that everybody is a human.

Therapist 2: Do you mean that because everybody is a human that everybody deserves respect?

Brent: I think so.

Therapist 2: But you're not sure, are you?

Brent: I think that he's right.

Therapist 2: I have to admit that I'm really confused here. It really sounds like your uncle Wayne believes that all people should be treated with respect.

Jordan: I've heard him say that too.

Therapist 2: Really?

Brent: Yep.

Therapist 2: Help us to understand here. It sounds like even though some members of your family think that you should stand up to people and in particular, girls and women, some of them don't believe that. How is that some of your family members have been able to stand up to aggression and disrespect?

Brent: Well, I think they just don't like it.

Therapist 2: I'm getting the sense that part of you doesn't like it either and doesn't really believe that you should be disrespectful to girls and women. Is that right?

Brent: I don't want to be mean.

Therapist 2: I can see that about you.

Therapist 1: I can too.

Therapist 2: What do you want your mom to know about how you feel about her?

Brent: I love her.

Jordan: So do I!

Therapist 2: Well, help me to understand how what you've done in the past—hitting her, threatening her, and verbally abusing her—let your mom know that you love her.

Brent: [crying] I'm sorry, Mom.

Stephanie: [crying] I know . . . but it really hurts me when you're mean to me.

(continued)

CASE EXAMPLE 6.3 *(continued)*

Jordan: [tearful] I'm sorry. We don't know what to do.

Therapist 2: It's okay. I'm going to let you in on something that you already know but don't know that you know. How's that sound?

Jordan: What is it?

Therapist 2: [Looking at both boys] Do you know what the word *inherit* means? [Both nod their heads "yes"] We all inherit different things from our families. I may not know you well, but it seems to me that you've inherited some of that compassion for others that your uncle Wayne has. What do you think, Daniel?

Therapist 1: I'm thinking the same thing.

Therapist 2: Now is the time to bring that out and use it and stand up to those ideas that have been hurting your mom, your family, and you. What do you think?

Jordan: Okay.

Stephanie: I've always known that the boys had it in them. I've seen traces of it here and there.

Therapist 2: And that's what we want to learn more about. We want to learn how you [Jordan and Brent] can use the qualities you already have within you—being respectful and kind—more often in the future. How does that sound?

Jordan: Okay.

Brent: Okay.

Therapist 2: We're very proud that you are taking a stand against disrespect.

The boys' previous violent and aggressive behavior toward their mother ceased. Over the course of five more sessions, their relationship with her dramatically improved. Stephanie reported that the most remarkable change occurred with Brent, whose relationship with his female teachers had been volatile. After the fourth session, she was contacted by one of Brent's teachers who said, "I don't know what has happened with Brent, but he has become quite a gentleman." The mother stated that it was the first time she has pictured Brent as a "gentleman."

The family in Case Example 6.3 had multiple contextual influences including family background, gender roles, and social relationships. Jordan and Brent were ultimately able to draw on their family background, which had at times negatively influenced their ideas about being a "man," as a strength and resource. It is important to understand the influences that shape the lives of individuals, couples, and families. When their perspectives are, for example, too narrow or restrictive or pose threat to self or others and contribute to "stuckness," therapists collaborate with clients to alter, shift, or expand those perspectives by finding valid alternative ones that open up possibilities for positive change. This collaboration allows for exceptions, alternative stories, and resilient qualities to emerge, which counter problem stories and themes. When magnified, these exceptions can lead to present and future changes in situations and relationships.

Clients' Theories of Change

A second aspect of clients' orientations relates to their ideas about how change might occur with their situations or lives. Sometimes referred to as clients' *theories of change* (Duncan, Miller, & Sparks, 2004), this aspect constitutes clients' ideas, attitudes, and speculations regarding how they situate themselves in relation to problems, at what rate and when change might occur, who might be involved, and what factors, including larger cultural and specific contextual influences, might be involved in facilitating change. Duncan, Miller, and Sparks (2004) discussed the importance of attending to clients' theories:

> Honoring the client's theory occurs when a given therapeutic procedure fits or complements the client's preexisting beliefs about his or her problems and the change process. We, therefore, simply listen and then amplify stories, experiences, and interpretations that clients offer about their problems, as well as their thoughts, feelings, and ideas about how those problems might be best addressed. As the client's theory evolves, we implement the client's identified solutions or seek an approach that both fits the client's theory and provides possibilities for change (p. 84).

Client theories are revealed throughout therapy in each interaction and interchange. They are filtered through cultural and contextual influences and help therapists to better understand clients' worldviews and how to help them. Recall that clients do not necessarily enter therapy with clear-cut ideas but give indications of how they view themselves and their situations by the words they use. Through careful listening, questioning, and direct inquiries, practitioners invite clients into conversations from which emerge details about how they feel and think their problems developed, what they have tried to resolve them (and to what degree those efforts have or have not been successful), what they have considered but have not tried, and what they might consider in the future to attain the change they desire. Much is to be learned about how clients expect change to occur.

Close attention to client theories reveals important information that assists therapists in selecting methods that are likely to provide a good fit for clients. To do this, orienting questions such as these can offer a glimpse of how clients see change in their lives in general.

- How do things usually change in your life?
- What prompts or initiates change in your life?
- How do you usually go about trying to resolve your concerns/problems?
- What have you done in the past to resolve your concerns/problems?
- What ideas do you have about how change is going to take place with your concern/problem/situation?
- What ideas have you considered that might assist with your concern/problem/situation?
- If someone you know had this concern/problem/situation, what would you suggest he or she do to resolve it?
- What has to happen before the change you are seeking can occur?
- At what rate (for example, slow or fast) do you think change will occur?
- Will change likely be in big amounts, small amounts, incrementally, and so on?
- Do you expect change to occur by viewing things differently? By doing something different? By others doing something different?

Clients' theories also reveal information about their coping styles. That is, clients typically have a coping style that is more internalized or externalized. Beutler and Harwood (2000) stated, "People cope by activating behaviors that range from and combine those that allow direct escape or avoidance of the feared environment (externalization) and those that allow one to passively and indirectly control internal experience such as anxiety (internalization)" (p. 80). Therapists can learn about clients' patterns and propensities by reviewing their histories of problem solving. This information can help therapists in systematically selecting methods that provide an increased degree of fit with clients. For example, clients with internalized coping styles may benefit more from methods that focus on internal experience such as feelings and thoughts. Clients with externalized coping styles are likely to respond better to methods that focus on behavior or action.

With information gleaned from the questions in this section and in Exercise 6.2, Learning Clients' Theories of Change, therapists use more specific ones to learn more about clients' ideas and to find pathways with possibilities for positive change. The following questions can help to shift attention from general ideas about change to those that relate to the problem(s) brought to therapy.

- What thoughts/ideas/theories have you been considering about how this problem has come about and what might put it to rest?
- Given your ideas about the problem you're facing, what do you think would be the first step in addressing it?
- What might you do differently as a result of the thought/idea/theory you've developed?
- What have you considered trying that is consistent with your ideas about what's influencing this problem?
- If you had this thought/idea/theory about someone else, what would you suggest that he or she do to resolve it?

Understanding Clients' Relationships with Concerns and Problems

Learning about clients' theories of change also involves gaining a sense of how they situate themselves in relation to their concerns (Bertolino, 2003). It is not a matter of whether or not clients are motivated, but what they are motivated about (see Chapter 5). Duncan, Hubble, and Miller (1997a) stated, "An unproductive and futile therapy can come about by mistaking or overlooking what the client wants to accomplish, misapprehending the client's readiness for change, or pursuing a personal motivation" (p. 11). Understanding clients' theories also means understanding the degree to which and ways in which they align themselves with problems and see others' roles in those concerns/problems. Because clients typically demonstrate varying levels of association with their concerns, practitioners want to increase their understanding of which part(s), if any, of the concerns presented, clients believe they play a role in. For example, some clients declare responsibility for the entirety of a problem by making statements such as, "I know I've brought this on" or "I'm the one who needs to make changes." Some decline any involvement but perhaps assign responsibility to others for the concern/problem by stating, "It's her fault" or "It's got nothing to do with me." Some clients align themselves with some portion or aspect of concerns: "We both have played a role in this mess" or "I admit that there are times when I've been unreasonable."

This information is of particular importance because it helps practitioners to better understand clients' views regarding who is involved and their degree of involvement. To identify responsibility, practitioners tune into clients' use of pronouns such as *I, me, mine, my, we, us, our, you, he/she, him/her,* and *they/them.* When clients use the any of the first seven pronouns listed, they are likely accepting some level of involvement with their concerns/problems and perhaps in bringing about change. The absence of self when using pronouns such as *you/he/they* can indicate that clients have removed or distanced themselves

Exercise 6.2

Learning Clients' Theories of Change

This exercise can help you to learn your clients' ideas about how they expect change to occur with the concerns that brought them to therapy. This information can assist in determining how to proceed and selecting methods. There are two parts to this exercise. Part 1 focuses on clients' experiences with learning and change. Part 2 involves specific questions to establish details about concerns and problems. The questions in both sections can be asked clients verbally or given to them to complete in a pencil and paper format.

Part 1

- I tend to learn best . . .
  By having something told to me over and over.
  By reading as much as I can on a subject.
  From the experiences of other people.
  By realizing rewards when I succeed.
  By making mistakes and learning from them.
  By being shown where I am wrong.
  Other (please describe): _____

- My therapist can be of greatest assistance by . . .
  Telling me what I should do.
  Asking me questions and encouraging me to look deeper into my own ideas.
  Sharing his or her ideas.
  Suggesting reading.
  Suggesting actions for me to experiment with.
  Just listening.
  Other (please describe): _____

- I expect change to happen . . .
  All at once.
  Step by step.
  In increments.
  Quickly.
  Slowly.
  Not at all.
  Other (please describe): _____

- I also expect change to happen by . . .
  Exploring and revisiting the past.
  Focusing on the present and future.
  Exploring and revisiting the past combined with focusing on the future.
  Other (please describe): _____

(continued)

Exercise 6.2 *(continued)*

- And I expect change to happen by . . .
  Gaining insight into how I got this problem.
  Identifying what's worked in the past and figuring out how to use it in the present.
  Trying new things until we find something that works.
  Other (please list): _____

- I think that I need to change . . .
  How I feel.
  Something deep in my personality.
  The way I think about or look at things.
  Some thing(s) that I do.
  Someone else.
  Other (please describe): _____

Part 2

- What ideas do you have about what is causing the concern(s)/problem(s) that you're facing?

  _____

  _____

  _____

- What ideas do you have about how change is going to happen with your concern/problem(s)?

  _____

  _____

  _____

- Given the ideas that you have about the problem you're facing, what do you think would be the first step in addressing it?

  _____

  _____

  _____

- What else might you do differently as a result of the theory you've developed?

  _____

  _____

  _____

from involvement with problems. Because clients' self-references are embedded in context, therapists must remain aware that various pronouns mean different things in different cultures (for example, the use of *you* by some Hispanic and other clients may include themselves: "When you get up in the morning, you need to have your homework finished"). The following questions can be useful in exploring how clients situate themselves and others in relationship to presenting concerns.

- Who would you say is involved with this concern/problem?
- What would you say is your part, if any, in all of this?
- What's your role, if any, in what's going on?
- On a scale of 1 to 10, how involved would you say you are with the concern/problem?
- In your estimation, who needs to do what about the concern/problem?

The preceding sections identified the importance of practitioners' exploring and attending to possible influences of context. They also discussed clients' theories in gathering integral information that will provide a link between what clients want to see to change and their ideas about how they expect change to occur. Without this information, therapists run increased risk of proceeding strictly on their own beliefs systems and theories. Although doing so may work randomly with some clients some of the time, it is an inadequate response and is likely to lead to mismatches between therapists and clients. In creating the best fit possible between their own approaches and clients' perspectives to provide the best possibilities for change, therapists must collaborate with clients to gather information and learn about their orientations and theories.

Framework Development through Secondary Matching

Thus far you have traversed the topographical landscape of factors that contribute to the creation of clients' concerns and problems. By exploring collaborative processes aimed at strengthening the relationship and alliance, gathering information, and exploring clients' orientations, you have learned about preliminary matching. The next task is to move toward *secondary matching* by selecting specific methods and techniques to facilitate change in the direction of clients' goals and preferred outcomes.

Secondary matching requires therapists to use information gained from therapeutic conversations and interactions as a guide for helping clients experience change in one more domains of their lives. These domains are outlined in Figure 6.1. This section discusses how to determine which domain(s) of change should be the focus of attention.

Domains of Change

Major models of therapy posit explanations as to why clients have problems and suggestions as to how problem resolution and/or solutions will occur. For example, experientially focused therapists emphasize the expression of emotion. Cognitively oriented therapists focus on changing thinking. Behaviorists target changes in behavior and action. Likewise, systemic family therapists work to change interactions between people. Although typically providing structured methods of intervention, therapists have also learned that theory-driven matching tends to omit the most significant contributors to outcome and clients from therapy processes.

Reconsider a point made previously: People are in a constant state of change and experience

Figure 6.1

Domains of Change

EXPERIENTIAL/ AFFECTIVE	COGNITION/ VIEWS	ACTION/ INTERACTION
♦ Feelings	♦ Cognitions	♦ Action patterns
♦ Sense of self	♦ Points of view	♦ Interactional patterns
♦ Bodily sensations	♦ Attentional patterns	♦ Language patterns
♦ Sensory experience	♦ Interpretations	♦ Nonverbal patterns
♦ Automatic fantasies and thoughts	♦ Explanations	♦ Time patterns
	♦ Evaluations	♦ Spatial patterns
	♦ Assumptions	
	♦ Beliefs	
	♦ Identity stories	

⬇   ⬇   ⬇

EXPERIENTIAL/ AFFECTIVE	COGNITION/ VIEWS	ACTION/ INTERACTION
♦ Give messages of: acceptance, validation, and acknowledgment	♦ Identify and challenge views that suggest: Impossibility, Blame, Invalidation, Non-accountability, or Determinism	♦ Find action and interaction patterns that are part of the problem.
	♦ Change cognitions (thoughts, perceptions, etc.)	♦ Suggest ways of disrupting problematic patterns
	♦ Offer new possibilities for attention.	♦ Find and use solution patterns.

change in different ways. Furthermore, people often find that making changes in one area of their lives influences change in other areas. This overlap is illustrated in Figure 6.2. Consider that an increase in insight (that is, a change in view) can lead a person to make behavioral changes (that is, action) or how a change in relationships with others (that is, interaction) can lead to a change in how one feels (that is, experientially). This is not a new idea: See the discussion of the increasing number of hybrid/ integrative approaches in Chapter 2.

Practitioners need to remain aware that because change is constant, it is crucial to tap

Figure 6.2

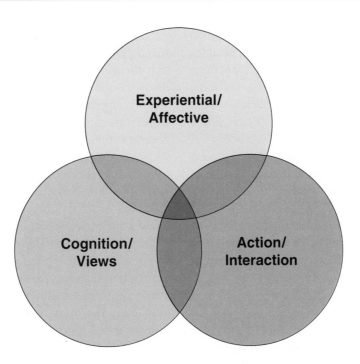

into the ways that clients have experienced change in their lives over time and in the past. In addition, recognizing that clients have different coping styles and are at different states of readiness for change should lead to the selection of methods that are in sync with their perspectives (and orientations to change), which can differ over time (from sessions to session, week to week, etc.). Including clients' histories of change—not just in the area of their current concerns—provides valuable information that will help therapists to determine what domain(s) of change will provide the best fit.

Stages of Change

One way to increase an understanding of clients' degree of readiness to change and to increase the factor of fit is by using the *stages of change* model (Prochaska & DiClemente, 2005; Prochaska et al. 1992; Prochaska & Norcross, 2002). Through their studies of both people who went through self-change processes (in other words, without therapy) and those who attended therapy, Prochaska and colleagues found that individuals tend to move through "stages" of change (that is, different levels of concern about ongoing and situational problems). They also experience different degrees of motivation and willingness to respond to those concerns. In addition, people are said to move through various stages of change in one of two ways. Some advance in a linear fashion, passing through one stage after another. More often, however, people go a second route: They progress, have setbacks, progress, have setbacks, and move through the stages in a "three-steps-forward, two-steps-back" process. For most clients, change is a process that unfolds over time.

The stages of change have been found to better predict outcome than other variables such as age, socioeconomic status, problem severity and duration, goals and expectations, self-efficacy, or social supports (Miller, Duncan, & Hubble, 1997). The Division 29 Task Force (see Chapter 2) of the American Psychological Association concluded that consideration of a client's stage of change in assigning insight or behaviorally oriented therapies provides a promising means for enhancing the factor of fit (Steering Committee, 2001). The stages of change framework provides therapists guidance about selecting and matching methods that is based on client feedback.

Precontemplation

Clients at this first stage of precontemplation are not aware or do not agree that a problem exists or acknowledge the presence of problems but do not usually see their roles in contributing to them. These clients often begin therapy involuntarily and are quick to reject responsibility. They may appear disinterested in discussing presenting concerns (which are often raised by those who initiated therapy), uncommitted and pressured to be in therapy, avoidant, and unaware of problems. As discussed earlier regarding clients situating themselves in relationship to their concerns, at this stage they use pronouns (*he, she, they*) that do not indicate ownership of those concerns. Instead they point to external factors (for example, other people, events, medication) as the reason for problems. Acknowledging the points of view of clients in the precontemplation stage without trying to get them to do anything is important. Instead, creating environments in which clients feel heard and understood and can consider the benefits of changing is essential.

Because clients at the precontemplation stage rarely initiate therapy and often attend only at the request (requirement) of others, they are commonly considered to be poor candidates for therapy. Some studies indicate, however, that clients who have been mandated to therapy do as well as those who attend voluntarily—so long as they feel connected with and understood by their therapists (Tohn & Oshlag, 1996). This finding supports clients' ratings of the relationship and alliance as being a consistent predictor of outcome (Bachelor & Horvath, 1999; Orlinsky, Grawe, & Parks, 1994). It also reflects the influence of expectancy and hope, which are likely to increase when clients feel connected with their therapists. Therefore, how therapists respond to clients who are mandated or involuntary participants, particularly during initial interactions, can make a significant difference in whether they move out of the precontemplation stage and remain in therapy or drop out.

Contemplation

Clients' recognition that problems are present and that change is necessary characterizes the second stage of change: contemplation. Often clients have ideas about goals and even know how to reach those goals but are not sure the change is worth the cost in time, effort, and energy (Miller, Duncan, & Hubble, 1997). Clients may appear to be attempting to evaluate and understand their actions, thinking about making changes, considering the pros and cons of their actions and the benefits and drawbacks of making changes, or thinking about when they made attempts to change in the past. As in the precontemplation stage, it is important to be patient with clients and not push them to change. It may even be useful to join clients' ambivalence about change by suggesting that they go slowly or by discussing the "dangers of change" (Fisch, Weakland, &

Segal, 1982). The latter is paradoxical and meant to match clients' teeter-tottering about change. By providing a supportive context, therapists can help clients at this stage to go at their own pace, thereby accommodating their varying states of readiness for change. Encouraging clients to think and observe change as opposed to suggesting that they take action to initiate it can also be helpful.

Preparation

By the time clients are at the third stage of change, preparation, they are less delicate, ambivalent and more open to divulging the details of their lives and accepting responsibility. Helping clients identify the change they desire and consider realistic strategies for attaining that change is important. Clients in the preparation stage are more likely to identify what they want different in their lives and the steps to achieve those changes. They may appear to be at the point of intending to change their behavior, on the verge of action in the direction of positive change, or in conversations as to how to bring about change. Many clients will have experimented—tried different methods of attaining change—to determine the results. Therapists can be active in helping these clients to identify past successes and problem-solving strategies and in exploring therapy options. In preparing clients for change, letting them know that there are many pathways and possibilities for reaching their desired changes is important.

Action

At the fourth (action) stage, clients are ready to do something to create positive change and reach their established goals. They appear to be determined by verbalizing their commitment to make change and undertaking specific actions to modify their behavior. Therapists accommo-

date this stage of change by helping clients implement strategies and follow through by modifying, altering, and changing such strategies based on the results achieved. Many clients move back and forth between preparing to take action and actually doing so.

Maintenance

In the fifth stage, therapists collaborate with clients to help them *maintain* the changes and gains that they have made and extend them into the future. Clients at this stage typically appear to be actively working to sustain changes achieved to date, giving considerable attention to preventing slips and lapses, and expressing anxiety about and/or fear of setbacks. Therapists can help clients, for example, by anticipating possible hurdles or obstacles that might occur "down the road" and developing prevention strategies or plans to "hold the course."

Termination

The sixth stage, *termination,* involves having complete confidence that a client will not engage in the old behavior. It has been deemphasized in recent years, however. Miller, Duncan, and Hubble (1997) note that this is more an ideal than a realistic or achievable state of change. Most clients remain in the maintenance stage and will "continue to be mindful of possible threats to their desired change and monitor what they need to do to keep the change in place" (p. 104).

The stages of change model provides markers to assist therapists in determining clients' readiness to become active change agents in their lives. To better assess clients' states of readiness, methods drawn from *Motivational Interviewing* provide an excellent resource (Miller & Rollnick, 2002). Table 6.1 offers a summary of suggestions from this approach.

Table 6.1

Exploring Client Readiness of Change

Disadvantages of the Status Quo

- What concerns/worries you about your current situation? How has that affected you?
- What hardships has your current situation contributed to?
- How has that been troublesome for you?
- In what ways does that concern you?
- How might it be a concern for you if you decided to leave your situation alone?
- What do you think will happen if you decide not to change anything with your situation?
- Advantages/Benefits of Change
- How would you like things to be different?
- What might it be like for you with your situation improved?
- Looking a few days/weeks/months/years into the future to a time when things are improved with your current situation, what might your life be like?
- What would be some of the advantages/benefits of things changing with your current situation?
- What would be advantages/benefits in your taking action to make changes?
- How might others benefit from changes you made?

Optimism about Change

- What affects your sense of optimism that you can make changes with your current situation?
- What makes you think that, should you decide to you can make the changes you want?
- What encourages you or gives you hope that you can achieve the change you want?
- How confident are you that you can make changes with your situation?
- What experience in making changes can you draw on that might be helpful to you with your current situation?
- What strengths might be helpful to you in making this change?
- What external resources (people, relationships, support systems) might be helpful to you in making this change?

Intention to Change

- What is your stance on your concern?
- What are your thoughts about it?
- What are your intentions about it?
- How important is it you for things to change with your current situation?
- What factors are currently influencing what you might do?
- What might you be willing to try?
- Of the possibilities discussed so far, which one(s) are most appealing to you?
- What would it take for you to begin to take a step toward changing your situation?

By understanding how clients view their problems and their degrees of motivation for various presenting concerns, therapists can choose methods within the domains of change to provide the best fit and opportunities for positive change to occur. Prochaska and Norcross (2002) related that clients in later stages are more likely to benefit from interventions that target behavior change whereas those at early stages are more likely to respond to conscious-raising or awareness-related methods. For example, clients at the precontemplation and contemplation stages are less likely to take action to make changes. Therefore, the therapist would focus on methods to help them to think about and view their situations rather than on ones to help them take an action. Clients at the preparation, action, and maintenance stages are not only candidates for changing their views of problems but are also likely to benefit from methods consistent with the action/interaction domain of change.

The stages of change framework can be particularly useful with clients who have specific and generally uncomplicated concerns. For example, some clients describe symptoms related to substance abuse, panic, anxiety, and depression that do not appear to be situated within or associated with other concerns. In other words, even though therapists may observe other problems in clients' lives, clients themselves do not share in these concerns and/or describe specific problems that meet specific criteria such as those outlined in the DSM. In such cases, therapists are encouraged to follow the underlying principles of SBE, explore clients' orientations, and use the stages of change to create an overarching therapeutic framework. In addition, specific, well-defined principles that complement and respect clients as well as their contributions to and roles in therapy could provide additional guidance. For example, Castonguay and Beutler (2006c) and colleagues have provided suggestions for matching therapy methods with clients who meet the criteria for several DSM-related disorders. Their suggestions are consistent with the stages of change and are designed to offer suggestions and guidance, not to serve as manualized protocols. Other systematic guides are also available to therapists working with clients with specific concerns (Beutler & Harwood, 2000; Seligman & Reichenberg, 2007).

Many clients experience complicated and multifaceted problems and therefore require more flexibility from therapists. When clients express higher-level or changing concerns or show no benefit from the approaches being used, therapists need to be able to switch out of specific modalities and/or abandon them completely, remembering that clients are the engineers of change.

Further Considerations in Matching

As discussed earlier and illustrated in Figures 6.1 and 6.2, clients experience change in one or more domains. Clients approach the domains in their lives and situations differently, and a change in one domain often immediately influences and/or triggers change in another. In determining the next step in facilitating change, therapists need to understand which domain(s) provides the most promising point of entry for a client. Answering this question requires answering a few other, basic ones:

- How does the client describe the concerns/problems (e.g., experientially, cognitively, in action or interactional terms, or in some combination)?
- What are client's ideas about change (i.e., how and under what conditions does the client expect change to occur)?

- What cultural influences might affect the client's perceptions about change?
- How does the client describe her/his relationships to concerns/problems (in other words, how involved does she or he see herself or himself with the concerns raised)?
- What is the client's primary coping style?
- In general, at what stage of change does the client appear to be?

The therapist's aim is to further elucidate factors that will help to determine pathway(s) that are most likely to facilitate change. With this information, therapists can move a step closer in selecting specific methods for addressing client concerns and promoting possible solutions as will be described in Chapters 7–10.

In Sum: Mapping the Client's Territory

Thus far the chapter has explored various elements that contribute to client perspectives and perceptions. Figure 6.3, "Mapping the Client's Territory," highlights these elements. Client factors represent the core of therapy with the therapeutic relationship and alliance serving as the balancing mechanism. Although many relationships can withstand and even benefit from some ups and downs, client-therapist relationships that are persistently out of balance are likely to result in negative outcomes. Other aspects in Figure 6.3 represent influential variables associated with increasing the factor of fit between therapists and clients. These ideas reflect data (see Chapter 2) indicating that client and relationship factors contribute most to outcome. These data suggest that therapy processes, including the selection of specific methods and techniques, should be primarily client, not theory driven. This does

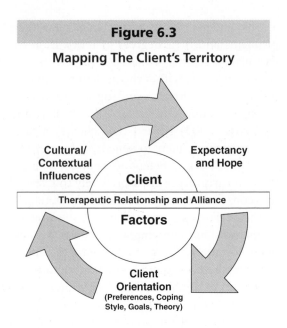

Figure 6.3

Mapping The Client's Territory

not mean that therapists should be passive participants in therapeutic processes but emphasizes the collaborative partnership in all aspects of therapy.

The data also underscore the importance of selecting and monitoring intervention strategies. McAuliffe and Eriksen (2000) estimated that up 50% of all mental health practitioners appear unreflective in selecting intervention strategies, which the authors defined as "adherence to a single technique, and/or maintenance of the status quo when more inclusive and socially critical interventions are needed" (p. 199). As you learned in Chapter 1, to increase effectiveness, therapists must be reflective in their practices.

Collaboration and Decision Making

Even the most collaborative therapists must make difficult decisions that can affect the selection of therapy approaches that match with clients. These decisions can result from a relative sea of information that flows from conversations and observations. Wading through a relative abyss of verbal and nonverbal information, therapists determine what to attend to and what to let pass or respond to at a later time. Therapists continuously assimilate waves of information, exploring possible areas of concern (for example, client concerns, safety risks) and strengths and resources. This brings to the forefront the therapist's philosophy (of people, change, and so on) and perceptions on which many decisions are based. After taking in and deciphering these data, the therapist needs to exercise judgment in assigning value to them.

All practitioners encounter situations that necessitate the use of higher degrees of structure or more directive action. For example, potential or explicit threats of harm to self or others in addition to issues regarding clients' cognitive, developmental, emotional, and physical capacities must be considered. To a lesser extent, ongoing decision making generally involves therapists' choosing paths that involve increased subjectivity, which may not always be in sync with clients. There will be occasions, for example, when therapists, either subtly or more directly, must challenge clients' perspectives, test ideas or hypotheses, or attempt to engage clients who are less verbal or conversational. Therapists might also deliberately shift conversations to maintain some sense of direction and keep therapy focused.

As a result of taking directive action, particularly when it comes to selecting specific methods, therapists' decisions and consequent actions could negatively affect the therapeutic relationship and perhaps outcome. Even the most skilled practitioners periodically face difficult choices and can veer off course from time to time. They must always exercise sound judgment, use intuition, and engage in supervision (see Chapter 13) when making critical decisions. In addition, maps provide only conceptual frameworks; they do not represent the territory. To ensure that they are on track from their points of view and help to minimize risks associated with course deviations, therapists must invite and encourage client participation and use feedback as a way to monitor clients' perceptions.

Collaboration in Case Conferences, Staffings, and Meetings

In many settings, staff gatherings provide opportunities to obtain updates on clients, discuss case planning, and coordinate therapy services. During formal and informal case conferences, therapists and others might talk about clients in ways that they would not if clients were present. In addition, when clients are not present therapists' points of view and preferences tend to be privileged, leaving clients out of the process. This can result in making decisions void of clients' input and without adequate attention to variables that can affect outcome.

Case planning is an integral aspect of coordinating services and in creating a good fit between the therapist, the client, and the approach employed. To ensure representation of clients' perspectives and preferences, the following ideas can be used as general guidelines:

- Include clients in meetings whenever possible.
- If clients cannot be present, invite them to contribute any thoughts or questions they might have.
- Share with clients any points that you would like to make as a therapist in upcoming meetings, providing rationale and allowing them the opportunity to edit your comments.

- Update clients on the outcome of case conferences or meetings including any ideas or questions that may have been generated.
- Act "as if" clients are present at meetings to keep conversations respectful and focused.
- Use clients' real names, do not use labels such as "the bipolar one," "the overreactive mom," or "the crisis-oriented family."

These general ideas help to establish a context that values clients and emphasizes collaborative partnerships. By including clients in meetings or ensuring that their perspectives are represented if they cannot attend, therapists increase the likelihood that what follows in therapy will be a good fit.

SUMMARY POINTS

- *Client orientations* form *preliminary matching* and include ideas about both the development of their concerns/problems and ways in which they expect change to occur, providing information that therapists use to improve the factor of fit of their approaches with clients' views.
- The two primary components of client orientations are *influences of context* and *theories of change.*
- *Influences of context* are microcosms of culture and refer to variables that may contribute to but not cause problems, possibilities, and solutions including—but not limited to—family history and background, social relationships, genetics and biology, religion/spirituality, gender, sexual orientation, nutrition, and economics.
- *Theories of change* refers to clients' ideas, attitudes, and speculations regarding how they situate themselves in relation to problems, the rate at which and when change might occur, who might be involved, and what factors, including contextual influences, might be involved in facilitating change.
- The *I-AM* approach includes *inviting, acknowledging,* and *matching.*
  - *Inviting* involves creating a context in which clients feel safe and open enough

  to communicate the details of their lives and situations.
- *Acknowledging* relates to an openness and commitment on the part of therapists to understand clients' views. Therapists do not have to agree with clients but must let them know that their perspectives are valid.
- *Matching* refers to therapists' use of processes and practices that are respectful of and consistent with clients' ideas about their concerns and problems, possibilities for attaining solutions, and the methods for achieving desired changes.
- *Secondary matching* involves selecting specific methods and techniques including *domains of change* and *stages of change* to facilitate change in the direction of clients' goals and preferred outcomes.
- *Domains of change* (see Chapter 2) refers to the major areas including experiential/affective, cognition/views, action/interaction in which therapists can work with clients to achieve change. Chapters 7–10 explore these areas in depth.
- The *stages of change* provide a template for describing how clients move to different levels of concern and degrees of motivation with problems. Some people advance in a linear fashion, passing through one stage after another while others have setbacks,

progress, have setbacks, and move through the stages in a "three-steps-forward, two-steps-back" process.

- All therapists encounter situations that necessitate increased structure or more directive action. Therapists' decisions and consequent actions, particularly in regard to selecting specific methods, can negatively affect the therapeutic relationship and perhaps outcome. Therapists always exercise sound judgment, use intuition, and engage in supervision when they must make critical decisions.

- Therapists must also keep in mind that maps provide only conceptual frameworks but do not represent the territory. For therapists to monitor their perceptions, participation and feedback by clients are necessary to minimize risks associated with course deviations.

- Include clients in case conferences, staffings, and meetings as a way to convey respect and ensure that their perspectives and preferences serve as guides to therapy.

DISCUSSION QUESTIONS

1. What are possible benefits and limitations of selecting individual models of therapy?

2. What are possible risks of forgoing structure and downplaying the role of theory?

3. What does *client's orientation* mean?

4. What are influences of context? Give some examples and explain how contextual influences factor into both client problems and solutions.

5. What is the client's theory of change? What are some areas of exploration within the client' theory of change?

6. What is *secondary matching*?

7. How can the stages of change be a useful template in therapy?

PART FOUR

Chapter 7

Changing Views and Perspectives, Part I

Exceptions and Differences

■ Fundamental to many therapy approaches is an emphasis on clients' perceptions, particularly cognition. Many cognitively oriented therapies focus on the development or expansion of insight or awareness. The idea that clients' problems are a product of what goes on in their minds is common to these approaches. Although "cognition" is an obvious area of focus in therapy, it also reflects a narrow view of perceptual processes. In addition to straightforward cognition, clients can also experience "stuckness" or change as a result of what they pay attention to and notice in their lives. One way to address this is to use a more expansive way to conceptualize cognitive processes by exploring the ways that clients *view* themselves, others, their lives, and/or situations. In the next two chapters, you will learn how therapists can assist clients in changing, altering, or shifting some aspect of their views, thereby bringing about the alleviation of symptoms and the problems that brought them to therapy.

It is important to note that the methods provided throughout this book, particularly those in this and Chapters 8–10, are general; however, their use in therapy is always specific. There are no "one-size-fits-all" methods; that is, there is no one correct focus of attention. Although therapists may have opinions as to what merits the most attention, ideations that are too dogmatic and leave clients out of therapeutic processes can be disrespectful and increase the likelihood of negative outcomes. Therapists' interest is in finding what works for each client, always keeping in mind that there are many pathways to the same point.

Orientation Toward Views: Negotiating the New

Let's first consider a fundamental idea: Some of the ways that clients view the world are helpful and direct them toward goals; others are not but contribute to distress, negative symptoms, and problems. When people become stuck, it is often due to rigidities in the realm of viewing. The French philosopher Émile Chartier summarized this rigidity well: "Nothing is more dangerous than an idea when it's the only one you have." As you have learned, the therapist's acknowledging the client's views is important although agreement with them is not necessary.

One task of therapists is to subtly challenge and deconstruct clients' perspectives so that they are able to save face (in other words, not experience unnecessary embarrassment, humiliation, or blame) and open themselves up to new ways to think about, perceive, and experience the world. Therapists accomplish this task by helping clients to change their views of problems and develop new ideas, patterns of attention, and identity stories. A change in views can enable clients to gain new perspectives and see new possibilities regarding their problems, which in turn can help them to experience themselves and/or their situations differently.

A focus on changing views is often a good place to stimulate change, especially for clients who:

- Use words that suggest they are at least, in part, perceptual processors (for example, *The way I see it; I think*).
- Indicate through conversations and/or orientations (including cultural influences) that they expect change to involve insight, awareness, or some form of explanation or change in perspective (for example, what they pay attention to in their lives).
- Have a more internalizing coping style (i.e., are more likely to experience hurt than anger, are quiet in social situations, worry or ruminate before taking action, prefer being alone, are introverted).
- Are at any level of alignment and degree of ownership with problems.
- Are at any stage of change.

A focus on views also is the first choice for clients who do not align themselves with or accept responsibility for any part of the problems discussed in therapy. These clients are most frequently at the precontemplation or contemplation stages. Many of them are in a state of inactivity and are less inclined to take deliberate action or steps. Although client states fluctuate and can shift quickly, using an approach that matches the client in a given moment or interaction is likely to provide the best fit, increasing opportunities for positive change.

Clients' Stories as Pathways to Problems and Possibilities

Chapter 4 explored multiple ways to strengthen the therapeutic alliance by attending to clients' use of language. Through subtle processes, practitioners acknowledge, validate, and inject possibility into otherwise closed-down client statements. As therapy progresses, clients' identity stories or narratives unfold, revealing rich descriptions of their lives and experiences. These stories reflect the views that they have of themselves or that others have of them. More dominant and often more consistent patterns or themes emerge in their stories. Attending to these stories that are embedded with strengths and possible areas of conflict has been a primary focus of this book and will be addressed further here. When experiencing pain, difficulty, or trouble, clients frequently have stories about themselves or others that are not helpful, contribute to problem maintenance, and close down the possibilities for change (Bertolino & O'Hanlon, 2002). Clients' identity stories influence how they approach their lives. Similarly, the stories that others hold regarding clients will affect the ways in which those others relate to those clients. *Problem-saturated* stories can lead to communication or interaction that is not helpful or is negative (White & Epston, 1990).

Although clients' views can contribute to stuckness, whether they are harmful is a matter of contention in therapy. A broad perspective on this issue involves two considerations:

1. What people do or do not do (in other words, their actions) is definitive. The most precise way to measure change is by examining what a person does over time—his or her behavior. Although misleading oneself or others through behavior is possible, maintaining this is difficult in the long term. Even for those who may be able to mislead themselves or others, the outcome is that their actions are acceptable (in other words, do not infringe on others' rights, create risk to self or others, or violate laws).

2. Some views that clients hold are helpful and some are not. Clients' views can contribute both to their problems *and* provide the keys to opening doors with possibilities.

Therapists' task is to identify aspects of clients' views that seem to contribute to their concerns and problems. One way to do this is to listen for how the views represent themes that limit or restrict the ways in which the clients interpret and experience the world around them. When clients are stuck, their viewing patterns generally represent at least one of four *problematic stories* (Bertolino & O'Hanlon, 2002). Once identified, therapists can work to change those stories that close down the prospects of change to ones that engender hope, possibilities, validation, and accountability.

Problematic Stories

Clients' stories (and others' stories about clients) yield descriptions of themselves, their lives, and situations. When clients are stuck, their stories are often problematic, indicating *impossibility, blame, invalidation,* or *nonaccountability.* By identifying stories that are troublesome, therapists can work to promote new ones that are validating, hold people accountable rather than blame them, and open up possibilities for change.

Stories of Impossibility

Consider the following story. Years ago a group of young men were part of the Flaming Arrow Patrol of Ingleside's Scout Troop 294. Located in the Phoenix, Arizona, area, the troop was supervised by various parents, one a man named Dick Hoffman. Over time, Hoffman developed a view about one particular member of the troop. In describing the young man, he stated:

> He seemed to go in fits and starts—he would dash from one thing to another. I thought it was a disability, not being able to concentrate the way the rest of us would. I knew he was wildly enthusiastic, but I didn't think he had enough ability to analyze things. . . . I thought, "When he grows up and gets into the real world he's going to have a tough time keeping up" (McBride, 1997, pp. 77–78).

At face value, this may appear a rather innocuous and unassuming story, but consider the implications of this perspective. How is it helpful? How might it affect attempts to facilitate change? Stories of impossibility suggest that people are unable to or are incapable of change. These types of stories can be readily identified through statements such as, "He'll never change"; "She's borderline"; "He can't help it, he's ADD"; or "You shouldn't expect much; she's always been that way." Here is an example:

> A 14-year-old was referred to therapy by a school counselor due to "chronic" truancy. On the referral form, the school counselor had written, "This adolescent has had a history of truancy since the age of 10. Given the chronic and ongoing nature of this problem, it is extremely unlikely that she will change her behavior anytime soon."

How might the school counselor's story affect efforts to help the adolescent? Where might this lead if others were to concur? Fortunately, not everyone around this youth subscribed to the story of impossibility. Others saw her as needing to be challenged more academically in school. As a result of talking with her and changing her classes, she became more interested in school, missing just one day the remainder of the year (about four months).

What about the youth from the Flaming Arrow Patrol? The troop leader ended his statement by saying, "I didn't dream anything would come of him." Of course, that was a complete misjudgment of the kid's personality" (McBride, 1997, p. 78). The youth was Academy Award–winning film director Steven Spielberg.

Stories of Blame

A second problematic story type imparts blame. Individuals tell stories of blame when they label themselves (or others label them) as having bad intentions or bad personality traits, suggesting that their intentions are not only bad but also purposeful, intentional, or preconceived. In regard to bad personality traits, the idea is that people are innately bad or have bad character. Stories of this type are evidenced by comments such as, "It's my fault that he hit me"; "I must be bad; otherwise I wouldn't have been sexually abused"; and "I don't deserve any better." They either perceive themselves as damaged goods or attribute bad intentions to themselves. Others can also convey stories of blame through comments such as "He has no intention of changing"; "He's always playing head games and is never serious about anything"; and "She's trying to make me miserable." A brief story exemplifies this. A couple came to therapy because of their "constant arguments." During the initial session, the husband stated, "She constantly puts me down and even tells others I'm no good. I feel like I can't get a break." The wife responded to his comments by saying, "It's all in his head. He's always imagining that people are out to get him." The wife's statement illustrates both stories of blame and invalidation, the next type of problematic story to be discussed.

Stories of Invalidation

Stories of invalidation characterize people as being abnormal or wrong in some way or give them the message that their perceptions cannot be trusted. This feeling often occurs when others undermine a person's internal experience or knowledge. Many clients feel invalidated by others who say they are wrong, make things up, make too much of something, or should just move on and forget about things. Stories of invalidation can be detected through statements such as, "You shouldn't feel that way"; "Just let it go"; "She's too emotional"; and "He needs to express his anger about his father's death; he just doesn't recognize how angry he is yet." Here is an example: A mother brought her teenage son to therapy. She remarked, "Lots of kids have fathers who aren't involved in their lives. He [her son] needs to just get over the fact that that's the way it is."

Stories of Nonaccountability or Determinism

The final type of problematic story relates to nonaccountability or determinism. People telling these stories reject responsibility for themselves and their actions. At times, they say things such as, "He made me do it"; "I was drunk"; or "I can't help it." People are accountable for the actions they take (in other words, what they do with their bodies) but not for what is done to them without choice or when they are intruded upon without their consent. In the latter case, the person(s) who committed the intrusive act(s) is(are) accountable. For example, a young woman attended a party with some friends. During the evening, she became intoxicated and started a fight with another woman. She thought the woman was trying to "steal" her boyfriend. Later that evening, as she was returning home, a man who had been at the same party raped her. The distinction here is that the young woman was accountable for what she did with her body when she had choices. These included becoming intoxicated and fighting with another woman. She was not accountable for what was done to her that she had no choice in—being raped.

When entering therapy, clients often have stories (ideas, beliefs, hypotheses) about what is contributing to their being stuck. These stories can be rigid, divisive, and get in the way of change. Left as they are, these views can continue to lead clients to ways that are not helpful in resolving their concerns. In essence, problematic stories can take on lives of their own, influencing clients' actions. A common thread among problematic stories is the creation of a mirage or smokescreen. They can appear to be so real that therapists can become entranced by them. This makes it important to first identify stories that suggest impossibility, blame, invalidation, and/or nonaccountability. To practice this, please complete Exercise 7.1, Identifying Problematic Stories.

In some situations, clients' (or others' stories about them) imply more than one type of problematic story. As they identify these stories, practitioners want to continue to acknowledge, validate, and hold clients accountable while remembering that every dominant story has other, "alternative," stories that offer different perspectives that contradict the problematic ones. Practitioners also respectfully challenge, create some doubt about, and offer new inroads that allow for the emergence of hope, resilience, and the possibility of change.

Cognition, Attention, and Reciprocation

What people notice and the ways they decipher and interpret information play a significant role in how they feel and act. When experiencing pain or suffering, people generally focus at least a portion of their attention on that pain or suffering. This focus serves as a form of "dimmer switch" with people having the ability to turn up or down symptoms (for example, anxiety, sadness, fear) and experiences through their thoughts and attention. In therapy, practitioners draw on methods for helping clients to shift their perspectives by changing patterns of thinking (cognition), attention, or both. Because cognition and attention are interwoven, a change in one is likely to affect the other.

For example, a client who changes negative self-statements (for example, "I'll never amount to anything"; "I don't deserve to be

---

Exercise 7.1

Identifying Problematic Stories

Clients' views can either open up or close down possibilities for change. When clients' statements reflect impossibility, suggest blame, invalidate, or remove accountability, practitioners want to cast doubt on those stories. To complete this exercise, please determine which form of problematic story is represented by the statement.

Statement: "He will never be even an average student."
Type of problematic story _____

Statement: "Without her medication she can't control what she does."
Type of problematic story _____

Statement: "It's been over a year now. It's time for her to get over it and move on."
Type of problematic story _____

Statement: "He always tries to make me look bad in front of others."
Type of problematic story _____

Statement: "He's ADD and always will be. It never goes away."
Type of problematic story _____

Statement: "She does that on purpose just to make me mad."
Type of problematic story _____

Statement: "Kids from broken homes are supposed to act out."
Type of problematic story _____

Statement: "There's no reason to cry about it. Just deal with it."
Type of problematic story _____

---

happy") to more positive ones (for example, "I am a capable person"; "I deserve to be happy") is likely to experience a change in what she notices in her life. This might be evidenced by noting that things look different in her environment or relationships. Conversely, a client's shift in attention to notice that at times others respond to him in ways he prefers (for example, smiling at him, starting casual conversations) might lead to a change in his thoughts (for example, "People can be friendly"; "I'm a likeable person"). Therapists' intention is to stimulate changes in view-

ing that will contribute to improvements with clients' concerns and problems.

A variety of cognitively oriented therapies, particularly those associated with the second and third waves (see Appendix), provides fertile ground for therapists seeking options for challenging problematic stories and views. Common to these approaches is an aim of helping clients to identify, challenge, and ultimately change underlying beliefs and thoughts. Emotions and physiological symptoms (primarily somatic) are considered entry points to cognitions, but clients' psychological

Figure 7.1

COGNITION/VIEWS

Cognitions—Points of view—Attentional patterns—Interpretations—Explanations—Evaluations—

Assumptions—Beliefs—Identity stories

- Identify and challenge views that suggest: Impossibility, Blame, Invalidation,

  Nonaccountability, or Determinism

- Change cognitions (such as thoughts, perceptions)

- Offer new possibilities for attention

---

constructions are seen as triggering these responses and it is therefore those constructions that are the focus of change. Because of this common feature among cognitive models, standard methods and strategies (although often named differently according to the model) are used to change "distortions" or "irrational" thinking. These methods and strategies include challenging *dichotomous thinking* (for example, seeing things as all or nothing or in extremes), *absolutes* (indicated, for example, by *always, never, everyone*), *overgeneralizations* (for example, reaching sweeping negative conclusions that go far beyond the current situation), *catastrophizing* (for example, "If I'm not completely successful, I'm a failure"), and *labeling* (for example, "I'm a loser"; "He's crazy") (Beck, 1995). Although some methods are unique to specific client situations and symptoms (for example, anxiety, phobias) (Castonoguay & Beutler, 2006b), most can be used in a variety of contexts. As you have learned, what seems to

matter most is that a particular method fits with a client and his or her orientation.

In selecting methods for helping clients change problematic views, it is important to ensure that observation and client feedback provide a rationale for the one(s) chosen. In addition, feedback processes should continue through the course of therapy as a means of evaluating the impact of methods. This feedback allows therapists to learn from clients what is working, what it not, and what can be done to create a better fit. (See Figure 7.1.)

The Matter of "Questions"

Language and interaction are therapists' primary methods for promoting change. Of the types of verbal communication employed, questions represent a significant—if not the largest—portion of their therapeutic repertoire. Questions, as discussed in previous chapters, are used to acknowledge, validate, prompt, expand, identify strengths and exceptions, and, as discussed here, help clients change their views.

To engage clients in conversations for change, beginning with questions that draw attention to the "unnoticed" can be helpful. These questions maintain interventive properties: They require clients to consider alternatives regarding their lives, concerns, or situations and can help to deconstruct problematic views that could lead clients to reposition themselves in relation to the problems that brought them to therapy. These questions are considered *exploratory* (or investigative) because they are posed to gather information (as a means of unraveling stories by ferreting out the details that compose them). They are also *generative* because they facilitate the construction of new meanings.

Consistent with those offered in previous chapters, the questions provided here are posed from a position of *neutrality*. The concept of *neutrality* is exemplified through the therapist's posture and is not intended to be interpreted in strict terms. It is impossible to be completely neutral; therapists influence others verbally and nonverbally. *Neutrality* refers to the therapist's overall position of asking questions as a means of evoking clients' views rather than imposing his or her own.

Tomm (1988) described four different categories of questions: *lineal, circular, strategic,* and *reflexive. Lineal* questions are investigative, straightforward ones intended to gather facts. They can be open or closed ended (for example, answered with "yes" or "no") and are most frequently cause-and-effect driven. Examples include these:

- What is most anxiety provoking for you?"
- How long has it been going on?
- Who else knows about your situation?

- What do you think about that?
- When is it most noticeable?
- Where does it happen most?
- How do others usually react when that is happening?

"Why" questions can also be useful, although they can spur client defensiveness because they require explanations. They should therefore be used in moderation.

Questions are considered *circular* when they are used to bring forth connections, such as those between persons, objects, perceptions, ideas, feelings, actions, and/or events (Tomm, 1988). Circular questions are primarily systemic: They are used to learn more about the relationship between things. In addition, they are also "4W-H questions" that ask who, what, when, where, and how. Examples follow.

- What do you when she does that?
- How does that affect you?
- What does your partner do when she sees you doing that?
- Who else does it seem to effect?

These questions are posed from a position of curiosity or conjecture in which therapists wonder about, rather than imply, associations.

Strategic questions propose options for viewing situations differently. Historically, they have been used predominantly as a means of instruction (in other words, the therapist behaves more like a teacher or instructor). Sometimes strategic questions can be used to move a stuck system and are intended to directly introduce different viewpoints. These are examples:

- What happens that you allow that to continue rather than stepping in?
- Wouldn't you rather feel less anxious and leave those thoughts behind?

- When are you going to take a stance against that?
- What would happen if you decided to take action?
- Is this habit you have something you are okay living with?

The therapist's intent obviously shapes the manner in which the questions are asked. When strategic questions provide a good fit for clients, they elicit useful information and stimulate change. Therapists should use discretion when using them, however, because they can lead to rifts and ruptures in the therapeutic alliance.

Reflexive questions are used to facilitate self-healing by creating new meanings that emerge from preexisting belief systems (Tomm, 1988). They are often used to help clients to create new meanings by viewing their lives and situations in a different light or from a previously unforeseen position. As discussed in Chapter 4, therapists who assume a more collaborative stance and focus on the creation of new meanings through conversation may find this a method that is a better fit for themselves and their clients. Reflexive questions represent a more inquisitive and "curious" stance on the part of therapists. These are examples.

- How do you think your life will be different when you've gained the upper hand with this concern?
- From where you stand, what might be a reasonable response to that situation?
- What else have you considered?
- Who is most likely to notice the change first?
- How do you think it would go if you were to take that step?
- What difference might it make if you were to do that?

Reflexive questions are process oriented and can be used to focus on the future, facilitate self-awareness, gather information, explore context, and so on (Tomm, 1988).

Questions used to initiate change in the realm of client viewing can span one or more categories and be helpful at different points in therapy. Because questions are the linchpins of methods, the intent behind them should be carefully considered. Whether used to gain information, highlight strengths and resources, make connections between things, subtly challenge ideas, or accomplish some other purpose, questions carry the capacity to bring forth new or different perspectives. To practice developing the four types of questions outlined, please complete Exercise 7.2, The Art of the Question. The next section discusses questions and statements and the specific methods they inform. These mechanisms can create new pathways of possibility for changing clients' views.

Identification and Building on Exceptions

This section goes beyond the traditional idea of identifying the errors in clients' thinking and attempting to explain the root of their problems to considering instead that clients' stories (their socially constructed realities) denote their best attempts at understanding and adapting to the world around them. These constructions, referred to as *clients' views*, may be helpful or not, depending on the context. Rather than focusing only on how these views can be problematic, therapists assume that there are already contexts and conditions (for example, moments, situations, events) in which clients have viewed the world in ways that are more helpful or beneficial. These represent exceptions, times when problems were

Exercise 7.2

The Art of The Question

This exercise is to help you develop four primary types of questions: lineal, circular, strategic, and reflexive. *Lineal* questions are straightforward and intended to gather facts. *Circular* questions are used to bring forth connections. *Strategic* questions are used to propose different ways to view situations. *Reflexive* questions facilitate self-healing through the creation of new meanings. To complete this exercise, please create one of each type of question for each statement provided.

Statement: "I'm in a complete downward spiral in my life. Nothing is going well and I feel like I can't do anything right."

Lineal   _____

Circular   _____

Strategic   _____

Reflexive   _____

Statement: "We constantly argue. She says something. Then I say something back. It just spins out of control after that."

Lineal   _____

Circular   _____

Strategic   _____

Reflexive   _____

Statement: "When I'm anxious, I can't focus on anything. My thoughts all run together, and I feel like I'm coming apart at the seams."

Lineal   _____

Circular   _____

Strategic   _____

Reflexive   _____

Statement: "He's always complaining about something. 'Get me this, get me that,' is all I hear. I'm sick of it."

Lineal   _____

Circular   _____

Strategic   _____

Reflexive   _____

less evident and intrusive or absent altogether. Exceptions can take on different forms, such on being spontaneous or deliberate (de Shazer, 1988).

The practitioner's first task is to be on the lookout for exceptions by exploring clients' lives not just in the area(s) of concern but also in other contexts. By identifying contexts (for example, situations, events, interactions, time, space) in which things have gone differently (and better), practitioners can work with clients to determine what specifically was different and how clients can employ those differences in present and future problematic situations.

Build Accountability through Language

Chapter 4 discussed ways to use language to acknowledge, validate, and introduce the element of possibility into otherwise closed-down situations. These methods are important because they provide respectful and subtle inroads for promoting new views. Often larger changes emerge through these smaller ones that are embedded in language. This section expands on the methods introduced in Chapter 4 and adds those that promote personal agency (in other words, responsibility and accountability). The aim is to invite clients into new ways of thinking and talking about their situations and lives.

As noted, clients commonly tell stories that suggest nonaccountability, nonchoice, and determinism. They (and sometimes others involved with therapy) at times attempt to justify actions or behaviors by attributing them to genetics, physiology, development, relationships (interpersonal), family, personality, or other influences. Keep in mind that although these forces can influence and/or shape behavior, they do not cause behavior with few exceptions (for example, certain intellectual and developmental disabilities). Examples of client statements that might indicate nonaccountability follow.

- I have a chemical imbalance. If I don't get my medication, I can't control what I do.
- He's ADD. He can't help it.
- It runs in my family—we can't stop drinking.
- That's the way I am. That's what us Bipolar's do.

We want to acknowledge and validate what clients feel experientially while inviting accountability for what they do. Let's explore ways to do this.

Reflect Back Nonaccountability Statements Without the Nonaccountability Part

When clients use excuses or explanations that contain nonaccountability, repeat back the statement without the nonaccountability part as in the following examples.

Client: Yeah, I told her I would try to be on time. But she knows I'm always late; that's the way it is in my family.

Therapist: You were late.

Client: He called me a name. So I hit him.

Therapist: You hit him.

Client: I didn't get my medication, so I forgot my appointment.

Therapist: You missed your appointment.

Use the Word *and* to Link Internal Experience and Accountability

When therapists hear statements of nonaccountability, reflecting back on what clients are experiencing internally and linking it to what they are accountable for can be helpful. This does two things. First, through acknowledgment, it lets clients know that the therapist is not trying to change how they feel. Next, it hold clients accountable for what they do—their actions and behaviors. To do this, therapists use the word *and*, not *but*. See the following example.

Client: I can't get anything done when she's always on my case.

Therapist: You can feel like you can't get anything done and you can get done what you need to get done.

Client: I get so upset that I just start cutting on my arm.

Therapist: It's okay to feel upset and it's not okay to cut on yourself or hurt yourself.

Client: What did she expect? She made me mad so mad I hit her.

Therapist: It's okay to be mad and it's not okay to hit her.

Find Counterexamples that Indicate Choice or Accountability

A third way to promote a change in viewing through language and invite accountability is to search for exceptions to the actions or behavior for which clients are not claiming accountability. Again, aside from certain identified conditions, therapists can make generalizations here because it is impossible for people to do negative behaviors 24 hours a day. Once exceptions have been identified, those exceptions can be amplified as in the following example to see how clients can become more accountable in the future.

Client: I was beaten when I was younger. The only way I know to handle my anger is to lash out—and it's mostly toward women.

Therapist: I'm sorry that you were beaten when you were younger. And it leads me to wonder about something your wife said yesterday. She said that last week, when she told you her paycheck was smaller than expected, you got as angry as she's ever seen you. Yet she said that you didn't take it out on her. How did you do that? What did you do instead?

Client: The drugstore was out of my medication. What was I supposed to do? It's the thing that calms me down.

Therapist: I'm a little confused. You said that your medication has been changed several times in the past few months—and while that was happening you managed to go without incident at work. Even though your medication wasn't regulated at that time, how were you able to keep yourself in check and at least to some degree, calm?

Client: It's a family thing. My father and uncles were alcoholics. I can't stop drinking—it's destiny.

Therapist: Your sense is that if it runs in the family, then you're predestined to have it run your life as well. And you mentioned last time that there was a period of time earlier this year when you didn't drink for a month. How do you stand up to destiny and take responsibility for yourself?

Now it is your turn. Please complete Exercise 7.3, Building Accountability, to further develop your skills in promoting accountability through language.

It is easy for therapists to become caught up in attempts to trigger sweeping changes with clients. Change can and often does happen quickly; however, the seeds of change are planted throughout therapy and sometimes need time to grow. By attending closely to how clients talk about their concerns, therapists can begin to identify ways in which they are inadvertently closing avenues of change. Language can offer possibilities in closed-down situations that clients have created through their statements.

Find Counterevidence to Problems

One way therapists can explore exceptions is to get clients (or others who know them) to provide examples that do not fit their problematic depictions and stories. To do this, therapists acknowledge clients and what they experience internally while working to identify evidence of alternative stories that counter problematic ones. For example, a therapist might say to a man who when angered has yelled at his wife and children, "So, you tell me that you were raised in a family in which the only way to express anger was through screaming and yelling. But I'm curious. You've mentioned your success in sales and I'm wondering, when you've been angry at work, have you screamed or yelled at your customers?" To a woman who is experiencing anxiety about taking an important exam, the therapist might

---

Exercise 7.3

Building Accountability

This exercise is to help identify client statements that may suggest nonaccountability—implying that clients did or do not have choice in how they behave. Practitioners keep in mind that although psychotropic medication and therapy, for example, can help clients *feel* better, they do not make decisions for clients, nor do they control behavior or actions. There are three ways to promote accountability in language. To complete this exercise, review each method and then following the examples, write your responses to the statements in the spaces provided.

- *Reflect back nonaccountability statements without the nonaccountability part.* When you hear a client use an excuse or explanation that conveys nonaccountability, repeat it while dropping the nonaccountability part.

Example

Client:	She kept talking trash, so I hit her.
Therapist:	You hit her.
Client:	He forgot to give me my medication, so I couldn't remember to come home on time.
Therapist:	You didn't come home on time.
Client:	I have ADD, so I couldn't do my homework.
Response:	_____
Client:	Alcohol is a disease, so how am I supposed to stop drinking?
Response:	_____

- *Find counterexamples that indicate choice or accountability.* Search for examples of clients behaving or acting in a way demonstrated accountability, thereby contradicting their claims of nonaccountability.

Examples

Client:	I can't help it; if I don't get my medicine, I can't control my anger.
Therapist:	I'm confused. Last Thursday you didn't get your medicine and you did a great job of controlling your anger. How did you do that?
Client:	I'll never get another job anyway, so why should I even try?
Therapist:	I must be missing something. How did you manage to get the past two jobs you've held?
Client:	If she makes me mad, she'll get what she deserves—a smack in the face.
Therapist:	_____
Client:	I can't help it; my teacher didn't remind me to bring my books home.
Therapist:	_____

(continued)

Exercise 7.3 *(continued)*

- *Use the word* and *to link together feelings and accountability.* Give clients permission to feel whatever they feel while holding them accountable for their behaviors and actions.

Examples

Client: He always makes me feel bad, so I call him names.

Therapist: It's okay to feel bad and it's not okay to call him names.

Client: My mom better change my curfew to midnight, or I'm going to be mad!

Therapist: You can be mad and you need follow the curfew your mom sets.

Client: If she would keep her mouth shut and not make me mad, I wouldn't go off on her.

Therapist: _____

Client: Drinking until I pass out helps me not feel sad.

Therapist: _____

---

say, "You've mentioned how this proficiency test has really raised your anxiety level and yet you've described how you managed to keep your focus and maintain a 3.97 GPA in college. How did you do that?" Another example is a parent who has described his son as being "out of control." The therapist might say, "You have said that he's out of control, and yet you mentioned that yesterday his teacher said he kept his cool when another boy taunted him in class." The following two examples demonstrate a search for counterevidence.

Father: (referring to his daughter) She never goes by the rules. In fact, I don't know why we even have rules. She doesn't think they apply to her.

Therapist: Your sense is that Jennifer really hasn't been up to par with the rules. Tell me a little about the particular rules she's broken that have been most bothersome.

Father: She doesn't do her chores. That's the main problem. I just can't get her to lift a finger.

Therapist: It seems like she hasn't helped out as much as maybe she should.

Father: Not at all. I'd settle for any effort at this point.

Therapist: OK, and when was the last time you can remember her pitching in?

Father: I don't know. Maybe a month ago she helped her mother with the dishes.

Daughter: A month ago! I did them yesterday! Are you blind?

Father: Wonders never cease. You should have done them anyway.

Therapist: (to daughter) Was that a fluke? Or do you sometimes do other things too and pitch in more?

Daughter: My room is always clean.

Therapist: Really? How do you keep it clean?

Daughter: It's easy. I just make sure I have it straight before I go to bed.

Therapist: Terrific. What else do you sometimes do?

Daughter: I take out the dog every morning.

Therapist: (to the father) Is that accurate?

Father: Well, yeah, she does. But she's responsible for doing those things.

Therapist: Right. There are some things that she's responsible for and it's been frustrating to you when she hasn't done them all. Is it safe to say that with some rules she shows more responsibility than others?

Father: Yeah, that's true.

The interchange began with the therapist acknowledging the father and tuning into his statements of impossibility (see Chapter 4). The therapist simultaneously introduced the element of possibility through subtle changes in language accompanied by a search for counterevidence. As the conversation progressed, evidence that contradicted the problematic story became apparent. This resulted in the emergence of an alternative story that created possible inroads for future change.

Client: It doesn't matter what I do, it's never good enough for my boss.

Therapist: It sounds like a tough situation. Please say more about that.

Client: I do my work. I turn it in on time, and I think I do a good job. He apparently doesn't see it that way. It's just not good enough for him and it's aggravating.

Therapist: I can see why it would be aggravating. It seems like whatever you've done to this point hasn't been good enough for him.

Client: Right. It just seems like no matter how I try, I always fall short.

Therapist: Is that something you would like to spend some time on?

Client: Yeah, I mean I don't like it.

Therapist: OK, tell me more about how this has affected you.

Client: Well, he gives me things to do at the start of each day and he always finds something wrong with each of them.

Therapist: Can you give me an example?

Client: Yeah, yesterday I handed in two charts that took me all day and he just ripped me up and down on the one on cost analysis.

Therapist: I'm sorry that happened to you. It sounds like a tough situation. (*client nods in agreement*). And I'm curious, what happened with the other chart that you turned in yesterday?

Client: He just glanced at it and then threw it into a pile.

Therapist: He didn't say anything. . . like you need to redo it?

Client: (pondering the question) Nope. No, he just tossed it in a pile.

Therapist: What did that mean to you?

Client: Well, that's kind of his way of saying that the work is acceptable.

Therapist: I see. So he's not the kind of person who really gives out praise. He just lets you know that the work is okay by not saying much about it.

Client: Right. He just ignores it.

Therapist: It sounds like sometimes your work passes through without him coming down on you. What do you suppose was different about the chart that he tossed into the pile yesterday and with those past assignments he didn't say much about—the ones that seem to pass his litmus test?

Client: I guess sometimes my work meets his expectations.

Therapist: Sometimes your work is up to par in his eyes—not as often as you'd like—but on occasion he's as pleased as he's going to be.

Client: That's right. I hadn't considered that.

Therapist: It doesn't mean that's as good as it gets—it just helps us both to understand that sometimes your work is up to par with your boss' standards. But from what you've said it's hard to know when that's the case whereas it's clear when he's unhappy.

Client: Precisely. And I'd really like to know how I can meet that standard more often.

Therapist: That sounds good. What will that do for you when it's happening more often?

Client: I'll be less frustrated, less aggravated.

Therapist: And what will be happening with you instead?

Client: I'll feel better and I think more satisfied with my job. And you know, I think it would help my attitude about the rest of my life.

Therapist: That makes sense to me and sounds like a terrific thing to work toward.

Client: That's what I think.

As in the previous example, the client in this illustration held a story that reflected impossibility. His view was that his work was never good enough for his boss, implying that this had been a pattern with his boss that would continue into the future. In response, the therapist did several things: acknowledged and validated the client, injected the idea of possibility into impossibility-laden statements made by the client, and—a crucial element—searched for and was able to find that there were times when the client's work was acceptable to his boss. With the counterevidence identified, the therapist inquired about the effect of such a change (as a means of identifying possible benefits). The therapist then subsequently used this opening to move the conversation forward to learn more about what the client wanted. To accomplish this, the therapist posed questions aimed at determining what the client wanted *instead* of what he did not want. As discussed in Chapter 5, this helps clients to achieve and progress as opposed to trying to rid themselves or their lives of something.

Starting in the present and working backward can be helpful in searching for counterevidence because the more recent the evidence that counters the problematic story, the more powerful it tends to be. Sometimes the therapist will need to go back a few weeks,

months, or even years to find such evidence. It is perfectly acceptable to explore the past as much as is necessary to search for counterevidence. Evoking general learning experiences that most people have had (for example, learning to read, write, ride a bike) can also be helpful. See the following example.

> When most people were very young, maybe in early grades like third, fourth, and fifth, they did a lot of learning in school. You see, one thing that I know about you is that you've been learning for many years. If that weren't true, you never would have learned your left hand from your right, the alphabet, and the difference between upper- and lowercase letters. You wouldn't have learned how to form words, to make sentences, and to read and write. Somehow you learned these things even when you thought they were so hard that you'd never figure them out. The thing is you've never stopped learning; it's just that now you're facing a new challenge.

After reorienting the client to some previous learning experience, the therapist can continue with questions such as, "How far back would you have to go to a time when you were doing better in [the particular activity]?" followed by "What do you remember doing that helped you to learn things that you didn't think you would ever learn?"; "How did you manage to learn things that you didn't think you would be able to learn?"; or "How far back would you have to go to find a time when things went just a little better in regard to the problem you're facing?" These questions help clients to notice what was different about times when they had some influence over the problem. They can be followed up with inquiries as to what the person *did* differently at those times, which can help to identify actions that the client undertook as a result of a different view. Often clients can then begin to utilize past actions that were helpful in managing the problem and moving in preferred directions. To practice searching for exceptions, please complete Exercise 7.4, Exception Seeking.

The idea of exception seeking is to be persistent and to work to evoke and elicit exceptions to problematic stories that represent abilities that have been covered up or gone unnoticed. These exceptions are important because getting clients to do what has worked for them in the past is generally easier than trying to teach them something completely new. If clients have already utilized skills in the past, as evidenced through exceptions, then they have demonstrated some ability in standing up to the influence of problems (Bertolino & O'Hanlon, 2002). At the same time, it is important to not become discouraged if questions for exceptions go unanswered. The goal is to have clients consider and reflect on times when things went differently from the problematic stories that have been dominating their lives. This process serves as a catalyst for clients challenging their own social constructions.

Draw Distinctions Between Multiple Statements, Multiple Actions, or Between Statements and Actions

Clients occasionally describe what they want to be different in their lives yet follow with actions that contradict those descriptions. In other situations, clients engage in actions that appear contradictory. For example, a client might get to work on time regularly but then consistently be late to the first meeting of the day. How therapists respond to such situations can make a significant difference in what happens next. From strengths-based perspective, such incongruities are not interpreted as client resistance, nor are they attended to as

lack of motivation or an unwillingness to change. They are seen simply as communication from clients with incongruities providing opportunities for therapists to subtly and respectfully draw out any inconsistencies between what clients say and what they do.

To do this, therapists avoid statements such as "You're saying [X] but you're doing [Y]" or "You're sabotaging yourself." Instead therapists assume a position of curiosity to learn more about clients' views and to subtly challenge any incongruities. Therapists respond with statements that highlight inconsistencies in the least inflammatory way. Examples include these:

- I usually understand things pretty well, but I must be missing something here. You've told me that you want to [X] in the future. But I need you to help me understand how doing [Y] is going to get you to where you want to be. What am I not getting right here?
- I've been trying to put this together in my mind, but it doesn't add up. You've described how [X] is important to you. I hear that loud and clear, yet what I'm seeing is [Y]. Those things seem at odds with one another. Can you help me to understand this better?
- You seem to have a plan, but others may not understand it as clearly as you do. How could you explain your plan for [X] in a way that others would get it?
- I've heard about so many things you've done to move yourself forward and in the midst of this seem to be these anomalies—things that don't fit with those changes. Have you noticed that?

The aim is to help clients to challenge their own views and corresponding actions. Sometimes this means helping clients to "save face."

Exercise 7.4

Exception Seeking

There are exceptions to problems. These are times when things have gone a little better or when problems have been less intrusive or absent altogether. To complete this exercise, follow the instructions and be sure to be specific with your answers, incorporating action-talk in your descriptions.

- First, write down today's date. Next, describe a problem. Then, on a scale of 1 to 10, with 1 representing the worst the problem could be and 10 representing no problem at all, rate the problem.

  Date: _____   Current Problem Rating: _____

  Problem: _____

  _____

- Over the course of the next two or three days (and up to a week), observe the problem that has been described.
- When the time has elapsed, look over the results and write your answers in the spaces provided.

  Date: _____   Current Problem Rating: _____

  What did you notice about the intensity of problem?

  _____

  _____

  _____

  Describe any moments when the problem wasn't as dominating or disruptive in your life. What specifically happened?

  _____

  _____

  _____

  If you had a difficult time with the previous question, how far back would you have to go to find a time when things went just a little better in regard to the problem you're facing? What happened? What did you do differently?

  _____

  _____

  _____

  What did you learn from your answers to the previous questions that might be helpful to you in the present?

  _____

  _____

  _____

  What might you do differently in facing your problem as a result of what you've learned?

  _____

  _____

  _____

Instead of imparting blame, practitioners create opportunities for clients to acknowledge what they have struggled to follow through with and to make necessary changes to be more successful. The following example illustrates this point.

Therapist: It seems that on one hand you've done some things that have really benefited you. You've stayed in school, raised your grades, and are now on a path to graduating. On the other hand, drinking and things like threatening others seem be lingering around and running interference from time to time. Have you noticed that?

Client: I guess. I don't know.

Therapist: It reminds me of the show "Sesame Street." Have you seen it?

Client: [Smiling and laughing]: Yeah.

Therapist: They have a skit where they sing, "One of these things is not like the other." To me, it seems like we have school and the gains you've made there and then we have the things that don't fit with that—drinking and making threats. Does that make sense?

Client: Yeah.

Therapist: Do you see any way that drinking and making threats benefit you?

Client: No, they don't.

Therapist: Okay, I just wanted to be sure I wasn't missing something.

In the process of drawing distinctions, following up with questions that evoke a sense of action can also be helpful:

- If you found that what you were doing wasn't working as well as you planned or was harder than you expected, what might you *think* about doing differently?
- If you were to *think* about making a change in your approach, how might you prepare yourself to follow through with it?

- What do you *think* would be a first step in making that happen?

Notice that these questions do not request that clients take action. They invite clients only to *think* about taking action. This is likely to create a better fit for clients who are not ready to take steps to make deliberate changes (for example, at the precontemplation or contemplation stages of change). In addition, even for clients who struggle to answer these questions, asking them can still be beneficial because clients think about what is asked, which is sometimes enough for clients to challenge any incongruities in their perspectives. This can open up new ways of viewing.

Use Splitting to Draw Distinctions

Another way to help clients to change their perspectives is to use splitting to draw distinctions between two things. *Splitting* involves taking aspects of a client's life or situation and creating separation between them. Therapists use numerous combinations such as distinguishing between the past and present, the present and future, "then and now," "this and that," the conscious and unconscious, and "inside and outside." For example, a therapist might ask, "What have you noticed about the way you were then and the way you are now?" or "When you consider where you are in school now and then fast forward to when you graduate and the opportunity to do what you've always dreamed about, what comes to mind?" The idea is for clients to notice the differences between things in their lives and how change is a constant factor. The following example is a brief client-therapist dialogue illustrating the use of splitting.

Client: Sometimes I really want to just get rid of those thoughts—the ones I have about my past relationship—but not always. Isn't that strange?

Therapist: It seems to me that it's just an indication of where you are.

Client: Probably so.

Therapist: At the same time, I was wondering, how about *keeping* the thoughts about your past relationship that are good for you and you *like* and *ridding* yourself of the ones that aren't good for you and you *don't like*?

Client: That's really interesting. I can keep what I want and let the rest go.

Therapist: That's right. And it's your decision as to which parts of the experience you want to keep and let go.

Find Alternative Stories or Frames of Reference That Fit the Same Evidence or Facts

Clients' stories are representations of their interpretations, explanations, and evaluations of themselves, others, events, or situations. When clients' stories become too restrictive, narrow, or problem saturated, they can close off the possibilities for change. These stories can be identified through both clients' statements and actions, which are consistent with closed-off views.

Problematic views are typically created over time through multiple experiences and interactions. It is important that therapists keep in mind that they are not trying to convince clients of (or "sell") new perspectives. They are *offering* new points of view that fit the same evidence or facts in an effort to dissolve problematic stories. In other words, therapists want to give clients the space to accept or reject all or part of the suggested interpretations.

In offering alternative stories or frames of reference, the therapist gives a more benevo-

lent interpretation through conjecture, which reflects a position of curiosity (Bertolino, 2003; Bertolino & O'Hanlon, 2002). Conjecture involves the use of phrasing that allows therapists to offer ideas without imposing them (see Chapter 4). This is typically done by beginning comments with sentence stems such as "I was curious" and "I wonder." In combining conjecture with interpretation, a therapist might say, "You've stated that you see your fear of large crowds as a weakness, something that interferes with you taking risks. From what you've described, it seems like there are times that it has stood between you and the opportunity to have new experiences. At the same time, I wonder if there are times that your anxiety acts as a safeguard of sorts—perhaps protecting you from taking leaps that may be a little too risky in a given moment."

Remember that therapists' stories are no more valid, correct, or true than clients' or vice versa; the point is that some stories open up possibilities whereas others close them down. Therapists focus on engaging in meaningful exchanges from which new stories of hope and possibility emerge and become the dominant narratives through which clients lead their lives. Another example of how a therapist might cultivate an alternative story is "You get the sense he just wants to do anything he wants when he wants to do it. And I'm wondering if he's trying to find a way to be independent and make his own decisions. When you come down hard on him, perhaps the only way he can see to show he's independent is to rebel and resist you, even if it gets him in trouble." In more traditional approaches to therapy, this method illustrated in the following example is sometimes referred to as *reframing*.

Adolescent: My mom doesn't have a clue about what's going on, but she thinks she does. What a joke! All she does is ground me and make rules and try to make my life miserable. If she wants me to hate her, she's doing a good job.

Therapist: It seems to you that your mother's mission is to put restrictions on you and make your life miserable.

Mother: I've tried to raise him to be respectful of others and look at the result! It's a rare day when he goes by the rules. All he does is fight with me. I'm very bitter about it.

Therapist: You've tried hard and it seems that your efforts to teach him so far haven't been as successful as you'd like—things haven't gone the way you'd like yet. I can see how that might make you bitter.

Mother: I am.

Therapist: (to adolescent) You know, your mom hasn't raised a 16-year-old boy before, and you haven't been a 16-year-old before. I wonder if your mom is doing what she thinks is best for you, and that maybe she will need some further education about what it's like to be a teenager in this day and age. No matter the age, we keep on learning. (to mother) You mentioned before that you have a 19-year-old daughter who is doing well. Perhaps you're finding out that it can be different to raise daughters and sons. Some of the things you've tried haven't worked and some have—because on those rare days you get through to him. So I'm wondering if you're still making the adjustments in raising a 16-year-old son versus a 16-year-old daughter.

The subtlety of introducing new interpretations is essential. Clients who get the sense that their experiences or views are being given short shrift or trivialized are more likely to close down. The way interpretations are offered is as important as the interpretations themselves. For this reason, it is important to employ ways to monitor the therapeutic alliance as a means of gauging how direct or indirect the introduc-

tion of an alternative story ought to be. When effective, a new interpretation of the same evidence or facts can lead to a new perspective for clients. If clients change their frames of reference, their actions are more likely to be in accord with those views. For example, a father who believes that his son's behavior is a result of manipulation will act in one way. However, if the same father sees his son's behavior as an indication that he needs more affection from his father, the father is likely respond in another way. Practitioners want to help clients to subscribe to views that will generate creativity, change, and possibilities.

Sometimes problematic stories become so entrenched and embedded in clients' lives that it becomes hard to see anything but the problems. When people seek or are referred for therapy, one of the major concerns is that they have started to organize their views of themselves and others' views of them as their illnesses. Pathologized people behave pathologically. The job of the therapist is to help such clients to change their views and to see and experience themselves as capable and accountable (Bertolino & O'Hanlon, 2002). Being treated with dignity can make all the difference. To practice finding alternative stories, please refer to Exercise 7.5, What's the Story?

Search for Hidden Strengths

At the heart of a strengths-based approach is the ongoing emphasis on learning about capabilities and resources. Chapter 5 discussed various ways to identify clients' strengths during information-gathering processes and use them to promote to change. Therapists can also search clients' lives to find out about hidden or nonobvious aspects that do not fit or are incompatible with their disempowered (hopeless, helpless, or stuck) views about themselves or their problems.

Exercise 7.5

What's The Story?

Because clients typically act in ways that are consistent with their views, their interpretations, explanations, and evaluations of themselves, others, events, or situations can close down the possibilities for change. The purpose of this exercise is to subtly challenge the problematic perspectives clients hold by offering new, alternative ones that have possibilities for change. If clients change their frames of reference, their actions are more likely change according to those views. It is important to note that alternative viewpoints are not stated as facts or truths but as possibilities. Therefore, clients have the space to accept or reject all or part of others' interpretations. To complete this exercise, please write the answer to the following questions in the spaces provided.

- Describe a problem. Be specific with your answers, incorporating action-talk in your descriptions.

  _____
  _____
  _____

- What explanation do you have for the problem(s) you just described?

  _____
  _____
  _____

- How does this explanation influence the approach to solving the problem?

  _____
  _____
  _____

- What other possible explanations might be worth consideration regarding the same problem? List five alternative explanations for the problem. Be creative.

  1. _____
  2. _____
  3. _____
  4. _____
  5. _____

- Go through the list of alternative explanations and rule out those that a neutral person would judge to be less than 50 percent likely.

- For each alternative explanation, list two ways that the behavior associated with the problem might change if this explanation were adopted.

  1. _____
     a. _____
     b. _____

Exercise 7.5 *(continued)*

2. _____
   a. _____
   b. _____
3. _____
   a. _____
   b. _____
4. _____
   a. _____
   b. _____
5. _____
   a. _____
   b. _____

- For each behavior change you listed in the preceding item, write what might be the effect of changing the behavior in that way right now.

1. _____
   a. _____
   b. _____
2. _____
   a. _____
   b. _____
3. _____
   a. _____
   b. _____
4. _____
   a. _____
   b. _____
5. _____
   a. _____
   b. _____

- To experiment and test alternative explanations, for the next few days or week, select one new explanation and try acting "as if" that explanation were true regarding the problem. Trying out alternative explanations or theories might bring about a different result with the problem. If one explanation does not lead to the desired outcome, try another. Pay close attention to those explanations that lead to the results for which you are looking.

By tuning their ears to the sounds of hope and possibility, therapists often hear things during the course of conversations or sessions that contradict the views that clients have of themselves or others have of them, such as being out of control, unable to change, or irresponsible. The process is similar to finding a picture of a polluted urban scene and noticing a pristine mountain lake stuck in the middle or sitting with a client who is wearing extremely wrinkled clothing but an exceptionally well-ironed tie that was put on perfectly. Therapists need to train themselves to notice what is right with clients (and what does not fit with the problematic stories).

Examples of questions that do this might include these. "You mentioned that your house is a mess. And yet in the picture I saw of you in your home office, I noticed how clean your desk was. How did you manage to keep it so clear?" To a client who has poor, nearly illegible handwriting and who says, "I just can't write!" the therapist could search for small indicators in his writing that show a hidden strength: "Take a look at that letter *g*. And also at that *j*. They are both well-formed letters and they sit well on the line. How were you able to write those two letters so well?" In searching for hidden strengths, therapists ask clients or those close to them how they explain the incompatibility. From there the practitioner can work to amplify and extend those aspects so that the exceptions begin happening more and more often. Upcoming chapters explore this further.

Foster the Person of the Client: The Q-As of Resilience

Time after time, clients demonstrate the ability known as *resilience* to face challenges that include managing, negotiating, and moving through difficult times, often marked by adversity. This ability refers to the positive role of individual differences in people's responses to stress and adversity. Everyone has the capacity to be resilient, yet it is most frequently identified with people who have lived or grown up in adverse conditions (for example, low economic resources, underprivileged circumstances, high-crime areas, abusive environments). Despite what sometimes appear as insurmountable circumstances and odds, such persons manage not only to survive but also in many cases thrive later in life (Wolin & Wolin, 1993). See Case Example 7.1 for an example.

Resilience is an aspect of client factors which is the largest contributor to outcome. Although resilience is acknowledged as being important to change, it is sometimes overlooked or missed in part because therapists focus on large, sweeping moments and examples of resilience. Although some examples are obvious and represented through ongoing life themes, more often resilience is evident in specific situations and contexts. To ensure that they identify it, therapists are encouraged to explore clients' lives for small, everyday indicators as opposed to more global ones.

Tapping into resilience has two components: (1) searching for *qualities* of resilience and (2) finding out about the *actions* that resulted from being resilient. Orienting clients toward these aspects of themselves and associated actions can help them to change their views of themselves and their situations and to use those resources to deal with future adversity. These questions can be asked to assist in identifying these components of resilience:

Resilience Qualities

- What qualities do you possess that you are able to tap into in times of trouble?

CASE EXAMPLE 7.1

I worked with a 12-year-old boy, Kelvin, who was in an outpatient psychiatric program. Prior to my involvement, he had been seen by more than 25 psychiatrists, psychologists, and therapists over a period of six years. Kelvin had been assigned different diagnoses at different times, which more often than not meant changes to his psychotropic medications. He had also been psychiatrically hospitalized five times. The youth continued in services due to persistent behavioral problems at home and at school.

Kelvin faced numerous challenges within his family. His mother had been diagnosed with several moderate to severe psychiatric disorders, including psychosis. Her emotional struggles were evident during therapy sessions. In addition, Kelvin's father battled severe alcoholism and was dealing with an assortment of ongoing health problems. The family also faced housing and financial stressors.

Despite the numerous factors posing challenges, Kelvin demonstrated remarkable resilience and ability to care for himself and, at times, others in the family. He reminded his mother of his appointments at the clinic and dealt with her unpredictable behavior on a daily basis. He helped his father even though he was frequently embarrassed by his episodes of drinking. Kelvin seemed to know how to get the help he needed, routinely seeking out people he knew could be counted on for support and help. These included teachers, neighbors, friends, and mental health professionals. Kelvin became known at the clinic for standing up to adversity. He not only met many of the challenges he faced but also progressed in therapy, overcoming the behavioral concerns that led to his initial referral. Kelvin mined his own resourcefulness, and in doing so, taught his parents and others how to do the same.

- What is it about you that enables you to keep going when you're facing everyday challenges?
- What comes to the forefront when you're facing difficult situations/problems?
- What is it about you that allows you to keep going despite all that you've faced?
- What would others say are the qualities that you have that keep you going?
- Who are you that you've been able to face up to the challenges that life has presented you?
- What does it say about you that you are able to face adversity?
- What kind of person are you that you are willing to stand up to life's challenges?

Actions Informed by Resilient Qualities

- What have the qualities that you possess allowed you to do that you might not have otherwise done?
- Given the type of person that you are, what do you do on a regular basis to manage the challenges that you face?
- How have you managed, in the midst of all that's happened, to keep going? How specifically have you done that?
- Tell me about a time when you were able to deal with something that could have stopped you from moving forward in life. What did you do?
- When you're feeling like things are becoming more difficult than usual, what

do you do to keep things from getting worse and to get back on track?

In asking questions such as these, therapists are not trying to convince clients of their resilience, nor are they implying or suggesting that clients should just take stock of their qualities and all will be well. Doing so would be invalidating to people who are suffering and in pain. Instead, clients convince therapists of their resilience through their actions, past or present, which are revealed through their answers to questions. This is why the questions listed here are designed to elicit and evoke from clients their inner qualities and the actions they have taken. Clients do their own self-inventories and tap into their personal resources. This allows them to shift views and attribute change or "control" to their personal qualities, internal abilities and resources, and actions (Bertolino & O'Hanlon, 2002).

Identify Valuing Witnesses

In the U.S. version of the movie *Shall We Dance,* a wife (Susan Sarandon) thinks her husband (Richard Gere) is having an affair and hires a private investigator to follow him. The PI learns that the husband is actually taking lessons in ballroom dancing. In the scene where the PI informs the wife what he has found out, the conversation turns to the idea of marriage. The wife asks, "Why do you think people get married?" The detective replies, "Passion." She disagrees and goes on to tell the man that she believes people need a "life witness." She states that people need others who will be present, take notice, and witness all the ups and downs that occur throughout life.

This notion has broad implications that extend beyond marriage. People are social beings and need some degree of connection with others. Connections can and often do vary and change over time, yet what remains constant is the need for others to be part of our lives. For clients, this translates to relationships with others who see them as capable and support them. Life witnesses, or *valuing witnesses,* as we refer to them here, are social supports who can be from the past or the present. They are people who can see beyond the problem to the person or who can remember the person before the problem occurred. Valuing witnesses can be friends, family members, teachers, coaches, or other meaningful short- or long-term acquaintances. The length of their involvement is not as important as the meaning that valuing witnesses bring to others' lives. Case Example 7.2 illustrates this point.

CASE EXAMPLE 7.2

While doing contract work for a local community mental health agency, I worked with youth who had been labeled severely emotionally disturbed (SED). Many of these children and adolescents had been given up on by other providers. Fourteen-year-old Quinton was referred to me after his family had moved to the area. The family lived in three different states over a period of two years, seeking mental health services (for example, individual and family therapy, psychiatric services) at each new place of residence due to Quinton's behavior. They had been through traditional office-based family therapy, intensive

CASE EXAMPLE 7.2   (continued)

home-based services, and medication management. Not even contacts with local law enforcement and the family (juvenile) court seemed to make a difference.

According to his mother, each time Quinton entered a new school, he would "have enemies within five minutes." He had been in numerous physical fights with classmates and neighborhood youth and had verbal altercations with school staff. He also had mostly failing grades, had been caught stealing, and would frequently come in after curfew. Quinton had been suspended from school 11 times in two years; his parents felt hopeless about the future.

While working with the family, I explored many different avenues. At times, Quinton appeared to have turned the corner and would do better for short periods of time, usually a week or two. However, it appeared to be two steps forward and three steps backward. Just when it seemed that things had improved, Quinton would get into a fight or some other type of serious trouble.

On one spring afternoon, Quinton and I were sitting on the front porch of his home when a purple truck pulled into the driveway across the street. This clearly sparked his attention. As man stepped out of the truck, Quinton yelled, "Hey Cole, what's up?" The man turned, waved, and replied, "Not much. Come on by later." When I asked Quinton who the man was, and he answered, "He's cool. He helps me out sometimes. I just like hanging out at his house."

After talking with Quinton, I asked his mother about Cole. I found out that Cole was in his mid-thirties, was married, and had a young child. Quinton's mother said, "He spends a lot of time over there and Cole doesn't seem to

mind. It's weird, but Quinton really listens to him and respects him." I then asked the mother if I could have permission to talk with Cole. I made it clear that Cole did not have to know the details of Quinton's trouble but suggested that since Quinton seemed to respond well to Cole, he might be a good resource. Quinton's mother readily agreed and signed a consent form giving me permission to talk with Cole.

The next day I met Cole after he arrived home from work. I introduced myself and said, "I've been working with Quinton and his family because things haven't been going so well lately. And the reason I've come to you is because I understand that Quinton really looks up to you." Cole smiled and added, "Well, he does spend a lot of time over here, and we like having him here." I followed, "It seems to me that he really gets something from his relationship with you, and even though I have no idea what that is, I think it could be a calming resource for Quinton. And what I'd like to know is, would you be willing to continue to be that positive influence in his life and perhaps teach him what you know about dealing with trouble and conflict?" I did not need to be any more specific. Cole knew what I was getting at. He smiled and replied, "I'd be happy to."

The events that transpired over the course of the next few weeks were remarkable. Quinton's behavior changed dramatically. His fighting stopped completely. He made more of an effort at school as evidenced by the elimination of suspensions and improved grades. He began helping out with his younger sister and coming home on time. Six weeks following the conversation with Cole, Quinton transitioned out of therapy.

The client's world outside of therapy is a powerful resource. Composed of significant others (for example, family, partner, friends, spiritual advisors, teachers, co-workers, classmates, scout leaders, coaches) and community resources, valuing witnesses are sometimes identified through conversations with clients. At other times, therapists need to ask about them. The questions can help to find out about such persons.

- Who have you met in your life that knew or knows exactly what you've been going through? How does he/she know that about you? How has knowing that he/she understood been helpful to you?
- Whom do you look up to? Why?
- Who has helped you through tough times? How?
- Whom do you feel you can count on?
- Who has the right idea about you?
- When you're struggling, who knows just what to say or do to get you back on track?
- What has this person(s) said to you in the past that was helpful?

If clients have a difficult time identifying people, searching for what they have found helpful rather than the helpful people themselves can be useful. A question to ask about this is "When things were going better for you, how did others make a difference in your life?" Through this form of inquiry, therapists can get an idea of what made a difference for clients and then work to establish possibilities in other contexts that could lead to positive connections. For example, therapists could suggest that clients become involved in activities that they previously enjoyed or might enjoy (for example, sports, clubs, hobbies, arts, support groups).

If valuing witnesses are available, they can be invited to sessions or meetings so the practitioner can get some evidence for this more hopeful, healthy view of clients. This method is akin to the idea of giving "living eulogies" when people come together to honor and speak about people *while they are still alive* (Albom, 1997). If witnesses are not available in person, clients can be asked to stand in for them. The practitioner might ask, for example, "If your best friend were here, what would she be able to tell me about the Sophia who was here long before schizophrenia arrived in your life? What kind of person is that Sophia?" The intent is to focus on what the relationship symbolized for the client.

In some instances, practitioners can help clients to connect with valuing witnesses. For example, they might talk about how in some cultures individuals who have passed on are seen as consultants who are available when people are struggling. Others might also be able to offer some of the same relational and supportive qualities that were important to the client. The practitioner might say, "You said that your mother was a person who understood you better than anyone else. She would let you know when you were out of line, but she did it in a loving way. Is that something you would like to experience again in the future?"

Through identification of valuing witnesses, therapists utilize and strengthen clients' social support systems and help to introduce new ideas to shift their views. An additional benefit is that the presence of valuing witnesses can help to both normalize and destigmatize. Because clients can feel increasingly isolated (and actually be isolated when experiencing problems), connections to others who have witnessed different aspects of their lives can let them know that they are not "mental," "crazy," or otherwise. Likewise, connecting clients with others who have had comparable experiences and have found alternative ways to think about them or deal with them can be helpful. Books, tapes, letters, and support groups can provide these types of connections. Whatever the mode, connections can help normalize the experience.

Life Stories Rewritten

A common thread in this book has been the idea of stories. People construct stories about themselves and others and interact with one another based on those stories. Therapists' aim is to help clients challenge problematic stories that suggest oppression, hopelessness, and impossibility. Because people can change, therapists hope that interactions with clients will help them to write new life stories that move them toward futures full of possibilities. This section discusses another way to help clients rewrite their lives with the idea of stories serving the backdrop. This helps clients to separate themselves from their problems through *externalizing conversations*.

The Person Is Not the Problem: Using Externalizing Conversations

One of the potential hazards of problematic views and stories is that they can take on a life of their own. It is as if people actually become their problems and in the process are depersonalized in some way. This situation is often evidenced by statements in which clients identify themselves as problems. They may use labels (for example, bipolar, alcoholic, ADD) or words (for example, *evil, crazy, mean*) with negative connotations that imply they are characterologically flawed or "bad." This also occurs when others refer to clients as problems

through negative descriptions such as, "He's crazy" or "Didn't you know she's borderline?"

As discussed, clients' stories represent the meanings they have created through relationships and interactions with others. Stories are never exact representations of clients' lives and often leave out crucial details and distort others. When stories become problem saturated, they can have debilitating effects. To cast doubt on negative stories and grow new stories of hope, practitioners can use a process referred to as *externalization* or *externalizing the problem* (White & Epston, 1990). This method helps clients to *restory* or reauthor their lives in ways that honor them and open up possibilities for change. It is especially useful when people already have diagnoses and labels, particularly ones that have not been empowering, validating, or facilitative of the change process (Bertolino & O'Hanlon, 2002).

Externalization is based on a crucial premise: *The person is never the problem; the problem is the problem*. Externalization can be a powerful process for empowering people to challenge the dominant stories about themselves, those around them, and society at large. Problems are considered manifestations of language and interaction that, in the worst cases, rob people of their character and personhood. Practitioners must acknowledge the power of labels while both avoiding the trap of reinforcing people's attachment to them and letting them escape responsibility for their behavior. By engaging in conversations that externalize problems, therapists can offer a way for clients to view themselves as having parts that the symptom has not contaminated. This automatically creates a view of clients' lives as nondetermined and accountable for the choices they make *in relationship* to problems.

Although therapists learn how to construct conversations that separate people from their problems, it is important to clarify that externalization is not a method per se. It is a *process* and the primary way through which narrative therapists facilitate change. Externalization is a way to create therapeutic conversations in which people are able to view themselves as separate from problems in order to challenge actions, interactions, and ways of thinking that are blaming or unhelpful. Through these conversations, people change their relationships with problems, allowing for the emergence of new views and stories.

Externalization can be used with individuals, couples, families, and groups (Freedman & Combs, 1996; Freeman, Epston, & Lobovits, 1997; Smith & Nylund, 2000; White, 2007). For the purposes of illustration, the process of externalization has been broken down into seven parts. It is possible to use different parts independently, depending on what fits best for clients.

1. *Collaborate with the person, couple, and/or the family to come up with a mutually acceptable name for the problem.* At various points in conversations with clients, their concerns and problems begin to become clearer and take shape. As conversations progress, the therapist's first task in externalizing is to clarify problems and give them names that best describe them. Naming problems most often emerges from conversations and in particular, the language used by clients. Through attentive listening, therapists identify key words clients use to refer to their concerns and then deliberately employ those words to begin personifying the problem.

For example, if a client says, "I'm just a depressed person," the therapist might say, "It sounds like Depression has made in-roads into your life." With an adolescent whose parent has said, "He's always getting into trouble," a response could be, "So am I correct in saying that Trouble has found a way to interfere in your son's life?" With a child who has been having temper tantrums a therapist might ask, "So, Anger has been convincing you to throw yourself on the floor and kick your feet, huh?" Some clients may persist in attributing the problem to themselves. In these situations, therapists are careful to not impose a shift in language. Instead the therapist gently persists, linguistically severing the person from the problem label so that the client can begin to take on the externalized view of problems.

Most names are derived directly from conversations; common ones are "Anorexia," "Anxiety," "Fighting," and "Anger." With younger clients, creativity can be a bonus. Names may be clever and humorous and involve playful discussion. Here are some examples that have been generated in therapy conversations:

- Depression—"the Downs"
- Temper tantrums—Mr. Tantrum
- Trouble sitting still—Ants (in my pants)
- Truancy—Ms. I. B. Truant
- Incomplete homework—Ms. Ing Homework

2. *Personify the problem and attribute bad intentions and tactics to it.* With the problem named, the process of externalization continues; the therapist talks with the person or family as if the problem were another person with an identity, will, tactics, and intentions that are designed to oppress or dominate the person or the family. For example, a client might be asked, "How long has Cocaine been hanging out with you?" Other examples might be "How long has Anorexia been lying to you?" or "When did Fighting first make an appearance in your life?" Here are some other questions to assist with this part of the process:

- How long has [X] been trying to convince you to lead a life you don't agree with?
- When did [X] first start appearing and running interference in your life?
- When did you first notice [X] lingering around and making noise?
- How long has [X] been recruiting you into a life that you don't want?

This part of the externalization process helps free clients and those around them from identifying the clients as the problems. Further separating clients from problems can involve a de-identifying effect in which problems are seen as challenges and threats to clients and *who* they are as persons. Externalizing questions separate clients' identities from problems and attribute bad and tricky intentions to those problems. This allows clients to transfer any energy previously used for defending themselves to standing up to the problems.

3. *Investigate how the problem has been disrupting, dominating, or discouraging the person, couple, and/or the family.* For problems to be problems, they must in some way interfere with certain aspects of clients' lives. In this part of the externalization process, therapists explore how clients have felt overwhelmed or dispirited by problems. Using externalization, therapists ask the persons in the room about the effects of the problem on the client and on themselves. This acknowledges each person's suffering and helps the therapist to better understand the extent to which his or her life and relationships have been limited by the problem. It also provides other opportunities to externalize the problem by asking more questions. These questions seek to understand the deepening of the

personification of the problem and the relationship between the client and the problem. Examples of questions therapists might use follow.

- How does Fighting convince you to do something you really know isn't right?
- What kinds of tricks does Anorexia use on your daughter to alienate her from those she loves?
- When Jealousy has found its way into your life, what kinds of thoughts does it lead you to?
- What kind of lies has Depression been telling you about your worth as a person?

These general questions can help with this part of the externalizing process.

- What tactics does [X] usually use to recruit you into a life you really don't want?
- How has [X] come between you and your [family/friends, etc.]?
- When has [X] tricked you into something that you later got in trouble for?
- How do you know when [X] is lingering around about to convince you to do something you shouldn't?

The use of language is a crucial point in learning about the effects of problems. Practitioners do not use language that is deterministic or suggests nonaccountability. Problems never *cause or make* people do anything; they only *influence, invite, tell, try to convince, trick,* or *recruit.* This type of language highlights people's choices and creates an assumption of accountability rather than blame or determinism. If the person is *not* the problem but has a certain relationship to the problem, the relationship can change. If the problem invites rather than forces, the person can turn down the invitation. If the problem is trying to recruit a client, he or she can refuse to join. An additional benefit of this process is it can increase the motivation between those involved with the therapy. The client, others, and the therapist can come together with the common goal of overthrowing the problem and its dominance in their lives.

4. *Discover moments when clients have not been dominated or discouraged by problems or their lives have not been disrupted by them.* This pivotal point involves therapists talking with clients and others who may be involved about moments of choice or success that have occurred in regard to the problem. These moments represent times when clients have not been dominated or cornered by problems and experienced things they did not like. Referred to as *unique outcomes* (White & Epston, 1990), such moments represent exceptions—times when clients have had the upper hand or stood up to problems, using their strengths and abilities to do so. Examples of questions/requests that explore unique outcomes follow.

- Tell me about a time when you haven't believed the lies Anorexia has told you and withstood to its attempts to draw you in.
- When have you been able to deny Depression from invading an event you were looking forward to?
- When have you seen Johnny stand up to the Temper Tantrum Monster?
- What's the longest time you have stood up to Cravings?
- When have you been able to stand up to [X]?
- What would be an example of a time that [X] was demanding your attention but you ignored it?
- When has [X] whispered in your ear but you didn't listen?

- Tell me about a time when you noticed [X], pushed it aside, and maintained the upper hand with it.
- Tell me about times when [X] couldn't convince you to [action].

By highlighting moments when the problem has not happened or when it has been successfully overcome, clients can begin to notice the influence they have over their problems versus the influence problems have over them. This process of separating clients from problems can create new social realities that reflect hope and possibilities.

5. *Find historical evidence to bolster the view of people as competent enough to have stood up to, defeated, or escaped from the dominance or oppression of problems.* The previous steps serve as the groundwork for this step. With identified moments when clients stood up to problems, therapists begin to help transform or rewrite clients' identity and life stories. The strengths, abilities, and exceptions gleaned from preceding conversations serve as a gateway to a parallel universe, one in which clients have life stories in which they are competent and heroic. To maintain the genuineness of these conversations and to prevent them from becoming simple reframings of clients' lives, therapists ask for stories and evidence from the past to show that clients were competent, strong, and spirited but did not always realize it or put much emphasis on that aspect of themselves. Therapists also invite clients and others involved to support and flesh out these views.

Searching for historical evidence involves finding out about the resilient *qualities* of clients that have allowed them to stand up to problems. This means learning about *who* clients are, drawing attention to change in clients' perceptions of self and in their identity stories. In addition to those offered previously, questions such as these help to learn about clients' qualities.

- What qualities do you possess that have helped you to stand up to [X]'s plans for you?
- Who are you so that you were able to reject [X]'s taunting?
- How do you explain that you are the kind of person who would lodge a protest against [X]?
- What is it about [X] that he/she was able to go on strike against [action]?
- What kind of person is [the client's name] so that he/she has been able to take his/her life back from the grasps of [X]?
- What other examples truly show the kind of person you are—the kind of person who knows when it's time to take a stand?

New stories can have a powerful impact on clients' current and past views of themselves. Therapists therefore ask questions that encourage clients to revisit past conceptualizations in ways that allow new stories of hope, change, and possibilities to take root. Here are some questions to help with this:

- What is it about your experiences in life that have aided you in rejecting [X]'s advances?
- What can you tell me about your past that would help me understand how you've been able to take these steps to stand up to [X] so well?
- Who knew you as a child/teenager/young adult and wouldn't be surprised that you've been able to reject [X] as the dominant force in your life?
- What do you think [person' name] would say if he/she could hear you talk about standing up to [X]?

- Who is someone who has known all along that you had the wherewithal to take your life back from the grasp of [X]?

6. *Evoke speculation from the person, couple, and/or the family about what kind of future is to be expected for the strong, competent person, couple, and/or the family that has emerged from the interview.* As new client stories take shape and become dominant, therapists help clients to speculate on what future developments will result now that client see themselves as being competent and strong. They also explore what changes will result as the clients keep resisting the invitations of problems.

- As you continue to stand up to [X], what do you think will be different about your future than the future [X] had planned for you?
- As [name of person] continues to disbelieve the lies that [X] have been telling him/her, how do you think that will affect his/her plans for the future?
- As [name of person] continues to stand up to [X], how do you think that will affect his/her relationships with family members?
- As you continue to keep the upper hand with [X], what do you think will be different about you compared to what [X] had planned for you?
- How do you think your strategy with [X] will help you in the future?
- What other possibilities do you see for yourself as you put [X] to rest?

As described at different junctures throughout this book, conjecture provides an excellent way to ask questions in a nonimposing manner. By speculating about possible changes and benefits, therapists further crystallize clients' new views of themselves and others' views of them.

7. *Find or create an audience for perceiving the new identity and new story.* The final part of the externalization process involves situating new stories in larger social relationships and contexts. Because clients' problematic stories developed in social contexts, therapists arrange for the social environment to be involved in supporting new stories or identities that have emerged in conversations. Possibilities for this include using letters, asking for advice for other people suffering from the same or similar problems, and arranging meetings with family members and friends. Questions that can assist with this include these:

- Who are people who have known you when you were not under the influence of [X] who could remind you of your accomplishments and that your life is worth living?
- Who else needs to know about the stance you've taken against [X]?
- Who would not be surprised to learn that you have gained the upper hand with [X]?
- Who needs to know that you've made a commitment to keep [X] from hanging out without parental permission?
- Who could benefit from knowing about your de-enlistment in the [X] club?

The idea is to continue until new stories have taken hold in clients' lives. This is evidenced in two ways: (1) Clients start viewing themselves in new, more competent ways, even when outside therapists' direct influence and (2) others report that things are changing for the better in relation to problems. This may happen within a few sessions or after a more extended process. To gain a better sense of how externalizing conversations unfold, you are invited to complete Exercise 7.6, Externalizing Problems.

Even though the steps described were presented linearly, externalization is a process that evolves over the course of therapy. Case Example 7.3 demonstrates its use as a process.

As discussed, if externalization is approached purely as a technique, it will probably not produce profound effects. It is necessary that therapists see problems as social and personal constructions that are changeable through language and interaction. In addition, externalizing language must fit with clients. Some clients will struggle with it and if it does not take, therapists should try something else. It is also possible to employ this unique way of using language without subscribing to the entire process. Subtle changes in language can help clients to gain a different view on problems.

Exercise 7.6

Externalizing Problems

Problems can take on lives of their own. In some cases, it can even seem as if people have actually become their problems. This implies that people are characterologically flawed or "bad." The person is never the problem. The problem is the problem. One way to change stories and views of problems is through the use of *externalizing conversations.* This exercise can help people begin to view themselves as separate from problems and, in the process, experience new relationships with problems allowing for the emergence of a new views and stories. To complete this exercise, take a moment to consider the following questions. Then write your responses in the spaces provided.

Exercise 7.6 (continued)

- *Name the problem.* Either as an individual or as part of a group, give the problem a name that accurately depicts it. The problem can be named with a straightforward description (e.g., Anger, Fighting, Overeating) or through a representation (e.g., Miss Fits, Mr. Temper Tantrum, The Troubles).

_____

- *Personify the problem and attribute bad intentions and tactics to it.* Consider how the problem has made its way into your life. (*Note:* The problem never *causes or makes* the person or the family to do anything; it only *influences, invites, tells, tries to convince, uses tricks, tries to recruit, etc.*)

Examples:

How long has [X] been trying to convince you to lead a life you don't agree with?
When did s [X] first come over to visit without permission?
When did you first notice s [X] lingering around and making noise?

_____

_____

_____

_____

- *Investigate how the problem has been disrupting, dominating or discouraging you and/or your family.* How have you felt dominated or forced by the problem or experienced things you didn't like. Be sure that each person who is involved has the opportunity to speak about the effects of the problem on him or her.

Examples:

How has [X] come between you and your family/friends, etc?
When has [X] recruited you into doing something that you later got in trouble for?
What intentions do you think [X] has for you?

_____

_____

_____

_____

- *Discover moments when the person or persons haven't been dominated or discouraged by the problem or have not been disrupted by the problem.* Describe moments of choice or success that there have been in regard to the problem.

Examples:

When have you been able to stand up to [X]?
When has [X] whispered in your ear but you didn't listen?
Tell me about times when [X] couldn't convince you to [take a specific action]?

(continued)

Exercise 7.6 *(continued)*

_____

_____

_____

_____

- *Find evidence from the past to support a new view of the person or persons as competent enough to have stood up to, defeated, or escaped from the dominance or oppression of the problem.* Search for stories and evidence from the past to show that the person was actually competent, strong, spirited, but didn't always realize it.

Examples:

What qualities do you think you possess that help you to stand up to [X]'s plans for you?
Who are you so that you were able to reject [X]'s taunting?
How do you explain that you are the kind of person who would lodge a protest against [X]?
Who is someone who has known all along that you had the wherewithal to take your life back from [X]'s grasp?

_____

_____

_____

_____

- *Speculate about what kind of future is to be expected from the person or persons.* Speculate on what future developments will result now that the person or persons are seen as competent and strong and the changes that will result as he/she keeps resisting the problem.

Examples:

As [name] continues to stand up to[X], how do you think that will affect her relationships with family members?
As you continue to keep the upper hand with [X], what do you think will be different about _____, compared to what [X] had planned for you?
How do you think your strategy with [X] will help you in the future?

_____

_____

_____

_____

- *Find or create a way to share the new identity and new story with others.* Using letters, asking for advice for other people suffering from the same or similar problems, arranging for meetings with family members and friends, or through other means, consider ways that others can experience the new story that has evolved.

Exercise 7.6   (*continued*)

Examples:

Who else needs to know about the stance you've taken against [X]?

Who needs to know that you've made a commitment to keep [X] from hanging out without parental permission?

Who could benefit from knowing about your de-enlistment in the[X] club?

_____

_____

_____

_____

CASE EXAMPLE 7.3

Ten-year-old Gerard was referred to me as a result of problems at school. According to his mother, Gerard struggled to sit in his chair in class, bothered other children who were trying to do their work, made animal noises, and talked back to the teacher. These behaviors had been reportedly carried over from the previous year and were increasing.

Early in the therapy, I asked Gerard, "What do you think we should call this problem?" When he appeared puzzled by this question, I asked, Remember *The Grinch Who Stole Christmas?* Gerard nodded that he did. I followed, "At first, the Grinch was pushed around by grumpiness. What's pushing you around?" Without hesitation, Gerard replied, "My mom says I got Ants in my pants." It was agreed that Ants were the problem and interfered with his life.

It was learned that Ants had been convincing Gerard to get out of his chair without permission, move around the classroom, disrupt others, talk back to his teacher, and do things that lead him to lose privileges in school. Although the Ants were very convincing, Gerard believed they were lying to him because he was in fact, getting into trouble and missing recess and activities on a regular basis.

Gerard and his mother were asked what things would be like in the future when Gerard is no longer being pushed around by Ants. Gerard stated that he would get to go to recess and have friends. His mother remarked that she no longer would be called at work with reports that Gerard had been in trouble.

As therapy continued, I asked Gerard about times when he had stood up to Ants' attempts to lure him into trouble. He replied, "Sometimes I just sit there and don't want to play Ants' game." "Really? How do you do that?" I inquired. Gerard answered, "I listen to Ms. Miller [Gerard's teacher] and do my work." His mother added, "Every once in a while I get a really good report from school. His teacher will call and say how he did his work and followed directions. It's really nice to hear those things. I just wish it were more often."

With evidence of how Gerard had at times been able to stand up to Ants, we then talked about how to do this more in the future. In a matter of three weeks, reports from his teacher and mother confirmed that Gerard had regained his life from Ants. His new story was shared with other family members and school personnel and Gerard was given a certificate in "debugging" for exterminating Ants.

SUMMARY POINTS

- Views and perspectives include cognition, interpretations, evaluations, assumptions, what people notice or pay attention to, and stories about self and others.
- Views can both open up or close down possibilities for change; however, views differ from actions, which represent a more precise way to measure change over time.
- A focus on views is indicated when clients maintain one or more problematic stories including stories of impossibility, blame, invalidation, or nonaccountability/determinism.
- Cognition and attention are interrelated—a change in one affects change in the other.
- Questions aimed at changing views and perspectives are typically *exploratory* and are used for gathering information or are *generative* in facilitating the construction of new meanings.
- Questions tend to fall into four categories—*lineal, circular, strategic,* and *reflexive. Lineal* questions are straightforward and intended to gather facts. *Circular* questions are used to bring forth connections. *Strategic* questions

are used to propose different ways to view situations. *Reflexive* questions facilitate self-healing through the creation of new meanings.
- One way to encourage a change in views and perspectives is for therapists to focus on *exceptions,* which represent contexts in which things have gone differently in clients' lives.
- Therapists work with clients to identify exceptions through methods that include *building accountability through language, finding counterevidence to problems, finding alternative stories or frames of reference that fit the same evidence or facts, searching for hidden strengths, fostering resilience,* and *identifying valuing witnesses.*
- *Externalizing conversations* offer a way to help clients to view themselves as separate from their problems. Instead of *being* their problems, clients are encouraged to explore their *relationships* with problems including how problems influence their lives and how clients influence problems.

DISCUSSION QUESTIONS

1. What criteria suggest a focus on changing views and perspectives?

2. What are the four categories of questions outlined by Tomm? List two examples of each type of question.

3. What are the four problematic stories described in this chapter? Give an example of each.

4. Counterevidence, alternative stories, and hidden strengths are elements of one pathway for

changing views. What do they exemplify? What is important to keep in mind when exploring these avenues? Give three examples of questions that are aimed at changing views and perspectives in this manner.

5. What is meant by *externalizing the problem*? What is the main premise behind externalization?

Chapter 8

Changing Views and Perspectives, Part II

Patterns of Attention

■ Exceptions provide an important pathway into times when things have gone differently in regard to clients' concerns. By identifying and amplifying exceptions, therapists can help clients use their strengths and resources and exert the influence they have over their concerns. This chapter builds on the use of exceptions by focusing on ways that clients can shift some aspect of attention to change their views and perspectives. The chapter also explores other variations for changing views that tap into both clients' and therapists' creativity. The final segment discusses the use of conversational and consulting teams to stimulate new perspectives.

Shifts In Attention

Consider the following scenario:

You are sitting in a theater preparing to watch a movie that you have really been looking forward to. You arrive early to be sure that you get a good seat. As you wait patiently through the many minutes of commercials and previews leading up to the start of the movie, you gulp down a large drink. Then it hits you—you have the immediate urge to go to the bathroom. There is only one problem: The movie is starting! You are uncomfortable but decide to wait just a few minutes. The movie immediately grasps your attention as you become immersed in a riveting scene. And along the way a strange thing happens. You forget that you have to go to the bathroom. You have unknowingly diverted your attention and are absorbed in the scene. At a later point, the movie hits a bit of a lull and your attention shifts back to the sensation of having to go to the bathroom and you do so.

Milton Erickson reminded people who were in pain that parts of their bodies were not feeling any pain at a given moment. For example, if a patient of Dr. Erickson's was experiencing leg pain, he might orient the person's attention to an arm or hand and have him notice how that extremity felt. By shifting his attention, the patient would feel less pain. Why? Because when people have problems, part of how those problems stay the same is that they fixate their attention on them. Shifting attention is an effective strategy for many clients because they have become entrenched in the way they view their lives and situations, which in fact is creating or at least increasing the intensity of problems to some degree. Consider the following scenario as a way to further understand the role of attention:

> A professional baseball player was having a breakout season. He was leading the league in hitting and was on top of his game. After missing a couple of games with a brief bout of the flu, he returned to the diamond only to have his hitting tail off. At first he chalked up his struggles to recovering from illness. When he continued to slump at the plate, he decided to go back and watch videotape of his hitting. As the player watched tapes of himself striking out and hitting weak ground balls, he noticed that he was lunging at pitches. He vowed to correct this problem and during the next few games he worked on keeping his hands back and waiting on pitches. There was only one problem: his hitting did not improve. The player realized that he must have missed something on the videotape and returned to viewing games that he played in following his illness.
>
> After further analysis, he realized he was moving his feet too much. He could not believe that he had missed such an obvious thing. So he quickly took the steps to correct this habit as he played the next few games. Despite this "correction," his hitting continued to suffer, and he began to get more and more frustrated. Feeling as if he must still be missing something, he asked the team's hitting coach to watch a tape with him and perhaps give him a second opinion.

> The player turned on a videotape he had selected and sat back, waiting to hear the coach's advice.
>
> After a few seconds, the coach asked, "Why are we watching this?"
>
> "What do you mean? Haven't you noticed that I'm hitting poorly? I've got to review these tapes to figure out what I'm doing wrong. I thought you could help," explained the player.
>
> The coach replied, "How come you're spending time watching yourself taking poor swings and struggling? You ought to be watching tapes of yourself prior to when you got the flu—ones that show you playing the way that you're capable of. Study the tape that shows your ability. Study tape of you making good, sound, fundamental swings and hitting the ball the way you are capable of."
>
> The player had not thought of that before. He did as the coach had suggested and within a few short games his hitting was back on track again.

As you have learned, there are no "wrong" views; however, some are more helpful, healthy, and safer than others. For many clients, specific fixations of attention are largely responsible for the problems that brought them to therapy. Therapists serve as anthropologists, investigating where clients are focusing their attention, particularly during problematic times. They also explore where clients give attention when things are better. Therapists can help clients to shift their attention in several key realms. Although not an exhaustive list, the realms typically include:

- Time (past, present, or future)
- What clients (or others) do well rather than mistakes or problems
- Actions instead of explanations

- Sensory perceptions (visual, kinesthetic, auditory, gustatory, or olfactory)
- Internal or external focus

It is possible to work within multiple realms simultaneously although often a shift in one is sufficient to bring about a change in others. To determine which realms provide the best fit, practitioners work collaboratively with clients and pose their ideas tentatively. Conjecture has been identified as an excellent vehicle for asking questions, making interpretations, and offering new perspectives. Recall that conjecture reflects the therapist's position of curiosity or wonderment, offering alternative views as possibilities rather than "truths" or "facts." For example, a therapist might say to a client, "The next time you notice yourself drifting back to the time of the abuse, I was wondering if you might consider noticing what else was happening at that time in your life." In this way, clients can accept or reject what has been offered.

Practitioners merely suggest possibilities that clients can try as a way to change their attentional focus and then notice and learn from the clients whether these suggestions helped them solve the problems at hand and move toward their preferred futures. What follows in the next several sections is various ways to help clients shift their focus of attention by making changes in one or more of the key realms described.

Finding a Vision for the Future

A dominant theme born out of psychoanalytic thinking is that the past is the primary determinant in how people function in the present and will in the future. Contradicting this notion is a growing body of research (see Chapter 2) indicating that a future focus is an important component of change. This is also supported by numerous major models of therapy (for example, Adlerian, cognitive, behavioral, reality, solution-focused/oriented, strategic) that emphasize a present-to-future focus. These approaches suggest that it is not the events in people's lives that matter as much as their perceptions of those events and the meanings they attribute to them. Moreover, with a future vision, people's views of both the present and past can change.

One of the leading advocates of a future focus was the Viennese psychiatrist Viktor Frankl (1905–1997), the creator of an existential approach called *logotherapy* (see Frankl, 1963, 1969). He spoke of the importance of meaning in people's lives, which became a cornerstone of his work. In a keynote address at the second Evolution of Psychotherapy conference in 1990 in Anaheim, California, Frankl spoke about meaning and a future focus as he told the compelling story of his life. He described the terrible things that happened to him while he was imprisoned in different Nazi concentration camps, including how he nearly died many times and was physically and psychologically abused and tortured. During his address, he described one day in particular that seemed to be etched deeply within him.

On a wintry day in Poland, he was being marched through a field with a number of other prisoners. He was dressed in thin clothing, with no socks on, and holes in his shoes. Still very ill from malnutrition and mistreatment, he began to cough. The cough was so severe that he fell to his knees. A guard came over and told him to get moving. He could not even answer because his cough was so intense and debilitating. The guard began to beat him with a club and told him that he would be left to die if he did not get up. Dr. Frankl knew this was true because he had witnessed it before. Sick, in pain, and being hit, he thought, "This is it for me." He did not have the wherewithal to get up.

He lay on the ground in no condition to move on. Suddenly, he was no longer there. Instead, he found himself standing at a lectern in postwar Vienna giving a lecture on The Psychology of Death Camps. He had an audience of 200 rapt with attention. The lecture was one that he had worked on the whole time he was in the death camp. He talked about the psychological factors behind dehumanization. He then described why, in his view, some people seem to survive the experience psychologically and emotionally better than others.

It was a brilliant lecture, all in his mind's eye. He was no longer in the field (he was dissociated) but vividly involved in the lecture. During the lecture, he told the imaginary audience about the day Viktor Frankl was in that field being beaten and was certain he did not have the strength to get up and keep walking. Then, exactly at the moment he was describing to his imaginary audience finally being able to stand up and start walking, his body stood up in the field. The guard stopped beating him and he began to walk; haltingly at first, then with more strength. He continued to imagine this lecture all the while he was doing the work detail and through the cold march back to the death camp. When there, he collapsed into his bunk, imagining this brilliantly clear speech ending with a standing ovation. Many years later and thousands of miles away, in 1990 in Anaheim, California, he received a standing ovation from 7,000 after his speech.

Viktor Frankl spoke of the importance of vision, which people who are experiencing pain, suffering, and difficulty often lack. He believed that out of vision emanates meaning, hope, and possibilities. Central to this idea is envisioning a future that differs from the past, one in which things work out for the better—a preferred future. That future vision was a starting point for Frankl's personal journey; it was so compelling he *had* to get up and walk. Had he not, he never would have given that brilliant speech. His vision led him to take action in the present to make it reality in the future. To do this, the first order of business was getting up off the ground and starting to walk.

A well-articulated and strong connection to a future with possibilities is missing for many clients. The absence of a vision for the future leaves some of them in a state of "going nowhere fast." For others, the lack of a future vision can have much more debilitating effects. For example, many clients experiencing suicidal ideation have a distinct absence of a vision of the future without pain and suffering. The same can be true for clients who have been sexually abused or traumatized in some way. They do not want to go on because of the intense pain they are experiencing and the lack of a sense that things will get better in the future. Waters and Lawrence (1993) stated, "One of the great deficits of most therapy is the lack of a proactive vision of what people need to move towards instead of a sense of what they need to move away from" (p. 9). Clients who have a sense of the future can be helped to further develop their visions and map out actions to move them toward those futures. For others, the path begins by imagining that it is possible to have a future that is different from or better than the past. Chapter 5 discussed the importance of a future focus in relation to information-gathering processes by which clients gain a sense of direction by knowing what they want different in their lives.

Therapists can help clients with an improved sense of the future to work backward to the present to determine (from that direction) what the next steps might be to make those visions reality. For example, if a client who is shy envisions a future in which she is in a romantic relationship, what would be an appropriate step to take when she meets someone she is interested in? Perhaps instead of her usual strategy of looking away and becoming quiet, she might make eye contact and say "Hi" or could attend a social event rather than staying home as usual. She might take a course in public speaking to help overcome her reluctance to speak in social situations. The point is that if she is beginning to get a new sense of her future, new actions probably would arise from that new sense.

Bringing a preferred future alive in therapy has three aspects. The first is to help clients to connect with and articulate their preferred future vision or sense. The second step is to identify possible barriers, either internal (for example, stories, beliefs, fears, self-imposed limitations, restricted views of one's identity) or external (for example, lack of money, lack of skills, lack of knowledge, prejudices or biases in the world). To deal with making the preferred future a reality, the third step is to create an action plan to negotiate or overcome the barriers and begin to move toward that future. This overall process is *future pull* (O'Hanlon & Bertolino, 1998, 2002). To assist with each aspect of future pull, some possible questions follow. These questions should be changed and reworded depending on both the fit for clients and the therapist's personal style.

Creating a Vision for the Preferred Future

This first list of questions is aimed at helping clients create a vision of the future and what they want for themselves and, perhaps, for others around them.

- What is your life purpose?
- What is your vision of your preferred future?

- What dreams did you or do you have for your life?
- What are you here on the planet for?
- What are human beings on the planet for in your view?
- In what area could you make a contribution?
- What is your bliss?
- What kinds of things compel you?
- It's 2/5/10 years from now and you have made a decision to go in a particular direction (for example, stay in a relationship or leave it). How does that feel and look to you?

Identifying Barriers to the Preferred Future

Beyond having a sense of where they want to go with their lives, some clients perceive barriers in their way. They feel or think that they are inadequate to the task of making their vision happen. Other clients believe that certain things must happen before they can pursue their preferred futures and dreams. The next questions can assist with identifying and negotiating perceived barriers.

- What, in your view, stops you from realizing your dreams or getting to your goals?
- What are you afraid of?
- What do you believe must happen before you can realize your dreams?
- What are the actions you haven't taken to make your dreams and visions come true?
- What are the real-world barriers to deal with to realize your dreams and visions?
- What would your role models, mentors, or people you admire do to realize this dream or vision if they were you?
- What are you not doing, feeling, or thinking that they would in this situation?
- What are you doing, feeling, or thinking that they wouldn't?

Making an Action Plan to Reach the Preferred Future

The questions in the two preceding lists will be enough for some clients to trigger a change in their views and help them move forward but not for others who need to do something to make their visions reality. They need to make a plan of action. This final series of questions can help clients to clarify the actions they need to take to make their preferred futures happen.

- What could you do in the near future that would be steps toward realizing your visions and dreams?
- What would you do as soon as you leave here?
- What would you do tonight?
- What feeling would you have in your body as you took those steps?
- What would you be thinking that would help you take those steps?
- What images or metaphors are helpful to you in taking these steps?
- Will you make a commitment to me or someone else to take those steps by a specific time?

- Who would be the best person to keep you on track, coach, and monitor you?
- When will you agree to take these steps, and how will the follow-up happen to ensure that you have taken them?

Implementing the Vision

This process can be followed as outlined; however, it is not necessary that the questions be applied systematically or in sequence. An alternative is to intersperse future-focused questions periodically as they fit a particular situation. The intention is to create pathways that provide opportunities for clients to orient their views from the past or present to the future. This can represent a major departure for clients; it can expose them to new possibilities that were not apparent to them previously. It can also clarify directions for therapy, introduce meaning and purpose into clients' lives, and lead to a restoration of hope. To learn more about how to explore client visions of the future, it can be helpful to do it personally. You can do this by completing Exercise 8.1, Articulating a Vision for the Future.

Exercise 8.1

Articulating a Vision for the Future

A well-articulated vision for the future can have an affect on current actions and how to interpret the past. The purpose of this exercise is to learn more about how create or rehabilitate a vision for the future and to determine steps to turn that vision into reality. To complete this exercise, please write your answers to the questions in the spaces provided.

- *Creating a vision for the preferred future.* It is first important to create a sense of what you would like to have happen in the future.

  What is one area that you would like to develop, improve in, or move forward with in your personal or professional future? Please be specific.

  To able to chave I job That I enjoy and Can Comfortably support my family

Exercise 8.1   (continued)

- *Identifying barriers to the preferred future.* Next, consider the areas, situations, or other barriers you may encounter and negotiate in achieving your vision for the future.

  What, in your view, will you need to address to realize your dreams or goals?

  Time; $ For The Education; Missed time W/ My Keds and Time

  What do you believe must happen before you can realize your dreams?

- *Making an action plan to reach the preferred future.* The final aspect is to articulate and clarify steps that need to be taken to make your desired future happen.

  What could you do in the near future that would be steps toward realizing your vision and dream?

  What will be different for you when you have made the commitment to take the actions outlined?

  What is one thing you can do right away to begin to move one step further toward your vision of the future?

Suggest That Clients Focus on What Has Worked Rather Than What Has Not: If therapists keep an eye out for them, they can find exceptions to problems in many areas of clients' lives. One particular area relates to what has worked previously but has been lost. It is as if people develop amnesia in the midst of problems and forget how they resolved their concerns or at least kept them from getting worse. This is a common occurrence and in part can be attributed to society's emphasis on problems and analyzing them. As a result, clients frequently become stuck trying to break down *why* something has not worked or is not working. Although it can be helpful to learn about why something is not working, doing so can also lead to overlooking previous solutions and possibilities.

Therapists can suggest that clients focus on what they have done previously in regard to their problems that worked to any degree. There are two ways to do this. One is to focus on specific solutions to specific problems. This can help clients to recall what they have already done that has been successful. For example, with a divorced client who wants to return to dating but does not think he will attract suitors, a therapist might say, "You mentioned that you used to date a lot when you were in college prior to getting married. How did you go about getting dates? What did you do?" The second way is to search for examples of solutions to any problem to help clients orient more toward the solutions than the problems. For example, a therapist might say to a client who doubts her ability to adapt to a new job, "Tell me about a time when you had to adapt, in some way, to a change around you. It could have been in school, a previous job, in a relationship, or some other life experience. How did you do that?" The following examples offer ways to do this.

A couple came to therapy with the complaint that they could not resolve their current argument about where to buy a house. During the course of therapy, each of them was asked to think about and write down a time when there had been a significant disagreement between them that involved a major life transition. Next, they were asked to write down how it was resolved and who did what. Each named the same situation, deciding where to get married. It turned out that the couple resolved the problem by visiting multiple possible venues and then talking it over. They had both forgotten about this effective strategy and began to make plans to visit, survey, and write down the pros and cons of different places that both deemed acceptable.

A teenager who was routinely being suspended from school for physical fighting was asked to in detail about the times he had felt as if he would get into fights but had done something else. He was able to describe several times that he had either left the scene instead of losing control or was prevented by friends from going to where the fighting would have occurred. This had the effect of convincing him that he had a choice not only about whether or not to fight but also about developing a plan for increased self-control and social support in the future.

It is understood that past solutions do not always fit neatly into the present tense. Therapists' intention is to help clients to recognize that they have dealt with difficult situations that eventually worked out. Although the resolution of current situations may not be derived exactly from previous ones, orienting clients toward previous solutions and solution patterns (for example, ways to think and view situations) can help. This can get the creative juices of change flowing and shift clients out of perspectives that are contributing to their problems.

Suggest That Clients Think of at Least One Thing That Would Challenge or Get Them to Doubt Their Thoughts: Although therapists frequently challenge clients' thoughts, having them undertake this process can also be useful. By disputing their own constructions, clients can create new perspectives for themselves. One way to do this is to suggest to clients that every time they have recurring thoughts or obsessions they think of at least three things they could do in the present or the future that could change their situations for the better. The following example is a specific illustration of how to have clients challenge their own thoughts.

> A male accountant was concerned that he would never meet a woman who liked the things he liked, such as sports. To "corroborate" his view, he was asked to go to a bar of his choice (which he loved to do, so this was not considered a task) on a weekend night to watch a game he wanted to see. He was then to notice how many of patrons in the bar were women and how many of those women showed at least minimal interest in the game he was watching. When he returned to therapy, he informed the therapist that there had been 67 patrons including 27 women. Of the women present, according to the client, 11 showed at least minimal interest in the game he was watching. After a pause, the client said, "Hey, that's around 40%. Those are better odds than I realized!"

Suggest That Clients Recall Other Aspects of Situations They Are Remembering: It is common to notice and focus attention on certain parts or aspects of situations. Clients often delete (in other words, omit), distort (in other words, modify descriptions), or generalize (in other words, make general conclusions about) parts of an experience (Bandler & Grinder, 1975) that they remember. The resulting constructions lock them into unhelpful views. One way to have clients challenge their own views is to help them notice aspects of a situation that they had not noticed previously. See the following example.

> A man who had been physically abused during his youth by his father felt guilty. He felt especially guilty about not having defended his siblings when his father turned on them. In describing various situations when his father had been violent toward both him and his two younger brothers, he happened to remember a time when he stood between his father and his brothers until they could get out of the room safely. This challenged his view that he never defended his siblings and relieved him of his guilt.

Suggest a Change in Some Quality of Remembered Experience: The quality of remembered experience, including both how people remember events and situations and what they remember, plays a significant role in the intensity and level of intrusiveness associated with negative experiences. It is not a matter of establishing *what really happened* in a factual sense but of *how events are experienced when they are recalled*. The *how* represents the ways in which people experience events, for example, visually, auditorally, or kinesthetically. This relates to *what* people remember, which also can be in the form of sights, sounds, bodily sensations, and so on. When clients convey their experiences, they describe certain aspects that are more prominent than others. For many of these clients, the intensity of their experiences lessens when they change one or more of the qualities associated with a situation or event. They can do so by focusing on how (for example, the length of experience) something is remembered or what is remembered (for example, sensory aspects). The following examples illustrate both.

> A man who had been neglected and locked in his bedroom as a child would experience bouts of panic when in small rooms. He would recall, vividly, his bedroom and the intensity of fear he had experienced as a child. In therapy, it was suggested that he change two things about his bedroom represented in the memories. The man first chose to move the placement of his bedroom door. He then changed the entire bedroom from being in color to black and white. By changing these qualities, he was able to change his associations with his bedroom, leading to a reduction in the intrusiveness of his memories.

> A client who had been attacked in her house by an intruder experienced intense visualizations and flashbacks of the events around the attack. Her memories were consistently between 20 and 30 seconds in duration and would leave her severely frightened and shaking profusely. Her therapist suggested that she imagine watching herself (dissociation) in a movie theater on a movie screen. She was then to review the attack in "fast-forward" mode, collapsing it into five seconds. By changing the rate of how she remembered the experience, she was able to change its intensity.

Identify and Integrate Unincorporated Aspects of Self: A commonality among some therapies (for example, Jungian analysis, Gestalt, internal family systems) is the integration of different aspects of self or personality. One way to think about this is to consider that everyone has different aspects of self that are recognized and acknowledged. These aspects show up more or less in different contexts, but they are nonetheless recognized as part of who the person is. When faced with events or situations that are perceived as negative or threatening, however, people, as living organisms, go into a protective mode. In some cases, such as extreme stress, experiential or physical intrusion, boundary violations, or threats, people split off aspects or parts of themselves. That is, one or more of the person's aspects (such as thoughts, memories, sensations, or feelings) go unacknowledged or missing and, therefore, are out of alignment with the rest of the person's self (O'Hanlon & Bertolino, 1998, 2002). For example, a person who was physically punished whenever he expressed anger may have split off anger, believing that it is a useless emotion and denying that he ever becomes angry. A woman who had been sexually abused may lose physical sensations when being intimate with her partner.

The irony is what has gone acknowledged or missing typically shows up in the person's life in a repetitive manner. It is turned down (in other words, lack or absence of feelings, sensations, memories) or up (such as flashbacks, intrusive thoughts, compulsive behavior, rage, somatic symptoms) in the person's experience or both up and down. These aspects of self are present but unacknowledged and outside of the person's awareness. Therefore, certain connections (for example, sights, smells, images, environments, conversation) trigger and reawaken these experiences and interfere in people's lives, over and over. This can affect clients' views and is usually evidenced by statements such as, "I don't get angry"; "I'm just a bad person"; or "Feeling sexual is bad." In addition, clients typically experience a lack of physical sensations, compulsive thinking, or disconnectedness with emotions such as anger and sadness.

One way to help clients is to help them integrate aspects of self that may have been split off. To do this, therapists work with them to acknowledge the existence of unintegrated aspects, make room within their boundaries of self for those aspects, and ultimately embrace and incorporate them. The following example illustrates this idea.

> A man was referred to therapy after multiple altercations with co-workers. In his initial session, he stated that he did not get angry and, in fact, thought anger was both a "petty" and useless emotion. When asked about the incidents at work, however, the man commented, "I just snap sometimes and lose it." He further remarked that his boss told him that he was tired of him "flying into fits of rage." As therapy progressed, it was learned that the man had been physically abused by his stepfather throughout his adolescence. While being abused, he was told by his stepfather, "This isn't anger. Anger is weakness. This is how I keep you in line." The man was then able to identify anger as an acceptable emotion, one that can be useful as long as it is not used to hurt self or others. He was then able to allow it to exist within himself, embrace his anger, and express it in positive ways.

Shift between the Past, Present, and Future: Freudians focus on the past; behaviorists emphasize the present. Solution-focused therapists aim for the future. Each of these approaches has a degree of validity depending on the client and the situation. At the same time, too much focus on one realm can become part of the problem. For example, there is such a thing as being stuck in the past, too much in the present, or overly daydreaming of the future. The point is that some clients can benefit from shifting from one realm to another, which might bring about a change in perspective in relationship to their concerns and problems.

To use this method, practitioners collaborate with clients to determine which realm may be associated with their stuckness. Determining which realm can be a useful way to help clients shift their views. Many combinations are possible, including but not limited to shifting from the past to the future, the present to the past, the future to the present, and so on. For example, if a client is exploring and analyzing her past to the degree that she is becoming increasingly depressed, the therapist might suggest that she consider what she is aware of and thankful for in the present and what she experiences when she connects with those feelings. Another possibility is to have the client who becomes anxious when focusing on his current situation focus on a time in the future when his anxiety is less present or absent altogether. The therapist needs to take care to invite clients into other ways of viewing and experiencing their lives and situations rather than impose ideas on them. The following example shows how this method works.

> A young woman came to therapy feeling overwhelmed about the prospects of her future. According to the client, her parents had "great expectations" for her and "constantly reminded" her that she needed to think about the future and prepare for it. Although the young woman enjoyed thinking about the future and what it might bring, she felt like that was all she ever did and had a difficult time appreciating much of anything. Given her affection for the outdoors, it was suggested that she go to a place she found tranquil and relaxing and stare out into the scenery, focusing only on the sights and sounds of the environment, and appreciate the moment as much as possible. By doing this, she was able to gain relief in the present

whenever necessary and appreciate the future in a way that was right for her.

Suggest that Clients Shift Focus from their Internal Experience to the External Environment or other People or Vice Versa:

Some people tend to spend more time in their inner worlds whereas others focus on what is going on around them. Depending on the context, too much of one or the other can spell trouble. It is not a matter of being introverted or extroverted but where someone places attention. As a means of helping clients to become unstuck, having them shift from focusing internally to externally or vice versa can be useful. The first example illustrates shifting from internal to external; the second example illustrates shifting from external to internal.

A young man was referred to me because he had been sexually abused by a male adult while in foster care. The client was experiencing severe anxiety that seemed to be triggered by flashbacks. It was learned that just prior to his flashbacks, he would become very internally focused. The young man stated that he would become "trapped" in a place that was "hard to get out of." He wanted to be able to "feel better" and reduce the intensity of the flashbacks.

Through further conversation, it was learned that there were variations with the client's flashbacks ranging from very intense (hyperventilation) to low intensity (only mild agitation). The client remarked that the intensity seemed to increase when he was "really trapped, focusing inside." He also stated that the intensity decreased "when I can get out of my mind." Based on his orientation to his concern, a plan was created to help him shift the focus of his attention from an internal to external. He was able to do this by recognizing the first signs that he was beginning to "go inside." This included

becoming very quiet and still and then increasing his breathing rate. The client had learned that in the past, he had been able to reduce the level of intensity by recognizing these things and then deliberately looking at the things around him (in other words, in the physical environment) to remind himself that he was in the present, not the past.

A man who was a supervisor to more 20 employees routinely got feedback that he was insensitive. He was asked to spend 20 minutes each day meditating and noticing his own feelings. As a result, he began to notice others' feelings more acutely when he was in touch with his.

Suggest That Clients Shift Their Sensory Attention:

Another potentially powerful method in shifting from one form of attention to another involves having clients transfer their attention from one sensory modality to another. This includes shifting from seeing things to listening, from listening to touching, from touching to smelling, and so on. Once again, the method can help clients who seem to be stuck in one specific realm to alter a problematic pattern of viewing. See the following examples.

A woman was experiencing flashbacks associated with years of sexual abuse. At a moment's notice, she would become overwhelmed with vivid memories that had a paralyzing effect on her. In exploring different possibilities, it was learned that her deceased mother had been a constant source of support and comfort for her. The woman had kept many gifts from her mother. One that she treasured the most was a bracelet her mother had given to her on her 21st birthday. She began wearing the bracelet every day, and when she would start to have flashbacks, she would physically touch the bracelet. This would shift her attention from the visual to the kinesthetic realm, bringing her out of the flashbacks.

A man reported having a "continuous" dialogue of negative self-statements running though his mind. He stated that he had tried "thought stopping" and other methods to no avail. It was suggested that he instead shift to some other form of sensory attention. The man stated that he really "soaked up" things when he was able to see them. Based on this, it was suggested that when he had negative self-statements, he shift to noticing the scenery around him. This helped distract his attention and break the cycle of self-recrimination.

Orienting Toward Balance

Existentialists have discussed the idea of "being-in-the world" and the responsibility people have for their existence (Binswanger, 1975; May, Angel, & Ellenberger, 1958). This idea is represented through three different types of relationships: (1) to self, (2) to others, and (3) to the biological world or environment; some also refer to a fourth type of connection: relationship to spirituality. The overarching idea is that for people to have balanced lives, it is necessary that they maintain their connections in these realms. Existing primarily in one or two areas but being disconnected from another can have negative effects. Examples of this include a person who focuses primarily on others at the expense of self or a person who is so focused on self that there is an absence of connection to the natural environment. In such cases, helping clients shift their attention to other forms of connection in order to achieve better balance in life can be useful. See the following example.

A client had been experiencing a significant decrease in energy and was feeling more and more overwhelmed at work. He remarked that he felt he was always doing for others. When his therapist inquired what he did for himself, he stated that he worked out and liked to read and made time to do those things, but nevertheless, something was missing. Further conversation identified that the man used to spend time hiking and fishing but had to "cut out" those activities and replace them with things he could do with "what time" he had. As the discussion progressed, the client noticed that what had been missing was the presence of the outdoors in his life. Although he still made time for himself, his connection to the outdoors had dissipated. He decided that he would address this by going for walks during his lunch breaks and plan at least one outdoor activity each weekend. His energy increased, and work became more manageable within a few weeks of his changes.

The intent behind the methods offered in this section is to assist clients to shift their attention away from areas that are contributing to problems. Sometimes this means noticing "what else" may be happening; at other times, it is to alter an unhelpful pattern of viewing. To practice various methods outlined, please complete Exercise 8.2, Shifting Attention.

Combining different methods (including others not mentioned here) can be useful. By shifting their attention, many clients achieve problem resolution. For other clients, different methods are necessary to help them change their views and associated actions. To determine the degree of change in viewing needed, therapists are encouraged to notice how clients talk about their lives and situations over time and the actions they take (for example, those that are helpful, productive, goal oriented, or counter to those actions). Stories are generative and unfold over time, meaning that therapists

Exercise 8.2

Shifting Attention

What is given attention is magnified. When faced with problems, people can fail to notice or block out certain aspects of situations, sometimes things that correspond to possibilities and solutions. Because problems can negatively dominate views, it is important to help reorient people to other aspects of situations, events, and their lives that are going or have gone differently. The purpose of this exercise is to learn how this shifting of attention can lead to changes in perspective and the alleviation or resolution of problems. To complete this exercise, please write your responses to the questions and in the spaces provided. (Be specific with your answers, incorporating action-talk in your descriptions).

- Describe a problem.

_____

_____

_____

Consider the following realms for shifting attention:

- Time (past, present, or future)
- What clients (or others) do well rather than mistakes or problems
- Actions instead of explanations
- Sensory perceptions (visual, kinesthetic, auditory, gustatory, or olfactory)
- Internal or external focus
- Choose one or more of the following methods for the problem identified.
- Focus on what has worked rather than what has not.
- Think of one thing that would challenge or cast doubt on the thoughts surrounding the problem.
- Recall other aspects of the situation.
- Suggest a change in some quality of remembered experience.
- Identify and integrate an unincorporated aspect of self.
- Shift between the past, present, and future.
- Shift from focusing on a client's internal experience to focusing on the external environment or other people or vice-versa.
- Shift sensory attention.
- Orient toward balance.

- List the method(s) chosen.

_____

_____

_____

- Utilize the method or methods chosen and monitor the results. This can be done immediately or after a designated amount of time has expired. Describe the results of each method used.

_____

_____

_____

Exercise 8.2   *(continued)*

• Describe what was learned as a result of the exercise and how this might affect what is done in the future.

_____

_____

_____

_____

_____

---

should take care not to view methods as magic wands but as processes that help to open up new possibilities in otherwise closed-down perspectives. This requires patience and persistence on the part of the therapist.

Stories and Metaphor

One particular pathway for changing views has more historical roots than others—the use of stories and metaphor. For centuries, stories have entranced people of all ages in various cultures and civilizations. Stories, including fairy and folk tales, myths, and metaphors, represent a universal means of communication and are accepted parts of society at nearly all levels. Although the degree to which they are used varies from society to society and culture to culture, the healing value of stories is widely recognized.

Because of their appeal, stories capture people's attention, thereby increasing the likelihood for the creation of new meanings and understandings. Stories have no one correct meaning but multiple interpretations, and people often construct different meanings from a single story. As a medium for facilitating

change, stories offer a means of accessing multiple pathways, which can help to:

• Normalize clients' experiences
• Acknowledge realities and experiences
• Offer hope
• Offer new perspectives and possibilities
• Bypass everyday conscious ways of processing information
• Remind clients of previous solutions and resources

Stories can have a normalizing effect because they convey the sense that others have had similarly difficult or traumatic experiences. Stories can also help clients to feel a little less ashamed and isolated and can provide a way to acknowledge their experiences and let them know that they have been heard. Using stories can strengthen the client-therapist relationship. Stories can also generate hope in clients that there are possibilities in the future and give the sense that things can change; stories offer new perspectives and possibilities, reminding clients of previous solutions and resources and providing a way to shift patterns of attention, possibly resulting in the creation of new, hopeful narratives. Case Example 8.1 illustrates a few of these points.

CASE EXAMPLE 8.1

Isaac, a 14-year-old, was brought to therapy by his mother after missing 45 days of school since his holiday (Christmas) break. Throughout the initial meeting, Isaac did not speak. I met with him both alone and with his mother and his response was the same. He did not talk. His mother spoke and expressed her concern that family court would take Isaac and place him residentially. I wanted to assure him that I believed in his ability to make choices and was not there to lecture him. So I said to Isaac, "If you think you should let the court process take its course, that's your choice. I'm not here to tell you otherwise. I'm just not convinced that you're convinced that that's what you should do."

His mother believed that Isaac had not gone back to school because some classmates had been picking on him. Isaac did not respond when he was asked about this. It would have been easy to view Isaac as a youth who was resistant, noncompliant, or delinquent. Yet none of those descriptions offered me possibilities for working with him. Therefore, based on what I knew about Isaac (which I had learned from his mother), I chose to explore various possibilities that might invite him back into school. I wanted to do this in ways that help could him eliminate any shame or guilt and, ultimately, save face. Furthermore, I hoped that the decision to return to school would be his and one that he made because it was right for him, not because he was forced.

One of the ways I did this was to tell him a story about a star college football player who had made the decision to stay in school for his senior year. He had forgone what surely would have been a lucrative contract and the promise of immediate stardom. The reason for this was in part due to his parents' advice. They told him that he would become a professional football player (barring a career-ending injury) but

would never have another senior year. Who knows what he might miss if he decided to leave school early? When Isaac did not seem to respond to the story, I simply moved on.

My sense was that I did not really know what might touch him in some way and it was my responsibility to continue to explore other possibilities that might invite him back to school. Another way that I did this was to use stories to remind him that it could be a challenge to return to something after time off. For professional athletes, this meant the off-season. For Isaac it meant summer, holidays, spring break, and so on. Despite having experienced many breaks, Isaac had always found a way to get back to school. I focused on his absence from school as the exception by reminding Isaac that he had been a "routine" student during his school career. He had never missed more than two days in a row and a few days overall in any school year. He was a ninth grader who had demonstrated competence in school attendance. My reminder was an attempt to let him know that he already knew something about attending school regularly.

There were other stories, anecdotes, and offerings during the initial session. Following the first session (which was on a Friday), I told the mother to call me on Monday. Although I had a full evening schedule, I could see her and Isaac in the morning if he had not gone back to school. When Monday came, the mother called and stated that Isaac had not returned to school. So she and Isaac came in for a second session. Just as in the first session, Isaac did not speak. So I continued to explore ways of inviting him back to school.

At the end of the second session, I told the mother that I would be gone for the remainder of the week but would be available to see them the following Monday morning if Isaac had not

CASE EXAMPLE 8.1 (continued)

gone back to school. Once again, I asked the mother to call me on Monday.

When the mother called, she stated that Isaac had returned to school. When asked what happened, she said she didn't know. However, she stated that something very strange had happened. On Sunday evening, Isaac approached his mother and told her the story of the college football player who had remained in school for his senior year. She related that she was confused because she knew the story and could not figure out why he was telling it to her again. As he did so, it then became clear to her that Isaac did not recall that it was a story that had been told in

therapy. According to the mother, when Isaac finished his story, he told the mother, "You never know what you might be missing." The next day he retuned to school.

A third session was scheduled with Isaac and his mother. Much to my surprise, the moment Isaac came into the room, he began talking. He spoke about returning to school and the reactions of his classmates. Although he certainly was not excited, he persevered. It was never learned why Isaac missed so many days of school. For the remainder of his school career, he did not miss more than his usual few days a year due to illness. Isaac graduated a few years later, on schedule.

In using stories therapeutically, practitioners should be aware of structure. Stories typically have a beginning, middle, and an end. The beginning draws clients in by offering them opportunities to explore other worlds, situations, and people. Because stories are not specifically about clients themselves and do not require them to speak, stories often contribute to a more relaxed atmosphere, taking pressure off clients to have to do anything. Stories also "hook" clients in and have them wondering, "What's next?" "What's going to happen?" The middle parts of stories typically include challenges, hurdles, and obstacles that are faced on the way to some form of problem negotiation or resolution. By the time the ending of stories comes around, many clients are on the edge of their seats with anticipation. They then learn about how characters use their strengths and resources to stand up to, overcome, and move past various challenges.

It is hoped that clients will connect with some aspect of stories that is meaningful.

Stories will resonate with people in different ways. At times, stories that therapists believe have the potential to create a significant impact and benefit clients seem to go in one ear and out the other. Other times what are thought to be rather elementary and unremarkable stories have profound effects with clients who come back for future sessions (a few days, weeks, or even months later) and report how stories helped them to see their lives or situations in new ways. Therapists want to pay attention to clients' verbal and nonverbal responses to stories because stories reach clients at different levels of experience. These responses inform therapists as to how to proceed (in other words, whether to tell more or fewer stories and what kinds of stories).

Therapeutic or healing stories come from different cultures, disciplines, and experiences. Many therapists build personal repertoires and in some instances categorize stories for use with specific clients and concerns. Some therapists retain stories rather easily and recall them in therapy as needed. Others may need to write them down and refer back to them when they believe the stories will provide opportunities to facilitate change.

Storytelling has been used effectively in a variety of contexts. Community-based projects, health promotion, and disease prevention have used a variety of stories on issues ranging from grief and loss to depression to family problems (Parker & Wampler, 2006). Stories are metaphors that provide a unique way to build rapport and understanding while opening up new possibilities for viewing.

Metaphors are used in everyday life to make comparisons, draw analogies and parallels, and describe experience. Let's take the example of water which is often used as metaphor in the banking industry. We can *float* a loan; have *liquid* assets, *slush* funds, *hard* cash, and rising *liquidity*; and can *freeze* accounts (Bertolino & O'Hanlon, 1998). The following example shows how to tap into a client's use of metaphor.

> I met with a family consisting of a mother, her 15-year-old daughter, and 12-year-old son. The mother sought therapy after the kids had taken her car out for a "joyride" in the middle of the night. While on their excursion, they caused an accident with another vehicle, abandoned the car, and left the scene. In addition to the incident, the mother reported that her daughter and son had been stealing from her and were "constantly in trouble."
>
> During the session, the mother was tearful and seemed distraught. She stated, "It's all too much. I feel like I'm on a roller coaster."
>
> "If you could get off the roller coaster and change rides, what would you choose?" I asked.
>
> The woman pondered the question then replied, "Well, I've never liked roller coasters. I prefer the calm rides—maybe a riverboat ride."
>
> "How might a riverboat ride be different from a roller coaster?" I followed.

> "Roller coasters move too fast and they go up and down too much. There are just too many hills and dips," she continued, "Riverboat rides can be bumpy, but not too bumpy, and they're slower."

Some therapists and models have even been developed around stories and metaphors (Lakoff & Johnson, 2001). Milton Erickson's therapy, for example, was based almost exclusively on stories, metaphors, analogies, and indirect suggestion (Haley, 1973; Rossi, 1980). Lankton and Lankton (1983, 1986) also developed an approach based on Erickson's work involving the use of multiple embedded metaphors. This approach might begin with a metaphor used to evoke emotion, then shift to one associated with changing cognition, followed by another encouraging action. Although this is an oversimplification of the model, it demonstrates how stories and metaphors can be used to facilitate change in multiple realms of clients' lives. Case Example 8.2 illustrates how metaphors can be used as a framework for promoting a change in viewing.

Other Media for Change: Written Word, Music, and Film

Just as stories are part of rich traditions in many cultures, written word (for example, stories, poetry, song lyrics), music, and film extend across and captivate people of all ages and backgrounds. These media can strengthen the client-therapist relationship; normalize and acknowledge clients' experience; instill hope; offer new possibilities and perspectives; bypass everyday conscious ways of processing information; and remind clients of previous solutions and resources. These ways to open up new pathways of viewing are especially useful because they can be adapted for individuals,

CASE EXAMPLE 8.2

A 14-year-old, Jeremy, was brought to therapy by his father after receiving poor grades, sneaking out at night, and smoking marijuana. About to be a freshman, Jeremy wanted desperately to play football for his high school team the upcoming school year; however, his father would not let him try out unless he improved his grades and behavior. It was the beginning of summer, and the teenager was required to go to summer school to make up classes and improve his grades. Jeremy was unhappy with this and wanted to give up. Knowing his love of football, I asked him what he thought the preseason in football was all about. He said it was a time for the players to get into shape. I agreed and added that the regular season could be a long one and without being in shape it, could be tougher. But there was more to it. The preseason was also a time to connect with other players and coaches and learn the playbook and any rules that go along with the game. This is particularly important for those players entering the pros from college. I finished by talking about how players were graded on their performance

and that would factor in to whether or not they would make the cut.

I shifted the conversation by talking about how the preseason was a time to gradually build up strength. It did not have to come overnight, but there was a time frame in which players needed to be ready for the regular season. I then speculated out loud. I wondered what kind of preseason Jeremy would have. How would he connect with other "players and coaches" (students and teachers)? How would be learn the "playbook" (school studies)? How would he adjust to and "learn the rules" (be at school on time, turn in assignments, etc.)? How would he make the "grade" (grades in summer school)? Finally, would he truly be ready for the "regular season" (the upcoming school year)?

Jeremy did wonderfully in summer school and raised his grades. His father let him play football, which began the last few weeks of summer. A week prior to the start of the school year, he came to therapy and I asked him, "Are you ready for the regular season?" he replied, "I've been in game shape for weeks!"

couples, families, and groups. Let's briefly explore some applications of these media.

Written Word

The use of written word in therapy has increased. *Bibliotherapy,* as it is commonly known, refers to the use of literature such as books, articles, and poetry in therapy. For some clients, the use of literature triggers new ideas and perspectives. Whether the reading is done by clients on their own or as a result of therapists' recommendations, therapists can ask

questions such as these to determine what new meanings may have been derived:

- What stood out for you as a result of your reading?
- What did you learn?
- What difference did/does that make for you?
- What might you do as a result of what you have learned?

Written word can also be used as an indirect path to change. For example, the practitioner might recommend that a client read *Alice in Wonderland* and say, "There is something in the book that I think will stand out for you. I'd like you to read it and tell me what it is." As a result, the client might return to therapy and reveal, "You know, when Alice peered through the looking glass, I felt like it was me looking at my life." The practitioner then follows up with some of the aforementioned questions. This form of indirect suggestion is, of course, open ended and has many possibilities. It is crucial to understand that the intent of indirect methods is not to be manipulative but to facilitate the creation of new meanings and views for clients. In addition, therapists best serve their clients when they are able to use literature that reflects the cultural metaphors of those clients (McCoy & McKay, 2006).

Music

Music can be used to promote relaxation, shift attention from other sensory modalities to auditory (listening) realms, or create new meanings by noticing experiential differences as a result of feeling, hearing, seeing (for example, live performances), and/or playing music. If you have ever found yourself lost in music in some way, this method is likely to be familiar to you. In fact, music therapy has become part of different therapy regimens in hospitals.

One way to use music is to have clients choose songs that are meaningful to them and then ask questions such as:

- What did you notice about yourself as you listened to the music?
- What stood out for you?
- How does that way of feeling contrast with what you feel when you experience [X]?
- What difference might that make you for you if you were to listen to music when you are experiencing [X]?

Another possibility is to use song lyrics as a basis for discussion. For example, if working with a group of adolescents, the therapist could ask that the group talk about the lyrics to a particular song. These conversations often prove surprising because the lyrics can spawn comments about life, change, hope, and so on. If conversations turn negative, therapists should acknowledge differing perspectives and ask questions to introduce new ways to think about the lyrics.

Film/Movies

One of the most frequently used media is film (movies)(cinematherapy/film work). Like music, many different genres are available and offer various therapeutic possibilities. In addition, movies are a flexible medium; DVD versions, for example, often contain language and subtitle options for persons with a hearing disability. Movies can be used in both general and specific ways. In a general sense, they can be used to evoke emotion, create connections between people, and/or bring them together. The following example illustrates the influence of movies.

> Some years ago I was teaching a workshop in the southeast part of the United States. During the break just prior to the final segment of the presentation, a woman approached me. She was in tears and initially struggled to find her tongue. I asked her, "Are you okay?" After gathering herself, she replied, "Yes. I have to tell you something. I've seen the movie (*Good Will Hunting*) you just showed a clip from at least a half-dozen times. But today was different. When I saw it, I had an immediate response. I saw it in a way I hadn't seen it before and it hit me hard. It made me feel and think things I hadn't in a long time. But these are tears of joy. What came out for me is good. I needed it. Thank you." Such is the power of movies.

In much the same way that written word can be used indirectly, a therapist can suggest that a client watch a film with the idea of seeing or hearing something that is meant for her. This *presupposes* that the client will find some meaning regarding some aspect of the movie watched. In such cases, therapists should take care to choose movies that exemplify the desired behaviors and interactions. In this way movies can also be used to model behavior or interactions.

In follow-up sessions, clients can be asked what stuck out or resonated with them. They most often describe situations or characters. These conversations involve searching for new views that clients may have developed as a result. The following questions can assist with this.

- What stood out most for you about that [character/scene/situation]?
- Why did [character name] act the way he/she did?
- How do you think [character name] got the idea to act that way?
- In your experience, where do people get the idea to act like [character name] did in the movie?
- Have you ever felt like [character name] in the movie? What was that like for you?
- What is one thing that is likely to remain with you as a result of seeing the movie?
- What difference might that make for you?

If clients respond to questions with "I don't know" or "Nothing," it can be helpful to switch to another character, scene, or situation in the movie. If clients continue to respond in the same manner, therapists can ask questions that build on positive outcomes that occurred in the movies or search for possible alternative views and actions that clients might consider in the future. Here are some questions to assist with this.

- Would you have done the same as [character name] did in the movie? If so/not, why?
- What could he/she have done differently?
- What would you have done if you were [character name] in the movie?
- What do you think it would have been like to be in the situation [character name] was in the movie?
- What ideas do you have about what you might do if you were in the situation portrayed in the movie?
- Would you want to be seen as being like [character name] in the movie? If so/not, why?
- To be seen in that way, what would you need to continue to do or do differently?

Movies can also be used with clients experiencing specific issues such as loss, grief, depression, anxiety, and divorce (Bertolino, 2001; Bertolino & Schultheis, 2002; Gabbard & Gabbard, 1999; Hesley & Hesley, 2001; Solomon, 2001; Wedding, Boyd & Niemiec, 2005). The following example illustrates the use of movies in this manner.

> A couple brought their seven year old son to see me. The child had been isolating himself from others and appeared sad. I learned that the couple had adopted the child when he was three years old and from time to time he would say things such as, "My family didn't want me" and "I don't have a family." One of things I did was to suggest that as a family they watch "The Tigger Movie." The movie is based on a story about the character Tigger's search for his family. In the end Tigger realizes that his "family" is Winnie the Pooh and his other friends from the 100 Acre Wood. After watching the movie the young boy came to

his next therapy session with a big smile on his face. He announced. "I have a family just like Tigger and they love me!"

The following considerations serve as a guide for therapists using movies with specific therapeutic issues:

- Normalize the idea of doing an exercise around watching a movie. Assure clients that film work has been used with other clients and the results have been positive.
- Select effective role models from films. Identify the character(s) that the client should note. What are some similarities between the client and character?
- Match the content of a film with therapeutic issues. Provide a rationale for why a particular film is being suggested.
- Pick films that clients will enjoy.
- Choose films that evoke inspirational moods.
- Show characters solving problems.
- Discuss scenes that might be offensive. Language, sex, nudity, and violence are hot points. Switch films if clients object to the one selected.
- Clarify the intent when assigning a film in which a client might mistake the role identification.
- Tell clients to turn off a film that they strongly dislike. Admit inevitable mismatches quickly.
- Take advantage of powerful indirect effects.
- Ask clients to be on the lookout for films that may be therapeutically useful. When possible, let clients select films.
- Clients can derive multiple meanings from movies, which provide opportunities for clients to create new views, learn more positive actions, and deal with adversity or problems in the future. Moreover, using movies is an excellent way to indirectly address problems with clients for whom direct methods do not seem to work.
- To explore the media of change suggested in this section, please refer to Exercise 8.3, Meanings through Multiple Mediums, which can help stimulate ideas to use with clients.

Conversational and Consulting Teams (CCTs)

Both clients and therapists can become mired in views that close down avenues of change, so the injection of other ideas can trigger new possibilities. One particular effort that has influenced many others is the use of the one-way mirror, which was employed during the second wave (see Appendix) and revolutionized in the 1970s and 1980s as a vehicle for teaching and training family therapists. From behind the one-way mirror, supervisors would observe therapists working with families and in doing could develop and then phone in directives. In this process, supervisors gave therapists instructions about how they were to intervene with families. Consistent with the first and second waves, practitioners were seen as the experts in the therapeutic milieu and responsible for producing change in others.

As the use of one-way mirror gained prominence in family therapy, variations evolved from its original form. A specific outgrowth was to have a team of therapists observe a session from behind the mirror (Boscolo, Cecchin, Hoffman, & Penn, 1987; de Shazer, 1988; Selvini Palazzoli, Boscolo, Cecchin, & Prata, 1980; Tomm, 1984b). This created space for multiple perspectives. The team's goal was to select a perspective that provided the best fit for the family, although the same concept would be later used with individuals and couples. To employ this approach, a

Exercise 8.3

Meanings Through Multiple Media

In the process of negotiating new meanings and perspectives, it can be particularly useful to explore different media, particularly the written word, music, and film. The purpose of this exercise is to assist in developing resources to help facilitate change in therapy. To complete this exercise, please write your responses in the spaces provided.

- Choose a specific concern and write it using action-talk in the space provided.

  _____
  _____
  _____
  _____

- Consider three examples of written word, music, and film that might help to think about, attend to, or open up a new perspective for the concern.

- Written word

  a. _____
  b. _____
  c. _____

- Music

  a. _____
  b. _____
  c. _____

- Film (including television and video)

  a. _____
  b. _____
  c. _____

  How did you come up with the examples you listed?

  _____
  _____
  _____
  _____

  Give an example or two of how you might introduce any one of the examples you developed if you were working with a client with the concern you described.

  _____
  _____
  _____
  _____

(continued)

Exercise 8.3 *(continued)*

- In this final section, list one or two possible examples of written word, music, or film you might offer for each specific concern specified. (Keep in mind that the following issues are all general and would require further elaboration in terms of clients' experiences and what they would like to have different in their lives.)

Physical abuse   _____

Divorce   _____

Anxiety   _____

Depression   _____

Substance Abuse   _____

Anger   _____

Family Problems   _____

Death   _____

Life Transitions   _____

With what other concerns might you use these media?

_____

_____

_____

_____

---

break is scheduled in the session at which time the therapist consults with the team. During this break, the selected frame (in other words, hypothesis regarding the family's interactions) and a task (in other words, how the problem could be solved) based on that frame would be discussed with the therapist. The therapist would then return to the session and deliver the feedback and task to the family. This was considered a breakthrough with the exploration of multiple viewpoints and the therapy office becoming a place of consultation.

As the third wave emerged, therapists continued to move from seeing family systems as essentially stable with governing homeostatic mechanisms to evolving and changing. People were also viewed as having resources within themselves and their social systems to solve problems. This movement represented a significant departure from previous thinking and brought with it a focus on the way language and interaction could lead to the creation of new meaning.

This shift also influenced the use of the one-way mirror with teams when Norwegian psychiatrist Tom Andersen (1991) introduced the concept of the *reflecting team*. Andersen offered a way to make therapy more strengths based by flattening the hierarchy between clients and therapists, making therapy more collaborative and conversation oriented. Perhaps most noteworthy were the philosophy and accompanying prescribed format in which clients were no longer offered what was deemed the *best* idea by a supervisor or team but would hear *all* of the team's reflections and choose which ones fit then best. Andersen (1993) stated, "Reflecting processes . . . are characterized by the attempt to say everything in the open. Everything the professional says about the client's situation is said so that the client can hear it" (p. 306). Instead of attempting to "sell" clients prescriptions for change, reflecting teams highlighted differences and events that did not fit with the dominant problem-saturated stories. It was hoped that the introduction of new ideas would lead clients to create new meanings and ultimately, new life stories. These new stories of hope and possibility could then pull clients toward their preferred futures. It was further hoped that therapists would gain new perspectives and ideas for working with clients.

Since its introduction, the reflecting team has evolved into *conversational and consulting teams* (CCTs), expanding their scope of use while keeping the underlining philosophy intact (Bertolino, 2003). CCTs are based on creating meaningful exchanges between therapists and clients, therapists and other professionals, and so on. CCTs can be used therapeutically at any juncture (at the beginning and during transition, or crisis intervention) and in a variety of contexts and formats (Friedman, 1995). Research has supported the efficacy of CCTs (Sells et. al, 1994; Smith, Yoshioka, & Winton, 1993) with clients who have become stuck in their problem-saturated stories.

Introduction of CCTs to Clients

Although CCTs have become more commonplace in therapy, their use will be foreign to many clients. Practitioners want to introduce CCTs as a possibility, not as a requirement for

change. As with all practices, therapists remain collaborative, letting clients choose which ideas align most with their perspectives and offer the best fit. The idea of using a team can be introduced to clients in different ways. The following example shows one way.

> Sometimes when we become stuck, it helps to get a few more ideas. One of the ideas we have here is that three (or four or five) heads are better than one. That said, I'd like to talk with you about our consulting team process. We have a team of between three to five therapists who come to therapy sessions and sit behind a one-way mirror and observe. The purpose of the team is to come up with new ideas and ways to look at things and to share those ideas with us. It takes about the same length of time as one of our therapy sessions, and a specific structure is followed. First, we meet together while the team listens to and observes our conversation. After about a half an hour or so, we switch places with the team. They come into the office and we go behind the mirror. The team then shares its observations, talking about what they heard and noticed. The team does not tell anyone what to do, pass judgment, or point out problems; instead its focus is on highlighting what is working and offering suggestions and ideas that we can accept, modify, or disregard. This process takes between 8 and 12 minutes. We will then return to the office, and the team will go back behind the mirror. There will then be an opportunity to share any thoughts about what stood out for you.

Client responses to the introduction of CCTs can vary, but common comments include these: "Great, we get four therapists for the price of one!"; "That sounds good"; or "We'll try anything." Some clients have some apprehension, mostly about what the team members might think or say. Some client responses are "They're really going to think we're crazy" or "That sounds intimidating." Much of this concern can be neutralized by helping the clients to have a better understanding of the process and realize that the team members will not criticize or judge them. It is therefore important to detail the process as much or as little as necessary depending on clients' concerns.

Foundational Ideas

Consistent with a strengths-based perspective, CCTs operate under the philosophical principles outlined in Chapter 2. Within those principles, the following ideas are underscored:

- No objective reality or truth exits in human social realities. Each person creates his or her own new meaning or "truths" based on the distinctions he or she draws from personal experiences, beliefs, and social contexts.
- In the therapeutic system, the therapist is a participant in the social construction of the therapy system's reality.
- Meanings and behaviors interact recursively. Each can change and influence change in the other.
- Positive connotation is extremely important. It is difficult for people to "leave the field" or to change under negative connotation.
- A stuck system needs new ideas. Thus, the goal is to provide a context in which clients can see and hear differently so they can understand their situation differently.

Preparation and Posture of the CCT

The team enters the session with as little previous knowledge about the client individual, couple, or family or possible. Team members do not review files as notes, nor have they been briefed. Their job is to respond only to what occurs in the room. The team also adheres to following operational points:

- Comments are based on what actually happens in the room, wondering about and giving personal responses to what occurs in the session.
- Ideas are situated in each person's own experience with the belief that this invites clients to adapt what is said to fit their personal experience.
- Comments are nonevaluative. Team members wonder about or focus on differences or new occurrences around which individuals or family members may choose to perform meaning.
- The team has a conversation to develop ideas rather than compete for the best idea.
- Team members address other team members rather than the individual/couple/family through the mirror.
- Efforts are made to respond to everyone in the family.
- Team members do not talk behind the mirror under the assumption that this keeps their conversations fresher and more multifaceted.
- There is an emphasis on brevity, especially if there are small children.
- Efforts are made avoid instructing or leading the individual/couple/family, striving instead to elicit many perceptions and constructions so that individuals can choose what is interesting or helpful to them.

The team is not trying to identify truths, give advice, or instruct. Members phrase comments from a position of speculation, and clients can accept or reject them. Reflections include new perspectives and punctuations given from a positive frame of reference and tap into clients' strengths, resources, positive attributes, and good intentions. Speculations are in the form of tentative offerings that are not evaluations or judgments. Andersen (1987) stated: "The reflecting team has to bear in mind that its task is to create ideas even though some of those ideas may not be found interesting by the family, or may even be rejected. What is important is to realize that the family will select those ideas that fit" (p. 421).

To remain nonevaluative, the team members use conjecture and curiosity and sentence stems such as: "I noticed that. . . ."; "I wonder if. . . ."; "I was curious about. . . ."; "I was struck by. . . ."; "When I heard [X] say, I wonder if he /she thought. . . ."; "I wonder what would happen if. . . ."; or "Perhaps it is. . . ." By maintaining a posture based of wonderment and emphasizing the generation of new ideas, team members contribute to a climate that has an increased likelihood that one or more ideas will "stick." Bateson (1972) famously spoke of the "difference which makes a difference" (p. 453), describing how one bit of information is distinguished from another. In this context, an idea always has the potential to resonate with others but is influenced by factors including who conveys it, who hears it, how it is said, and so on. In other words, two team members can make similar comments but many factors will influence how they are interpreted.

The Format

As described earlier, CCTs have a basic format that is open to variation. This format involves a team of therapists which observes the therapy session, usually from behind a one-way mirror, although it can also be done without a mirror in a large room. Variations may involve videoconferencing or using video- or audiotape or the telephone. It is recommended that the team consist of three to five clinicians. Too few or too many can affect the degree and quality of the conversation.

In the initial part of the session, the therapist meets with the individual, couple, or family for 30 to 45 minutes. The therapist begins by introducing each family member or invites each person to say his or her name. Then the therapist asks the family questions, such as, "Who would like to talk about how we can best use this time?"; "What is most important for us to focus on during this time?"; and "What kind of feedback would we like from the team?" The therapist and clients can use the time in whatever way they deem appropriate (which may have changed since the meeting with the team was arranged); however, it is suggested that there be a focus to the session so that the team can be as helpful as possible. At the end of the initial segment, the therapist says, "I wonder what the team heard or noticed about our conversation. If it's okay with you, I'd like to invite them to switch places with us so that we can listen to their conversation." Clients are then invited to listen to the team, choose anything that fits, and leave the rest behind.

Once the transition has been made, the team members introduce themselves. They then engage in an 8 to 12 minute conversation (which can be adjusted depending on the context) about what resonated or stood out for them. Team conversations tend to evolve based on what each person has written and what has just been said by other team members. For example, one team member may make a comment that he or she had written down, which triggers a thought in another team member who continues the conversation. This allows for spontaneous and creative conversations.

The team may wonder out loud through conjecture-laced, open-ended questions or statements (for example, "I wonder what will be different when things start to turn the corner"; "I was curious about how Jennifer has been able to keep her head above water with all that has happened"; "I was struck by how Desmond acted so quickly in when his mother asked for help with the yard work. I wonder if he noticed that."). The team members may also reflect the experience, feelings, or perspectives they had while observing (for example, "I was really moved when Nate told his father how much he cares about him"; "I can see why this is so important to Vinnie. I could hear the pain in his voice when he talked about the loss of his friend. It really struck a chord with me."). Team members' comments are used to validate, encourage, and widen the view of the situation. Hearing the perspectives of different people almost invariably shows that there are multiple valid ways to view and construe the situation. The conversation ends with the team thanking the clients and wishing them well. The CCT and client-therapist teams then switch places for the final part of the session.

In the final part, the therapist invites the clients to share any thoughts or comments that they might have as a result of experiencing the team's conversation. This part should take no more than five or six minutes and is meant to provide an opportunity for brief reflections. During this time, the therapist asks questions such as, "What was your experience in observing the team?"; "What stood out for you?"; "What did you hear/see/feel/notice?"; "What made sense to you?"; and "What was the process like for you?" Each person should be given space to share his or her experience; however, some will have little or nothing to say. Interestingly, it is common for clients to have more to say in future situations once they have had time to digest the events of the session. It is important that in this last sequence therapists avoid having clients fall back into problem-talk. It is not a time to rehash but to reflect on what stood out, including any new meanings or experiences that have emerged. Therapists can also revisit this in detail with clients in subsequent sessions.

One of the major benefits of using CCTs is flexibility. As noted, many possibilities in terms of variations can be utilized in different contexts. CCTs also provide an excellent vehicle for training new therapists, particularly in how to use language in respectful and strengths-based ways. The use of teams as a supervisory or consultative tool will be discussed in Chapter 13.

SUMMARY POINTS

- In addition to the ideas provided in Chapter 7, therapists can help clients to change their views by shifting their attention in areas related to *time, what clients do well, actions instead of explanations, sensory perceptions,* and *internal or external focus.*
- *Stories and metaphor* provide a pathway to changing views and perspectives by *normalizing, acknowledging, injecting hope, offering new possibilities, bypassing everyday conscious ways of processing information,* and *offering reminders of previous solutions and resources.*
- *The written word, music,* and *movies* are other media that can offer clients new ways of viewing.
- *Conversational and consulting teams* (CCTs) offer a structured way to offer feedback to open up new perspectives for clients and therapists. CCTs are flexible and can be used at different junctures of therapy and in different contexts.

DISCUSSION QUESTIONS

1. Focusing on shifting attention is a pathway for changing views and perspectives. What are different methods that therapists can use to help clients shift their attention?

2. Describe a situation in which you might use one or more ways to help a client to shift his or her attention. What method(s) might you choose?

3. In what ways do metaphor and stories facilitate change and healing?

4. What are examples of other media that can help to change clients' stories and facilitate healing?

5. How can conversational and consulting teams (CCTs) be used at one or more points in therapy? What are examples of situations in therapy in which CCTs can be useful?

Chapter 9

Changing Actions and Interactions, Part I

Identifying and Altering Repetitive Patterns

■ As you have learned, people can experience problems and solutions in multiple realms. Chapters 7 and 8 explored ways to promote change with clients whose views have become problematic. A change in this realm will be sufficient to resolve many clients' concerns. In at least two situations, however, an additional or alternative realm provides a better fit than other approaches and needs to be explored. One situation involves clients who have made changes in their perspectives but need to take *action* to have those new views influence their lives significantly. For example, a client may identify exceptions to a problem but needs to employ them more deliberately in the present to achieve her desired change—this requires taking action. A second scenario involves clients whose situations have problematic patterns of action or interaction. For example, a couple may have arguments in which one of them engages in patterns that trigger the other, leading to escalations. In these situations,

working to change *how* they interact as a means of deescalating their arguments can be helpful.

Behavioral, marital, and family therapists focus on the ways that patterns of action and interaction influence the development and maintenance of problems. They focus on how clients *do* their problems as opposed to trying to explain them. Other therapy approaches (for example, cognitive-behavioral, rational emotive behavior, reality, solution-focused, multimodal) also emphasize, at least in part, behavioral and/or interactional change. A concurrent idea with these approaches is that clients need to undertake some form of action in their lives so they are able to experience the benefits of change. The belief is that it is not enough to think differently; people need to *act* differently.

This chapter moves into the realm of action and interaction to explore ways to change and alter problematic patterns. It first investigates how problems are constructed. Then it discusses the identification of problem patterns. The remainder of the chapter focuses on specific methods for collaborating with clients to help them alter, disrupt, modify, and ultimately change the ways of acting and interacting that are contributing to, maintaining, or sustaining problems. The chapter also considers how to investigate potential solution patterns and the ways in which clients can use those solution patterns to initiate change in the present. See Figure 9.1 for a visual representation of the action/interaction realm.

Action and Interaction in Context: The Construction of Patterns

Take a moment to think about the everyday actions you engage in. You are likely to identify a few or more routines that you follow. Delving a little deeper, you may notice that you approach situations in your life (for example, dealing with conflict, completing tasks) in certain ways. You may follow these ways more or less loosely, but nonetheless, they involve some form of action and therefore, patterns. Life requires action, and actions are rarely random. They are patterned and, in many cases, predictable.

Patterns are part of our everyday lives. In some instances, however, patterns repeat in unhelpful ways. In a sense, people become frozen in time without a way to escape (O'Hanlon & Bertolino, 1998). As discussed in Chapter 3, John Weakland of the Mental Research Institute (MRI) was fond of saying that life is just one damn thing after another. Just when it seems everything is sorted out, we reach a different developmental stage and life ushers in new dilemmas. For people who seek therapy, life has taken on a more troublesome tone: It has become the same damn thing over and over. Out of this comes the sobering perspective—the job of therapists is to help clients to move from the same damn thing *over and over* back to one damn thing *after another*.

Figure 9.1

ACTION/INTERACTION
Action patterns—Interactional patterns—Language patterns—Nonverbal patterns—
Time patterns—Spatial patterns

▼

- Find action and interaction patterns that are part of the problem

- Suggest ways of disrupt problematic patterns

- Find and use solution patterns

Context is of particular importance with patterns. As discussed in Chapter 6, behavior cannot be understood void of context. Konrad Lorenz (1997), the Nobel Prize-winning ethologist, made this point explicitly in a story about his theory of imprinting. He observed that baby goslings would follow anything less than a certain height that made quacking noises and appeared in front of them in a certain time period after they hatched. On his farm in Austria, he had some geese. He isolated all objects that could fit the imprinting criteria before the critical imprinting period after the latest group of goslings hatched. He became the goslings' "parent" by parading in front of them, crouched and quacking. The goslings began to follow him, which excited Lorenz immensely. Invigorated with finally demonstrating his theory, he began wandering around his farm. Some time later, he looked up to notice that a tour guide and a group of tourists were observing him with concern. Lorenz realized that he had wandered into a field of tall grass in which the goslings could not be seen. What the observers saw was what appeared to be a madman, crouching in the grass making quacking noises and every once in a while leaping about in joy, clapping his hands and yelling in excitement.

In traditional models of family therapy, context and environment, in particular, became primary considerations regarding families. These models were based on the idea that interpersonal relationships held the key to understanding individuals' behaviors. This widening of the inquiry and focus to include context and environment was a major step forward in not assigning simplistic single causes to peoples' distress, which therapy did in its initial form. This was a significant stride in challenging monolithic individual psychodynamic explanations for problems; unfortunately it kept the pathologizing bias of that earlier approach (see the Appendix). A new currency of descriptors, such as "schizophrenogenic mothers" and "dysfunctional families," replaced previous ones such as "hysterics" and "neurotics" as family therapy gained prominence.

As family therapy (and behaviorism to some degree) evolved and addressed inherent biases (see the Appendix), the roles of action and interaction became more important. Similar to molecules, which can change in composition (for example, from solid to liquid to gas), problems were seen as patterns of action and interaction that could be changed. Clients' stories and first impressions may suggest that problems are set, but under close observation, it is clear that the patterns of action and interaction involved in problems are anything but static. Patterns, which maintain the shape of problems, can be changed and thus lead to problem resolution.

It is essential that therapists keep two things in mind: (1) the interpersonal settings in which behaviors have been occurring must be examined and (2) problematic patterns of action and interaction are not always recognizable to those who engage in them. Clients become entrenched in *doing* their problems and unaware that their actions may be sustaining those problems. There is the saying: *Insanity is doing the same thing over and over again and expecting different results.* The task of therapists is first to identify and second to change the patterns that are contributing to clients' problems. It is as if some logs get jammed up in a bend in the river and therapists want to remove the fewest number of logs to break up the logjam. They do not have to take every log out or catalog when each log fell into the river, nor do they need to get into the river and push the logs down every week. They merely need to help break up the pattern that keeps the logs stuck. A small change is often all that is necessary to alter a problematic pattern. Erickson (1980) held the idea that "maladies, whether psychogenic or organic, followed definite patterns of some sort, particularly in the field of psychogenic disorders; that a disruption of this pattern could be a most therapeutic measure; and that it often mattered little how small the disruption was, if introduced early enough" (p. 254).

Because each client has a different situation, therapists collaborate with clients to learn the nuances of their concerns. Therapists then select methods that fit with clients and are respectful of their orientations to change. This keeps therapy focused and client driven.

The Landscape of Action and Interaction: Identifying Problematic Patterns

Because problems do not exist in a vacuum, the more therapists can flesh out the dynamics that surround them, the more opportunities there are to influence and change them. These dynamics are represented through patterns—*how* people do their problems. Richard Bandler who with John Grinder (Bandler & Grinder, 1975; Grinder, DeLozier, & Bandler, 1977) meticulously studied Milton Erickson's work, often asked clients, "If I were you, how would I do your problem?" In much the same way, therapists study the landscape and map out clients' problems. O'Hanlon and Bertolino (1998) wrote: "We explore with clients the negative problem patterns that seem to be inhibiting or intruding in their lives. We seek to be geographers, exploring the topography and the coastline of Problem-Land. We want to know the details of the problem or symptom, *and* help the client to find ways to escaping it" (p. 66).

Previous chapters discussed the use of action-talk in ferreting out clients' problem descriptions and goals. Action-talk is essential to learning about clients' patterns because it elicits detailed, sensory-based descriptions. Action-talk (and video-talk) moves clients from vague descriptions to clear, observable ones. From these descriptions, therapists can search for any contextual aspects of problems that repeat. These repeating sequences are related to time and space and represent the patterns that therapists work in collaboration with clients to alter, modify, disrupt, and change. To identify problematic patterns, therapists explore the following areas:

- What is the *frequency* (rate) of the problem? How often does it typically happen (once an hour, once a day, once a week)?
- What is the typical *timing* (time of day/week/month/year) of the problem?
- What is the usual *duration* of the problem? How long does it typically last?
- What is the range of the problem's *intensity*?
- *Where* (location and spatial patterns) does the problem typically happen?
- *Who else* is involved? What do others who are around or involved usually do when the problem is happening?

These questions are not random but reflect a position of curiosity on the part of therapists. Their intention is to gain clarity about the specific ways that problem patterns play out in clients' lives. Case Examples 9.1 and 9.2 illustrate inquiring about the details that surround patterns.

The exchange in Case Example 9.1 indicated that many aspects of the client's problem patterns were related to time, space, and relationships. For example, the client's anxiety is work related. It most frequently occurs and is

CASE EXAMPLE 9.1

Therapist: Can you say more about the anxiety you've been having?

Client: I get real anxious when I'm around others.

Therapist: When did this first become apparent to you?

Client: I guess three or four years ago when I was in a hotel where I was staying for a business trip and I started to panic.

Therapist: By "panic" you mean what, specifically?

Client: I felt like I was being suffocated by people around me. I couldn't move. It was so crowded and I felt like I was going to pass out. I was overwhelmed.

Therapist: It sounds overwhelming. What did you do?

Client: I was able to get to the men's room and sit in a stall until I was calm.

Therapist: That's good. If it's okay with you, I'd like to ask you a few more questions so I have a better understanding of the circumstance of what you experienced.

Client: Sure, go right ahead.

Therapist: Thank you. How often have you experienced that kind of anxiety since then?

Client: It's happened quite a few times—mostly when I've been around lots of people.

Therapist: Okay. Where else has it happened other than the hotel?

Client: Let's see. At a convention I went to. I thought I was going to pass out then too.

Therapist: What happened?

Client: A friend helped me by getting me to a quiet place.

Therapist: Where else?

Client: One other time that I can remember was in a narrow hallway in my office building. Now I just don't use that corridor. I go a different way.

Therapist: That sounds like good choice. I'm very curious about something that I'd like to ask you more about but first I have one other question. You told me earlier that you are a season ticket holder for the Cardinals. How have you managed the crowds at the stadium without incident?

Client: I'm not sure. I never really thought about it. I mean, I love baseball.

Therapist: Okay, what about when you've gone to the movies or shopping. . . can you recall any incidences of anxiety that parallel the ones you described?

Client: Not any that come to mind. I don't really like crowded places in general, but it's not a problem for me.

Therapist: Here's where my curiosity may be getting the best of me. Do you see a connection between the events you've described?

Client: Not really.

Therapist: Each one of the anxiety-provoking events you described was work related. Does that make sense?

Client: Yes. I think that's right—they all are.

Therapist: Okay—that's part of the picture but let's get a little more specific. How often would you say you've felt the kind of anxiety you've described?

Client: Maybe once a week.

Therapist: Does it vary? Are there some weeks that you have more episodes than others?

Client: Yes. You know, now that I think of it, I feel more anxious when I have more stress at work.

CASE EXAMPLE 9.1 *(continued)*

Therapist: What might contribute to your stress?

Client: If I feel pressure from my boss—like if my sales are a low for the week.

Therapist: So when you've felt less pressured, you've been less stressed and had fewer anxious moments?

Client: Right.

Therapist: When you've felt panicked in the past, has there been a specific time of day?

Client: Usually in the morning. Well, early morning, actually. I can't remember feeling anxious or panicked any other time.

Therapist: What is it about the mornings?

Client: That's when our sales figures are given to our boss and if he is going to say something, it happens right away—first thing in the morning. He comes right to us—all of us in sales—and let's us know how unhappy he is. If we're away on business, he calls. It's like clockwork.

Therapist: And how often does he come to you with information on sales figures?

Client: Always on Mondays.

Therapist: Have you felt anxiety on any other day but Mondays?

Client: Yeah, but it's nothing I can't handle. Mondays are the worst.

Therapist: I see. So do you feel anxious before or after he comes to you or calls you or both?

Client: Hmm. Definitely before. Because I know when my sales are down and it's like waiting to see the principal.

Therapist: Okay. What happens after you speak with your boss?

Client: Well, then it's over. Once we've talked, I'm okay.

Therapist: How long would you say your anxiety lasts afterward?

Client: I hadn't really thought about it before now, but I actually feel better right away. Because once I've heard the news, I know where I stand and can get on with my day. It's the not-knowing that drives me crazy.

Therapist: And what have you noticed helps to curb your anxiety just a twinge leading up to the Monday sales report?

Client: Being with other salespeople.

Therapist: How does that help?

Client: I think it's because I'm with others and if our sales may differ, we're all in it together. We've all faced the wrath of our boss.

Therapist: I see. You can support each other.

Client: Right.

Therapist: What else helps just a bit?

Client: If I call my co-worker, Reg, before we have to face the boss. He has a great outlook and always puts things in perspective. He doesn't panic like I do.

Therapist: That's great. So both group and individual support helps. . . .

Client: . . . yes, they both help a lot.

most intense on Monday mornings. Although he may experience anxiety at other times, it is not the debilitating kind he experiences on Mondays. In addition, the onset of the anxiety has been prior to a meeting with his boss before a discussion of sales figures. Other information indicated that the client's anxiety dissipated once his boss had spoken with him.

The details described helped the therapist to understand the context of the client's anxiety. His anxiety was not random. There were specific elements related to where, when, and under what conditions he would feel most anxious.

CASE EXAMPLE 9.2

Therapist: You mentioned that you'd like to work on eating less so that you can lose weight. Please tell me about that.

Client: Well, I just eat too much.

Therapist: What are your eating habits like? Do you eat regular meals?

Client: I eat three meals a day.

Therapist: Okay, and do you have snacks in between or eat at other times?

Client: I occasionally have snacks but nothing big.

Therapist: Okay, three meals and snacks here and there. When you say you eat too much, do you mean at your regular meals?

Client: Yes. At those three meals I eat too much.

Therapist: Tell me more about that.

Client: Well, when I sit down to eat. . . I eat real fast. I'm always done before everyone else, so I eat more.

Therapist: So when you sit down to eat, you take a regular size portion, but you eat it faster than the others who are eating with you?

Client: Exactly.

Therapist: And then you get another helping. . .

Client: . . . yeah, I may have two or three more helpings.

Therapist: Is it only with specific foods?

Client: It's really with all foods. I'm not choosy.

Therapist: And how fast is eating fast . . . how long does it typically take you to eat that first portion?

Client: Oh, about five to seven minutes.

Therapist: What about the second and if there's a third?

Client: The same. I just keep eating until everyone else is done.

Therapist: How long does that typically take?

Client: About 20 minutes or so.

Therapist: Where do you usually eat your meals?

Client: Mostly at home, but at work I eat with my co-workers.

Therapist: At home, do you eat in the kitchen?

Client: Yeah.

Therapist: Is anyone with you?

Client: My husband and two kids.

Therapist: Do they stay the whole time?

Client: Oh yeah, they can't be excused until we are all done.

Therapist: What do they do while you are eating?

Client: Nothing really. They just eat too. I think they're used to it.

Therapist: How often do you eat alone?

Client: Rarely.

Therapist: Is there anything different about the how quickly you eat or the amount of food you eat when you're alone as opposed to with others?

Client: No, not that I can think of.

CASE EXAMPLE 9.2 *(continued)*

Therapist: And in regard to work, do you bring extra food. . .

Client: . . . No, I don't have to because there are always goodies sitting around—donuts, cookies, cake.

Therapist: But as you said, you don't really eat that much at other times . . . outside of your meals . . . you just eat a lot when having actual meals.

Client: Yes. I'll eat whatever is around.

Therapist: And do you eat at the same rate at work?

Client: Yep, and when I'm done, I grab cookies or whatever else is around.

Therapist: How much time do you have to eat lunch at work?

Client: A half hour, but I wind down after about 25 minutes so I can clean up and get back to my desk.

Therapist: What are your eating habits like at restaurants?

Client: I think I eat less. We don't really go out that much because our budget is tight, but when we do, I usually just order a regular meal.

Therapist: Does that work for you?

Client: It does. I'm sometimes still hungry, but I get over it.

Therapist: How do you do that?

Client: Well, it's easier because the amount of food is limited. I don't like buffets so that's not an issue for me. I just order once and they control how much you get.

Therapist: So there are times when you really get the upper hand with eating, and one way to do that is by ordering one time and having someone else prepare the food and be in charge of portions?

Client: Yes.

Therapist: What about home or work? What have you noticed about times when you've eaten a little less in either of those places?

Client: That's hard. At home, I'm the one who makes the food so I always prepare a lot. At work there's always extra stuff in the lunchroom. But I have noticed that I eat less when it's just not around. I guess that's a simple way to looking at it, but it's true.

In Case Example 9.2, information about the client's problematic pattern was obtained by asking questions that focused on time and space. For example, the client reported that she ate quickly and for approximately 20 to 25 minutes whether at home or at work. The therapist also learned that she does her pattern three times a day—only at meals. In addition, there is at least one context in which her eating habits vary. Given this information, the therapist has various places to intervene with this client. Once a problematic pattern is identified, the aim is to find someplace (and sometimes more than one) in that pattern in which the client can do something different. We revisit Case Examples 9.1 and 9.2 later in this chapter to learn about possibilities for pattern intervention. At this juncture, to practice identifying problematic patterns, please complete Exercise 9.1, Identifying Problematic Patterns.

Exercise 9.1

Identifying Problematic Patterns

Life is composed of routines and *patterns*. This exercise is to help identify patterns that maintain problems. It is important to recognize that problematic actions and interactions are *contextual*. Problems and solutions occur at certain times, in certain places, with certain people, last for different lengths of time, and so on. To determine how to proceed, it is first important to explore the patterns surrounding problems. Use of 4W-H questions that ask who, what, when, where, and how helps to learn about patterns. With this information and when necessary, therapists can then work to change, alter, and disrupt those patterns. You may complete this exercise by yourself or with other persons. Please answer the questions by writing your answers in the spaces provided. (Be specific with your answers and incorporate action-talk.)

- Describe a problem.

  _____

  _____

  _____

- How often does the problem typically happen (once an hour, once a day, once a week)?

  _____

  _____

  _____

- What is the usual time (of day, of week, of month, of year) of the problem?

  _____

  _____

  _____

- How long does the problem typically last?

  _____

  _____

  _____

- Where does the problem typically happen?

  _____

  _____

  _____

- What do you [or the person(s) with the concern] do when the problem is happening?

  _____

  _____

  _____

Exercise 9.1 *(continued)*

- Who is usually present when the problem is happening?

_____

_____

_____

- What do others who are around when the problem is happening usually do or say?

_____

_____

_____

- What have you learned as a result of completing this exercise?

_____

_____

_____

Preparation for Movement: Orienting Toward Action

Being collaborative involves taking care to honor and respect clients' orientations to change. Using the I-AM framework described in Chapter 6, practitioners invite, acknowledge, and match clients' perspectives and select methods based on their preferences. Although ongoing change requires some form of action, many clients are not in a state of readiness to take action in their lives. For those clients, the methods outlined in Chapters 7 and 8 may provide better opportunities for change. For clients at the *preparation* and *action* stages of change, practitioners can encourage ways to change action and interaction in addition to methods associated with changing the viewing. A focus on this realm is indicated with clients who:

- Have a more externalizing coping style. In other words, they are more socially gregarious, seek activity, and tend to take charge and focus more on external factors as influences (Beutler & Harwood, 2000).
- Use words that suggest they are, at least in part, action and interactional processors (for example, "I really need to do something about this"; "I do this and she does that").
- Indicate through conversations and/or orientations (including cultural influences) that they expect change to involve doing something different—taking action, changing behavior, or making some form of change involving movement.
- Indicate a degree of ownership with problems (for example, use of "I," "me," "we").

Although these criteria for focusing on this realm offer general rules of thumb, therapists should keep in mind that what people say they are willing and planning to do is not always the same as what they actually do. This is a crucial point because clients may leave sessions with seemingly good plans of action and come back in future sessions not having implemented them. This will be discussed in subsequent chapters; however, it is important to note that this is attended to as communication, not resistance. Because they hold the idea that methods need to fit with clients' orientations, therapists attend to these moments as client feedback or information. This information provides opportunities to revisit clients' orientations to renegotiate the means and methods that offer the best probability of achieving desired change.

Therapists are not searching for correct methods but ones that are respectful and effective in opening up possibilities for change. The best methods are the ones that work for clients. Crucial to methods aimed at addressing patterns of action and interaction is the idea that clients are capable of making changes on their own. Traditional models that have placed therapists in the role of designing and implementing strategies often have done so without providing a rationale to clients. This has contributed to the notion of therapists as shamans and the only experts in the therapeutic milieu. Such thinking raises the risk of client dependence, downplays client strengths, and, more important, conveys the message that clients are incapable of understanding and implementing ideas introduced in therapy.

At times indirect, "back-door" methods (for example, paradox, which is described later) are appropriate in helping clients to change pervasive patterns. At the same time, therapists should use education as an important measure in creating contexts in which clients are encouraged to be creative. This requires taking the time to explain the rationale behind methods. By modeling and inviting creativity, therapists are conveying self-sufficiency and independent thinking, allowing clients to tap into their capacities to resolve their own concerns. To further invite creativity, sometimes giving clients examples of things that others have tried can be

useful. At other times, stories can be used to trigger movement or experiments. No matter the inroad, clients are treated respectfully and partnered with in making change to *their* lives.

There are two primary pathways—depatterning and repatterning—used to facilitate change with client patterns of action and interaction. *Depatterning* involves altering repetitive patterns of action and interaction by changing one or more aspects of problem sequences. *Repatterning* works to establish new patterns by identifying and encouraging the use of solution patterns of action and interaction. Depatterning will be explored in this chapter in detail. Repatterning will be discussed in Chapter 10.

Depatterning of Repetitive Action and Interaction Patterns

Inherent to behavioral and family therapy approaches is a focus on—and changing—behavioral sequences. Behaviorists target individuals and ways to positively or negatively reinforce their behaviors. Strategies implemented are based on systems of rewards and consequences. Family therapists (primarily systems theorists) identify problems as the result of problematic patterns of interaction (in other words, what occurs between people). Although the two approaches are vastly different in principle, they share common ground that change involves what people do, whether it is as individuals or in relationship to each other.

One approach to changing action and interaction is *depatterning*. It involves altering or disrupting the patterns involved in surrounding problems. Therapists can then notice whether problems change or not. Depatterning in a predominantly behavioral or interactional sense would most likely take place at therapists' directives. In other words, therapists would design and implement strategies based on their conceptual maps of change. From a strengths-based perspective, therapists collaborate with clients and learn what they think will work best for them. Doing so involves finding out from clients what they have tried to solve or resolve their concerns in the past, including what has or has not worked to any degree. Therapists also ask questions to learn more about what clients feel might work and what is acceptable to them prior to offering any suggestions. As discussed, therapists do not want to suggest things that clients have already tried or are completely out of the question in terms of their orientations to change.

For clients who are stuck in patterns that metaphorically speaking appear like "broken records" or are engaged in "more of the same," depatterning offers an excellent way to change problem sequences. Within every problematic pattern are typically several places to suggest changes to alter or disrupt it. Depatterning can be accomplished in 11 different ways. As a means to elucidate the method being outlined, one or more case illustrations will be provided.

Change the *Frequency/Rate* of the Complaint or the Pattern Around It

One method of depatterning involves changing how a particular aspect in a problem sequence occurs. This can be done by encouraging clients to do the pattern more or less. The following example illustrates suggesting that clients speed up or slow down some aspect of the sequence or pattern.

An extremely bright and creative man who had a deep appreciation for language sought therapy for the concern of talking very rapidly when he became nervous. This presented difficulty because he was up for a promotion that would involve periodic public speaking.

He was concerned that he would be passed over for the promotion if he could not overcome his nervousness. Rather than directly target his nervousness, the therapist suggested that the man "give others the opportunity" to learn from his knowledge. He was then encouraged to give each word the respect he believed it deserved. No word deserved a quick pass over. To do this, the man agreed to slow his rate of speech down so that he spoke no more than 10 words in a sentence and no more than five sentences in a minute. He then mapped out a future speech and rehearsed it to ensure that it was within the parameters he had set with his therapist.

Change the *Location* of the Performance of the Complaint

Problems often have a physical location (environmental) component. They occur in some places but not in others. For problematic patterns that have this dynamic, practitioners can invite clients to continue the complaint but in a location in which the problem has not occurred. See the following example.

A family of four came to therapy with the chief complaint that they could "not work things out." When asked about this, the parents concurred that dinner was a "nightmare." The mother stated that there were "constant" arguments that made it "nearly impossible to enjoy each other's company." The family was asked various other questions about the length of their arguments, the general sequence of events, and so on. It was learned that although other periodic conflicts occurred, dinner was by far the most troublesome time of day. It was suggested that the family have dinner as usual, but as soon as an argument began, they were all to proceed directly to the garage (which was connected to the kitchen), which was deemed the "crisis room." Once there, they were to continue the argument until each person had a chance to fully express himself or herself or agree to refrain from arguing. They were to take as much time as possible and return as many times as necessary to restore peace to dinner time.

Change the *Duration* of the Complaint or the Pattern Around It

Problem patterns are often consistent in terms of length. Although a degree of variance may exist, they run their course in predictable fashion. A possibility, then, is to either increase or decrease the length of the problem pattern. Increasing the length may initially appear illogical (paradoxical) to some clients. After more discussion, many clients will understand that this particular method often removes the spontaneity associated with patterns. See Case Example 9.3.

CASE EXAMPLE 9.3

Gerard, a 10-year-old, was brought to therapy by his mother because he would scream very loudly when he did not get his way. His mother had grown tired of this behavior and was at her wits end. I explored the pattern of interaction and the sequence of events that seemed to occur between the mother and her son. I learned that the longest Gerard had screamed was about 30 seconds (with short breaks to breathe) because his mother would give in each time. She said, "I just can't take it, so I give him what he wants."

Several aspects of the concern offered possibilities for changing the pattern; however, the mother continued to go back to the length of the screaming. Based on this, I asked her if we could spend some time exploring that aspect of the concern. She agreed. I proceeded by asking if she had any specific ideas about what might work. She replied that she was "out of ideas but was "open to any and all suggestions." I then encouraged her to consider the possibility of changing the length of the time that Gerard spent screaming. I said, "This may sound weird, so please bear with me. You said that the longest Gerard has screamed for is about 30 seconds. It becomes too much for you and you give in. What do you think would happen if you encouraged him to scream for

a longer period of time?" Her immediate reaction was to say, "I couldn't do that. I couldn't take it." Noting her concern, I followed, "I certainly can understand that. But do you really think he would?" The mother smiled, "I see what you're saying. He wouldn't expect me to tell him to scream longer because I always tell him to stop." "That's what I was thinking," I replied.

The conversation continued, and we talked about the importance of thinking as creatively as possible without trying to find a correct answer. A further consideration was that whatever we came up with needed to be something she fully agreed with and knew she would follow through on. We also agreed that if something did not work, we would modify or abandon it. The result was a plan in which the next time Gerard did not get his way and began to scream, his mother would wait him out. To do this, she would focus on her watch and time the length of his scream. When he quit, she would encourage him to scream longer, perhaps for two or three minutes.

That evening, following the session, the mother told Gerard "no" and he began to scream. At first she felt herself drifting back into her old pattern of trying to plead with him to stop, but she quickly caught herself, sat down in

CASE EXAMPLE 9.3   (continued)

a chair, and glanced down at her watch to keep time. Gerard seemed surprised by this. He looked at his mom, tried to distract her, and then stopped screaming. His mother immediately responded to his silence, "Twenty seconds of screaming isn't enough. You need to scream for at least two minutes to make sure you got it all out. You owe me another minute and 40 seconds." Gerard was shocked by his mother's reaction. After a few moments, he grunted and left the room. A short while later, his mother told

Gerard "no" for something else and as he took a deep breath to scream, she looked down at her watch. Gerard stopped in his tracks and again left the room. The pattern had been disrupted.

In the next session, I talked with Gerard about his feelings and how it was fine for him to become upset. However, there were better ways to let his mom know how he felt. We then worked on ways that he could let her know how he was feeling and what he needed without screaming.

Change the Complaint's *Time* (Hour/Time of Day, Week, Month, or Year) of the Pattern Around It

One of the more predictable elements of problematic patterns is time. Like changing the location of complaints, small changes in time can be enough to disrupt repetitive sequences. Time includes small (for example, seconds, minutes, hours) or large (days, weeks, months, years) increments depending on the problem. See the following examples.

> A husband was upset that his wife wanted to talk about "serious" issues as soon as they went to bed. He stated that that should be "together time," not "serious time." It was suggested that he request "serious time" with his wife between 8:00 and 8:30 P.M. each night. She agreed, and after two nights, they were able to increase their "together time."

> A woman brought her 12-year-old son to therapy because he would sneak out late at night. It was suggested that she schedule "sneak out" time each morning. She was to wake him up at 5:00 A.M. every morning and

sit on his bed until he got up and went outside for at least 15 minutes. Her son was annoyed with being waked so early each morning and quit sneaking out.

Change the *Sequence* (Order) of Events Involved in or Around the Complaint

Because patterns involve events, an obvious point of entry is the sequencing of those events. Once patterns are mapped out, therapists collaborate with clients as in the following example to determine what might be changed in the sequencing of problematic patterns.

> A woman was concerned that each time she tried to get in a word with her father, he would start giving her advice. The sequence was that she would make a comment, he would begin to give advice, she would try to interrupt and tell him what she needed, and he would talk over her. She appreciated his advice but was not always asking for it. Sometimes she just wanted him to listen. The end result was her giving up on conversations. It was suggested that she determine what kind of conversation she wanted with

her father prior to calling him. Then, she was to call him and before raising an issue, tell her father what she needed from him, thus changing the sequence of their conversations. If he continued to talk over her, she was to tell him she had to get off the phone. After getting off the phone one time, her father began listening to her requests and accommodating them in conversation.

Interrupt or Otherwise Prevent the Occurrence of the Complaint

One way to change problematic patterns that are predictable is to interrupt or stop the complaint altogether. This is often done by "beating the other person to the punch." When problem patterns have been identified, therapists encourage clients to either prevent complaints from reappearing or to reduce their intensity. See the following example.

> A teenager would come home from school each day, throw her books on the floor and say, "I'm not going back! I hate school." Her mother would then have problems getting her to do her homework and getting her to attend school the next day. It was suggested that the mother change the sequence of interacting with her daughter. She was to meet her at the front door and before the daughter could say anything, she was to blurt out, "I can't believe the day you've had! How did you make it through it?" The first time the mother tried this, her daughter was surprised and said, "Mom, it wasn't that bad." The second time, the daughter responded with, "Mom, get a life." The problems with school ceased.

Add a New Element to the Complaint

Aspects of patterns can vary yet at core remain consistent and predictable. When patterns are routines that help people to function, disruptions to those patterns can in fact create problems. Other times, it is the patterns themselves that are problematic and can be disrupted by introducing new elements. The hoped-for result is that clients find new and more effective ways to dealing with their concerns. See Case Example 9.4.

CASE EXAMPLE 9.4

A woman came to therapy because of a concern with her 11-year-old son. When her son did not get his way, he would latch on to her clothes. He would grab her clothes and proceed to yell at her to let him do whatever he wanted. She reported that he would not let go of her clothes until she gave in. She did want to keep giving in to him, and her clothes were getting ruined from her son hanging on to them, stretching and occasionally tearing them. The woman was extremely frustrated to the point of tears.

As we got to know each other, I learned that the woman was in a symphony orchestra. She had a deep love of and appreciation for music. As she spoke about music, her eyes lit up and she seemed to become more relaxed. I asked her, "What does your family think about you being in the symphony?" "My husband loves it, but my son can't stand classical music," she replied. "That must make it hard to practice at home," I followed. The woman smiled and said, "No, it doesn't, because I don't practice at home. I practice at our rehearsal site." Confused, I inquired, "Well how do you know that he doesn't like classical music?" "Because every time I turn it on at home, he leaves the room or, should I say, he runs out of the room,"

CASE EXAMPLE 9.4   *(continued)*

she answered. As the mother spoke, she began to smile and laugh. It was as if a "light bulb" went on. She said, "I know what to do the next time he grabs my clothes. I'll just go into the living room and turn on classical music." I acknowledged her creativity and encouraged her to follow her idea. I also recommended that she exercise patience if her efforts did not bring immediate results.

The next session with the woman was scheduled for two weeks later. She began by describing how one evening she told her son he could not go to a friend's house after dark. In predictable fashion, he reached for and grabbed her clothes. Because she waited to tell him "no" until she was in the living room, the woman as able to reach over and turn on the stereo. When the classical music came on, the boy let go of her clothes and yelled, "Turn that crap off!" After some hesitation, he then lunged toward her in an attempt to grab her clothing again. This time, however, the woman responded differently. Whereas in the past she would have withdrawn and moved away from his attempts to grab her clothes, this time she moved toward her son and said, "Do you want to dance? I love to dance and your father's not here. . . ." She proceeded to reach for his arms as if to dance with him. The boy immediately pulled his arms back and said, "What are you doing? You're a freak!" and ran out of the room.

The woman then turned the music off and proceeded to leave the room. As she did, her son came back around the corner and went after her. She again pursued him and said, "I don't need music to dance. C'mon!" Once again, her son ran from her, this time standing behind the kitchen table where she could not reach him. From that point, the pattern of her son grabbing her clothes until he got his way had been altered.

Break Up Any Previously Whole Element of the Complaint into Smaller Elements

Another way to change problem sequences is by breaking them up into smaller parts. This can be an effective approach because it takes people out of the rhythm and spontaneity associated with their patterns. People can become unknowingly caught up in the blow-by-blow of problematic patterns. Building deliberate breaks into patterns makes it difficult for clients to both maintain patterns and the intensity that can accompany them. See the following example for an illustration of this.

A husband and wife came to therapy with the complaint that they were having disagreements over various household concerns. Each time they would try to discuss a topic, it turned into an argument. The therapist suggested that the couple get a timer, set if for two minutes, and allow each person that amount of time to state his or her point of view. Once the timer went off, it was the other person's turn. The couple was to argue one point at a time.

Reverse the Direction of Striving in the Performance of the Problem

Perhaps one of the most controversial methods is reversing the direction of striving. Known in various approaches under different names such as *paradox* or *prescribing the symptom,* the central idea is to encourage the continuation of problems that clients are complaining about. Sometimes just suggesting that people do what they do not want to do often disrupts problem sequences. The intention behind this method is not to deceive but to change pervasive patterns that have not responded to other methods. Although a flexible method, it should never be used with behaviors that are dangerous to self or others, present some form of risk, or are illegal or unethical. See the following examples.

> A man would become anxious—sweating profusely and stuttering—when his boss approached him. He was worried that others would notice his strange behavior, thereby making him more self-conscious. It was suggested that he practice producing his anxiety when at home so that he could become anxious with every person he meets. In this way, he would relate to each person in the same way, and no one would be able to notice the difference. The man abandoned his anxiety.

> Nelson, a 12-year-old who resided in a short-term residential program, would hide his books and assignments and refuse to do his homework. When Nelson and I met for therapy, I told him that he was predictable and that I knew exactly what he would do. That evening at study time he would hide his books and refuse to do his homework. I added that I was smarter than he was because I was older and had been to college. I then suggested that he continue to hide his books so there would be even more proof about how smart I was and how predictable he was. Nelson was not impressed by my comments. He informed me that he was not predictable and that I had no idea what he was going to do that evening regarding his homework. I told him to continue his "game" and I would continue to be smarter than him.

> The next day I arrived for therapy appointments. I was told by a youth care worker that Nelson had been eagerly awaiting my arrival. Nelson raced through the door after school and blurted, "Ha! I'm smarter than you! I'm smarter than you!" "How's that?" I asked. "I did my homework! Ha, ha! I'm smarter than you!" I told him that I would need to verify it. Nelson had in fact completed all of his homework, apparently without hiding his books or any delay. I then spoke to Nelson about his accomplishment, "This is amazing. I can't believe it. I've never been outsmarted by a 12-year-old. Congratulations. But we both know it won't happen again. I'm sure it was all luck." "No it wasn't. You'll see!" responded a riled-up Nelson. He was right. Nelson maintained his new homework practices and thrived on the praise staff gave him for completing his homework. He found that positive attention felt much better.

Link the Occurrence of the *Complaint to* Another Pattern That Is a *Burdensome Activity*

From clients' frames of reference, there are patterns that may not be experienced *as problematic enough.* Sometimes patterns have become such a part of people's lives that they seem satisfied with their continuation. Although varying perspectives explain this behavior, from a strengths-based perspective, therapists maintain the stance that people do want their lives to be different; they do not want to feel bad and have negative symptoms. Conversely, change can sometimes be difficult, especially if people have been living with problems for extended periods of time. One way to address this is to use *ordeals* (unfavorable or burdensome activities) that are more trouble than they are worth. The idea as illustrated in the following example is to link an ordeal with a complaint behavior so that the client comes to the conclusion that giving up the problem is a better choice than maintaining it with the ordeal.

> A 14-year-old came to family therapy with his mother and stepfather. According to his mother, the teenager had been breaking curfew, was failing five out of six subjects at school, was consistently tardy to class, and was not completing homework. There was also suspicion that he might be smoking marijuana. It was suggested that his parents contact the school and find out how many minutes he had been tardy for that particular day of school. When he came home, they were to go to his room and read to him for the amount of time that he had missed class. If he took off, they were to get up when he returned home, no matter what time it was. They were to read to him and make sure that he got his "education." Because the teenager did not bring books home, they were asked to read from encyclopedias. They agreed that any education that he could get from the reading would be beneficial because he had been doing poorly at school and not completing homework. The parents informed the teenager of their plan, but they never had to use it. The young man stopped coming in late because he did not want to be bothered by his parents reading to him at all hours.

Change the *Body Behavior/Performance* of the Problem or Complaint

It is not uncommon for people to develop patterns that involve actions specific to their bodies (for example, hair pulling, nail biting, self-mutilation). When clients engage in behaviors that pose threats to themselves, therapists need to ensure that they are safe. In circumstances in which behaviors are troublesome but do not represent a threat to self, suggesting that

clients change how they perform problematic patterns can be helpful. The following example illustrates this.

> A woman would cut her arms when she became upset or anxious about things in her life. She said that she did this to release the pain she felt inside. She would proceed with cutting until she drew blood. Instead of cutting herself, she was instructed to use a red lipstick to mark on her arm.

The methods outlined represent general categories to change problem sequences. Some methods overlap with others, and it is possible to combine two or more at the same time. It is also possible, although unnecessary, to target multiple aspects of problem patterns. Small alterations are usually sufficient to trigger changes in the performance of symptoms. To practice selecting and applying the methods described, please complete Exercise 9.2, Depatterning Through Context, and Exercise 9.3, Depatterning Through Interruption and Disruption.

Depatterning can be used to change virtually any aspect of a problem sequence. For example, a person who chewed his thumbnail might be encouraged to chew on the one fingernail for a set period of time or as an alternative, chew every fingernail for a minimum of five minutes each per day. Another example is to suggest that a person who straightens her belongings compulsively create one "junk" drawer or cabinet in her kitchen. Milton Erickson might get a person who smokes to put his cigarettes in the attic and matches in the basement. He once suggested that a compulsive hand washer change the brand of soap she used to wash her hands. He also worked with a man who had insomnia and had him agree to wax floors all night (a task he hated) if the man wasn't asleep within 15 minutes of going to bed. After the third night of waxing, the man

Exercise 9.2

Depatterning Through Context

Problems occur at certain times, in certain places, last for different lengths of time, and so on. This also means that at times, places, and so on they do not occur. Changing any one element—whether it is time, location, or some other aspect—can be enough to disrupt a problematic pattern. This exercise can help to make small changes in a number of areas that can ultimately lead to the resolution of the problem you are facing. To complete this exercise, review the different aspects of context that are listed. Consider which one, two, or three might apply to the identified problem. Then write your response to each inquiry in the space provided. (Be specific with your answers, incorporating action-talk in them.)

- Describe a problem.

  _____

  _____

  _____

- Notice the usual timing of the problem—when it happens, how long it lasts, or the frequency. Write one small change that could be made to alter the timing.

  _____

  _____

  _____

- Notice the usual location of the problem or the spatial arrangements of it (e.g., where it occurs). Write a change that could be made with the location or spatial arrangement.

  _____

  _____

  _____

- Identify the usual way to relate to others who may be involved with the problem. Pay close attention to voice tone, the words used, and nonverbal behaviors. Write one small change that could be made in the current pattern of relating.

  _____

  _____

  _____

- Select one of the ideas you have written and during the next week, put it into action. Track the effect of this action. If this does not bring about the desired results, try modifying or changing another aspect of the problematic pattern.

did not have trouble going to sleep again (O'Hanlon & Hexum, 1990).

It can be helpful to think of depatterning as "running interference" in problem sequences. It can present a challenge for clients whose patterns have become extremely embedded in everyday life. Because patterns represent what is familiar, trying something different or new can be difficult. As an experiment, try saying the word "yes" while shaking your head from

Exercise 9.3

Depatterning Through Interruption and Disruption

Either consciously or unconsciously, we engage in patterns that we believe will bring about the results we desire. In some instances, attempts at solution actually keep problems going and sometimes make them worse. This exercise will help change repetitive patterns by doing something different. It is important be creative in doing this exercise. In addition, if an attempt to interrupt or disrupt a problem sequence does not bring about the desired results, other possibilities should be explored. (Be specific with your answers, incorporating action-talk in them.)

- Describe a problem.

  _____

  _____

  _____

- Interrupt or prevent the occurrence of the problem. Write in the space provided one way that the occurrence of the problem could be interrupted or prevented.

  _____

  _____

  _____

- Add a new element to the problem. Write in the space provided one way to add a new element to the problem.

  _____

  _____

  _____

- Break up the problem into smaller elements. Write in the space provided one way to break the problem into smaller elements.

  _____

  _____

  _____

- Create an ordeal by linking the problem pattern with some burdensome activity. Then write in the space provided an ordeal that could be used to disrupt the problematic pattern.

  _____

  _____

  _____

- Select one of the ideas written here and during the next week, put it into action. Track the effect of this action. If this does not bring about the desired results, try modifying or changing another aspect of the problematic pattern.

left to right indicting "no." Or do the opposite by saying "no" and moving your head up as if to indicate "yes." What was that like? If it felt awkward at all, you can relate, on some level, what it is like to change a pattern.

There are considerations when determining which routes are indicated. First, to ensure that they are on track with their concerns, therapists summarize what they have heard from clients. Next, they invite clients' ideas about how their problems might be best approached and any ideas they might and/or want to explore on their own or with therapists' support. Therapists want to encourage clients to consider new ideas without worrying about finding the right ones. It is also important to be mindful that clients are typically more invested in trying something new if they feel that they have made a contribution to the idea's development. When clients have ideas, therapists want to draw them out by asking them to tell more, following with:

- How might that work for you?
- What do you need to do to make that happen?
- What will be your first step in putting this idea in motion?
- What, if anything, can others do to help to put this idea into motion?

Clients sometimes have trouble coming up with ideas or would prefer that therapists come up with them. Therapists accept these challenges, reminding clients that they are the "bus drivers" and the ones to decide whether an idea is a good fit or not. In addition, clients must decide whether or not they are willing to carry out suggestions. With this in mind, it can be helpful to say to clients, "Change involves work." Practitioner recommendations or suggestions for changing patterns represent ideas that they believe may be helpful but are not

directives. Practitioners offer them from a position of conjecture by telling one or more stories offering metaphorical possibilities and solutions, offering straightforward anecdotes about how other clients solved similar problems, or making suggestions based on how they understand the problematic pattern (Bertolino & O'Hanlon, 2002). With these considerations in mind, let's return to the first two case examples provided in this chapter to examine some possibilities for changing the doing of problems through depatterning.

In Case Example 9.1, the client was engaged in a pattern in which he would become anxious on Monday mornings prior to meeting with his boss to discuss sales figures. Several elements within the client's problematic pattern could provide points of entry. These included but were not limited to time (Monday mornings), space (work or business-related contexts), and relationships (with boss, co-workers). Examples of changing this pattern might be to suggest that the client call his co-worker at the first twinge of anxiety before the pattern becomes full blown. He might also schedule 15 minutes of "anxiety time" to take the spontaneity out of the symptoms, or he might create an anxiety space where he could go to "let it out." Finally, he might interrupt his anxiety, prevent its occurrence, or reduce its duration or intensity by listening to music or doing something be found relaxing. Beyond these ideas, encouraging the client to more actively and deliberately use his co-worker support system would be a good idea. The therapist could also pursue other angles (as described in Chapter 7) such as identifying specific precipitating factors (triggers) or further exploring exceptions. Further exploration of the pattern might also reveal other possibilities.

In Case Example 9.2, the client's problematic pattern contained strong elements of time, duration (planned meals, length of time spent eating each helping and the overall meal, and number of helpings) and space (who was present, physical contexts of home, work, restaurants). More conversation might have led to more options, such as determining how much and the kinds of foods the client ate, differences in unexplored contexts (others' homes), and so on. Based on what was learned, several possibilities for changing her eating patterns exist. One might be to suggest that she position herself where she can see a clock while eating. Then she would take just one regular size bite of food every minute—no more, no less. She could eat the same foods but at a different rate of ingestion. Or she could eat at the same rate but only foods with less calorie content. She might also be encouraged to eat in sequence with another

person at the table. For example, when that person takes a bite, she takes a bite. This might alter the timing around the problematic pattern. Finally, it could be suggested that she eat with whichever hand is not her dominant one (for example, eat with her left hand if she is right-handed), thereby changing the body behavior/performance of the complaint.

In both case examples, more exploration would likely lead to other ways to alter or disrupt the problem pattern. Throughout therapy, practitioners continue to elicit client feedback to understand what is working, what is not, and what might provide improved opportunities for change in the direction of their preferred futures. If one method is not working, something else needs to be tried. Allegiance to clients precedes allegiance to methods.

SUMMARY POINTS

- For some clients, a change in perspective is not sufficient. They need to take action.
- A point of convergence among behaviorally oriented and systemic approaches is a focus on changing patterns of action and interaction.
- The realm of action and interaction includes patterns related to behavior, relationships, language, nonverbal communication, time, and space.
- Behavior can be understood only in context; all behavior is shaped by numerous contextual influences (see Chapter 6).
- To identify problematic patterns, therapists explore specific areas including their frequency, timing, duration, intensity, location, and other persons involved.
- A focus on changing patterns of action and interaction is indicated when clients use words that suggest they are action and interactional

processors; convey through their orientations that they expect change to involve taking action or making movement; and demonstrate a degree of ownership with problems.
- It is important for therapists to collaborate with clients when helping them to change actions and interactions concerning a rationale for methods and encouraging creative action so that clients take initiative to change problematic patterns themselves in future situations.
- A primary way to facilitate change with client patterns of action and interaction is through *depatterning*.
- *Depatterning* involves altering, interrupting, preventing, or modifying repetitive patterns of action and interaction by changing one or more aspects of problem sequences such as its frequency/rate, location, duration, time, or sequence.

DISCUSSION QUESTIONS

1. What criteria suggest a focus on changing action and interaction should be used?

2. What are areas of consideration in identifying potential problematic patterns?

3. For which stages of change is a focus on action and interaction most indicated?

4. What is *depatterning*? List two examples of how it might be used to change a pattern of action or interaction.

5. What is a situation when you might use one or more ways to depattern? What depatterning method(s) might you choose?

Chapter 10

Changing Actions and Interactions, Part II

Identifying and Amplifying Solution Patterns

■ Chapter 9 introduced changing patterns by depatterning. This chapter explores *repatterning,* a second way to change patterns by establishing new ones in place of problematic ones. Repatterning is accomplished by identifying and encouraging the use of existing solution patterns of action and interaction. The chapter also discusses how to create action plans and collaborate with clients on tasks to accomplish goals. These processes can assist therapists in helping clients to change patterns by accessing solutions and possibilities that already exist within themselves and their social relationships and systems.

Repatterning through Solutions

Repatterning incorporates processes of eliciting, evoking, and highlighting previous solution patterns, abilities, competencies, strengths, and resources. It casts therapists as detectives who investigate areas that are likely to yield exceptions and contexts in which clients have demonstrated competence and mastery over problems. Repatterning involves identifying previously successful strategies that clients have used to deal with or resolve the problems that brought them to therapy. This is of particular importance because problems can create the illusion that they are present 24 hours a day, rendering clients helpless. When caught up in their problematic patterns, clients perpetuate this illusion by not recalling times or situations when things have gone differently or realizing the wealth of experience they have available. This also clouds their ability to identify actions that have been crucial to past successes with problems.

A chief philosophical underpinning of repatterning is the focus on asking questions that evoke a sense confidence and gather information in ways that highlight client competence. Therapists do not try to convince clients of their strengths or imply that all they need to do is think positively. Clients can interpret what may appear from therapists' perspectives as innocuous statements (for example, "All you need to do is step up to the plate and hit a home run"; "I can see you're full of strengths"; "Just go out there and do it") as invalidating, condescending, disingenuous, or as a form of "false cheerleading." As discussed throughout this book, being strengths-based means evoking what clients *have already done* that demonstrates competencies and solutions. When clients are able to connect with concrete examples of solutions, strengths, and resources through repatterning processes, they are more likely to convince themselves of the influence they have over problems. To prepare for the methods that subsequent sections will discuss, please complete Exercise 10.1, "Identifying Preliminary Solution Patterns."

Methods That Elicit Patterns for Solutions

The next sections discuss five methods used to evoke solution patterns.

Find Any Helpful Changes That Have Happened Before Therapy Began

One of the keys to collaboration discussed in Chapter 3 emphasized the role of helping clients to notice differences and variations in their concerns prior to starting formal face-to-face therapy. For some clients, the road to positive change starts *prior* to the first therapy session. Researchers refer to this phenomenon as *pretreatment change* (referred to in this text as *premeeting or presession* change), and studies indicate that up to two-thirds of clients coming for their first sessions report positive changes in reference to the complaints that brought them to therapy (Lawson, 1994; Weiner-Davis, de Shazer, & Gingerich, 1987; Ness & Murphy, 2001). As with exceptions, determining what clients *did* differently is important in addition to identifying presession change and corresponding solution patterns. To invite clients into conversations about presession change, therapists ask clients what they noticed happening between the time that they made the appointment for therapy and the first session. The following questions can assist in identifying presession change:

- What's been different between the time you made the appointment and now?
- What have you noticed that's been just a little better?
- What ideas do you have about how this change came about?
- What did you or others do differently?
- What difference has the change made for you?
- What will it take to keep things going in a better direction?
- What will you need to do to make that happen a little more beginning today?
- What else will you need to do?
- What, if anything, can others do to help you to continue to move forward?

The following example illustrates how therapists can identify and build on presession change.

> A young woman, Kylie, had been feeling down for several weeks. After talking with friends, she finally agreed to talk with a therapist. She made the appointment for two weeks later and then when about her business. Time passed until one day Kylie was having a lunch with a friend. Her friend inquired, "How did it go with your therapist?" A shocked Kylie exclaimed, "Oh no! The appointment is in 20 minutes!" So

Exercise 10.1

Identifying Preliminary Solution Patterns

This exercise is to identify preliminary exceptions and solution patterns to problem sequences. These identifiers illustrate times when things have gone differently and more important, what was different. They can serve as building blocks for future change. As with problematic actions and interactions, exceptions are *contextual.* Solution patterns occur at certain times, in certain places, with certain people, and so on. 4W-H questions, which ask who, what, when, where, and how, are useful in gathering information about patterns of action and interaction. You may complete this exercise by yourself or with others. Please answer the questions by writing your answers in the spaces provided. (Be specific with your answers and incorporate action-talk in them.)

- Describe a problem.

  _____

  _____

  _____

- When and where does the problem happen rarely or not at all?

  _____

  _____

  _____

- What is different about those times?

  _____

  _____

  _____

- What constants are present when the problem doesn't seem to be happening or is happening less frequently?

  _____

  _____

  _____

- Who is present or absent when the problem isn't happening or is happening less? What do people who are present do that helps?

  _____

  _____

  _____

- What are you [or you or the person(s) with the concern] doing when the problem is less noticeable or absent altogether?

  _____

  _____

  _____

- What did you learn as a result of completing this exercise?

  _____

  _____

  _____

she rushed over to see the therapist with whom she had she made the appointment. After sitting down she revealed, "I made this appointment a few weeks ago and I was really down. But things have changed. It's weird." The therapist proceeded to ask Kylie what had happened between the time that she had made the appointment and the actual appointment. She stated that she had changed jobs and starting journaling again. Kylie hypothesized that making the appointment had "jump started" her life. Before ending the session, the therapist talked with Kylie about how she might jump start herself in the future if she felt herself slipping back into her old patterns. To this Kylie replied, "I could just make a phantom appointment!" The therapist followed, "Terrific! And I'll send you a phantom bill!"

By drawing on presession change, practitioners are encouraging solution patterns in two ways. The first is by highlighting what clients have done to "get the ball rolling" to make positive strides in relation to their concerns. With the expectation of starting therapy as a kind of "flossing" effect (flossing more vigorously or more often in preparation of visiting the dentist), clients begin to direct more attention and effort to their problems (Bertolino & O'Hanlon, 2002). Asking about positive presession changes can yield important information about how people solve their problems or make changes. Practitioners can then assist clients with ways to utilize this information more deliberately in the future.

A second way to encourage solution patterns is by giving clients credit for their actions. When positive change is already in motion, therapists can talk with clients about how that change came about and what they did. As discussed in the next chapter, talking about how change occurred is essential because the more clients attribute change to themselves and their

actions rather than external factors or chance events, the more likely the change is to remain in the long term.

Find out about Previous Solutions to Problems (Exceptions), Partial Solutions, and Partial Successes and Actions Associated with Them

In Chapter 7, you learned about a direct pathway to solutions by focusing on exceptions to problems. All patterns of action and interaction have exceptions—it is just that they are more difficult to notice in the midst of problems. To reorient clients toward previous exceptions and successes, practitioners use a posture of *investigation through invitation*: inviting clients to reexamine, not reprocess, events to flesh out details that run counter to problem descriptions and patterns. In searching for exceptions, the therapist might say, "Tell me about a time when you expected the problem to (surface, get worse, continue) but it didn't." This would be followed by questions that identify *how* and *what* clients did—the competencies associated with those exceptions. Specifically, the therapist asks, "How were you able to do that?" and "What did you do differently?"

This process seeks more than an attentional shift that comes from asking questions that elicit exceptions. The intent is to tap into clients' motivation to take action. This requires therapists to maintain their investigative stance and identify those actions and interactions that represent the influence clients that have had in the past over their problems and that can be reengaged in the future. These questions can elicit exceptions.

- Tell me about a time during the past (day/week/month) when (the problem) happened to lesser degree or not at all?

What happened? What specifically was different? Who did what?

- Tell me about a time when (the problem) happened and you were able to get somewhat of a handle on it. What was different about that time? What did you do?
- You said that you've felt a little better over the past (days, weeks, months). What has been different? How did that happen?
- You mentioned that you've had trouble with (the problem) three of the last four days. How did you manage to (hold the problem at bay, stand up to the problem) on that one day?
- You commented that you and (other person's name) have had a lot of conflict recently about (problem). Yet when (the problem) came up you said that you didn't (fall back into the old pattern, engage in the conflict as in the past). What happened so that the situation didn't (do that, get stuck in the conflict)? What did you do? What did (other person's name) do?
- You told me that you've done (action) (two, five, ten) times in the past week. Even though you had the chance and may have thought about it, how did you manage to keep from drifting back into the old pattern the rest of the time?
- You didn't (action) last night. How did you keep yourself from doing what you usually have done? What did you do this time instead of (action)?

Because problematic patterns have exceptions, therapists assume that there have been times when things have gone better and problems have been less apparent and influential in clients' lives. Therapists do not ask *whether* but *when* things have gone differently. In effect, they *presuppose* exceptions and move to gain clear action descriptions of what clients did when things went a little differently in regard to their problematic patterns. This involves gaining details about what happened, when it happened, and what needs to happen in the future so the solution patterns occur more deliberately and with more frequency. Case Example 10.1 illustrates this idea.

CASE EXAMPLE 10.1

Therapist: Please tell me more about what you mean when you say your "world is crumbling."

Client: I feel like I can't keep up. There's work, the kids, bills . . . you name it.

Therapist: Of all the things you're trying to keep up with, which one or two comes to mind most?

Client: That's easy—it's not having enough time with my kids.

Therapist: You'd like to do be with them more but that hasn't been the case lately.

Client: Yeah. It's frustrating.

Therapist: When recently have you been able to spend time with them, even though it may not have been as much as you would have liked?

Client: Last weekend we went to the zoo and to lunch and that was fun. I wish it could have been longer.

Therapist: I can hear how important this is to you. And I wonder how you were able to create the time last weekend to be with your kids for the time you did.

(continued)

CASE EXAMPLE 10.1 *(continued)*

Client: It took some creative scheduling.

Therapist: Given what I know about your work, I have a sense of what you mean. That's what makes me even more curious. What did creative scheduling involve?

Client: I had to arrange to change shifts with some of my co-workers.

Therapist: How did you do that?

Client: I talked with them way ahead of time.

Therapist: So you did some planning ahead?

Client: I did.

Therapist: What else?

Client: I offered to switch with them in the future if they needed my help.

Therapist: That was very thoughtful of you.

Client: I have good relationships with my co-workers. We all get along well.

Therapist: It sounds like you've got some strong ties. And those relationships have helped you when you needed it.

Client: Definitely.

Therapist: And even as busy as you've been and the feeling you've had that your world's crumbling, you've found a way to keep some pillars in place. You planned ahead, used some creative scheduling, and were able to spend some time with your kids. I'm wondering to myself how you'll be able to do that more in the future.

Client: I think planning ahead is the key. If it's important to me, I'll do something about it.

Previous solution patterns are often subtle and need to be drawn out. It is frequently a good idea to break problem patterns into smaller elements and focus on exploring just one element, particularly one that clients identify as most significant. The following example illustrates how to encourage solution patterns.

Therapist: You said that there have been times when you've been so upset that you've said things that you later regretted. But last weekend, when you were told that you weren't going to get the raise you were expecting, you didn't say anything to your boss. How did you do that?

Client: I was still mad.

Therapist: Right. You were still mad, yet you didn't react as maybe you had in the past. I'm curious about what was different about this time.

Client: I can't lose my job so I didn't go off.

Therapist: Is that what you told yourself? "I can't lose my job."

Client: Yeah.

Therapist: And even as angry as you were, what did telling yourself that do to help you through that moment?

Client: Well, it helped me remember that I have kids to feed, bills to pay.

Therapist: I see. You remembered your kids and bills. What did that allow you to do instead of going off?

Client: I called my friend Felicia. She's always there for me.

Therapist: Okay. So then you called Felicia. How is that different than what you've done at other times?

Client: Well, I don't always talk to people when I get mad. I usually just go off but by calling her, I didn't blow my top and risk my job.

Few people begin therapy by focusing on what is going well and what is working. As a result, it is not uncommon for clients to focus primarily—and sometimes almost exclusively—on what is not going well in their lives and situations. This makes a shift to focusing on solutions a major shift in attention. Practitioners do not want to force solutions on clients but want to help to reorient them to other aspects of the problem that have gone unnoticed and abilities that have been underutilized. Exception-oriented questions provide a doorway for clients to reorient themselves to moments when they had influence over the problems. It also can be helpful for therapists to offer multiple-choice options to clients to see whether something that emerges from conversations resonates with clients and to offer other possibilities for future situations. The therapist in the previous example might have said, "I'm curious as to whether it was thinking about your kids and bills, or calling Felicia, or something else that made a difference for you." Clients will frequently affirm one of the choices or respond, "No, what really helped me was (action taken)."

The following points can serve as guides in focusing on previous solutions patterns and associated actions.

Ensure That Clients Feel Acknowledged and Validated: Therapists remain client-driven and use feedback processes to ensure that clients feel heard and understood. A push toward solutions can lead to invalidation, discouragement, and what can appear to be resistance. Refer to the processes described in Chapters 4 and 5 and continue to employ feedback processes on an ongoing basis.

Explore Shades of Difference by Working from Worst to Best: Before exploring any shades of difference regarding the intensity of problems, clients need to feel heard, acknowledged, and validated. Creating this feeling can help to let them know that the severity of their concerns has been noted. To do this means learning from clients how "bad" problems are, including how they affect their well-being and everyday functioning. Reflecting, paraphrasing, and summarizing are used to convey this understanding. Therapists can then begin to move toward differences in problem intensity in ways that are less abrupt. The following example illustrates how a client might not feel heard or understood and how a therapist might respond by working from worst to best.

Therapist: You've said that William's behavior has been very bad lately and you're most worried about his tantrums. When he's had these tantrums, he's scratched and kicked you. Is that right?

Client: Yes. He scratches and kicks.

Therapist: Tell me about a time recently when he seemed a little more manageable.

Client: I don't think you understand. His tantrums are always bad. They're very bad. They just go on and on.

Therapist: Okay. Help me to understand what you've been going through with William because I don't think I'm getting how it's been affecting you.

Client: Well, it's just flat out frustrating. He just seems to be getting worse.

Therapist: I can see and hear your frustration.

Client: It's been really hard because it doesn't seem to let up.

Therapist: It seems like it's always there. . . .

Client: . . . exactly . . . it's like it's always there.

Therapist: How have you managed to hang in there?

Client: It hasn't been easy.

Therapist: That's what it sounds like . . . and I'm wondering, because you've been through so much, how you think I might be able to help you with this?

Client: If we could just see any change with him, then I think I would have some hope.

Therapist: I see. If it's all right with you, I'd like to ask you a few more questions to help me better understand how it's been with William.

Client: Sure.

Therapist: So which day this week was the worst regarding William's scratching and kicking you?

Client: Thursday. Definitely Thursday,

Therapist: What happened on Thursday?

Client: He kicked me so hard that he bruised my arm. It also took me a long time to calm him down once he got going.

Therapist: Are you okay?

Client: Oh yeah. It'll go away.

Therapist: I'm sorry that Thursday was such a difficult day.

Client: Thanks. I'm guess I'm used to it.

Therapist: Well, I appreciate your persistence. And I'm curious as to how the other days stacked up against Thursday—because that was the worst day.

Client: You know, Tuesday wasn't quite as bad.

Therapist: What happened on Tuesday?

Client: He slept more and the one time he started to get riled up, he calmed down pretty quickly.

Therapist: How did that happen?

Client: I think maybe I caught it as he was getting riled up and I distracted him with a puzzle.

Clients who do not feel listened to are more likely to shut down verbally, give up, and drop out of therapy. They can also appear to therapists to be resistant and unmotivated. The therapist in the preceding example moved forward toward exceptions before the client was ready, recognized this, and backtracked to ensure that the client felt heard and understood. This was done by attending more to the problem and then by searching for a small opening to create an inroad for exploring exceptions.

Focus on Small Changes Instead of All-or-Nothing or Sweeping Changes: When answering queries such as "Tell me about a time recently when you didn't have the problem?" or "When have things been better?" clients' responses are not surprising. They say, "I always have the problem!" or "It's never better!" This happens because these types of questions represent too big a leap for most clients. Because they are generally oriented toward problems and what is not working, it is too much for them to turn 180 degrees and consider when problems are completely absent and what is working. Instead, therapists search for small movements and indicators of success as opposed to sweeping, all-or-nothing exceptions. To do this, therapists ask questions such as, "Tell me about a time recently when things went a little better" or "What's been different about the times when the problem has been a little less dominating in your life?" Smaller increments of change when things were a little better or more manageable are typically more palatable for clients and easier to identify.

Work with Clients in Ways They Consider Helpful and Consistent with Their Orientations to Change: Therapists use many types of questions, all of which reflect their underlying ideas about change. Determining when and how to use questions is important. In general, some questions are consistent with a search for "problems" or a lack thereof; others emphasize "solution-talk" or the presence thereof. Therapists who focus more on the former are more likely to ask, "Tell me about a time when the problem wasn't quite as bad." In contrast, therapists using solution-talk would ask, "Tell me about a time when things were a little more manageable for you." Depending on the circumstances, both types can be useful; however, one orients clients to problems and what is not working and the other to exceptions, including possibilities, solutions, and what is working.

A focus on exceptions runs counter to some clients' orientations to change. Although this is rare, if clients persist in engaging in problem-talk, therapists should be respectful and accommodate these types of conversations. Ultimately, it is important to match language that fits with clients, so if an approach is not working for a particular client, the therapist changes what he or she was doing.

In sum, when exceptions are identified, therapists work to *reinforce, further explore,* and *extend* those exceptions into the future (De Jong & Berg, 2007). A therapist *reinforces* exceptions by showing interest both verbally and nonverbally by asking, "What was that like for you?" and by doing what naturally occurs when people reveal important things (for example, lean forward, raise eyebrows, take notes). *Further exploration* relates to asking questions about how exceptions occurred. Examples include "How did you did you make that happen?" and "What would (person's name) say you did that helped?" This also involves asking clients, "What else happened?" The intent is to investigate and amplify other changes that may have accompanied the primary ones. In *extending* exceptions, therapists employ ques-

tions that help clients to project exceptions and changes into the future. To do this, they ask, "What will it take for you to (action) tomorrow/next week/month, and so on?" Therapists make these efforts to help clients use exceptions as seeds for growing new stories of hope and possibility.

Search for Contexts That Indicate Competency and/or Good Problem-Solving or Creative Skills

Because problems can dominate attention, they often affect other aspects of client's lives. Problems can appear as all-encompassing, thereby clouding competencies that clients have used in other areas and contexts of their lives. These contexts can include employment, school, hobbies, sports, clubs, or other areas in which clients have special knowledge or abilities that they can tap into as resources for solving problems. These *contexts of competence* offer possibilities for transferring the ability from one area of a client's life to another in which it is not currently being employed. Practitioners use this form of "linking" to identify situations in which problems would not or have occurred and connect them with areas with present concerns. Case Example 10.2 demonstrates this idea.

The key to identifying contexts of competence is to be on the lookout for them. When clients say things such as "I don't know why he and I can't get along at home. I don't have these problems with co-workers"; "All he does is act out at home but the neighbors think he's wonderful"; or "I feel really anxious when I'm speaking to groups outside of school, but when I teach my classes, I'm fine." Abilities, strengths, and resources come out in different contexts. Therapists *assume* that clients have abilities. Asking questions can help to pan their lives to identify those abilities

CASE EXAMPLE 10.2

A high school junior, Maurice, was brought to therapy because of fighting at school. Although he had a history of problems at school, there were no reports of these problems when he played organized sports. Maurice had a vision of the future—to play college football. The following dialogue was taken from the second session with Maurice.

Therapist: How's it been going at home?

Maurice: Bad. . .

Therapist: How so?

Maurice: My parents won't get off my case about the fights. They just need to leave it alone and everything would be fine.

Therapist: They've been on your case a lot lately . . . mostly about the fights at school.

Maurice: Yep. They don't get it. If people say stuff to me at school, I'm gonna stand up to it. That's the way it is.

Therapist: I can see how that might get to you.

Maurice: It does.

Therapist: And so that's what happens in school. What about on the football field?

Maurice: What do you mean?

Therapist: Well, I haven't heard about you getting ejected from a football game for fighting. In fact, have you ever even had a personal foul called on you?

Maurice: No way.

Therapist: How come?

Maurice: I can't get kicked out the game—that's what happens when you get a personal foul in high school sports.

Therapist: So what? Haven't you been so mad that you felt like going after another player?

Maurice: Oh yeah, all the time.

Therapist: What do you do when there's an opposing player talking trash or one who shoves you after a play?

Maurice: I just ignore it and get back to business.

Therapist: How do you do that?

Maurice: I just focus on the next play and getting it done and I let it go.

Therapist: That's interesting. Tell me more about how you focus.

Maurice: I just focus in on the game and eliminate everything else.

Therapist: It sounds a bit similar to what I used to do when I was in high school. I played baseball and hockey, and on the days that I was pitching, people would say that it was like I was in a trance or something because I was sort of like a zombie. I was just focusing.

Maurice: Exactly! I do that too—it's kind of hard to do anything on game days.

Therapist: That's actually a very good skill that serves you well on the field. And it also raises my curiosity about you. What if you were to get suspended from school for fighting during football season—what would happen?

Maurice: I'd miss a game—at least.

Therapist: Are you willing to risk that?

Maurice: No way.

Therapist: OK, so what I'm wondering is how do you get yourself to focus on the field in those moments when you really need to?

Maurice: It's the bigger picture. I've got a job to do—to help my team to win.

Therapist: What about at school? What's your job there?

Maurice: I guess to get an education.

CASE EXAMPLE 10.2   (continued)

Therapist: So fighting hasn't interfered with your job on the field but it has with your job in the classroom.

Maurice: Yeah.

Therapist: So how can that ability you have to focus on the field be helpful to you when you're in school?

Maurice: I see what you mean. Yeah, I think I just have to keep remember what my job is on and off the field.

Therapist: Your dad told me that you want to play college ball. Is that right?

Maurice: Yeah, I've got some colleges looking at me.

Therapist: That's terrific. And adding a new element to your overall game wouldn't hurt—showing the ability to focus in and out of school—on different things. That's why there are Academic All-American athletes each year in college sports. They do well in academics and in sports. I bet most coaches would find the ability to focus a wonderful quality in a player—maybe even a sign of maturity.

Maurice: That's what my dad would say. I know I can focus better in school, and I'm not going to ruin going to college because of some idiot who knows he can get me riled up.

Therapist: It's not worth losing your dream, is it?

Maurice: No way.

Maurice's behavior improved at school. He had no more fights and was able to maintain passing grades. A year later he was offered a scholarship to play football for a university with a nationally ranked program.

---

and then link them to problem contexts. The following questions assist with this process:

- How have you managed to hold the problem at bay when you're at (place)?
- What do you do differently when you're (action description) as opposed to (action description) that helps you to manage your life a little better?
- How can being able to (stand up to, better manage) the problem when you're (action description) be helpful to you in dealing with (problem)?
- How can you use that ability in standing up to (problem)?

In most instances, at least some part of the abilities utilized in specific contexts are transferable and provide solutions to problems experienced elsewhere. It can also be helpful to find out about times when clients or those who know them have faced similar problems and resolved them in ways that they liked. This provides a pathway for transferring knowledge and associated actions from one person to another.

Find Out What Happens as the Problem Ends or Starts to End

The problems that clients bring to therapy have endings or at least points at which they are much less evident and intrusive. One way to evoke solution patterns is to explore the sequences that lead to those endings. Once identified, therapists can work with clients to use those sequences in the present and future. The following questions elicit information about these solution sequences:

- How do you know when the problem is coming to an end?
- What do you do when this is happening?

- What is the first sign that the problem is going away or subsiding?
- How do you usually react to this?
- How can your friends/family/co-workers tell when the problem has subsided or started to subside?
- Is there anything that you or significant others have noticed that helps the problem subside more quickly?
- What have you noticed helps you to wind down?
- What is the smallest thing you could do when you notice the decline of the problem?
- What do you do when the problem has ended or subsided?
- What will you do in the future when the problem is no longer a problem or more consistently out of the picture?
- How might these problem-free activities differ from what you do when the problem is happening or present?

The following example illustrates how therapists focus on how a problem ends or starts to end.

> A 34-year-old man came to therapy with the worry that he would die very young, just as his father did (at the age of 47 of a heart attack). The man stated that he thought about it frequently, sometimes for hours at a time to the point that he would experience intense bouts of sweating, heaviness in his chest, and the sensation that he might pass out. Although his physician had told him he was in good health, the worries continued on a daily basis and were now interfering with his ability to work. One the questions asked of him was "Even though your breaks from it may be brief, what have you noticed brings your bouts of worry to a temporary end?" Initially, the man did not have an answer. The next week, however, he returned to therapy and volunteered that playing his guitar and listening to Bob Dylan helped. With a smile, he stated, "My Fender guitar pulls me out of it and so does a good Bob Dylan tune." The man was then asked to play his guitar several times a day to "Fend(er) off worry" and put Bob Dylan on his MP3 player so it would be available to him at all times should worry rear its head.

Find Out Why the Problem Is Not Worse: Using Strengths as a Countermeasure

A common misperception, particularly with certain concerns (for example, substance abuse), is that clients must get worse and perhaps "bottom out" before they get better. This generalization is not only empirically unsubstantiated but also can have negative consequences (Timko et al., 1999). Letting clients deteriorate without concerted efforts to intervene in their downward spirals raises serious ethical and legal concerns and can pose threats to their health and well-being.

One of the ways therapists can counter problem patterns that indicate client deterioration is by finding out *why things are not even worse*. This involves tapping into clients' resilience, including the ways they cope with and keep problems from completely overtaking them. The strengths and resources that clients use, often unknowingly, can serve as protective mechanisms that help them to maintain some degree of functioning. These resiliencies help to normalize clients' experiences without engulfing therapists in problematic stories that suggest impossibility.

By virtue of living life and facing a variety of circumstances, people develop experience in solving problems and managing adversity. The ability to do this serves as a reminder that the clients who come for therapy have had problems throughout their lives and will have other problems in the future. Their current problems may or may not be worse in intensity compared to previous or future ones. Clearly, clients have stored up some level of experience that can serve as an asset in halting downward movement. By accessing their knowledge, strengths, resources, and protective mechanisms, therapists can help clients to transition toward the future change they desire. These questions evoke those sensibilities:

- How come things aren't worse with your situation?
- What have you done to keep things from getting worse?
- What steps have you taken to prevent things from heading downhill any further?
- What else has helped things from getting worse/deteriorating further?
- How has that made a difference for you/with your situation?
- What is the smallest thing that you could do that might make a difference with your situation?
- What could others do?
- How could we get that to happen a little now?
- What might help you to hold the course you've set once you leave here today?
- What keeps you going when you feel like you're in a deep struggle?
- What specifically do you do?
- What do you do on a regular basis to keep things from getting worse?
- What could you do in the future if you feet yourself slipping?

Asking why things are not worse can seem counterintuitive to some clients who may be caught off guard, but they have not viewed their situations from that vantage point. The questions offered help orient clients to whatever aspects of themselves, others, or their sit-

uations, however small, have worked to any degree. The preventative mechanisms can help build hope for clients when they feel or think that nothing is going right.

The following example indicates how therapists can learn from clients what they do to keep problems from getting worse.

A family, consisting of a biological father, stepmother, biological mother, her boyfriend, and two boys, 14 and 9 years of age, came to therapy. The father initiated therapy as a result of the 14-year-old's stealing car stereos, breaking curfew, and doing poorly in school. Along with two other clinicians, I was part of a conversational and consulting team (CCT) (see Chapter 8) that worked with the family at a stuck point. During the initial part of the session, the mother stated that she felt as if things were "going down the drain." During the conversation between members of the CCT, I responded to this comment by saying, "You know those sticky things they put in bathtubs to keep people from slipping and falling? I wonder what the sticky things are in this family that even when they fall down, keeps things from going down the drain?" Later in the session the mother responded to my earlier statement. "I know what keeps things from going down the drain. We love each other," she stated. To this the therapist asked, "That's so nice to hear. And I'm curious, what difference does it make that you love each other?" "We can't give up," replied the mother, "So we pull together when things get rough." The therapist was then able to explore with the family members how they pull together during rough times and what they do differently when things start to get slippery. Then, at a later session, they were able to discuss how the family members can utilize that ability more in the future.

This form of counterevidence serves as a preventive measure and as a stepping point to positive change. To practice using counterevidence and other strategies outlined in this section, please complete Exercise 10.2, Repatterning Through Solution Patterns.

Rituals of Connection and Continuity: Balancing Security and Change

An important but often overlooked area of clients' lives is *rituals*. This book discusses various types of rituals. The focus here is on rituals of *connection and continuity*, which include action patterns that increase connection to others and offer stability and consistency. These rituals consist of activities that take place daily, weekly, monthly, yearly, seasonally, on holidays, or at other intervals with regularity. Examples include activities such as exercising, writing in a journal, having dinner with family, or going out for dinner with friends.

These rituals are, in effect, solution patterns that people can count on. In addition to connecting people with each other and bringing stability, they serve as protective factors in the face of adverse conditions such as child

---

Exercise 10.2

Repatterning Through Solution Patterns

This exercise is to evoke solution patterns through repatterning. Solution patterns include exploring changes made prior to therapy, previous solutions (including partial solutions and successes), skills and competencies used in other contexts, the way that problems come to an end, and why problems are not worse. Identifying these solutions and having clients employ them more deliberately in the future can change many problematic patterns of action and interaction. You can complete this exercise by yourself or with others. Please answer the questions by writing your answers in the spaces provided. (Be specific with your answers and incorporate action-talk in them.)

- Describe a problem.

  _____
  _____
  _____

- Consider any changes that have occurred with the intensity or presence of the problem prior to the start of therapy. What specifically was different? How is it helpful to you to notice that?

  _____
  _____
  _____

- Recall a time in the recent past when the problem happened but you (or another person) were (was) able to get somewhat of a handle on it, reducing its intensity or force. What specifically happened? How was this different than what has happened at other times?

  _____
  _____
  _____

Exercise 10.2   (continued)

- What influence did you have over the problem described in the preceding question? What specifically did you do differently?

  _____
  _____
  _____

- We use many abilities every day in other areas of our lives but do not necessarily apply them to problem situations when they arise. Take a moment to think about things that you are good at, skilled in, or able to do that you use everyday at work, home, school, and so on. How might you use those strengths with the problem described in this exercise?

  _____
  _____
  _____

- How do you know when the problem is coming to an end? What's the first thing you notice?

  _____
  _____
  _____

- What might you do with the information described in the preceding question?

  _____
  _____
  _____

- Think about your experience with a specific problem that you've been facing. Why aren't things worse with your situation?

  _____
  _____
  _____

- What specific action have you taken to prevent things from getting worse? Be as specific as possible.

  _____
  _____
  _____

- What does your ability and that of others' involved to prevent things from deteriorating further say about you and others? How is it helpful for you to know that?

  _____
  _____
  _____

abuse, neglect, substance abuse, divorce, or the loss. In fact, research indicates that everyday routines and activities that remain constant in the lives of children can contribute to increased levels if resilience in adulthood (Wolin & Wolin, 1993). Most people's lives involve some form of rituals whether they involve their families, friends, or others who are close to them. The following story illustrates this idea.

> When I was in the fifth grade, I met a kid named Steve. Because we both loved sports and lived within a half-mile of each other, Steve came to my house after school and on weekends. We'd throw a football around and hang out for hours. Steve's visits were routine and predictable. Most evenings he would show up at the backdoor of my home precisely as the family was beginning to have dinner. What my family came to understand was that while Steve's home life was often chaotic and unpredictable, at my home things tended to be routine, predictable, and consistent. Each evening my mom would make enough food for a small army, which was the case with seven children, and there was always plenty of food, conversation, and camaraderie. Steve was easily able to blend in as one of the family. Steve's routine remained consistent for several years until the end of my eighth grade, when my family moved to Massachusetts.
>
> After I graduated high school, some four years later, my family moved back to Missouri. Steve did not know this. One day, by chance, he spotted my sister Mary on the highway. Although several years had passed, he recognized her, turned around, and followed her home. As if picking up where he left off, Steve began to come around regularly again (especially around dinner time), and even lived with us for a while. It seems that Steve had found his stability again.

Rituals that connect clients who have come from chaotic, disruptive, and potentially detrimental environments to others provide consistency and can make a significant difference in helping them to deal with the adversity they face in life. The problem is that when disruptions occur, they disrupt clients' rituals as well. Part of what therapists can do is to help clients either restore rituals that have been interrupted by their life changes or help them create new ones.

Regardless of the context (for example, home, residential placement, foster care), therapists can help clients to create, implement, and engage in those activities that are meaningful, create stability, and increase connections (Bertolino & Thompson, 1999). These regular activities help to protect children and adolescents as well as people of all ages from some of the troubles that can plague them as they grow and develop and move through life. See the following example.

> Zac and his father had been very close since he was about seven years old. Zac would follow his dad around the house, and they would spend lots of time together. One of their favorite things was to attend baseball games together. As time passed, Zac began to spend more and more time with his friends. This meant less time with his father. Around the age of 15, Zac began getting into trouble. Initially, he was charged with stealing and breaking and entering. As a result, he was ordered to placement at a juvenile facility.
>
> Over the course of a year, Zac was able to earn the right to go on weekend passes with his father. One August weekend, Zac's father picked him up from the juvenile facility. As they were driving along not saying much, Zac noticed a pair of baseball tickets above his father's sun visor in the car. He asked his

dad, "How come you don't want to go to games with me anymore?" His father, surprised, responded, "When your friends changed and you started to get into trouble, it seemed like I was the last person you wanted to be around. So I just stopped asking." A tearful Zac sat quietly for a moment, then spoke, "I miss going to the games with you." The father and son restored their ritual of going to baseball games together. This helped to bring stability to Zac's life and reconnect father and son.

Many situations can disconnect individuals, couples, and families from their rituals. These events do not have to be traumatic, just unsettling in some manner. For example, events such as the birth of a child or the change of a job can disrupt them. As in the preceding example, rituals that help to reconnect people can also provide continuity (stability) to relationships. Rituals of stability can also help people to reconnect with themselves. People, like organisms, have a tendency to withdraw and protect themselves when they are traumatized. This means that some people withdraw from aspects of themselves or others and as a result struggle to reconnect. Therapists therefore want to encourage patterns that help clients to feel safe and secure and experience increased stability in their lives. See the following example.

> A woman accepted a new job with the promise of an exciting new career. Her new position required her to move to another state 800 miles from her family and friends. Although her job was all she had hoped for, she found herself slipping into a state of depression. Her therapist asked what she had done in the past when she was feeling down. She stated that she had never really experienced such lows because she had always felt connected to others. Additional discussion revealed that in the move, the woman had left two routines that had been essential to her well-being. One was a nightly phone call to one or more family members or friends. The other was lighting a candle, drinking a cup of tea, and reading a chapter of a book before going to bed. Although the woman periodically called others, she did not do so at a rate that was consistent with her previous pattern. In addition, she had completely stopped her bedtime routine. Her therapist suggested that she had been "on hiatus" from her routines long enough and that it was time to reinstate them. After two weeks, the woman reported that she was feeling much better and more like herself.

To learn more about rituals of connection and stability, please complete Exercise 10.3, Connection and Stability Through Rituals.

Rituals of Transition: Action Methods with Meaning

Transition rituals can be helpful when clients have identity stories or unfinished business that they feel a need to leave behind. Transition rituals offer people physical, action-based ways to disrupt old stories and create new ones and a renewed sense of self. There are two types of transition rituals: (1) *rites of passage*, which help to move people from one role or developmental phase to another and to have that validated and recognized by others in their social contexts and (2) *rites of mourning/leaving behind*, which help to facilitate or make concrete the end of some relationship or connection.

Transition rituals involve the use of symbols, which are physical objects that can be carried around, burned, or buried. These symbols represent the unfinished experience within clients and can be used to help them express that unfinished experience without doing it on their bodies or

Exercise 10.3

Connection and Stability Through Rituals

In most people's present and/or past histories, there have been specific events (for example, dinner times, certain meals on certain days, movie nights, vacations) that occur with regularity on a daily, weekly, monthly, seasonal, or yearly basis. These rituals provide consistency in people's lives. Research suggests that children who come from homes where there has been abuse, alcoholism, divorce, or some other disruption or trauma tend to do better as adults when they can keep their rituals in tact or put new ones in place. The purpose of this exercise is to help to identify rituals that bring about connection to others and stability in life. This can involve continuing rituals that have been in place or beginning new ones. To complete this exercise, please answer each question by writing your responses in the spaces provided.

- What are the current rituals in your life (and/or in your relationships)? You may want to think of rituals as routines or things that happen on a very regular basis. List each one.

   1. _____
   2. _____
   3. _____
   4. _____
   5. _____

- How does each of the rituals you listed bring some consistency to your life?

   1. _____
   2. _____
   3. _____
   4. _____
   5. _____

- What are some rituals that you used to have in place but for one reason or another were stopped or interrupted?

   1. _____
   2. _____
   3. _____

- Which of the rituals that you listed in the preceding question would you consider starting again?

   1. _____
   2. _____
   3. _____

- What difference might it make if you were to restart an old ritual?

   _____
   _____
   _____

Exercise 10.3   *(continued)*

- Consider meeting with those persons to whom you are close and who have been part of your rituals. Invite them to talk with you about new rituals that you might implement in the future. Then list those rituals here.

  1. _____
  2. _____
  3. _____

- Take one of the new rituals that has been decided on and try it a few times. Then write the results of that experiment here.

  _____
  _____
  _____
  _____
  _____

---

without getting stuck in their bodies. Symbols are most often chosen by clients but may arise out of therapeutic dialogues or suggestions of what other clients have tried. Symbols might include a picture, doll, plant, rock, or other object. Many clients also choose to write something (for example, a letter, poem, story) as part of their ritual. The following steps create a template to use for creating transition rituals:

1. *Introduce the idea of a ritual.* Develop clarity in terms of its purpose and what remains unfinished for the client. Collaborate with the client to determine what symbol might be used for the ritual.

2. *Prepare the client to perform the ritual.* Ensure that the client is emotionally and psychologically ready. The client needs to decide who is going to lead the ritual (i.e., a family member, friend, the therapist) or whether she or he wants to do it alone.

3. *Have the client(s) perform the ritual.*

4. *Create a respite experience.* The person completes the ritual and then does some-

thing else such as meditation, praying, or another form of self-care and respite.

5. *Celebrate the client's transition in life.* The final step in the ritual process can be a celebration—something that symbolizes that the person has moved on and has entered a new phase in life.

The following example illustrates the use of a transition ritual.

A man in his late 50s had experienced flashbacks dating back to his experience in the Vietnam War. The intrusive memories represented clustered experiences of situations he had been directly involved with or witnessed. Over the course of therapy, the man was able to gradually face the images until they were no longer intrusive and interfering with his life. He decided that he wanted to mark his transition "back to life" by putting "each pellet of pain to rest." He chose an old canteen he had been issued by the Army as his symbol and put one marble for each previously intrusive memory into it. When he was finished, the man took the canteen out into the ocean on his boat. He then gave the canteen and its contents a "proper burial at sea." Following the completion of the ritual, he continued on a trip through the Caribbean where he had always wanted to sail.

Rituals can combine transition with continuity. For example, having clients choose both *problem symbols* that they are going to leave behind and *solution or resource symbols* they are going to carry with them is a way to combine both. Rituals provide a way to give people something to *do* about the unfinished or disconnected feelings they have inside or to reconnect with their social environment after they have been cut off or disconnected by trauma or change in their lives (Bertolino & O'Hanlon, 2002). Transition rituals represent changing both views and actions associated with problem situations by performing some action that is imbued with meaning and symbolism.

Action Plans: Putting Ideas to Work

Some clients come to therapy expecting change to happen simply from attending sessions. Although practitioners should not be surprised when change happens quickly, most clients must take some action to ensure that the change they are seeking occurs. Change that extends beyond a temporary shift in attention or the short-term disruption of problematic patterns requires some form of action. Clients need to go beyond therapeutic conversations and put their ideas, actions, and interactions, old or new, into play. Encouragement may be enough for clients who are prepared to take steps to put their new ideas and skills to work. They demonstrate initiative and take action to

make changes in their everyday activities. Other clients are inclined to make changes but are unsure about how to proceed. Creating action plans can be helpful for these clients.

Collaboration serves as a cornerstone for determining what clients are motivated for and what might fit with them in terms of action planning. Recall that clients at precontemplation or contemplation stages are better served by attempts to help them change some aspect of how they view themselves, others, events, or situations. Therapists might say to these clients, "Between now and the next time we meet, I'd like you to notice what's different about the times when things seems to be going a little bit better for you." Clients who are at the preparation or action stages have a higher state of readiness to do something, so they are more likely to express interest in and follow through with plans of action.

Although specific tasks and action plans help to target specific problems and concerns, using more generic ways to initiate change can also be useful. For example, the "do-something-different" task provides a way to orient clients toward action in general (de Shazer, 1985). Clients are told "between now and the next time we meet, I would like each of you [or you alone] to do something different, no matter how strange, weird, or off-the-wall what you do might seem" (p. 123). Another possibility is to say to clients, "When you leave here, do one thing different that will be out of the ordinary in relation to how you've approached the problem you've been up against." These prompts can help clients be spontaneous and creative and can be enough for some to break out of problematic patterns.

Although therapists do not direct clients to do anything, their message should encourage clients to consider the benefits of experimenting with new actions and behaviors (in other words, being proactive) as opposed to waiting for change to happen to them (in other words, being reactive). As you have learned, such a perspective will not fit with clients' views at times and therapists want to be respectful and not impose their ideas. The intention is to do what is in the best interest of the client with an eye to exploring avenues that could lead to new possibilities.

Beyond the use of generic tasks, therapists can partner with clients to develop specific plans of action. Planning action is important because clients (1) often forget the precise ideas and/or instructions given or mutually decided on, (2) are often in such pain, anxiety, or confusion when visiting therapists that they are not always at their best intellectually, and (3) are more likely to follow through with specific plans rather than those that are vague or too general. Action plans involve determining and outlining steps designed to move clients toward their goals. These are not big leaps but small steps and tasks to initiate change and create momentum in the direction clients are seeking. *Tasks* are meant to help bring about changes in patterns of attention, action, and interaction around problems outside of therapy sessions.

Action plans should be focused, realistic, and reasonable for clients to follow through on in the midst of their everyday lives and responsibilities. The more clients are involved with and invested in the creation of plans and tasks, the more likely they are to try things. Therapists do this by listening closely to clients' ideas about what they have tried and what they think might work. In addition, as previously discussed, therapists *offer* different ideas to clients, always being mindful that clients make decisions as to whether the ideas discussed fit with their orientations to change.

To increase the likelihood of follow-through of plans and tasks, working with clients to create between-session action plans as opposed to only global, long-term ones is a good practice. This brings attention to the present and near future and allows therapists to monitor the effects of the actions targeted at specific concerns. Another way to increase the likelihood that clients will follow through is by writing action plans and the specific tasks that have been outlined. This ensures that tasks are clear, understandable, and meaningful to clients. It also serves to remind clients to do the tasks and therapists to follow up on them. Examples of both generic and specific action plans are provided in Figures 10.1 and 10.2.

The ways in which action plans are approached and discussed can affect how clients' proceed. For example, some clients may object or display dissatisfaction with the words *assignment* and *homework*, which can evoke recollections of meaningless time-consuming activities. An alternative is to use the word *task* or to frame action plans as involving experiments and ways to "try different things." Language again plays a pivotal role in determining how to approach clients to increase the chances of follow-through.

Consistent with a strengths-based philosophy, not following through with tasks between sessions does not imply client resistance. In such cases, therapists should talk with clients about plans to determine whether adjustments are necessary or tasks need to be abandoned altogether. If this does not lead to better follow-through, therapists should confirm that clients are really interested in taking action in the direction tasks are designed to address. To gain a better understanding of where clients stand regarding action plans, therapists can ask any of the following questions:

- We discussed the idea of your trying out something new between sessions and it

Figure 10.1

ACTION PLAN

Date: _____

1. Between now and the next session, I will interrupt _____ by _____.

2. I will follow through with this action at least _____ times between now and my next session. Each time, after completing the task, I will observe to determine the effect(s) it has had on my concern.

3. I acknowledge that I have the ability to take action that can change my situation and accept responsibility for following through with this task.

4. At my next session I will be prepared to discuss the results to date of the task(s) described in this action plan.

Date of Next Session: _____

---

didn't materialize. I'm getting the sense that I'm missing something about you or your situation. What do you think that I haven't yet understood about your situation?

- I'm getting the sense that maybe I'm not being as helpful as I could be. Can you tell me a little bit about what I'm doing (or what has been happening in sessions) that's working or not working for you?
- I'm wondering if you have some ideas about how to get this problem to fade from your life that I haven't already heard

about or understood clearly enough. What can you tell me that might help me to better understand how to approach your concern more effectively?

If clients make it clear that they do not have the time or do not see taking action as a priority, therapists should be sure that they are working with clients in ways they see as being helpful. This can be a good opportunity to ask more about what the therapist still does not know about clients' situations. As a result,

Figure 10.2

Completed Action Plan

ACTION PLAN

Date: _____

1. Between now and the next session, I will interrupt raising my voice at my son by either taking deep breaths to calm myself down and then speaking slowly to him or I will leave the room until I am calm and able to approach my son in that calm manner.

2. I will follow through with this action at least three or four times between now and my next session. Each time, after completing the task, I will observe to determine the effects it has had on my concern.

3. I acknowledge that I have the ability to take action that can change my situation and accept responsibility for following through with this task.

4. At my next session, I will be prepared to discuss the results to date of the task(s) described in this action plan.

Date of Next Session: _____

---

therapists may need to seek other forms of helping clients that are more consistent with their orientations to change.

Action plans and the tasks embedded in them are aimed at stimulating deliberate movement in the direction of goals. By doing something different, many clients experience small changes that can lead to bigger and often more significant gains. In addition to having obvious benefits, such as client improvement, action plans can strengthen the therapeutic alliance by increasing levels of client-therapist collaboration. Therapists may also note that some of the most effective tasks, in fact, are ones that clients do not follow through on in part because the creation of action plans can affect problems by removing the spontaneity of the patterns around them. Making clients more aware of problematic sequences and reflecting on the plans of action created with their therapists may be enough to interrupt those sequences from running full course.

SUMMARY POINTS

- In addition to *depatterning* (see Chapter 9), *repatterning* represents a second primary way to facilitate change with clients' patterns of action and interaction.
- *Repatterning* works to establish new patterns by identifying and encouraging the use of solution patterns of action and interaction by investigating any helpful changes prior to therapy, exploring for previous solutions to problems including partial solutions and successes, searching for contexts in which there is evidence of competency, finding out what happens as the problem ends or starts to end, and determining why the problem is not worse.
- *Rituals of connection and continuity* include action patterns that increase connection to others and offer stability and consistency. They consist of activities that take place daily, weekly, monthly, annually, seasonally, on holidays, or at other intervals with regularity.
- Research indicates that everyday rituals such as routines and activities that remain constant in the lives of children can contribute to greater levels of resilience in adulthood.
- Therapists encourage the continuation of current rituals, the reinstatement of past rituals that have been disrupted, and/or the creation of new rituals.
- *Transition rituals* can help clients who have identity stories or unfinished business that they feel a need to leave behind. They offer people physical, action-based ways to disrupt old stories and create new ones and a renewed sense of self. These rituals include *rites of passage,* which help to move people from one role or developmental phase to another and to have that movement validated and recognized by others in their social contexts and *rites of mourning/leaving behind,* which help to facilitate or make concrete the end of some relationship or connection.
- *Action plans* involve determining and outlining steps designed to move clients toward their goals; they include taking small steps and doing tasks to initiate change and create momentum in the direction clients are seeking.
- *Tasks* are meant to help bring about changes in patterns of attention, action, and interaction around problems. They seek to have clients make changes outside therapy sessions.

DISCUSSION QUESTIONS

1. What is *repatterning*? List two examples of how repatterning might be used to change a pattern of action or interaction.

2. Give a situation for which you might use one or more ways of repatterning? What method(s) might you choose?

3. Why are rituals of continuity and connection important to individual development and relationships?

4. How can action plans be used to promote change?

PART FIVE

Chapter 11

Future Interactions and Sessions

Patterns of Client Responses

■ This book has offered a myriad of methods for creating collaborative relationships. These methods provide specific ways to improve the factor of fit between clients' orientations and therapists' approaches as a means of facilitating positive change. Therapists' place their efforts on maximizing their effectiveness and the impact of therapy in each session to help clients improve their lives and the circumstances that brought them to therapy.

With few exceptions, therapists do not know whether they will see a client beyond the first session. In fact, the most common number of sessions that clients attend in therapy is *one*. This has both positive and negative connotations. On the positive side, some clients achieve what they hoped for in just the one session. This generally means that therapists were helpful in brief interactions. On the other hand, a percentage of clients drops out for other reasons such as not feeling heard and understood, having unmet expectations, and as mentioned, being mismatched with

therapists and their approaches. Ways to decrease the prospect of the latter have been addressed at length throughout this book.

This chapter begins with ways to approach clients at the end of initial sessions to ensure that therapists are in sync with clients' orientations. This can help to reduce premature dropout and negative outcomes. Therapists then learn about some general categories of client responses in subsequent sessions and how to continue to engage clients in ways that increase the likelihood of positive outcomes.

Continuous Engagement: Exploring Client Experiences and Revisiting Preferences

Over the course of therapy, what clients experience can change dramatically. This includes their perceptions of therapists, preferences for therapy sessions, views of problems and concerns, goals, and even decisions that were made prior to or early on in sessions. Clients usually make their thoughts known about dropping out, frequently early on, yet therapists do not always pick up on those signals (Piper et al., 1999). Thus, the only way to really know what is happening with clients is to ask them. Chapter 4 introduced ways to be process informed by asking questions to learn about clients' preferences. In addition, it also provided questions for periodically "checking in." Because clients' experiences and preferences can change quickly and outside of therapists' awareness, it is crucial that therapists not assume that what has been communicated earlier is the same at later points. By checking in with clients, therapists are able to gain feedback to help determine what should happen next in therapy. This is particularly important at the end of first sessions.

As first sessions come to an end, therapists want check in by using any of the following questions:

- How was the session/meeting for you?
- What was helpful or not helpful?
- Did we talk about what you wanted to talk about?
- Did we work on what you wanted to work on?
- How was the pace of our conversation/ session/meeting?
- Was there anything missing from our session?
- What, if anything, should I have asked that I did not ask?
- Is the way we approached your concern/ situation fitting with the way you expect change to occur?
- On a scale of 1 to 10, with 1 representing being completely off track and 10 being completely on track, how would you rate this session?

- What changes, if any, would you recommend if we were to meet again?
- Did you feel heard and understood?
- What, if anything, would you need me to do differently if we were to meet again?
- How would explain your experience in therapy today to others who may be curious?

These questions bring attention to clients' experiences, which as you have learned, are more accurate indicators of how therapy is going than therapists' perceptions. Based on clients' feedback, therapy can continue as is or with adjustments. The following example illustrates this notion.

> Myles, a 20-year-old college student, came to therapy with the concern that he was "angry all the time." He related that his anger was getting in the way of his studies. During the first few minutes of the first session, Myles stated, "I do not want to talk about my mom." I respected his wishes and considered that if his mom was factoring into his anger, we could revisit that at a later time when he was ready. At the end of the session, I checked in with Myles by asking him a few process-oriented questions. There was nothing remarkable revealed until I asked, "Is there anything you want to be sure we talk about next time that we didn't today?" To this Myles responded, "No not really. Well, maybe my mom." I was very surprised and rechecked with him to be sure I was clear, "So you want to be sure we talk about your mom?" "Yeah, I do," Myles answered. I followed, "Thank you for sharing that with me because I would have waited a bit longer based on what you mentioned early in the session." "Right, I didn't want to talk about her but I changed my mind," Myles remarked.

There is a saying "Let me hear what I say so I know what I think." As the therapeutic alliance strengthens and clients are able to self-reflect, this will change how they feel and view the world. Practitioners check in to ensure that they are working with clients in ways that they deem beneficial. Many times clients state that things are fine and no changes are necessary. If clients comment that they would like something to be different but their feedback seems vague, practitioners follow up with questions that help clarify what they mean. For example, if a client says, "I think we need to change our focus," the practitioner might respond, "Tell me more about that. What ideas do you have about what we should change our focus to?" This can clear up ambiguity that can lead to confusion about clients' preferences and can activate therapists' own theories. Once information is gained, therapists can respond by making changes to accommodate clients' preferences about directions, goals, and so on.

Remember that for various reasons, some clients offer little feedback. What remains clear is that that most clients do not volunteer information about their experiences if things are not going well. They will respond by not returning to therapy. Case Example 11.1 demonstrates this idea.

CASE EXAMPLE 11.1

A 10-year-old boy was brought to therapy by his mother. Her concern was that her son was having trouble "focusing" in school, the result being low grades. The therapist, a graduate student, noticed that the youth had trouble sitting still and answering questions. She attempted to engage him through stories and topics he might have interest in, but she was able to get only one-word answers. Sensing that the mother was distraught, the student tried to offer some consolation in the form of options, saying, "Your son's struggle with focusing is apparent. Have you considered having him evaluated by a psychiatrist? Some kids can benefit from medication." The mother responded, "Well . . . I hadn't really . . . well, if you think it might be a good idea. . . ." The therapist followed, "I can give you a referral for a few different psychiatrists, and you can choose one or someone else to your liking." The mother took the referral and a second appointment was scheduled for two weeks later.

When the scheduled appointment arrived, the mother and son did not show up. In supervision, the student expressed her disappointment with this, feeling that she had had a good "connection" with the mother. I told her that there are many reasons clients do not return for sessions, but perhaps it would be a good idea if we watched the videotape of the session. At the point of the session where the student introduced the idea of the youth being evaluated by a psychiatrist, the mother's expression changed. I asked the student, "What did you notice about the mother in that moment?" The student replied, "I can see it as plain as day right now. Her whole facial expression changed. When I asked her about a psychiatrist, she went from smiling to having a blank look. Maybe I jumped the gun."

I told the student that because there were many things to attend to in therapy, it is possible to miss something. I believed her intentions were good, but perhaps her suggestion was a bit premature given that there was more to be learned about the concern, the mother's expectations, what had been tried, and what ideas might fit best with the mother's beliefs. "Given this and what you saw on the tape, what ideas do you have about next steps?"

(continued)

CASE EXAMPLE 11.1 *(continued)*

I asked. The student answered, "I think I should call her and tell her that I think I was premature in suggesting a psychiatrist. I'd really like the opportunity to hear more about what she wants and thinks is a good way to proceed." I agreed.

The student called the mother and asked for the opportunity to meet again. The mother replied, "I'm glad you said what you did. You know, you're a nice person and clearly very smart and I didn't want to hurt your feelings, so I took the referral and we set an appointment.

But I've seen too many kids put on drugs and maybe it's helped them, but that's not the way I'm willing to go with my son. I want to try other things way before I would ever consider drugs as an option. So if you're willing to work with us knowing that, then we're all for it." "That would be great," followed the student. From that point on, the student checked in with the mother and son in each session to be sure they were working in ways that were both helpful and consistent with their beliefs.

In Case Example 11.1, the student approached the mother in a respectful way and had good intentions; however, the mother had different expectations of which the student was not aware. This led to a rupture in the therapeutic alliance. Fortunately, the student had a second chance and was able to repair that rupture and engage in processes that were acceptable to the mother. It is up to therapists to invite clients from the start of therapy to share their thoughts and feelings so they can have the best experiences possible and achieve their desired change. By being process informed, therapists utilize corrective mechanisms that tap into the most important contributors to outcome, their clients.

Another area that therapists should address at the end of sessions involves clients' preferences about how to proceed. Therapists commonly assume that clients want to schedule another appointment. The problem with this thinking is that it leaves clients out of decision-making processes. In much the same way that people go to see their physicians for single appointments and expect results, it is reasonable that many clients attend therapy with the mind-set that they may need only a single session. It is up to therapists to be aware of clients' expectations, not to assume that they will want or need subsequent appointments.

To determine how to proceed, therapists ask clients about their preferences in every session. Would the client like to schedule another session? If so, how soon? Some clients prefer to meet weekly; others request sessions every other week, and so on. When clients ask therapists to give their opinions, they should tell them. A therapist might say, "I recommend that we start with such and such a schedule if that makes sense to you." In some instances, based on their preconceived ideas about problems and other factors such as schedules and responsibilities, clients have ideas and may want to check with therapists to see if what they are thinking is acceptable. As discussed in Chapter 3 regarding *keys to collaboration*, therapists accommodate clients' preferences and let them know that adjustments can be made in the future regarding the frequency, timing, length of sessions, and so on. Now, please take a moment to complete Exercise 11.1, Reorienting to Process Feedback.

Exercise 11.1

Reorienting to Process Feedback

As therapy progresses, it is important to continue to monitor client's perceptions of the therapeutic relationship. This can help therapists to learn more about what is working *and* what is not. Therapists can use the latter information to make adjustments in an effort to repair any ruptures in the alliance. To complete this exercise, please generate a list of four to six questions that you could use to check in with clients about their perceptions of the format, timing, structure, or any other aspect of therapy. Then write your answers in the spaces provided. If needed, please refer to the collaboration keys outlined in Chapter 3. Remember that questions are to focus on the processes between clients and therapists, not personality characteristics, qualities, and so on.

Examples of Process-Oriented Feedback Questions

How would you like to proceed from here?
How did the meeting arrangements work for you?
On a scale of 1 to 10, with 1 representing a very poor session and 10 representing a very good sessions, how would you rate our meeting today?

- _____
  _____
- _____
  _____
- _____
  _____
- _____
  _____
- _____
  _____

Second Sessions: Continuing Conversations for Change

Second and subsequent sessions share similarities with first ones. Practitioners create space through conversation so clients can discuss what has transpired since previous sessions. Active listening and attending continues as practitioners acknowledge, validate, and introduce possibility into otherwise closed-down statements. They also invite clients' preferences, monitor goals, and use their orientations as compasses for change. Another important element is the incorporation of outcome-oriented feedback. As discussed in previous chapters, outcome-oriented feedback is instrumental in understanding, from clients' perspectives, the impact of therapy. It also provides crucial information about clients' progress that when incorporated into sessions affects how therapists proceed. The next sections explore how these points factor into second and subsequent sessions.

The Role of Outcome-Oriented Feedback Revisited

Recall that real-time feedback is made up of process- and outcome-oriented feedback. Process-oriented feedback, as previously described, is based on clients' ratings of the therapeutic alliance. Outcome-oriented feedback relates to clients' interpretations of the impact of therapy on major areas of their lives (in other words, individual well-being, interpersonal relationships, and social role functioning). As therapy progresses, outcome-oriented feedback becomes increasingly important because it is the best indicator of whether and to what degree clients are benefiting from therapy.

At this point, it is necessary to highlight two key terms. The first term is *the reliable change index* (RCI), a measure used to assess the magnitude of change necessary to be considered statistically reliable rather than due to chance or the passage of time. The RCI is an average based on the reliability or consistency of a measurement instrument. It represents the difference between two time points that would not be due to simple measurement error. The RCI can prove useful in separating successful and unsuccessful cases; however, it can also result in over- or underestimates of the amount of change depending on level of severity (Duncan, Miller & Sparks, 2004).

Another key term, *clinical significance*, refers to reliable improvement that also corresponds to a change in clinical status, which involves movement from a clinical (often referred to as *dysfunctional*) range to a nonclinical (*functional*) range. As with process-oriented feedback, outcome-oriented feedback is gathered on an ongoing basis, beginning with the first session. Because the general trajectory of change in successful therapy is highly predictable with most change occurring earlier rather than later in therapy, the majority of outcome measures are used minimally in sessions 1–3 and then at least in every third session thereafter (Brown, Dreis, & Nace, 1999; Hansen, Lambert, & Forman, 2002; Haas, Hill, Lambert, & Morrell, 2002; Whipple et al., 2003). The first few sessions are particularly important because predictive value has been demonstrated in the fit between client-therapist pairings and the client's experience of meaningful change early in therapy (typically the first few sessions) (Duncan, Miller, & Sparks, 2004). Although clients' ratings of improvement can significantly affect positive outcome, the absence of subjective improvement in the first few sessions suggests that the sessions are at much greater risk for negative outcome (Brown, Dreis, & Nace, 1999).

Outcome-oriented feedback is a consistent means of rating client improvement. It is therefore important that therapists employ strategies of monitoring outcome on an ongoing basis. Later sections will revisit the use of outcome-oriented feedback as therapy progresses.

Each Session as its Own Entity: Reorienting to Clients' Stories

Future sessions are not necessarily "continuations" of previous ones. Sometimes clients have entirely new concerns to discuss, emergent thoughts about old concerns, and so on. Because much can transpire between sessions, therapists begin by extending permission to clients to begin where they are most comfortable. Doing this helps to convey respect, enhance collaboration, and strengthens the alliance. Therapists continue to acknowledge, validate, and create a climate that promotes hope and possibilities for future change. In these sessions, therapists can use questions such as those posed in Chapter 4 or by asking, "How have you been?" or "Where would you like to start today?" Clients' responses to these questions can vary but tend to fall into one of four categories:

1. New concerns or problems (that differ from previously defined ones)

2. Ambiguous or vague (do not indicate directional change)

3. No change or deterioration

4. Improvement

The remainder of this chapter explores the first three categories of client responses and areas of focus associated with each. The fourth category will be discussed in Chapter 12.

Client Reports of New Concerns or Problems

Clients commonly begin subsequent sessions (and sometimes initial sessions) with what is foremost in their thoughts. They may speak about what happened days earlier or while driving to their sessions. Because practitioners create space for clients to begin where they feel most comfortable, many describe events or situations that on the surface may seem to have little to do with past conversations. These topics, however, can be meaningful for clients and a way to reconnect after time elapsed between sessions.

It is possible that some of these dialogues reveal what appear to be completely new concerns or problems rather than being connected with problem descriptions and goals established in previous sessions. Depending on what has transpired between sessions (for example, events, new meanings, changes), clients may delve into the details of specific conversational threads or graduate from one topic to another. Doing so can indicate clients' preferred ways to communicate, provide relief, be a means of "updating" therapists, or serve some other purpose. No matter what the rationale, practitioners let clients know that the best starting places are the ones clients are most comfortable with. Practitioners therefore acknowledge all concerns and make sure that clients feel that they have been heard and understood.

Through acknowledgment, many clients shift back to the concerns that led them to seek therapy in the first place. Without prompting, simply by feeling heard and understood, they reorient to their initial complaints and pick up where they left off in previous sessions. In other instances, clients' new concerns represent a theme or are connected to and consistent with previous ones. With further exploration, therapists can probe with clients any possible relationships that may exist between current concerns and those raised at different times. One way for therapists to investigate these connections is to check in with clients. The following example illustrates the checking in process.

Therapist: Based on what you've described so far, it seems like a lot has happened since our session last week.

Client: That's definitely true. This week has been crazy. It's hard to wrap my brain around it.

Therapist: I wonder whether you see any relationship between what you talked about last week regarding your job loss and what you've mentioned today in terms of being worried about your mother getting older and having more health concerns?

A client might answer this question in many ways. One is to say, "Actually, I do. There seem to be a lot of sad things happening in my life lately." Another possibility is, "Not really. I've just got a lot going on." What therapists want to do is determine from the client's perspective whether there is a connection between previous and current concerns. If clients note parallels or agree with therapists' observations, therapy may continue along the same lines with goals set in previous sessions. If not, relationships between concerns that are not evident may come to fruition at a later time.

New concerns raised during subsequent sessions have a more significant affect on some clients' lives. It is not always clear to therapists whether these new concerns are more significant than previous ones. In these cases, it is imperative that therapists talk with clients to determine the weight of their present concerns. One way to do this is to summarize both the goals that were previously set and the current complaints and then ask clients which ones are most concerning. Here are some ways to engage clients in these types of conversations:

- Would you say that the concerns you've been talking about today take precedence over the ones we discussed last week?
- In our last session, you mentioned that (problem) was really concerning you and was something that you wanted to focus our attention on. Based on the concerns you've mentioned today, do you think our time might be best spent on what we discussed last week or this week?
- If it's all right with you, I'd just like to make sure we're talking about what you want to talk about. I can see that you've got a few concerns. Would you rather spend this time talking about the concerns you're having now or the ones we discussed last week?

Also see the following example.

> During his initial therapy session, a 37-year-old man expressed concern about being "overwhelmed" with his responsibilities at work. He stated that he wanted to be able to manage his work better and be more efficient. At the start of his second session, he related that he was having trouble with his marital relationship. As the therapist listened, he described how he felt that his wife didn't value his opinion of things and therefore didn't involve him in important decisions. The therapist acknowledged this new concern and then followed, "This sounds important to you and I can understand why. And last week you described some things that were also of concern to you. These different concerns may or may not be connected to each other, but I want to be sure that we're using this time in a way that you think is most helpful to you. So if it's all right with you, while this can change at any time, I'd just like to check in with you to make sure we focus on what you feel like is most important at this time. With that in mind, would you rather spend this time talking about your sense of being undervalued and left out of important decisions in you marriage, or do you think it's more important to talk about being able to manage your work better and be more efficient, as we discussed last week?"

Some therapists choose to allow problem descriptions to change and ultimately dissipate as a result of ongoing conversations. They choose a less directive posture, responding to clients' as innocuously as possible. Anderson and Goolishian (1988) have described how through ongoing conversations, clients' problems will "dis-solve" and new meanings will be created. They base this observation on the notion that if therapists and clients remain engaged in dialogue, new stories will emerge. This may benefit those clients who have conversational styles that allow them to "talk through" their concerns.

A higher degree of structure is often important for clients to maintain a sense of direction in therapy. As discussed earlier, acknowledging clients' current concerns may be enough for them to return to previously established goals. For instance, the client in the previous example might respond with, "Well, I'm concerned about my marriage, but I'm more concerned about work. Let's talk about that." Or he could respond, "I'm really not worried about work now. How could I be? My marriage is a mess. I think we should talk about that." Another possibility is for the client to say, "I want to work on them both."

In the latter two client responses, the therapist would acknowledge a modification in goals. The first would involve a shift to focusing on client's concerns about his marriage. Although this could change again in future sessions, it is important to accommodate client preferences on an ongoing basis. The second example would entail expanding previous goals by adding the client's interest in focusing on his marital conflict. When there have been additions or changes in concerns resulting in multiple goals, it is a good idea for therapists to go a step further and ask, "Which of these concerns would you like to focus our attention on now/first?" In lieu of potential danger to self or others, clients choose the directions of therapy, including their conversational and relational preferences, which can and do periodically shift.

When client concerns and/or goals change, inquiring—at least minimally—about any changes that may have transpired in relation to previously established ones can be helpful. Doing so identifies positive change that may

have occurred that might otherwise be overlooked. Identifying progress can reinforce the concept that change is always happening, which can in turn serve as a source of encouragement and empowerment for future change. When clients are able to identify and connect with what they did to bring about change, they may be able to transfer those understandings into the present and future. See the following example.

A 15-year-old, Terrance, had been breaking curfew and staying out until 3 or 4 o'clock in the morning. Terrance's father indicated in the first session that this was his primary concern. Two weeks later at their next session, the father stated that Terrance had skipped school during the previous week. After acknowledging this new concern and learning more about it, the father was asked if he was most concerned with Terrance's staying out late or skipping school. The father responded that missing school was the bigger of the two concerns. Before proceeding, the father was asked, "Before we talk about this further, could you give a brief update on what's happened with the situation of Terrance's coming in late?" The father paused for a moment then replied, "Well, he didn't stay out late this past week, so that's better." The therapist followed, "Really? Were you surprised?" "A little," the father replied.

Before delving into the concern of truancy, Terrance was asked questions aimed at evoking exceptions and strengths to build from. These included, "What did you do differently?"; "What was different about the days last week versus days when you would have blown off curfew"; and "Even though you may have thought about staying out late during the past week, how did you get yourself to come in when you were supposed to?" And the father was asked, "What was it like for you to know that you son was safely inside last week at night before curfew rather than running around?" and "What did you do when you found that Terrance was coming in on time each night?"

Although therapy goals can change from session to session, therapists seek opportunities to identify indicators of change to build momentum in the direction of newly identified concerns. Therapists take care not to minimize clients' current concerns or move in directions in which clients are not interested; at the same time, brief reorientations toward previous goals can stimulate stagnant systems and create hope. By identifying positive changes, however small, therapists can help clients to notice that change is always happening and the influence they have over their concerns and problems. This can serve as a catalyst for future change.

Ambiguous or Vague Client Reports

Examples of a second way that clients respond in second and subsequent sessions are "I'm not sure"; "I don't know"; or "Kind of so-so." These responses may suggest indifference or reflect what appears to be lack of interest. Such responses present a potential hazard for therapists. In the process of acknowledging clients' experiences, they do not want to be drawn into stories of impossibility. They assume that there have been times when things have gone differently and therefore work with clients to identify and amplify any positive change, however small, that may have occurred. They are mindful to acknowledge the difficulties that clients face yet want to do this in ways that keep open the possibilities for positive change.

When clients provide vague responses, it is a good idea to use process-oriented questions, such those provided in Chapter 4, to check

in with clients. These questions can assist with this:

- In terms of our work together, what has been helpful or unhelpful? In what way(s)?
- Are there other things that you feel/think we should be discussing instead?
- Is there anything I should have asked that I haven't asked?
- What, if anything, anything has been overlooked?
- How satisfied are you with how things are going so far on a scale from 1 to 10, 10 meaning you are completely satisfied with things?
- What changes, if any, should be made at this point?
- What, if anything, should I be doing differently?
- Is the way we've approached your concern/situation fitting with the way you expect change to occur?
- Is there a way to approach your situation that we haven't yet considered?
- What, if anything, has been missing from our sessions?

Information gleaned from these questions can help therapists determine how to proceed. Another way to shift conversations from ambiguity is to reorient clients to previous goals through summarization. This reminds clients of specific concerns and allows therapists to search for minute changes. Here is a generic example of how to do this:

> The last time we met you mentioned that you were feeling/experiencing/thinking (description). You commented that you had (symptoms, negative reactions, thoughts). Tell me a little bit about what has happened since our last session.

It can also be useful to ask one or more of the following questions:

- How have things been in relation to the last time we met?
- What's been different since our last meeting?
- What's your sense about how things are going now as compared to last time?
- The last time we met, you mentioned that on a scale of 1 to 10, things were at a 5. Where would you say things are today?

If these general questions do not provide clarification, therapists can focus on *small* movements that are typically easier for clients to notice. Questions such as the following can assist with this.

- What have you noticed about your situation that's been *just a little surprising,* in a good way?
- How did you get that to happen *just a little bit?*
- What has been *minimally* better that could have otherwise gone unnoticed?
- What's *something small* that indicates to you that maybe things will turn the corner?
- What does noticing that do for you?
- What else have you noticed?

As with new or changing concerns, therapists are sure to acknowledge and simultaneously search for counterevidence, times when things have been different with regard to presenting concerns. The challenge for therapists is to acknowledge and search in ways that are not invalidating or suggest that clients should just move past or ignore their struggles. The difference is that therapists attend to struggles as hurdles, not barriers. Change is a possibility even with situations that appear outwardly closed down.

Integration of Outcome-Oriented Feedback to Clarify Ambiguity

The addition of outcome-oriented feedback offers therapists another form of information as a means of understanding how clients interpret their situations. Recall that standardized outcome measures have clinical cutoffs, meaning that some clients who enter therapy are not in a representative population that has been shown to do so. Statements from these clients tend to be more generalized and less descriptive. As discussed earlier, the reason for this is that they are reporting fewer symptoms and lower levels of distress—which translates to vague statements. Therapists should refer to clients' overall outcome scores to corroborate or refute what clients have said verbally or therapists have observed.

For example, if a client scores a 37 on the Outcome Questionnaire 45 (OQ-45.2), a 120-point measure with a clinical cutoff of 44 (Burlingame et al., 1995; Lambert & Burlingame, 1996; Lambert & Finch, 1999; Lambert et al., 1996), the therapist might say, "I noticed that your score on the outcome measure is in the lower range, suggesting that you're doing fairly well for someone who is in therapy. Yet you've stated that you're really stuck and haven't felt good. Can you help me to better understand what seems to be out of sync for you?" Another possibility is to say, "In looking at your outcome scores, it seems to make sense that you are feeling uncertain about where things stand. You've got some concerns, but it has been difficult to pinpoint exactly what they are. What ideas do you have about how we might proceed from here?" Some measures also have subscales that could clarify ambiguity. With this information, the therapist might say, "I noticed that your close and social relationships seem to be satisfactory to you, but your sense of self is diminished. Does it seem that way to you, or am I off in interpreting this?"

As you have learned, continuing therapy without clarity has risks. First, ambiguity can contribute to frustration for clients and therapists alike and result in misguided attempts to facilitate change. In addition, clients who score in the nonclinical range tend to have fewer beneficial outcomes because the severity of their problems is relatively low. Finally, change is predictable, and if therapists do not respond to an absence of subjective change in the first few sessions, the risk of negative outcome is significantly increased.

Therapists can respond to this type of ambiguity in several ways. One is to focus on helping clients to make small changes in how they view their situations (see Chapters 7 and 8). This approach may provide a better match if clients are at the precontemplation or contemplation stages of change. A second response is to talk with clients about whether therapy is right for them at that point in time. They may not be in a state of readiness and another form of help could offer a better fit. If clients' ratings of their relationships with their therapists indicate a poor fit, it may be necessary to refer them to other practitioners.

Client Report of No Change or Deterioration

A third way clients tend to respond during subsequent sessions is with reports that problems are the "same" or "worse." Clients make statements such as, "It's the same as last time"; "There's nothing new"; "It's continuing to go downhill"; and "It's worse than ever." These reports are not unusual because people experience their concerns along a continuum; sometimes they are near one end or the other, and at other times they fall somewhere between. The challenge for therapists is to be patient and remain focused on the possibilities of change.

It is important that therapists do three things. First and foremost is to continue to acknowledge and validate, conveying an understanding of clients' pain and suffering. Doing this provides a way to foster the therapeutic alliance and lets clients know that their experiences are valid.

Next, as has been discussed at various junctures, therapists check in with clients to learn their perceptions of therapy processes and the therapeutic relationship. This information is essential in determining any adjustments, modifications, or referrals that may need to be made to better meet clients' needs and provide a better fit. If a process measure is being used, the therapist can refer to the feedback provided by the client. Otherwise and/or in addition, therapists ask questions of clients to gain important feedback about their perceptions of the alliance (see Chapter 4). This information is essential in identifying ruptures in the therapeutic alliance, which can occur at any time and represent faulty expectations, ongoing problems in establishing an alliance, and moments when the client's interpersonal ideas about others are enacted in therapy (Harmon et al., 2005). Clients' expectations and preferences are crucial aspects of therapy, and ruptures in the alliance can contribute to frustration and demoralization if not resolved (Safran, Muran, Samstang, & Stevens, 2002). When ruptures or problems occur, therapists can consider doing the following:

- Discuss the here-and-now relationship with the client.
- Ask for feedback about the therapeutic relationship.

- Create space and allow the client to assert any negative feelings about the therapeutic relationship.
- Engage in conversations about the client's expectations and preferences.
- Discuss the match between the therapist's style and client's preferred ways to relate.
- Spend more time learning about the client's experience in therapy.
- Readdress the agreement established about goals and tasks to accomplish those goals.
- Accept responsibility for his or her part in alliance ruptures.
- Normalize the client's responses by letting him or her know that talking about concerns, facing challenges, taking action, and/or therapy in general can be difficult.
- Provide rationale for techniques and methods.
- Attend closely to subtle clues (e.g., nonverbal behaviors, patterns such as one-word answers) that may indicate a problem with the alliance.
- Offer more positive feedback and encouragement (except when the client communicates either verbally or nonverbally that this is not a good match).
- Engage in further supervision and/or training.

A third point for therapists is to remember that clients' perspectives are changeable. As you have learned, clients' perspectives represent their stories, which are socially constructed realities. Therapists continue to acknowledge clients' perspectives while searching for moments when new possibilities can be introduced into conversations. This can lead to the creation of new stories that highlight exceptions to problems, previous solutions, and clients' strengths and resources.

With both kinds of reports—lack of change or deterioration—therapists take care to acknowledge what clients experience and learn more about what specifically appears to be the same or worse without losing sight of possible exceptions. Therapists identify what has or has not worked to any degree and how clients may have used strengths to counter deterioration. These questions can assist with this process:

- How have you managed to keep things the same?
- What specifically has been worse?
- How so?
- How has that affected you?
- What is one thing that you've noticed about your concern that tells you things haven't gotten out of hand?
- What prevented things from deteriorating even further?
- How did you do that?
- Who specifically did what?
- How did that help?
- How might you get that to happen in the future?
- What kind of help from others, if any, do you need to ensure that that happens?
- What else might help in the future?
- What is a step that you can take after leaving here today that might help things to get back on track (or keep them from slipping again)?
- What do you need to set that in motion?

These questions are particularly important in identifying small movements that the client may not have noticed. Although it may seem to clients that from one session to another their situations are unchanged, that is not possible. As you have learned, problems are contextual and have variations regarding where and when they occur, their intensity, duration, and so on. When clients report stagnation or deterioration, *beginning with the worst* and then gradually identifying *shades of variance* with problems can be helpful. The following example illustrates this idea.

Client: Nothing has improved. I still feel like crap. I'm just always depressed.

Therapist: You've been quite depressed.

Client: Yep and nothing has worked for me—it's bringing me down.

Therapist: Nothing's worked so far. . . . I can see why that would bring you down.

Client: I just want to feel better.

Therapist: I want you to feel better too. Tell me about a time in the recent past when you felt a little bit less depressed or like you had your head slightly above water.

Client: There hasn't been a time. I'm always depressed.

Therapist: It would be helpful if you could tell me a little more about that. Let's start with last week. Even though they were all depressing, which day was the worst—the most depressing day?

Client: Saturday.

Therapist: Tell me about that. What was it like?

Client: I couldn't get out of bed until real late . . . the phone rang, I don't know how many times . . . but I didn't answer it. I also didn't eat until that night . . . it was a wasted day.

Therapist: I see. Not the kind of day that you want to repeat too often.

Client: Definitely not.

Therapist: Okay, then tell me about Friday or Sunday because even though you were depressed on those days, it wasn't as bad as Saturday. What was different during those other times?

Client: On Sunday I slept too long too.

Therapist: I see. How was Sunday different than Saturday?

Client: Well, I did eventually get up at one o'clock in the afternoon. Saturday I didn't get up until six in the evening.

Therapist: How did you manage to get yourself up earlier on Sunday?

Client: I just knew that I had to function at least a little on Sunday so that I could get to work on Monday.

Therapists cannot afford to become hypnotized by these kinds of problematic stories or they will be as stuck as clients have become. By starting with the worst it has been, there is only one direction to go. Once variations in context have been identified, therapists can work to amplify and expand those exceptions. It is not just clients' perspectives that interfere with change. As discussed throughout this book, therapists must also be aware of their own perceptions and how those perceptions can affect the way that therapy proceeds, including closing down possible avenues for change. The following example exemplifies this point.

A father, mother, and their 17-year-old son, Darren, came to therapy. The parents had divorced three years before but were very invested in the well-being of their son and attended all sessions together. They had initiated therapy with concerns that Darren had been failing several classes, smoking marijuana, coming in very late each evening, and not getting a job to help pay for his car insurance. There had been small indicators of change over the course of about several months; however, I felt as if we were stuck and not making enough progress. It seemed to me that when change had occurred, it was minimal and was often overridden by some sort of crisis between sessions. I finally decided to express this concern in a session by saying, "I wanted to share something with all of you. I've been thinking about it for a couple of weeks now. I don't really feel like this [therapy] has been helpful to you. It seems to me that things get a little better, but then they slip back—like we're in quicksand in some ways." Following my statement, the mother remarked, "I think coming here has been very helpful." Surprised at this, I asked, "In what way?" "Darren has been doing much better in English and Math and it looks like he has a chance of graduating now. We couldn't have said that before," she replied. Darren then added, "Yeah, I'm going to pass and I've got a job interview next week." The father also spoke up, "And he does at least tell me when he's going to be late now. That's a miracle in and of itself." It was clear that each of the family members had different ideas about how the therapy had been proceeding and the changes that had occurred. I was then able to learn what specifically had been helpful and what I needed to do more of in the future. Had I not asked, I might have made changes that were not helpful in the family members' eyes.

As discussed earlier in this chapter, it is imperative that therapists respond to the absence of change or deterioration in therapy in a timely manner. The risk of negative outcome with clients who do not show improvement in the first few sessions is significantly high and can increase if therapists continue with the status quo.

It is up to therapists to talk with clients about their perceptions of therapy including their states of readiness for different methods, determine what might provide a better fit, and continue to evaluate the effects of new methods. Therapists may also need to talk with clients about whether therapy is right for them at this point in time, which may lead to a referral.

Asking Coping Sequence Questions

Chapter 7 discussed the idea of finding *counterevidence* to problems. Sometimes referred to as *coping sequence questions*, this technique offers an excellent way to acknowledge pessimism while maintaining an eye on possibilities. When clients respond with statements such as, "Every week it's the same old same old"; "Nothing is going to work"; or "Yes, but . . .," therapists combine acknowledgment with questions that identify qualities and actions that keep clients going. This can foster resilience and draw out underutilized strengths and resources. For example, a therapist might say to a client, "From what you've described, things have been worse. I'm sorry to hear that things have been sliding downward. I'm also curious about what has kept things from completely bottoming out. How have you done that?" These questions help with this process:

- Why aren't things worse with your situation?
- What have you done to keep things from deteriorating even more?
- What steps have you taken to prevent things from heading downhill any further?
- What else has helped things from getting worse?
- How has that made a difference for you/with your situation?
- What is the smallest thing that you could do to slow down this slide even more?
- How might that make a difference with your situation?
- What could others do?
- How could we get that to happen a little now?

Therapists do not try to convince clients that things are better than they perceive them. This can prove invalidating. Instead, they assume there are exceptions by virtue of the fact that *things can get even worse*. Therapists' questions are aimed at helping clients to do their surveying *to convince therapists* of their abilities by identifying what they have done to keep things from getting worse. The following example demonstrates this idea.

> A 16-year-old boy, Harrison, was sent to therapy after being charged with breaking and entering and felony theft. According to his mother, Harrison also had a history of taking drugs and stealing from her. During the third session, his mother said, "It can't get any worse. I've just had it." I acknowledged the mother's feelings and then asked Harrison, "How come you're not already locked up?" He seemed confused by my question. I continued, "I see quite a few teenagers, and by the time they've done what you've done, they're either headed for out-of-home placement or have already been there. What's kept you from being sent away?" Harrison's demeanor changed and he looked down. "Apparently someone believes that you should have another chance and has given you a pass. And I wonder how you have kept things from getting any worse, knowing that one more charge would most certainly get you placed?" Harrison replied, "I don't want to be sent away." I replied, "I hear you. Tell me what have you done since your last offense to prevent that from happening?" "I've listened to my mom more" he answered. This began a shift to focusing on what Harrison had been doing and could do in the future to get his life back on track.

Joining the Pessimism

No matter how insightful, articulated, or well positioned an approach or line of questions may be, some clients will remain steadfast in their perspectives. Therapists are challenged to avoid the pull of impossibility in believing that clients are resistant or unmotivated or that their situations, circumstances, or problems are unchangeable. When clients respond to therapists' attempts to elicit exceptions or differences with negative or closed-down statements, clients are often communicating that therapists still need to learn more about their concerns, orientations, and theories. Clients are letting therapists know that their ways of relating to them are not working and that therapists need to interact with them differently.

When all paths seem to have been exhausted, joining clients' pessimism can prove beneficial. An example might be for a therapist to say, "You've convinced me just how bad things really are. I don't think I understood at first. Even though I think things can get better, I really don't have a clue as to what to do to help you. I'm sitting here wondering what I must be missing about your situation and where to go with this." Another option is to say, "It really does sound like a dreadful situation. I think maybe I didn't see that at first. Maybe we should spend more time on this so it really sinks in with me." Statements should match clients' degree of pessimism and not trivialize their concerns. The following example illustrates this.

> A couple sought therapy for "bitter arguments" that resulted in yelling and one or both people feeling hurt and angry. The arguments had become extremely intense and accordingly to both parties, their relationship was beyond repair. The therapist asked various questions to elicit exceptions such as, "When have things been just a little better between the two of you?" and "What is different about times when your arguments are less intense?" The therapist's questions were met with terse, often one-word answers that things are "never better" and "will always be that way." It seemed that no matter what the therapist

tried was met with trepidation. In response, the therapist shifted his approach to join the couple's pessimism. The therapist remarked, "You've convinced me." The couple looked surprised, and the wife inquired, "Of what?" "Well, you've convinced me that there isn't a single reason you should be together." Appearing even more surprised, the husband and wife looked at each other. Almost in unison, they both replied, "It's not that bad." To this the therapist responded, "What's not that bad? I haven't seen one indication that you are able to handle your disagreements in any other way but to argue until one or both of you suffers." The room fell silent and then the wife spoke, "Actually, there have been a couple of times recently when we've been able to stop things from getting too bad." This created an opening for the therapist to pursue exceptions.

By joining the pessimism, therapists can strengthen both their relationships with clients and understandings of their experiences. As a result, some clients reverse gears, and exceptions to their problematic stories become evident. These exceptions can then be amplified and built upon.

Responding to "No-Talk" Clients

It is not unusual to periodically encounter clients who speak very little or not at all. Although this often changes sooner rather than later, it can result in stagnation in therapy. It can also lead to frustration for both therapists and clients. Although there may be additional options with more verbal clients, therapy can still be beneficial for those who choose not to speak.

The first response in these situations is it to give the client permission not to speak. A therapist might say, "It's okay if you don't want to talk. Sometimes I feel that way."

Another possibility is, "You're the only one who will know when it's right for you to talk. I'll leave it up to you" or "If you want to talk later that's fine. If you don't, that's okay too." Stories and self-disclosure also can be used to invite clients into conversation. The best asset therapists can have is their belief that under the right conditions, people can experience positive change, even when clients are less verbal. The following example illustrates the importance of maintaining this belief and how it can affect therapy.

An 11-year-old boy was brought to therapy because he had been isolating himself from other children and appeared despondent. When he did not speak or respond verbally to questions, I said, "I just wanted to let you know that it's okay if you don't want or feel like talking. I've felt that way at times. And, if you want or feel like talking later, that's okay too—but there's no pressure to have to say anything. And you know, today might be a good day to not talk. You know why? Because I have a lot to say! You see, I wanted to tell you about this TV show I saw last night. It was about UFOs. It was really cool but weird too." As I continued to talk, the young man smiled and seemed ready to say something so I said, "Ah, you know what I mean. But hang on, I'm not quite finished yet." By the time I finished, just a minute or so later, he was bursting with excitement and couldn't wait to tell me about his favorite movie, which was about aliens coming to earth. The rest of the sessions and those that followed were filled with conversation.

Being less verbal does not mean that clients do not want things to change. The key is to focus on finding out what might stimulate movement while not knowing what might resonate with clients. This is accomplished by implementing processes that invite change without becoming infatuated with the methods themselves. Therapists expand on the subtle openings that emerge from problematic stories to create new stories that emanate hope and possibility. To practice using the methods provided in this and the previous two sections, please complete Exercise 11.2, The State of Progress.

Negotiating Impasses

In addition to the ideas offered earlier in the chapter regarding possible ruptures in therapeutic alliance, therapists can consider the following strategies when therapy appears to remain at a standstill:

- Revisit the current stage of the client's change. (Ask: What is the client's state of readiness for change?)
- Focus more on the client's view of the problem or situation—this will not require action.
- Ask open-ended questions that will allow the client to notice one or more aspects that have been downplayed or have gone unnoticed about the situation (take care not to imply that the client's perspective is

---

Exercise 11.2

The State of Progress

Clients return to second and subsequent sessions with varying reports of their progress in therapy. Therapists want first to learn clients' perceptions and explore them further to determine whether clients' reports involve new concerns, ambiguity, no change, deterioration, or a combination of these. To complete this exercise, pair with another person. One of you should role-play a client and the other a therapist. You can also choose to do this exercise individually. In using pairs, consider your role-play a second or subsequent session. Begin the role-play session as you typically would. At some point, the client is to respond in one of the ways described previously. In the following spaces, the therapist is first to write the client response and the category of response (for example, report of new concerns, deterioration). Next, the therapist determines a way to respond to the client. This response (and there may be more than one) should be listed. Finally, write the result of the therapist's response. You may repeat the last two parts of this sequence numerous times if necessary. If you are completing this exercise individually, think of possible statements clients might use in second or subsequent sessions. Write two or three for each client. Then follow the rest of the exercise as outlined. (*Note:* You will not be able to complete the "results" section without a partner.)

Example:

Client response:	"Not only is my boss increasing my workload but now my wife is threatening to leave."
Category of response:	Client reports new concern or problem.
Therapist's response:	Acknowledge client's new concern; ask client to say more about his new concern to determine whether it is just on his mind or something he would like to talk more about in therapy.
Result of therapist's response:	Client gave details of relationship concerns with wife.
Therapist's response:	Inquire about whether the client's previous concern of an increasing workload or more recent concern of his wife threatening to leave takes precedence.
Result of therapist's response:	Client stated that he was concerned about work but felt it was most important to talk about his relationship with his wife.

Exercise 11.2   (continued)

1

Client response: _____

_____

Category of response: _____

_____

Therapist's response: _____

_____

Result of therapist's response: _____

_____

Therapist's response: _____

_____

Result of therapist's response: _____

_____

Therapist's response: _____

_____

Result of therapist's response: _____

_____

2

Client response: _____

_____

Category of response: _____

_____

Therapist's response: _____

_____

Result of therapist's response: _____

_____

Therapist's response: _____

_____

Result of therapist's response: _____

_____

Therapist's response: _____

_____

Result of therapist's response: _____

_____

"wrong"; try only to introduce other ways of viewing that may offer new possibilities or will encourage the client to talk about the problem or situation differently).

- Help the client to weigh the possible positive and negative effects of his or her behavior.
- Help the client to weigh the possible benefits and drawbacks of change.
- Offer straightforward feedback without imposing it (for example, "From where I am standing, I'm concerned about what might happen if this continues. Of course, that is for you to decide, but I believe it's my responsibility to speak about it.") (*Note:* Always provide more directive feedback and make necessary safeguards if there is risk of harm to self or other.)
- Demonstrate genuine confidence that the client has the strength to face his or her challenges.
- Avoid a "solution-forced" situation when the client's conversational preference is to talk more about problems and his or her ambivalence.

- Acknowledge further—ensure that the client feels heard and understood and verifies this either verbally or nonverbally (ask questions or use an alliance measure as needed).
- Reorient to the client's concerns to ensure that you and the client are focusing on the same issue.
- Discuss with the client whether the level of services is a good fit and/or whether he or she is ready to be in therapy.

In stuck situations, there are no single correct questions to ask clients. There are, however, questions that draw attention to therapy processes and encourage other conversations about what is working, what is not, and possible corrective actions. Therapists focus on ensuring that clients feel heard and understood and on creating the best fit possible between clients' orientations and therapists' approaches. This requires that therapists create a climate that is responsive and based on continuous client-therapist feedback loops.

SUMMARY POINTS

- Client engagement processes continue in subsequent sessions and throughout therapy.
- Therapists check in with clients to monitor their ratings of the therapeutic relationship and alliance.
- Client feedback is incorporated into sessions on a real-time basis.
- Outcome-oriented feedback represents the most consistent means of rating client improvement; early ratings are predictive of outcome.

- Two essential terms associated with outcome-oriented feedback are *the reliable change index (RCI)* and *clinical significance*.
- *The RCI* is a measure that assesses the magnitude of change necessary to be considered statistically reliable and not due to chance or the passage of time. It is an average based on the reliability or consistency of a measurement instrument and represents the difference between two points in time that would not be due to simple measurement error.

- *Clinical significance* refers to reliable improvement that corresponds to a change in clinical status, which involves movement from a clinical (often referred to as *dysfunctional*) range to a nonclinical (*functional*) range.
- Client responses in subsequent sessions fall into four general categories: *new concerns or problems, ambiguous or vague, no change or deterioration,* and *improvement* (discussed in Chapter 12).
  - When clients report *new concerns or problems,* therapists acknowledge and collaborate with them to determine the relevancy of those new concerns and make any necessary adjustments to goals and directions in therapy. Therapists also take care to explore any changes with concerns raised in previous sessions because there may be moments of positive change to be highlighted and amplified.
  - When clients offer *ambiguous and vague* responses, therapists work to clarify those statements and ensure that they are on track.
  - When clients report *no change or deterioration,* therapists acknowledge and validate, check in with clients to learn their perceptions of therapy processes and the therapeutic relationship, and recognize that clients' perspectives are changeable.

DISCUSSION QUESTIONS

1. What do the terms *reliable change* and *clinical significance* mean? Why are these terms important?

2. What are some of the common client responses in second and subsequent sessions?

3. When faced with ambiguous client responses, what are ways that therapists can gain clarity?

4. How can therapists determine ruptures in the therapeutic alliance? What are potential risks of inadequately responding to a problem with the alliance? What are ways in which therapists can respond to such problems?

5. What are three possibilities for negotiating impasses?

Chapter 12

Emerging and Evolving Stories

Building on Progress and Change

■ Chapter 11 discussed three general categories of ways in which clients often respond during subsequent sessions and interactions. This chapter explores a fourth category: when clients report improvement or others identify it. Because evidence of change can take many forms, therapists' aim is to be clear about what specifically has improved, how it occurred, the meaning of change in clients' eyes, and its overall relationship to the goals of therapy. This chapter also explores ways to prepare clients for transitions, manage setbacks, and anticipate future hurdles.

Reports and Identification of Improvement

When clients report change or therapists identify it, therapists seek to amplify that change and explore ways in which it affects clients' lives now and can in the future. To identify change, therapists scan clients' lives for exceptions, indicators of improvement in relation to the problems described in therapy. These questions can assist in identifying change:

- What have you noticed that has changed with your concern/problem/self/situation?
- What specifically seems to be going better?
- Who first noticed that things had changed?
- Who else noticed the change?
- When did you first notice that things had changed?
- What did you notice happening?

Once change has been identified, focusing on how it occurred can amplify it. This process involves asking questions that draw on specific actions of clients and others who may be involved. In addition, therapists emphasize any differences that the change has made in clients' lives and in relation to their goals.

Questions such as the following are used to amplify change:

- How did the change happen?
- What were the influences (for example, family, culture, spirituality)?
- What did you find worked for you?
- What did you do?
- How did you do that?
- How did you get yourself to do that?
- How did you get that to happen?
- How was that different than before?
- How did that help you?
- Where did you get the idea to do it that way?
- What did you tell yourself?

Clients' answers to these questions can help them to better understand how they use their strengths and resources to manage problems. This is an integral part of change processes because it often helps clients to recognize abilities that have gone unnoticed or underutilized. Because clients can respond to questions about improvements in ambiguous ways (for example, "I just wanted things to change"; "I worked at it"; "I knew it couldn't continue the way it had been"), therapists continue to follow up to translate vague descriptions into clear, concrete ones. Questions that focus on how and what are pivotal to gaining clarity. To practice amplifying positive changes, please refer to Exercise 12.1, Identifying and Amplifying Change.

If clients struggle with these questions, they may be too global or sweeping. In such cases, looking for smaller changes may prove a better fit. To do this, therapists might say, "How did you get that change to happen *just a little?*" or "What did you do *a little differently* than in previous situations?" Notice that the questions in this section focus on clients' actions as opposed to external variables. What

clients attribute change to is crucial to whether it will last in the long term.

Using the Dynamic Duo: Attribution and Speculation

Notice that the questions in the previous section—and throughout this book—have emphasized clients' roles in change processes. There many reasons for this. First, therapists help to create the conditions in which clients are more likely to experience positive change; however, they do not make clients change. All change is self change. Therefore, what clients *attribute* the significant portion of positive change to is crucial. If clients see therapists, others, medication, or other external entities as *primarily* responsible for their improvements, the likelihood that the change they have experienced will last in the long-term decreases. This is in part because clients may deny accountability once external factors have been removed or diminish as causal agents of change.

Whether change happens before or during therapy, results from clients' or others' own actions, or occurs by happenstance, therapists want to enhance the effects of change by helping clients to see change and its maintenance as a consequence of their own efforts (Duncan, Miller, & Sparks, 2004). They want to attribute the major part of the change to clients' individual actions and *who they are as people*. In a sense, therapists *blame* clients for changing for the better. To do this therapists ask questions to assist in assigning change to clients:

- How is that you have been able face so many challenges and not lose sight of (X)?
- Who are you such that you've been able to (X)?
- What does the fact that you've been able to face up to (X) say about you?

Exercise 12.1

Identifying and Amplifying Change

This goal of this exercise is to help identify and amplify positive changes in second and subsequent sessions. *Identify* refers to noticing positive changes, however small, and exploring how those changes came about. *Amplify* means determining the benefits of the change and how those changes might affect people's lives in the future. To complete this exercise, choose a concern and answer the following questions in the spaces provided. Be as specific as possible, listing each behavior, action, or interaction by using clear, action-based descriptions.

• What have you noticed that has changed for the better with the problem you've been facing?

_____

_____

_____

_____

_____

• Who first noticed that things had changed? Who else noticed?

_____

_____

_____

_____

_____

• When did you first notice that things had changed? What did you notice happening at that time?

_____

_____

_____

_____

_____

• How did the change happen? What did you do? What did others do?

_____

_____

_____

_____

_____

• How did you get yourself to do what you did?

_____

_____

Exercise 12.1 *(continued)*

_____

_____

_____

6. How does what you did differ from what you've done in the past?

_____

_____

_____

_____

7. How has the change been helpful to you? To others around you?

_____

_____

_____

_____

8. What will be different in the future as these changes continue?

_____

_____

_____

_____

9. Who else might benefit from these changes? How?

_____

_____

_____

_____

- What kind of person are you that you've been able to overcome (X)?
- Where did the wherewithal come from to (X)?

Therapists do not dismiss the contributions of external factors that serve as catalysts for change. Therapists' aim then is for clients to attribute the major portion of change to their own actions. They convey the idea that even though external factors may be triggers in producing change, it is clients themselves who are in charge of their lives. The following questions can assist in both identifying the contributions of external factors and promoting accountability and self-efficacy:

- You mentioned that you feel/think that (for example, medication, therapy) is helping. How are you working with the (medication, therapy) to better your life?
- In your mind, what does (medication, therapy) allow you to do that you might not have otherwise done?
- What percentage of the change you've experienced is a result of (medication, therapy), and what percentage do you think is the result of your own doing?
- As a result of *feeling* better from (medication, therapy), what are *you* then able to *do* as a result?

Even the most experienced therapists encounter clients who are unable to identify what has brought about or contributed to positive change. For example, clients, particularly adolescents, often respond to therapists' questions with "I don't know." This does not mean that clients are withholding information or are resistant; they may not have given much thought to it, do not know, or perhaps are not interested. What seems to make a difference is how therapists attend to these kinds of client reports. *Speculating* about how the change might have come about can be useful (Bertolino, 2003). For example, a therapist might have a client speculate or guess by asking, "If you had to guess, and there were no wrong answers, what would you say made a difference for you?" or "If (for example, a close friend, your partner, mother, boss) were here, what would he/she say has contributed to things changing?" If this does not reveal anything, therapists can do their own speculating, "What do you think about the idea that you might have

had a role in your situation improving?" These questions assist with using speculation:

- I'm wondering if perhaps part of the reason things are going better for you is that you are becoming (for example, more in tune with what you want, more responsible, more mature, wiser, growing up). Perhaps you are becoming the type of person you want to be and learning new ways of managing your life. What do you think about this idea?
- Is it possible that the change you've experienced might be related to your (action)?
- What do you think about the idea that the change you've experienced might be related to your (for example, wanting to lead a different life, being ready for the next stage of your life)?
- What do you think about the idea that the change you've experienced might be an indication that you're taking back control of your life?
- How might the change you've experienced be a sign of a new, preferred direction for you?

Therapists speculate from a position of curiosity or conjecture, leaving clients to either accept or reject the speculations depending on whether they fit. It is interesting to note that because therapists' speculations involve the attribution of positive qualities and actions, they are less likely to be rejected. It is unlikely that a client will say, "No, I'm becoming less responsible." Even if speculations are off target because they highlight competencies, clients will at least ponder them. This may trigger new client-initiated speculations. It is hoped that therapists' speculations will lead clients to come up with their own. See the following examples.

A woman came to therapy stating that she was "depressed." Exploration of her concern revealed that she had suffered a series of events including the loss of her job. After making gains and then experiencing periodic setbacks, she accepted a new job that paid less but had the potential to be more fulfilling. At first the woman seemed to remain mired in self-defeat; then over the course of two weeks, her depression seemed to lift. This was evidenced by a change in her demeanor, voice, and posture. As the next few weeks passed, the woman's physical appearance changed as she took more of an interest in her self-care. After two months, the woman was back in charge of her life. Her therapist asked her, "How did you get your life back from the throws of depression?" She replied, "That's a good question. I've actually thought about that but I'm still not sure." The therapist asked, "I've been wondering to myself if something inside you, that's been dormant for a while, came to life. Perhaps you realized that it was time to reclaim your life and that meant using your wherewithal and what you've learned over the years." Now in tears and seeming to connect with the therapist's words, the woman followed, "I think you know me better than I know myself."

Trent, a 14-year-old, was mandated to therapy by the family court. He and a friend had stolen his friend's mother's ATM card and withdrawn more than $2,000. Trent had also been failing his classes at school. Over the course of seven months, Trent made amends and paid restitution for the theft and raised his grades in school. He did this by turning in his homework and doing extra credit. To his mother's surprise, he also began helping out at home by mowing the lawn and cleaning. When asked what he thought led him to make so many changes, Trent appeared somewhat confused and answered, "I'm not

sure. I guess I just did it." I followed this by speculating about some possibilities by saying, "I wonder if it's because you are becoming more mature and responsible. Maybe you're also thinking more about others, like your mom." His eyes glistening, Trent leaned forward and said, "Yeah I think that's part of it. I also think I'm just seeing that things need to be done and no one can do them but me. I've done it and I'm proud."

Attribution and speculation draw attention to clients' roles in creating positive change. They also support evolving new stories of growth, resiliency, and hope that run counter to the problem-saturated ones that brought them to therapy. This serves as a way to "anchor" the change, meaning that clients are better able to connect with their internal experiences, including feelings and sensory perceptions (Bertolino, 1999). By moving to an experiential level, the change may be more profound. To further assist clients in connecting with internal experiences, therapists ask questions such as these:

- When you were able to (action), what did that feel like?
- How did you experience that change inside?
- How was that feeling similar or different than before?
- What does it feel like to know that others may also benefit from the changes you've made?

Asking these questions makes it possible to evoke feelings and sensations of joy, comfort, reassurance, and hope that have been lost or buried as a result of the oppression of problems. This idea is illustrated in the following example.

A couple came to therapy concerned with increasing conflict in their relationship. This had resulted in arguments and decreased time spent together as a couple. Both members of the couple described how strong their relationship had been and how their conflict had become more apparent since having children. During therapy, they were able to change various aspects of their interactions, build in more "together time," and reconnect by reinstating previous rituals of connection that had disappeared over time. As it came time for the couple to make the transition out of therapy, both members were asked what they had experienced. The wife stated, "It's like *déjà vu*. It takes me back to what brought us together to begin with. Some of those old feelings are there again. I don't know that they ever went away—they're just back." The husband agreed, "It's easy for those feelings to go missing. When I take the time to really appreciate what we have, it all comes rushing out. It's invigorating."

Sharing Credit for Change

Although change involves individual actions, it can be particularly helpful to share the credit for it, especially with couples and families. Unlike attribution, sharing the credit involves focusing on relationships and acknowledging each person's contribution to improving overall situations. Sharing the credit serves several purposes. First, as you have learned, the quality of the client's participation in therapy is an important factor in outcome. When clients are left out of therapy processes, they can appear as noncompliant, resistant, and unmotivated. By recognizing clients' contributions, therapists are extending change to those who may be more peripherally involved but are nonetheless important to the stability of clients' relationships and/or social networks.

A second purpose of sharing the credit is to use it as a countermeasure in situations where positive change has occurred but is being negated in some way. This is evidenced by client statements such as, "It will never last"; "He's done that before"; or "You haven't seen the real (name) yet." These comments often come from clients who do not feel as if they have made a valued or positive contribution to change.

To better understand these kinds of responses, consider what a person or caregiver, such as a parent, might experience when change has happened quickly in therapy. Although problem resolution is the goal, it can also raise feelings of blame ("I'm a bad parent"; "I clearly did a bad job") or inadequacy ("I obviously don't know what I'm doing"; "Anyone could do a better job than me"). It may appear to someone that therapy was the reason change occurred and that the other person's efforts over the years or course of the relationship were futile. Some clients experience both feelings of being a failure for not being to resolve problems and then invalidation when a stranger—a therapist—is able to "fix" the situation.

Client experiences of invalidation and feelings of failure can undermine therapy. The irony is that although family members are often pointed to as the cause of problems, they do not always get credit for their individual contributions when things go better. By identifying the contributions of everyone who may be involved, therapists counter negative statements that can minimize change and prove invalidating. There are several possibilities for sharing the credit for change. One way is to give others involved with therapy credit by saying:

- I wonder how you were able to instill the value of (specific value) in (name).
- Like you, (name) seems to hold the value of (specific value). I can't help thinking that he/she learned it from you.

- It seems to me that (name) has learned the value of (specific value) from you.

A second possibility is to evoke from those involved something that they feel contributed to the change process:

- How do you think your (relationship, parenting, etc.) has contributed to (name)'s ability to (action)?
- In what ways do you think you have been able to help (name) to stand up to adversity?
- In what ways do you think you were of assistance in helping (name) to stand up to (concern/problem) and get back on track?

A third way is to ask the primary client what contributions others have made to his or her life and then to share the answers with others who are involved:

- What did you learn from (name) about how to overcome (concern/problem)?
- Who taught you the value of (specific value)?
- From whom did you learn about (action, thing)?

These questions do not create conflict in attributing change to the qualities and actions of individuals but offer "both/and" as opposed to "either/or." Therapists both attribute the major portion of significant change to individuals and share the credit with those who have provided care and support. Doing so can neutralize each person's feelings that their efforts have been acknowledged but are valued negatively. As a result of sharing the credit for change, it is not uncommon for clients and others who are involved to experience a new sense of togetherness or spirit of family.

Continuing Conversations to Build on Change

In identifying and amplifying change, it is important to keep in mind that a change in one area can lead to one or more changes in other areas. Therapists continue to scan for ways in which positive change may be creating a "ripple effect." Like a snowball traveling downhill, expanding as it gains speed and momentum or a domino starting a chain reaction of knocking over others, therapists search for other changes in clients' lives. These questions assist with this:

- What else have you noticed that has changed?
- What else is different?
- How has(have) that(those) difference(s) been helpful to you?
- What difference has the change made with employment/school/home life, etc.?
- Who else has noticed these other changes?
- Who else has benefited from these changes?
- What difference has that made for him/her/them?

Consistent with exploring changes that have occurred in relation to goals, therapists clarify ambiguous responses to understand "what" is different and "how" those changes came about. In addition to recognizing the changes themselves, therapists orient clients to other changes in their lives. See the following example.

> A woman in therapy related that she was feeling "overwhelmed." She spoke about various concerns among which was working to raise two very young children as a single parent and maintaining her sobriety. In her third session, she appeared cheery, smiling, and laughing as she reported that things were "100 percent better." Thinking that this comment had something to do with her initial concerns, the therapist asked the woman,

"What's changed?" "I got a new job with a good raise!" she exclaimed. The therapist was then surprised to learn that although nothing specifically had been done regarding her primary concerns, her outlook on them had greatly changed. The woman remarked, "I feel like I can handle things a lot better now."

Although specific goals are identified during therapy, it is not uncommon to learn that secondary concerns or areas have been affected and changed in some way. This suggests that although identified goals are the main focus, therapists must remain on the lookout for ways to promote change in general. Doing so can indirectly lead to gains in meeting established goals. Thus, it is crucial to ask clients about positive changes or benefits that may have occurred elsewhere in their lives and how those might relate to the concerns that led to therapy.

Making New Connections through Linking

Another way to build on client improvement is through *linking*—joining two things that have not been joined together previously (O'Hanlon, 1987). One of the benefits of linking is that it orients clients to other changes that may be occurring concurrently but perhaps without notice. There are two ways to link. The first involves using words including *as, while,* and *when*. For example, a therapist might say, "*As* you continue to improve your eating habits, you can notice how those changes affect more than your weight." Or "*While* you are appreciating how you feel without flashbacks, you may also notice the affect it has on your relationships."

The second way to employ linking is by using phrases such as *the more this, the more that; the less this, the less that; the more this, the less that;* or *the less this, the more that.* For example, a therapist might say, "The *more* comfortable you become with your anger, the *more* accepting you may be of your other feelings" or "The *less* anxiety you experience, the *more* you can appreciate the gains you have made." The idea is to help clients to notice that change in one area of their lives can trigger change in others.

Revisiting Outcome-Oriented Feedback

Outcome-oriented feedback provides information about clients' concerns. When changes are reported or identified, this feedback can be used to gain clarity about the degree of change from clients' perspectives. Using the sample parameters described previously with the OQ-45.2 (for example, 120-point scale, clinical cutoff of 44, RCI of 10) (Burlingame et al., 1995; Lambert & Burlingame, 1996; Lambert & Finch, 1999; Lambert et al., 1996), let's suppose that the client from the previous example had a first session score of 61 and then scores of 60 and 43 in sessions two and three, respectively. The client's verbal statements combined with her cheery appearance and an 18-point improvement (which is clinically significant on the measure) substantially corroborate improvement. With this information, the therapist would want to follow up with questions that reflect the changes. The therapist might say, "It sounds like you've really experienced some wonderful changes. I have not only heard about these changes but also can see them written on your face and in your voice. You also indicated this on your outcome form. You moved 18 points. Does that seem like a small or large amount of change for you? What does it mean to you?" The therapist would continue to work to understand what the change means to the client and what difference it might make in relation to the overall goals of therapy.

For the sake of deepening your understanding, let's consider two other examples of alternative outcome scores and how this might influence follow-up questions. With the same client, imagine that the scores for sessions one through three were 61, 55, and 34. The therapist would explore the variations in scores between each of the sessions. For example, what kind of changes occurred between sessions one and two? Regardless of the numbers, does the client consider that a small or large degree of change? It is also noteworthy that the client would have gone from the clinical to the nonclinical range. As part of continuing conversations, the therapist would want to find out what the relationship of that change is to the overall goals of therapy and what else the client would like to see improve.

Let's consider a final example with scores of 61, 65, and 56. Once again, it would be important to talk with the client about what transpired between each of the three sessions. For example, what happened that lead to an increase in scores and possible deterioration between sessions one and two? Furthermore, even though the client improved overall from session one to three, what is the meaning of that change? If the client verbalizes changes that are not reflected in instrumentation, the therapist wants to inquire about that.

Because real-time data provide snapshots of recent times, therapists are reminded that single scores can indicate one-time fluctuations. Large changes in scores are likely to reflect situational changes (for example, positive events, crises) that may not give an accurate depiction of clients' lives in general. Therapists serve clients best by comparing and contrasting scores over several sessions. Improvement, deterioration, or flattening of scores (in other words, very small changes over a span of multiple sessions) is likely to provide a more reliable picture.

Outcome data represent just one form of information. Although the data offer a general direction about whether clients are on positive or negative trajectories of change, suggesting that therapists continue as is or change their approaches, the data does not tell them what to do or how to do it. The information needed to determine what is working and what is not comes from feedback in conversations with clients.

Situating Change in Relation to Goals and Preferred Futures

Therapists should be reminded that therapy begins by identifying concerns and complaints but clients determine relative significance of positive change. The task of therapists is to engage clients in conversations to understand the meaning of change. A central question involves how the change that has occurred relates to established goals. Have the concerns or problems been resolved? What else needs to happen for therapy to be considered successful/for goals to be met? To understand how change is situated in relationship to goals, the following questions can be helpful:

- What difference has the change made in your life?
- How are you benefiting from the change you've experienced?
- What will be different in the future as these changes continue to occur?
- In the future, what other changes do you think might occur that might not have otherwise come about?
- Who else might benefit from these changes? How?
- In the future, what will indicate to you that these changes are continuing to happen?
- How does the change that's happened relate to the goals that we set?
- What difference has this change made in relation to your goals for therapy?

- To what degree have things improved?
- Has the problem that brought you here been resolved?
- What else needs to happen to cause this problem to fade from your life?
- What else, if anything, needs to happen so that you'll feel/think that the problem you came here for is manageable without therapy?
- What else, if anything, needs to happen so that you'll be convinced that the problem no longer exists?
- Last time, you indicated that if you were able to (action), you would know that things were better. Now that you have achieved this, how do you see things?
- At the start of therapy, you told me that things were at a 4 on a scale of 1 to 10. You also mentioned that you would know that therapy had been successful when (action). That would represent an 8. Now that those things have happened, does that indicate to you that things are at an 8? What else, if anything, needs to happen for you to feel that you have met your goals?

Change should be evaluated in the context of both goals and outcomes. When improvement has occurred, therapists collaborate with clients to determine what else, if anything, needs to happen in relationship to goals. The achievement of goals is only one determinant in therapy; the other is outcome. Of primary concern is that clients can meet goals without necessarily having improved outcomes. For example, a client may report that he is meeting goals such as getting to work on time, completing his tasks on schedule, and getting better evaluations. However, if the same client does not report improvement (in areas such as individual, relational, and social role functioning) on an outcome measure, further exploration is

necessary. This is necessary because the client may reach concrete goals yet remain depressed or anxious or continue to have trouble in relationships with co-workers, and so on. If goals have been met but are inconsistent with outcome scores, therapists discuss these inconsistencies with clients.

Suppose the client previously described has met his goals but remains in the clinical range in terms of outcome scores and has not achieved reliable and clinically significant change. The therapist might approach the client by stating, "You've accomplished the goals you set out to achieve and yet you've expressed some (describe what has been indicated in the outcome measure, for example, anxiety, discomfort with close relationships, anger, trouble sleeping) in the instrument you completed today. Please tell me about that." The opposite can also occur when outcomes improve without goals being met. Therapists must determine what is a sufficient indicator of change. They must not overly interpret any one form of information but to bring it to clients' attention and let them provide the meaning.

When improvement in the context of goals and outcomes has occurred, initiating conversations about how clients can begin to make the transition to higher levels of independence and out of therapy can be a good idea. These conversations can identify concerns of clients who may have fears about the sustainability of the changes they have made and about leaving therapy in general. Therapists should do their best to reassure clients that the decision to end therapy will be a collaborative one.

In beginning transitions to less intensive services therapists can proceed in several ways. As discussed in Chapter 3, incorporating clients' preferences in terms of meeting is important. Because these preferences can change, therapists want to check in with clients at the end of every session. One way to begin transitions is by gradually allowing more time to elapse between sessions so that clients can gain more independence and, it is hoped, confidence in their abilities to maintain and further their changes.

Although there is a focus on transitioning clients out of therapy, the more flexible therapists are, the better they will be able to accommodate clients when there are "bumps in the road." They will be able to change the frequency and length of sessions as needed. Knowing that there will be periodic "check ups" can also provide a connection and security for clients. The reminder that they will see their therapists some time in the future can help clients with severe or chronic concerns, children, and adolescents to stay on track and hold course with the changes they have made.

Whether gradual or quick, therapists need to keep in mind inherent risks that can occur as transitions begin. For every combination of therapist and client, there is a maximum amount of benefit that can be achieved in therapy. One indicator that clients may have reached this point is when their concerns become more generalized and vague. For example, a client may have achieved a goal of improving her social relationships by making more friends. This may be supported by improved outcome scores that move her into the nonclinical range and are both clinically significant and reliable. The client, however, comes to therapy feeling that there is "something else" that she needs to work on. The therapist and client talk about this, yet the client cannot quite put her finger on it.

If the therapist and client are not able to negotiate a new goal in a reasonable amount of time, several possible risks are possible. First, a distinguishing factor between therapy and other forms of support is the focus on a problem or concern in therapy. The client may be satisfied in continuing therapy because it offers a form of support; at the same time, the therapist may experience increased frustration in not knowing "what else" needs to happen. This situation can lead to dependency, randomness in conversation, and perhaps the "discovery" of new problems that may not be problems at all.

Outcome-oriented feedback becomes invaluable in such situations. If the client's scores on a measure have flattened out and remained relatively stable over the course of a few sessions (in other words, some variance but no major ups or downs), this is another indicator that she has probably reached the significant portion of change she is likely to make with her therapist at this time. She may improve a few points outcomewise, but if she remains in therapy too long without significant gains, the likelihood that she will experience regression increases. This is primarily due to time. Over time people will have many experiences some of which will be problematic. Therefore, the longer people remain in the therapy the more the likelihood that some form of problems will arise.

People go through individual, relational, and familial developmental changes and face hurdles at different junctures. Therapy can be helpful in negotiating these changes so individuals, couples, and families can continue to grow. Once concerns have been resolved or sufficiently addressed, most people make the transition out of therapy. What must be determined is whether the risk that clients will get worse is worth the cost of their remaining in therapy too long. This is not just a decision for therapists. Clients are consumers and should be treated as capable of making decisions that are right for them. Therapists' responsibility is to talk with clients about the possible benefits and drawbacks of continuing therapy once goals have been met and improved outcomes have been achieved. If clients are continuing to make periodic gains, however small, are willing to accept the risk of regression, and want to be in therapy, this may be of little consequence. To address this, the idea of an "open-door" perspective was introduced in Chapter 3. This perspective, which involves offering a flexible transition into and out of therapy, can counter clients' fears and provide a responsive system. The end of this chapter revisits the open-door perspective.

Extrapolations: Growing New Stories

As clients progress, therapists search for opportunities to grow new stories and help them to take "root" in clients' lives in addition to amplifying and expanding exceptions and differences. Therapists do this by highlighting positive decisions clients have made, promoting accountability, and drawing on strengths and resources. They accomplish these in two ways: *writing therapeutic letters to clients* and *documenting new life stories.*

Writing Therapeutic Letters to Clients

Therapy can affect the way people think, feel, act, and interact. What happens in sessions can resonate immediately, in the long term, or can pass through and be paid little attention. Sometimes clients reflect on moments and conversations and say, "I wish I had written down what you said (about X)" or "I've been trying to remember what you said." When different exchanges prove meaningful to clients, further accentuating those conversations and points associated with them can be helpful.

A creative way to highlight key points is to write therapeutic letters to clients. These letters can be used at any point in therapy when therapists feel that they may be therapeutic. Letters, which are a flexible medium, highlight client

abilities and resources. They also amplify what is working and encourage more of those favorable actions. In addition, letters to clients orient them toward goals and presuppose future changes. They can be tentative and speculative, meant to work beyond therapy sessions and "thicken" preferred stories in clients' lives.

To illustrate how therapeutic letters to clients can be used to highlight and facilitate change, refer to Case Example 8.2, involving Jeremy. To recapitulate, Jeremy was brought to therapy by his father because of having poor grades, sneaking out at night, and smoking marijuana. Jeremy wanted to play high school football, but his father made this contingent on improved grades and behavior. Although unhappy about it, Jeremy attended summer school to make up classes and improve his grades. An analogy was used to draw a parallel between the football preseason and summer school with suggestions about getting shape for the upcoming school year, referred to as the "regular season." Other analogies were offered, in particular, about the necessity to connect with others, focus on studies, and so on. Letters to Jeremy were used to highlight his gains and extend them into the future. Case Example 12.1 includes a series of three of these letters.

Although letters are not a good fit for all clients, their value to some clients is often compelling and worth the time and effort. Client reports suggest that letters can be worth anywhere from 3 to 10 sessions of face-to-face therapy (Freeman, Epston, & Lobovits, 1997; Nylund & Thomas, 1994; White, 1995). Some have even indicated that letters were the most therapeutic aspect of therapy. Whereas the impact of therapy may or may not remain once sessions have ended, clients can refer back to letters over and over, recalling those qualities and skills that they utilized to stand up to adversity. Now, to practice writing

CASE EXAMPLE 12.1

During Jeremy's second session, we talked about the upcoming professional football season. He was a big fan and passionate about playing. Following session two, I wrote Jeremy the following letter:

Dear Jeremy,

You're may be surprised to receive this letter, but I felt compelled to share some thoughts with you after our last meeting.

I've been so impressed with how you've made an effort to make it to summer school on time. I realize that this must be quite a new game for you. It sort of reminds me of a player being traded to a new team. He has new coaches, new teammates, a new stadium or practice field, and even a new playbook. You've accepted this challenge and have been holding your own. I'll be wondering between now and the next time we meet what other changes you'll make to prepare for the next school year. See you soon.

Sincerely,
Bob

Jeremy continued to make progress, and I employed more football analogies, accentuating the notion of summer school as the "preseason" and the fall as the "regular season." Between sessions five and six, I wrote Jeremy the following letter:

Dear Jeremy,

I wanted to drop you a brief note to share some thoughts with you.

At the start of therapy, you mentioned that last school year was a tough one. You had a hard time keeping up with your studies and getting your homework handed in, and

that hurt you when it came time to play football. But this year has been different. You started off summer school with a bang and used your preseason well to prepare for the regular season. Now that you're on a roll, I wonder how good a shape you'll be in when the regular season starts in the fall. It seems that you've got some momentum going now.

I keep wondering how you're going to use the new learnings you described to me. I hope that you'll let me know somehow. It's exciting to think that I may be reading about both your academic and sports achievements in the newspaper. Keep me posted!

Sincerely,
Bob

Jeremy attended a total of 11 sessions over the course of the summer and up to the start of the new school year. Following his last session, I sent him this letter:

Dear Jeremy,

You've certainly made the transition from the preseason to the regular season. And I keep wondering what other changes will happen now that you seem to have secure footing. Who else will learn about these changes? Who else will learn about the kind of person that you are—the kind of person that you've demonstrated that you can be over the past few months? Of course, I don't expect you to have the answers off the top of your head. Bit by bit perhaps, the answers to these and other questions will become clearer as time moves on.

I want to mention something that you taught me. I learned from you that sometimes

(continued)

CASE EXAMPLE 12.1   *(continued)*

we have to make smaller changes to get to bigger ones. I also learned from you that even if others are skeptical about the changes you make, if you keep moving forward, their ideas about you change. You're living proof of that. I don't think I've ever had a teacher tell me that her student was a "hidden gem!"

I want to wish you the best in the future. Please know that we all believe in you and are here if you need us in the future. Take care.

With appreciation of your efforts,
Bob

Jeremy raised his grades and was able to play football.

therapeutic letters to clients, please complete Exercise 12.2, Therapeutic Letters to Clients.

Documenting New Life Stories

Chapter 7 explored ways to use externalizing conversations to separate clients from their problems. Such conversations help in the growth of new stories that engender hope and run counter to problem-saturated ones. In a sense, clients experience positive changes in their life scripts and rewrite identity stories. These new, emergent stories emanate hope and possibilities and reflect clients' renewed sense of selves. To help clients to develop their life scripts, therapists can ask the following questions:

- What does your decision to stand up to (X) tell you about yourself?
- Now that you've taken your life back from (X), what does that say about the kind of person you are?
- How would you describe yourself now as opposed to when you began therapy?
- What's it like to hear you describe yourself as (X)?
- What effect does knowing that you've put (X) to rest have on your view of yourself?
- Can you speculate about how this view of yourself as (X) is changing how you're relating to me right now?

- What do you think (X) would say/think about you since you have come to think of yourself as able to stand up for yourself?
- How do you think my view of you has changed since hearing you describe yourself as (X)?
- How do you think (names) will be able to treat you differently now that they know that you see yourself as a person who is capable of getting the upper hand with (X)?

Inviting others who may have some involvement in therapy (for example, friends, family members, teachers) to share their views regarding new, evolving stories can also be meaningful. This can be done by asking the following questions:

- What do you think (name)'s decision to stand up to (X) tells you about him/her that you wouldn't have otherwise known?
- What effect might (name)'s decision to regain his/her life back from (X) have on your relationship with him/her?
- How do you think (name)'s new sense of self as being (for example, capable, independent, responsible) might affect your relationship with him/her?
- What other changes do you foresee as (name) continues to on this new path?

Exercise 12.2

Therapeutic Letters to Clients

Therapeutic letters to clients can serve numerous purposes. For example, they can be used to acknowledge clients' efforts, highlight changes, and speculate about the future. These letters also provide points of the reference that clients can refer back to time and time again to remind themselves of their resiliencies, strengths, and past changes. They can also be used at any juncture of therapy, making therapeutic letters to clients a flexible therapy strategy. The purpose of this exercise is to write a "mock" or practice letter to a real or fictitious client. To complete this exercise, please write a brief letter to a client in the space provided. In your letter, you can choose to highlight, acknowledge, summarize, and so on. When addressing concerns, goals, and changes, be specific and use action-talk. When speculating about meanings, drawbacks, benefits, and future change, use a position of curiosity rather than one of expertise.

Date: _____

Client Name: _____

Letter: _____

_____

_____

_____

_____

_____

_____

_____

_____

_____

_____

_____

_____

_____

_____

_____

_____

_____

_____

_____

_____

_____

_____

Signed: _____

One of the ways that therapists can further encourage new stories to "take" hold" is through mediums in which change is documented. Growing up, people often had papers, reports, transcripts of grades, certificates, awards, and other documentation of their abilities and progress. These may have been posted on refrigerators, framed and hung on walls, kept in scrapbooks, and so on. Others may have kept personal journals, written letters to themselves or songs, or captured their experiences on video. Like therapeutic letters to clients, these "collections of competence" remain physical representations of change that serve as reminders of what has been accomplished and possibilities for the future (Bertolino, 1999). To orient clients to documenting their new life stories, therapists can ask:

> Down the road, others may be curious as to how you went about overcoming (X). Sometimes people write letters to themselves, others keep journals, diaries, or scrapbooks, or create new ways to keep track of the changes they've made in their lives. What might help you to document this journey you've been on?

Although this idea may not apply to all, it is flexible and can be used with clients of all ages. The following example illustrates how documenting new life stories helps to solidify present changes and contribute positive views of the future.

> A 24-year-old woman came to therapy reporting that she had been feeling "depressed" and "isolated." She had been severely physically abused as a child and stated that she had felt "disconnected" as a teenager, never really fitting in. She was now an aspiring musician whose original songs were deeply personal and somber. She stated, "That's just who I am." After a few weeks, the woman began to experience a lifting of her depression.

> Her therapist was struck by the woman's presence and how she seemed to "glow" and radiate warmth. This was a side that the therapist had not seen previously. In supervision, it was suggested that the therapist share this observation with her client. In their next session, the therapist said, "I don't know if this will mean anything to you, but recently I have seen a side of you that I hadn't seen previously. Last week and today as well, you seem to have this glow about you. You seem to be in a very different place. I can feel an energy and warmth radiating from you." The young woman smiled and spoke about how she felt like she was "coming out of years of darkness." The therapist then wondered aloud if this other part of her client might be expressed somehow—perhaps in her music. The woman replied, "I've thought about that. I've always written what I feel, but this is different for me. I'm not sure where to begin." The therapist replied, "It's all you, so maybe it's best to start with whatever comes out spontaneously." About two weeks later, the client brought her guitar to the session and played a new song she had written. It was called, "Everything That Glows." The client said the song was a reminder of "what can be."

Whether through writing, art, music, or other mediums, it is important for clients to select something that they enjoy and/or have interest in pursuing. Therapists can ask clients the following questions about ways in which they might document progress:

- What have you done in the past to remind you of what's important in your life?
- How are you able to remember what you've accomplished and hold the feelings that come with those accomplishments?
- What could you do now or in the coming days to remind yourself of the progress that you've made?
- What will help to remind you of where you're heading in the future?

- What will help you to reorient to what's worked for you should you hit some turbulence in the future?
- How will that help you?

The documentation of new life stories can be a one-time or ongoing process. More important, it serves as a resource when clients encounter challenges or bumps in the road. In times of trouble, people can refer back to the documentation and be reminded of their resiliencies, abilities, and strengths. Whether verbalized, documented, or both, new life stories can also be shared in larger contexts; this can benefit both clients and others who may be experiencing similar difficulties. Akin to the idea of *social interest,* it has been suggested that people focus not only on how they can make personal changes but also how they can further the well-being of others (Adler, 1956). Public speaking, volunteering, writing for a story for a newspaper, and so on offer opportunities to share the stories. People do not have to be on television or write lengthy biographies for their stories to touch others. To pursue this idea, therapists can ask:

- Who else needs to know about the changes that you've made?
- What difference do you think it would make in others' attitudes toward you if they had this news?
- Who else could benefit from these changes? How so?
- Would it be better to go along with others' old views about you or to update them on these new developments?
- What ideas do you have about letting others know about the changes that you've made?
- What might be a first step toward making this happen?

With clients who are able identify ways to share change with larger social contexts,

therapists investigate how to put those ideas into action. A unique way to apply this idea is to have clients become consultants to others. Epston, White, and "Ben" (1995) stated:

> When persons are established as consultants to themselves, they experience themselves as more of an authority on their own lives, their problems, and the solution to these problems. This authority takes the form of a kind of knowledge or expertise which is recorded in a popular medium so that it is accessible to the consultant, therapist, and potential others (pp. 282–283).

To explore the idea of clients as consultants, therapists can ask:

- Periodically I meet with others who are experiencing the same or a similar problem to the one you've faced. From what you now know, what advice might I give them about facing their concerns?
- If new clients were to ask me to tell them how previous clients have solved similar problems in the past, what would you suggest that I say to them?
- What suggestions would you have for therapists or other mental health professionals who in the future might work with clients who have experienced the same or similar problems?

Clients' new stories can be shared with others in different ways. However, therapists must respect that change is often a deeply personal experience and one that people may prefer to keep to themselves. Therapists' allegiances are to clients and what they find most meaningful.

Preparation for Transitions

Each session represents a step toward the end of therapy. Therapists need to think about preparing clients for "transitions" rather than "termination." This could mean a transition out of therapy or into another form of service. In a larger sense, therapists help clients to achieve more satisfactory degrees of individuation and connectedness. Although therapy involves specific concerns and problems, therapists must be aware that people have separate lives and pursuits *and* are connected through meaningful relationships. They are able to connect and disconnect without becoming overly fused (lack boundaries and sense of self) or disengaged (have boundaries that are too rigid and are emotionally cut off). Therapists therefore must be aware that experiences, thoughts, and actions are influenced by social interactions and the meanings derived from them.

Therapists' focus in each session is to maximize their effectiveness. They maintain an eye on what will constitute success, including the construction of goals, ways to accomplish those goals, and recognize when progress is being made. In preparing for transitions, therapists consider how to *manage setbacks, anticipate perceived hurdles and barriers, extend change into the future,* and *use transition/celebratory rituals.* The following sections discuss each of these points.

Putting Change in Context: Managing Setbacks

Change is constant with an infinite number of contextual influences that can shift its course. Although periodic setbacks and new challenges are to be expected, setbacks (often referred to as *relapses*) rarely indicate a return to full-blown problems. Taking the time to talk with clients about the possibility of fluctuations is important. Essential to these conversations is an emphasis on the notion that difficulties and setbacks do not have to knock people off course. Clients have abilities and resources available to them should challenges arise.

Consistent with the *maintenance* stage of change, therapists emphasize clients using their "muscles of resilience" and strategies that they have used previously to minimize the impact of setbacks and get back on track (Bertolino, 2003; Prochaska & DiClemente, 2005). When clients experience difficulties or setbacks, therapists use those setbacks as opportunities to learn more about the terrain of clients' lives, including what is working and what is not. They orient sessions toward clients' ideas and expectations, explore exceptions and differences, and use methods outlined in previous chapters. Case Example 12.2 illustrates how a therapist might work with a client experiencing a setback.

CASE EXAMPLE 12.2

After seeing her therapist for six sessions, a woman remarked, "I feel like my old self again. I'm doing so much better." At one time, the woman had been cutting her arms with broken glass or scissors, skipping her university classes, lying to her parents, and putting herself down through self-talk such as "I'm no good"; "I'll never amount to anything"; and "I'm a

failure." It seemed as if she had finally turned the corner.

Two weeks later, the woman came to her next session. She was in tears. As she sat down, she struggled to talk about what was happening with her. As the conversation unfolded, the therapist was able to explore with the client the setback she had experienced:

CASE EXAMPLE 12.2   (continued)

Therapist: It's okay to cry.

Client: [sobbing] I know. I just can't believe it.

Therapist: Tell me about that.

Client: Everything's changed.

Therapist: Something's changed . . .

Client: . . . Yeah, I was doing so good and now . . . I'm back to where I was.

Therapist: I don't understand. Can you tell me what has given you the idea that you're back where you were?

Client: Everything was going fine. Then yesterday I found out that there was no way to pass my communications course because I've missed too many classes. Why should I even bother?

Therapist: How did you find out about that?

Client: My professor told me.

Therapist: I'm sorry to hear that. What did you do when you got the news?

Client: I had to go to my next class.

Therapist: You went to your next class? How did you muster up the strength to do that after what you had been told?

Client: [wiping her tears] Well, I can still pass my other two classes.

Therapist: So even though you were feeling bad, you went to class. A few weeks back, you would have just gone home and given up.

Client: I would have.

Therapist: What did you do to get yourself together so quickly?

Client: I went home and called my mom.

Therapist: What happened?

Client: She told me not to worry about it. I was doing better and that I could retake the class. But I still feel like I failed.

Therapist: I understand. It's still a letdown to you after you've made so many changes. Yet in the midst of the news you got, you knew what to do—to reach out to your mom.

Client: I did.

Therapist: And when you called your mom, you were honest with her about not being able to pass the class this semester. Is that right?

Client: I was. I told her the truth.

Therapist: Even though you could have made something up.

Client: Yeah.

Therapist: Okay, did you cut your arms?

Client: No.

Therapist: So as upset as you were, you went to class and called your mom and were honest with her. You took care of yourself in good ways, not through old habits like cutting.

Client: Uh huh. I did take care of myself and didn't slip back.

Therapist: Even though you were understandably upset, you kept things from becoming worse. Can you tell me more about what else you did that helped you before coming here today?

Client: I went to bed early. I felt a little better this morning, but then got sad again later.

Therapist: So sleep helped a little. What else?

Client: Just talking to my mom. I'm going to call her again after this.

Therapist: It sounds like you and your mom have been getting along better lately.

Client: We have. I think because I'm more honest with her now.

Therapist: Okay. So getting sleep and talking with you mom helped. And what will it take for you to continue to do those things in the next short while?

Client: I think staying focused on what's important to me, like finishing school and having a good relationship with my parents.

To help clients manage their setbacks, it is necessary to acknowledge and search for counterevidence and exceptions just as it is when there are reports of new concerns or problems. Acknowledgment can cause many concerns to vanish or dissipate. When setbacks appear more chronic or patterned, therapists use methods aimed at identifying small differences such as how clients have managed those setbacks to any degree. These questions can be useful in exploring exceptions to setbacks:

- Given what you've been through, how did you manage to (continue to work, make it to this appointment, etc.)?
- When you hit that rough spot, what kept things from going downhill any further?
- How did you manage to bring things to a halt?
- What did you do?
- What helped you to bring it to an end?
- Who else helped you?
- How were those persons helpful to you?
- How might they be helpful to you in the future?

- What signs were present that things were beginning to slip?
- What can you do differently in the future if things begin to slip?
- What have you learned about this setback?
- What will you do differently in the future as a result of this knowledge?
- What do you suppose (name) would say that you will do differently as a result of this knowledge?
- What do you suppose will be different as a result of your doing things differently?
- What might be some signs that you were getting back on track?
- How will you know when you're out of the woods with this setback?

Referring to information gained from outcome measures can also be helpful. For example, clients who experience periodic crises may have elevated scores during those more difficult times. When patterns emerge, therapists can ask clients to reflect on them and perhaps determine a more effective way to prevent setbacks. Case Example 12.3 illustrates this.

CASE EXAMPLE 12.3

A man had been attending weekly therapy sessions for five months. He had made significant strides toward his goal of at least seven hours of undisturbed sleep per night. His sleep pattern improved to at least six hours of undisturbed sleep per night that he maintained for three straight weeks. At his next session, the client reported that he had experienced three nights of "poor" sleep (in other words, less than four hours of undisturbed sleep) in a row. After his therapy session, he was able to reinstate his pattern of "good" sleep, which remained for several weeks until he experienced a similar setback. This pattern occurred for the next two months. The client would have several weeks in a row of quality sleep and then experience an interruption that lasted two or three nights. When the therapist noticed a pattern of spikes in the outcome scores during the weeks the client experienced poor nights of sleep, he asked the client what he saw when he looked at the scores. The client immediately identified the higher scores and asked the therapist for the specific dates of the previous sessions that corresponded with the higher scores. The client then proceeded to check his date book. After a long sigh, the client said, "Each of the times my scores went up was right

CASE EXAMPLE 12.3 *(continued)*

after or during one of my bouts with insomnia. That's obvious. But what I hadn't realized until now was that my sleep problems have always started on specific Sundays—ones that I hadn't been able to go to church because my kids have been with me on those weekends. Church has been a support for me." When the therapist asked why his children didn't go to church with him, the man replied that he thought they were too young. The client was asked about child care at the church during services. He responded that he felt using it would "take time away from them" on weekends.

As the discussion progressed, the client and therapist engaged in conversation about how loss of sleep affected the quality of time he had with his children. When he had not had enough sleep, he felt he was not "present" enough. He was asked whether he thought a full night's sleep and being present with his children were sufficient reasons for him to attend Sunday services on weekends his children were with him. The client appeared apprehensive so the therapist suggested that the client consult with the pastor of his church, which the man thought was a wonderful idea. During their conversation, the pastor said two things that seemed to be meaningful to the man. First, he said that the man's children deserved to have their father emotionally present in their lives. Next, the pastor told the man. "To be supportive, you need support." The man began attending church every Sunday. His "good" sleep pattern stabilized and he made the transition out of therapy six weeks later.

Outcome scores can be helpful with clients who attend therapy sporadically (that is, their periodical attendance is mixed with cancellations and "no shows") and then contact their therapists in crisis. Exploration of their scores often reveals distinct patterns that may be helpful in predicting more challenging or stressful times and an increased risk of setbacks. Therapy becomes more preventative when possible "trouble zones" are identified and plans are created by which clients use their strengths and resources to stay on track.

Anticipating Hurdles and Perceived Barriers and Extending Change into the Future

Beyond problem resolution, several other aspects of positive change can be of benefit in the future. First, clients can use their new understandings and skills to *anticipate perceived*

hurdles and barriers that may pose a threat to maintaining the changes they have made. A second benefit is that therapists can help clients to *extend change into the future* by building on small changes.

Anticipating Hurdles and Perceived Barriers

As clients move closer to transitions from therapy in its typical state, some identify hurdles or perceive barriers that may pose a threat to maintaining the changes they have made. At other times, therapists initiate conversations about possible areas of future concern. Clients are not told that they *will* hit roadblocks but that they *might* experience future challenges. Because clients do not generally expect their lives to be problem free, this is not necessarily newsworthy. By discussing possible future hurdles, therapists maintain a focus on prevention and normalize apprehension and fear about what may come down the road. This can also increase the likelihood that current changes will continue in the future.

To engage clients in conversations about possible future hurdles or perceived barriers, therapists can ask, "Is there anything that might come up between now and the next time we meet that might pose a threat to the changes you've made?" or "Can you think of anything that might come up over the next (few weeks/months) that could present a challenge for you in staying on track?" If a client responds "yes," the therapist and client then explore, in detail, what those challenges might be and how the client will meet them. The following questions help to identify and address perceived hurdles or barriers:

- What have you learned about your ability to stand up to (X)?
- What might indicate to you that the problem was attempting to resurface?
- What might be the first sign?
- What will you do differently in the future if you face the same or a similar problem?
- How can what you've learned help you in solving future problems?
- If you feel yourself slipping, what's one thing that can stop that slipping and get you back heading in the direction you prefer?
- What's one thing that can bring a slippage under control or to an end?

Therapists can also create specific scenarios that would require a client to use new understandings and skills in the future. For example, a therapist might say, "If you were to encounter a new concern such as (X) and it caught you off guard, how might you use what you've learned to keep it from overwhelming you?" See the following example.

A 16-year-old boy was brought to therapy for fighting at school. During his last session, he was asked if he could think of anything that might throw him off track. When he said he couldn't think of anything, he was asked specifically how he might handle things in the future if someone were to start something with him. He immediately said, "That already happened. A kid threatened to pop my bike tire. I stood back and told him to go ahead. I wasn't going to fight him. The kid walked away."

It is not necessary to consider every possible situation that could pose a threat to clients. Therapists want to remind clients to use what they have learned more automatically in the future. What is important is helping clients to connect with their strengths and resources on a regular basis so that desired actions become the rule, not the exception.

Extending Change into the Future

Change in the present can benefit clients beyond the concerns that brought them to therapy. By asking questions that orient clients toward future change and progress, they often become more resilient to everyday problems. It is as if clients' psychological and relational immune systems are less likely to be compromised because they are focusing on health, well-being, and the future. To invite clients into conversations to explore how change can be extended into the future, therapists ask:

- How can you put your new understandings to work in the future?
- What have you been doing that you will continue to do once therapy has ended and in the future?
- How will you continue to solidify and build on the changes that you've made?
- What will you be doing differently that you might not have otherwise been able to do?

- After you leave here, what will you do to keep things going in the direction you prefer?
- What else will you do?
- How will you keep things moving forward?
- How will you make sure that you will do that?
- How will you keep your eyes on the road ahead instead of staring into the rearview mirror?
- What do you need from others?
- How might they be of help to you?

These questions encourage clients to consider how other areas of their lives can improve in the future as a result of the changes they have made in the present. As discussed in Chapters 5 and 8, a vision of the future can have an effect on how people act in the present and view the past. Instead of focusing on how they are held captive by past events, clients focus on where they are going and the kind of futures they want for themselves. People can respect and embrace history without letting it own them and determine their futures.

Engaging in Transition/ Celebratory Rituals

Chapter 11 explored various forms of rituals that facilitate connection, continuity, and transition. This section discusses a different form of *transition rituals* and *celebratory* rituals. These rituals are rites of passage, helping people to move from one role or developmental phase to another. In therapy, transition/celebratory rituals can be particularly helpful in signifying the achievement of goals, in accentuating changes clients have made, and in making the transition out of therapy. Context is the determinant in how and to what degree such rituals are used. For example, in residen-

tial placement facilities, transition/celebratory rituals are commonly used to symbolize the mastery of skills or movement from one program level to another (Bertolino & Thompson, 1999). Rituals offer a person a means of marking transitions; however, it is important to engage clients in conversations to determine whether and what kinds of rituals would be meaningful for them. To do this, they can say to clients:

> It often helps people to mark the changes they have made or the ending of therapy with something symbolizing that they're moving on into the future. Is there anything that we might do here to put an exclamation point on the changes you've made or your transition out of therapy?

Some clients will want to move forward without any symbolic event, preferring that their transitions be subtle. Other clients request things such as exchanging cards or sharing stories. See the following example.

> In his second-to-last session, a man who had experienced severe combat-related trauma requested that his therapist write down five things that he felt the client had improved on during therapy. The therapist agreed and at the final session presented the client a journal. On the first page was a list of the things he felt the client had accomplished. The therapist then said to the client, "Now it's up to you to write your story and all that you accomplish in your life."

Other possibilities for celebratory rituals are therapeutic letters to clients and certificates. The latter is consistent with certificates given for achievement in academics, sports, volunteering, good citizenship, heroism, and so on. Certificates can be particularly meaningful to younger clients and used as a means

Figure 12.1

CERTIFICATE

of

EXCELLENCE

in

_____

This certificate is hereby awarded to

_____

On this day, _____, _____

For demonstrating his/her ability to

_____

Signed: _____

to document change. Figures 12.1 and 12.2 offer examples of certificate templates.

The methods detailed in this section are just a few ways that therapists can help clients to transition from therapy. Other possibilities can be found in specific therapy approaches. To practice the ideas outlined in this section, please complete Exercise 12.3, Transitions.

Figure 12.2

CERTIFICATE

of

CHANGE

_____

This certificate is hereby awarded to

_____

On this day, _____, _____

For standing up to

_____

and reclaiming his/her life.

Signed: _____

States of Transition: In through the Out Door

Everyone exists in states of transition. We move from one thing to the next. In therapy, clients make transitions to different degrees of services ranging from intensive inpatient programs to periodic check-ups with their therapists. As clients meet goals and outcomes, they also make a transition out of therapy and reengage again if needed. It is not the length of time spent in therapy that is important but

Exercise 12.3

Transitions

To prepare clients to transition to less intensive or other forms of services or out of therapy, several approaches can help them to tap into their resiliencies, strengths, and resources. The purpose of this exercise is to develop a few of these approaches for use with future clients. To complete this exercise, please respond to each prompt by writing your answers in the spaces provided.

- Create three questions that focus on how clients have managed setbacks.

Examples: How did you manage to keep things from getting worse? How did you put the brakes on when things started to slip?

1. _____
2. _____
3. _____

- Create three questions that clients can use to anticipate and manage perceived barriers and hurdles.

Examples: What is one possible situation that might contribute to your slipping just a little in the future? What future situations could leave you most vulnerable to a setback?

1. _____
2. _____
3. _____

- Create three questions that can be used to extend change into the future.

Examples: How will you take the changes you've made into the future? How might you keep your feet moving forward and build on the changes you've made?

1. _____
2. _____
3. _____

- Create a list of possible transition/celebratory rituals.

Examples: Letters, certificates, etc.

_____   _____
_____   _____
_____   _____
_____   _____
_____   _____

whether clients experience an improved quality of life.

Consistent with this idea but potentially in conflict with third-party regulations is the opportunity for clients to move in and out of therapy as needed. As discussed previously, therapy needs to be similar to the general practitioner model used by primary care physicians; allowing clients to reenter therapy with minimal hurdles can improve individual well-being and relational functioning while reducing overall medical expenditures, days of work lost, and so on. Because people experience different problems at different times in their lives, it is necessary that psychotherapeutic systems of care be responsive and flexible.

One way to move toward this ideal is to create therapy contexts in which people are able to transition out of and return to therapy in the future if they needed. This does not guarantee that clients will see the same therapists they originally worked with but that they are welcome back and that every attempt will be made to meet their needs. This may be done by talking on the phone, starting therapy again, or making referrals elsewhere. This open-door system provides a respectful and responsive way to meet clients' needs in an ever-changing world.

Subsequent sessions provide fertile ground for furthering therapeutic change. Therapists continue to collaborate with clients to determine what is working and what is not while keeping an eye on helping clients to reach their goals and achieve higher degrees of functioning. When changes are identified, therapists use processes to amplify those changes and grow new stories of hope and possibility that counter problematic ones. In lieu of positive change, therapists make adjustments based on client feedback and continue to monitor the effects of those adjustments. By utilizing respectful and responsive practices, therapists increase the opportunities for successful outcomes and encourage future change.

SUMMARY POINTS

- Client engagement processes continue and therapists check in with clients to monitor their ratings of the therapeutic relationship and alliance.
- Therapists continue to incorporate outcome-oriented feedback into sessions.
- When *improvement is reported or identified,* therapists amplify those changes and use methods such as attribution, speculation, and sharing credit for change. Emphasis is also on determining the relevance of change in relation to previously established goals.
- To help changes take "root" in clients' lives, therapists write letters, document new stories, and use other means to share new, evolving stories with others.
- To prepare clients for transitions into other services or out of therapy, therapists focus on how clients can *manage setbacks, anticipate perceived hurdles and barriers, extend change into the future,* and *use transition/celebratory rituals.*
- An open-door environment is encouraged to enable clients to return to therapy in the future as needed with as few hurdles as possible in reinstituting those services.

DISCUSSION QUESTIONS

1. Why is client attribution to change important in therapy?

2. What are ways that therapists can encourage internal attribution?

3. How can therapists help to accentuate change and help to grow new client stories?

4. What are some ways that therapists can help to prepare clients for transitions?

PART SIX

Chapter 13

Evolution in Context

Constructing New Worlds through Respect and Integrity

■ This book has been about *possibilities*. It has been about how practitioners can help people to change their lives and the lives of others through processes that open up avenues for change. If each one of us accepts the idea that possibilities exist within people and their lives, then we can determine what kind of world we want and how to go about making that world a reality.

This chapter concludes your journey by exploring ways that therapists can further negotiate stuck points and create possibilities at the individual, relational, and social levels. It begins by considering how therapists can attend to and navigate personal patterns that can hinder change. Following this, it discusses how ideas offered throughout this book can be utilized in supervisory relationships. Next the chapter explores ways to incorporate strengths-based ideas at the organizational level as a means of improving overall services. The chapter and this book end where they began: by reorienting ways

in which therapists can remain connected with their philosophical beliefs.

Changing Therapists' Views and Patterns

In the Greek myth, the sculptor Pygmalion created a statue of a beautiful woman (Galatea) and then fell in love with it. The god Aphrodite took pity on Pygmalion and brought the statue to life. Although theories and methods are important to therapy processes, therapists must exercise care in determining how and when to use them without falling in love with them. A risk of aligning too much with theories or methods is that they can distort therapists' perceptions. What is observed can seem real in the eyes of therapists. Theories are social constructions and therapists' methods are means of facilitating change. Even so, therapists at times develop patterns of practice that are not necessarily helpful to clients. Just as clients can become stuck, therapists are at risk of working in ways that can hinder progress. Possibilities for preventing therapists to align too much with theories or methods include *engaging in ongoing self-reflection, using frameworks to stimulate new ideas, participating in supervision,* and having *reflecting consultations.*

Ongoing Self-Reflection

As you have learned, a primary way to monitor for and manage stuck points is by checking in with clients. Because clients are the most important contributors to outcome, their feedback is necessary in determining what is working, what is not, and what the next steps are. Chapter 1 discussed the value of *ongoing self-reflection,* which provides therapists a crucial way to think about sessions at a later time. Although "in-the-moment" revelations often prove helpful in sessions, therapists should set aside time on an ongoing basis to self-reflect outside sessions. Doing so offers the opportunity to reflect without taking focus away from clients.

During self-reflection, considering various *pathways of impossibility* that can contribute to therapy impasses can be useful (Duncan, Miller, & Sparks, 2004). As with the client problematic stories described in Chapter 7, therapists can become stuck by viewing situations as impossible and unchangeable. Four pathways to impossibility can inhibit therapists' attempt to promote change.

Anticipation of Impossibility

Through preconceived notions, case reports and assessments, language, interaction, diagnosis, descriptions, and other avenues, therapists can unintentionally create problems or situations that appear to have no solutions and suggest impossibility. When problems or situations are deemed impossible, therapists often begin to label clients as "resistant," "unmotivated," "noncompliant," and "unwilling to change." Evidence that therapists anticipate impossibility is most commonly found in their practices, which inhibit rather than encourage and promote change.

Theory Countertransference

As in the myth of Pygmalion and Galatea, therapists are at risk of bringing their theories to life in clients. They can become convinced that the observations they make throughout therapy are real and objective. Although traditions, including theories, are important in all human pursuits, they can also inhibit change and even have damaging consequences (Bertolino & O'Hanlon, 2002). *Countertransference* refers to an emotional, largely unconscious process that takes place in the experience of therapists and is triggered in relationship to clients and intrudes in therapy. Likewise, the theory of countertransference takes place in the theoretical realm when clinicians unconsciously intrude on clients with their theoretical biases and unrecognized assumptions. To challenge this pathway to impossibility, therapists remain aware of how their theoretical constructs influence the content, process, and direction of therapy and work to form collaborative partnerships that honor clients' orientations.

Repetition of Unhelpful Methods, Techniques, and Practices

Patterns in the form of routines and habits are a part of everyday life. Chapters 9 and 10 discussed how clients' actions and interactions can repeat and become problematic. In much the same way, although many of the methods that therapists employ do facilitate change, some can become problematic and contribute to stagnation or even inhibit change processes. It is therefore important that therapists develop awareness around their patterns of practice, noting any that may be repeating in ways that are not helpful.

Inattention to Clients' Motivation

A final pathway of impossibility occurs when therapists use their goals and ideas about change instead of tuning into clients' goals and ideas. Impossibility can result when clients are left out of therapy processes and not consulted about their perceptions and preferences. When excluded or only minimally involved, clients can appear unmotivated. As you have learned, it is not a question of whether clients are motivated but what are they motivated about.

The four pathways of impossibility can occur within or outside therapists' awareness. Processes that promote self-reflection offer therapists ways to better monitor personal patterns that can interfere or undermine attempts to facilitate positive change. In addition to maintaining awareness of ways that can inhibit change, therapists also use ongoing self-observation to identify what they have done well in sessions. This can be done when therapists ask themselves:

- What did I do well?
- How do I know it was helpful to the client?
- What should I consider doing more of in the next session?
- What should I consider doing differently in the future?
- What changes should I consider making in the next session?
- What difference might that make?

Because self-reflection is based on hindsight, it can be helpful to audiotape or videotape sessions. Therapists do not always recognize when they are working in ways that are or are not helpful while taping can reveal aspects of sessions that they might not otherwise remember or have their attention drawn to. The therapist reviews the tape and considers some of the aforementioned questions and might also ask, "What did I see or hear on the tape that did not stand out for me previously?"; "How might this information be useful?"; "What might I do with this information?" Therapists can watch the therapeutic discourse unfold from a different position, which can help to generate new ideas and possibilities for future sessions. Self-reflection is always based on perceptions; therefore, getting a second perspective from supervisors or colleagues can also be useful. Again, by using the same or a similar set of questions posed earlier, new ideas can be generated about what might be helpful in future sessions.

As discussed in previous chapters, new ideas are considered tentative and are treated as such when offered to clients. Therapists do not consider new ideas as truths but as ways to generate possibilities. They also strive to present multiple ideas as opposed to just one or two. For example, a therapist who was using a video might say, "I reviewed the videotape last week and had some new thoughts that I would like to share with you." In consulting with a colleague or supervisor, a therapist might say, "I reviewed the tape from last week with a colleague/supervisor who had a few ideas that I would like to share with you if that's okay." By presenting multiple ideas, therapists increase the chances that one or more will resonate with clients and jump-start positive change. As new ideas are presented, therapists follow up with all or some of these questions:

- Which, if any, of these ideas resonate most with you?
- Which one(s) specifically stands out the most for you?
- What comes to mind for you as a result?
- What else comes to mind?
- How might that be helpful to you?
- What other ideas do you have as a result of what you heard?
- What might you do with this new information?

The questions outlined in this section can help to stimulate new ideas and help therapists to shift out of unhelpful patterns that may contribute to stuck situations.

Use of Frameworks to Stimulate New Ideas

Considering how various theoretical frameworks might offer therapists alternative ways to view client concerns can also be useful. Methods discussed throughout this book (particularly in Chapters 7–10) provide possibilities for helping clients to change views and actions, and therapists can use these and other frameworks to reconceptualize stuck situations. In other words, models can be used to stimulate new perspectives and inject the element of possibility. Examples of specific frameworks and sources therapists might find helpful include these:

- *The attempted solution is the problem*—consider how clients' previous attempts at solution may actually be contributing to their problems (Watzlawick, Weakland, & Fisch, 1974)
- *Symptoms as metaphors*—consider how client symptoms might represent or symbolize other problems (Haley, 1987)

- *Striving toward balance*—consider how clients' concerns might stem from expending to much or too little energy on one aspect of their lives at the expense of other aspects (Carl Jung) (De Laszlo, 1991; Bugental, 1987; Yalom, 1980)
- *Body to mind*—consider how clients might benefit from focusing on becoming more "settled down" and relaxed in their bodies (in other words, their physiological states) before delving into more cognitive or intellectual aspects (in other words, their psychological states) (van der kolk, 1994)
- *Classes of problems and classes of solutions*—consider how problems may exist in opposite yet corresponding classes (for example, anxiety might be in a class that includes increased heart rate, increased blood flow, or rapid thoughts; the corresponding class of solution includes the opposite: decreased heart rate, decreased blood flow, or slower thought processes) (Bertolino & O'Hanlon, 2002; O'Hanlon, 1987)
- *Integrating "parts"*—consider how unacknowledged and unintegrated aspects of self could be embraced and integrated to help clients experience wholeness and an increased sense of self (O'Hanlon & Bertolino, 1998, 2002; Schwartz, 1995)
- *Shift from one domain to another (e.g., from cognitive to behavioral, or affective to cognitive)*—consider how focusing primarily or exclusively on one domain may not be effective; switch to a different domain or type of processing (Beck, 1995; Ellis, 1996; Meichenbaum, 1977)

Many possible frameworks can be used to think differently about clients and their situations. Therapists are reminded that these frameworks are not based on irrefutable scientific evidence, nor are they representations of truth or reality. Instead, they provide therapists alternative viewpoints, which can be enough to help move a stuck situation forward. To practice this idea, please complete Exercise 13.1, From a Different Perspective.

Supervision as a Parallel Process

Supervision offers an excellent forum for self-reflection, identifying unhelpful patterns, and generating new ideas. Baldwin, Wampold, and Imel (2007) have suggested that therapists

---

Exercise 13.1

From a Different Perspective

Just as clients can become stuck in their views, therapists can experience stagnation when their perspectives are too narrow or restrictive. The purpose of this exercise is to help generate new ideas by using various therapy frameworks to think differently about closed-down situations. To complete this exercise, please follow the instructions and write your answers in the spaces provided.

- Describe a stuck situation you are experiencing with a client or in your personal life. Be specific and use action-talk.

  _____

  _____

  _____

  _____

  _____

- Consider that the attempted solution to the problem has become the problem. Choose two of the following three frameworks as ways to view the situation you described.

  a. Shift away from the domain (i.e., cognition, behavior, affective) you have been primarily focused on to another.

  b. Consider that the problem falls into a particular class with a corresponding solution class that is the opposite of the problem.

  c. Create your own framework that is different than the one you have been using.

- Write the letter for each framework chosen on the blanks as indicated and three new ideas for each you have developed. The ideas should represent alternative ways to view the stuck situation.

  Framework _____

  1. _____

  2. _____

  3. _____

  Framework _____

  1. _____

  2. _____

  3. _____

who routinely experience low client alliance ratings may benefit from supervision. Key to the effectiveness of supervision is the underlying philosophy that informs it. The principles described throughout this book apply not only to therapy but also to supervisory processes. Referred to as *isomorphism,* supervision processes parallel those of therapy. White and Russell (1997) stated, "When the supervisory system is mapped onto the therapeutic system, the roles of the supervisor and supervisee correspond to those of the therapist and client, respectively" (p. 316). Accordingly, the first task of therapists is to learn about and accommodate their supervisees' preferences. The following considerations can serve as a guide for supervisors:

- What does the supervisee want from supervision?
- What does the supervisee want to have happen as a result of meeting with the supervisor?
- How can the supervisor be helpful to the supervisee?
- What will indicate to the supervisee that supervision has been helpful?
- In what ways does the supervisee learn best?

- What methods of supervision—for example, case discussion, theoretical conversations, audio/videotape consultation, team approaches, discussion of readings (this can vary from session to session— does the supervisee prefer?
- (If the supervisee has had previous supervisory relationships) How have previous supervisors been helpful to the supervisee?
- What does the supervisee feel/think that he or she does well in the therapeutic milieu?

Supervision is a collaborative process in which supervisors work to create contexts in which learning can take place, accountability can be ensured, and new ideas can be generated. Supervisees, in turn, are responsible for their preparedness in supervision: Supervisees articulate ways that they believe their supervisors can be most helpful. It is understood that supervisees learn differently and, therefore, some methods of supervision provide a better fit (Bertolino & Caldwell, 1999). Supervisors who maintain the same flexibility with their supervisees as they do with their clients increase the likelihood that supervisees will benefit from supervision. Case Example 13.1 illustrates this concept.

CASE EXAMPLE 13.1

A graduate student in social work was meeting with me for her weekly supervision. During our meeting, the student described a client with whom she had been struggling. The student described how she felt "stuck" and did not know how to proceed. After gaining some details about the situation, I asked her, "How can I be most helpful to you with this?" She thought for a moment and said, "I'm not really sure." I followed, "There are different ways that

we can approach this. It's not about choosing the right way but about approaching it in a way that helps you most. So let's talk about some possibilities. As we do this, I'd like to hear your thoughts. Is that okay with you?" The student agreed that it was and I continued. "One possibility is for us to continue to talk, as we are now, and come up with some ideas that you can take into your next session. Another is that we could arrange for me or another supervisor to

CASE EXAMPLE 13.1 (continued)

observe from behind the one-way mirror. By having another set of eyes and ears, some new possibilities might arise. We could also set up cotherapy and I could be in the session with you." At this point, the student smiled and said "that's what I was thinking but didn't know we could do that." "We can. Tell me more about what you were thinking," I said. "If you were in the session, I feel like I could get some ideas by observing," she stated. I clarified this further by asking, "Would you prefer to lead the session and have me there to support you? Or would you want us both ask questions of the client?

Or would you want me to lead the session and you mostly observe?" Without hesitation, the student responded, "Actually I would prefer to observe and learn from you."

The student checked with her client to see whether she was comfortable having me sit in and lead a session. The client agreed, and the session went forward as planned. Following the session, the student stated, "That was extremely helpful. I not only learned a lot but the experience also validated so much of what I was thinking. I'm more confident now about the next session with my client."

Supervision has many aspects. Supervisors have different responsibilities and need to be direct at times with supervisees. This can be the case when risks of harm to self or others exist or when supervisees need more direction. This also, of course, depends on the experience, training, and skill level of supervisees. In general, however, supervisors should encourage supervisees to step outside their comfort zones from time to time to help them increase their effectiveness (Miller, Hubble, & Duncan, 2007). One way to this is by cross-referencing supervisees' reports of client progress with established goals and outcome data. This is also a good quality assurance practice, ensuring that supervisees are not only gathering outcome data but integrating it into sessions. Case Example 13.2 illustrates how client outcome data can be useful in the supervisory context.

Although supervisory styles vary, it is important that supervisors be able to adapt to the different ways their supervisees communicate. To monitor the supervisory alliance, supervisors ask process-oriented questions

such as those offered in Chapter 4. For example, a supervisor might ask:

- Are there certain things you want to be sure we talk about today?
- What ideas do you have about how we might best use our time together today?
- Have we been talking about what you want to talk about?
- What, if anything, should I do differently?

These questions draw attention to supervisees' experiences of supervisory relationships and provide information that supervisors can integrate to increase their helpfulness.

Reflecting Consultations

Chapter 8 discussed the idea of using conversational and consulting teams. This team approach can be helpful for situations in which clients, therapists, or both are experiencing impasses. Because stuck systems can benefit from alternative viewpoints, a team format provides an excellent avenue for opening up

CASE EXAMPLE 13.2

A supervisee was concerned about how to proceed with a client who had been in therapy for nine sessions over the course of three months. The supervisee stated that the client had reached her goals by session three but was still expressing concerns with "not having enough time to get everything done." Though he had tried to clarify what this meant, the supervisee stated that the client would give only ambiguous responses. I then reviewed the client's outcome scores, and a pattern quickly became apparent. I asked my supervisee, "What do you notice when you look at the scores over time as opposed to just each session as a single entity?" The supervisee glanced at the scores, chuckled and said, "Wow. I don't know how I didn't see that. She made a lot of progress up to session four—about a 25-point change. Then her scores leveled out. They haven't changed but for a point or two since. Now I know why it's been so frustrating to get her to clarify her ambiguous statements." I then asked my supervisee, "Right. So what can you do with this information?" He answered, "First I need to make sure she has seen the scores and we talk about them. But I want to find out from her what else she thinks needs to happen because if we continue at this rate, she could regress." "Okay, good. What else?" I asked. "I'm not sure," he answered. I added, "I would encourage you to consider multiple possibilities. One may be that there is something else that needs to happen for her to make other gains. It could be that she's just at transition point. Another could be that she has achieved the maximum benefit from meeting with you that she is going to reach at this point in time. What is important is to do what you said a moment ago; to take the information back to her and see how she responds."

The supervisee met with his client. She stated that the scores made sense to her. The client related that she felt she had made "excellent progress" and that her situation had improved "dramatically." She also revealed that she is the kind of person who wants "everything to be perfect" even though that was "a tall order." After further discussion, the therapist and client agreed that she was ready to make the transition out of therapy. The client was reminded that she was welcome back for a check-up in the future, if needed.

new possibilities. In this context, consultation teams can be used to help therapists view or think about therapy situations from different perspectives.

Consultation teams usually consist of two to four therapists or other practitioners. The process begins with the team listening as a therapist describes a situation in which he or she would like feedback. During this time, the therapist covers several key areas, including:

- A brief description of the problem.

- What would the therapist like to be different or have change about the concern/problem/difficulty.
- What has been tried so far to achieve that change.
- What kind of feedback would the therapist like from the team.

The therapist takes 6–10 minutes to cover the areas and add anything else he or she believes to be pertinent. The team members listen from a "not-knowing position," assuming no prior knowledge about the client(s). They are only to listen, not ask questions. The team's task is to generate new ideas as a way to help move the therapy along or get things unstuck.

After the therapist has finished, the consulting therapists have a conversation with one another. During this 4–8 minutes process, the therapist listens to this conversation, considering which ideas, if any, resonate with him or her. Following this, the therapist takes a few minutes to reflect on what stood out. As an alternative, another therapist who has not been involved can interview the therapist and ask questions such as:

- What stood out for you?
- What was new to you?
- What else was new for you?
- What did you hear?
- What else did you hear?
- What new ideas do you have as a result of listening to the conversation?
- What will you consider doing differently as a result of having these new ideas?

Such reflective conversations can be used in different variations and contexts. The purpose is to help therapists expand or shift their views of stuck situations. The generation of alternative perspectives can help therapists explore new possibilities with clients and negotiate impasses. To practice reflecting consultation, please refer to Exercise 13.2, The Reflecting Consultation.

Identifying Characteristics of Successful and Effective Therapists

Much has been learned about what contributes to success whether with by athletes, educators, musicians, or businesspersons. Research has challenged the common assertion that people are wired at birth or possess natural gifts or "talent" that leads to their success (Ericsson, Charness, Feltovich, & Hoffman, 2006). Instead, research suggests that high performers are made. They share commonalities such as working hard, continuously practicing, and adopting new mind-sets. Research specific to therapists has found that factors such as personal attributes and education have little influence on success rates. It is clear that the best clinicians, sometimes referred to as "supershrinks," share characteristics echoed across professional literature (Miller, Hubble, & Duncan, 2007; Ricks, 1974). Highlighted throughout this book, these characteristics include:

- maintaining a posture of awareness, being alert, observant, and attentive in therapeutic encounters.
- comparing new information and what is learned with what is already known.
- remaining acutely attuned to the vicissitudes of client engagement—actively employing processes of gaining ongoing formal feedback and incorporating that feedback into therapy on a consistent basis.
- consistently achieving lower scores on standardized alliance measures at the outset of therapy because they are more persistent and perhaps, more believable, when assuring clients that they seek honest feedback, enabling them to address potential problems in the working alliance (therapists with lower rates of success, by contrast, tend to receive negative feedback later in therapy, at which point clients have already disengaged or are at heightened risk of dropping out).
- spending more time on strategies that might be more effective and improve

Exercise 13.2

The Reflecting Consultation

Stuck systems can benefit from the injection of new ideas. One way to do seek new ideas is by using reflecting consultations. The purpose of this exercise is to use conversation as a vehicle for generating new ideas and possibilities for the therapist experiencing the stuckness. You will need a minimum of three but no more than five people for this exercise. To complete this exercise, please follow the instructions.

- Choose one person to present a stuck situation involving a client or personal situation. The other two or more members will form the team.
- The person presenting the stuck situation is to take 6–10 minutes to focus on the following aspects of situation:

  1. A brief description of the problem
  2. What he or she would like to be different or have change about the concern/problem/difficulty
  3. What has been tried so far to achieve that change
  4. What kind of feedback would he or she like from the team

The presenter may also add in other details *as time permits.*

- During the presentation of the stuck situation, the team is to observe, listen, and take notes but not to ask questions or talk to one another.
- When the presenter has finished, the team is to take 4–8 minutes to have a conversation among itself. The team is to consider the content areas described in the stuck situation, adding what stood out and resonated with each team member. As general guidelines, team members' responses should:

  1. Be from a "not-knowing" position (assuming no prior knowledge about the situation discussed)
  2. Address only what was stated during the presentation
  3. Highlight strengths
  4. Be framed from a position of conjecture (e.g., "I was curious," "I wonder")
  5. Be tentative

The presenter is not to ask or be asked questions during this process.

- The presenter then takes 2–5 minutes to reflect and convey what resonated with him or her. There is no dialogue between the presenter and team during this process.
- When the process is complete, the presenter and team take time to debrief and ask whatever questions they have of each other.
- After completing the exercise, write any key ideas that came across for you as the presenter or a team member.

_____

_____

_____

_____

_____

Exercise 13.2 *(continued)*

- What was the experience like for you?

  _____

  _____

- What did you like most about the exercise?

  _____

  _____

- What did you like least about the exercise?

  _____

  _____

- What was most surprising to you about participating in the exercise?

  _____

  _____

- How might this type of consultation be useful to you in the future?

  _____

  _____

---

outcomes as opposed to hypothesizing about failed strategies and why methods did not work.

- expanding awareness when events are stressful and remaining open to options.
- evaluating and refining strategies and seeking outside consultation, supervision, coaching, and training specific to particular skill sets.

Although the nature versus nurture debate continues, what is known is that through increased effort, interest, consistency, and self-motivation, therapists can improve their rates of success. As in other fields, working hard and demonstrating interest in outcome are clearly characteristics of effective therapists. They go several steps beyond what other therapists do. This requires ongoing self-examination and exposure to feedback that although sometimes painful, contributes to growth. There is no known shortcut to this kind of commitment to excellence in helping relationships.

Effectiveness, Longevity, and Self-Care

It is also apparent that part of maintaining effectiveness and long-term success as a therapist involves good self-care. This means working in climates and with others who are supportive, using methods such as self-reflection and supervision, and taking time for oneself. In addition, therapists can do the following to create balance within self and in relationship to others:

- Believe in what they do.
- "Walk the talk" by practicing what they preach both personally and professionally.
- Be action-oriented.
- Stand by their word.

- Be an energy-giver, not an energy drainer.
- Be a source of optimism, inspiration, and support to others.
- Give their unconditional energies (body, mind, heart, and soul).
- Be strengths based, not just "positive."
- Recognize what others have to offer— their contributions to change.
- Be a resource to others (clients and colleagues).
- Check in with themselves (What kind of day have you had? What else is going on with you?).
- Build in restorative "recovery time" every day.
- Find what inspires them and gives them hope–this can create more personal energy.
- Remember that hope is contagious!

Creating Strengths-Based Organizations: We All Go Together

Whether in agencies, organizations, institutions, private practices, hospitals, schools, or other settings, the support of colleagues and staff is essential to individual well-being and the overall success of services. Lack of support and negativity, in particular, can prove devastating to organizations, often leading to "staff infections" (Bertolino, 1999, 2003; Bertolino & Thompson, 1999) that occur when negativity becomes pervasive, interfering with relationships, and spreading through an organization or setting. Sometimes slow to develop, other times spreading like wildfire, staff infections can create distress in relationships and affect the quality of direct service provision.

As you have learned, therapists should take the time to learn about the organizations with which they choose to work. The lifeline of an organization is represented by the people who work there. The underlying philosophy is its "pulse." Unabated negativity can decimate people, programs, and organizations. Although funding may be the most consistent external concern, negativity can permeate organizations and practices and represents the most significant internal threat.

A strengths-based philosophy is not simply a response on a case-by-case, individual level but provides the background for organizational success. There exists, however, a dominant culture in mental health and social services that continues to emphasize deficits and pathology. Madsen (2006) stated:

> While there is growing institutional support for strengths-based practice, a discourse of deficits receives considerable institutional support from managed care requirements (the need to show medical necessity for reimbursement), clinical licensing requirements (the requirement of diagnosing clients), and professional training (the prevalence of courses that emphasize psychopathology) (p. 47).

The dilemma of developing and implementing a strengths-based culture often exists within preexisting and often outdated philosophical underpinnings and practices. To face this challenge, it is necessary to create organizational cultures that are based on *feedback, proactive inquiry, philosophy in action,* and *people in places.*

Culture of Feedback

Culturally responsive and respectful organizational climates include multiple levels and systems of feedback. Throughout this book, the role of individual feedback to providers has been discussed. This information helps therapists create a better fit between their approaches and clients' orientations, thereby increasing the prospects of successful outcome. Again, merely utilizing real-time feedback processes has been demonstrated to significantly improve outcomes (Miller, Duncan, & Brown, 2006). This process-oriented feedback can also be integrated at the supervisory level and in any form of meeting in which an impasse is apparent.

Organizationally, a culture of feedback allows staff at all levels to better understand the experiences of clients served, including what is working and what is not. Examples of questions organizations might ask of themselves include:

- How do we ensure that the voices of our clients contribute to our understanding the quality of services we provide?
- How do we develop feedback measures and processes that are culturally sensitive, respectful, and responsive to our clients and their needs?
- How do we monitor our intentions, purposes, and values as we review current possibilities and consider future ones for sustaining a culture of feedback?

Specific process-oriented feedback mechanisms may also be used at the end of therapy or services to invite clients to share their views about their overall experience. This feedback is not aimed only at clients' experience with individual therapists but also staff at all levels. This can be obtained by asking clients to respond to points such as:

- I felt heard and understood by staff.
- I felt accepted for who I am as a person by staff.
- I felt understood by staff.
- I felt my concerns were taken seriously.
- I felt that my strengths, resources, and wisdom were acknowledged and honored by staff.

- I was invited to be an active participant in our work together.
- I was encouraged and given the opportunity to give feedback during the process of therapy.
- I was consulted about goals.
- I was consulted about ways to meet goals.
- I was treated respectfully.
- Staff made an effort to understand my uniqueness.

Clients should be offered options for rating these areas (for example, from very high to very low). Space on forms can be provided for clients to give specific examples; however, the longer that measures become and the more time and effort involved in completing them, the more likely it is that clients will bypass open-ended questions. Though general, information from transition measures and others designed to elicit client feedback provides organizations with opportunities to track, monitor, and respond to trends and patterns.

Why is this so important? As you learned in Chapter 3 with Addressing Service Expectations, people often enter therapy with perceptions and expectations. These perceptions are not random and represent previous experiences (for example, previous therapy encounters, interactions with others, information from media). Because perceptions of interactions with therapists change over time and can influence the course of therapy, they need to be tracked individually in real time. Likewise, by the end of therapy, clients will have created overall perceptions that are based on interactions with other staff members, including office, intake, and administrative staff. These perceptions can affect what people do in the future, including how they approach services and what they communicate to others about their experiences with a particular organization. In other words, people seek services from people and organizations they value and with whom they have personal connections; therefore, reputation matters.

Proactive Inquiry

An organization's success in providing mental health and social services depends largely on the climate created within it. The long-term sustainability of programs requires not only secure funding but also a clearly articulated mission, vision, and set of principles that drive those entities. An organization's core philosophical principles should be timeless and enduring, although the means and ways to carry them out may vary (Collins, 2001, 2005). As an example, please take a moment to review the core principles of SBE outlined in Chapter 2. These principles are not associated with any one theoretical model or approach but provide a foundation for respectful and effective service provision.

In defining the core principles that drive services, organizations engage in proactive processes that see strengths as keys to success. This means shifting from a "fix-what–is-broken" model to a "discover-what-works-and-design-what-will-work-better" approach. This translates to identifying the strengths and gifts of organizations. Organizational personnel ask themselves:

- What are the strengths and gifts of the organization?
- What has contributed to the strengths and gifts of the organization?
- What gives the organization spirit and life?
- Who contributes to that spirit and life?
- What does organization do well?
- How can the organization keep up the good work?

- How can the organization develop those good practices even further?

Such questions can generate enthusiasm and encourage deeper levels of staff involvement and commitment. Continuing on this path and consistent with the ideas presented throughout this book, it can be helpful for organizations to approach identifying core principles by considering the following:

- Every organization has strengths and something that works.
- What is focused on and given attention becomes a socially constructed reality.
- There are many perspectives and ways to understand a situation.
- Inquiry, the act of asking questions of an organization or group, influences groups in some way.
- Respect toward others and in relationships facilitates cooperation.
- The past informs but does not determine the future—bring forward the best from the past.
- Envision the future.

An organization's mission, vision, and philosophical principles are the driving forces behind its services. When core principles have been developed, articulated, and disseminated, organizations then take steps to "walk the talk." Doing this means ensuring that the philosophy is being carried out in all aspects of an organization and its services. The result is that policies, procedures, and quality assurance practices are evaluated in terms of their fit with the organization and its mission.

Philosophy in Action

For ideas to matter and make a difference, they must be put into action (Bertolino,

2003). Overarching questions related to this include:

- How are staff strengths identified and utilized?
- What processes are used to ensure that relationships are honored and valued?
- How are everyday organizational dilemmas approached from a strengths-based perspective?

In their primer to *Appreciative Inquiry,* Cooperrider and Whitney (2005) described the "4-D Cycle," which can be helpful to organizations in putting a strengths-based philosophy to work a structured way:

Discovery (of what has worked and represents the best of the past)

Discovery involves having staff determine what from the past typifies the values of the organization and has worked to any degree. All organizations have things that have worked and that can be used as stepping stones to future successes. Identification of specific examples including "what" and "how" contributed to those successes is essential. This is a way to conduct a strengths-based inventory that identifies foundational asset.

Dream (what is possible)

As therapists do with clients, organizations focus on developing a well-articulated vision of the future. What kind of organization is wanted? If things were the best they could be, what would be different? From here, they further develop a vision that is clear, realistic, and attainable.

Design (the processes and structures that support the organization's best dream)

To achieve a vision of the future, processes and structures need to be outlined. This includes what people's various roles and responsibilities are within an organization. It involves clearly delineating action steps and applicable time lines.

Deliver (the destiny)

This facet in the cycle requires commitment to accomplish the design. Systems of accountability and recognition must be created and standards established for continuous innovation and alignment with core values. Doing this ensures a proactive atmosphere in which an organization is always monitoring for changes and adjusting to those changes to better meet the needs of clientele, staff, and the community at large.

These facets occur at all levels of organizations—from front-line staff to the board of directors. All voices are heard, honored, and respected. Involvement is critical in creating respectful, responsive, and highly energized climates.

People in Places

What seems to be problematic for some organizations is a lack of consensus as to what kinds of persons offer the best fit. Stronger infrastructures are created when the "right" people are in the "right" places and carry out the organization's philosophy in all aspects of their jobs. To meet this challenge, an organization may identify the core qualities that are sought in staff. For example, an organization may identify compassion, ability to deal with ambiguity and to manage diversity, and integrity and trust as core qualities, values, and competencies. These qualities are agreed upon, outlined, articulated, and followed in everyday hiring practices and then in services. Because of their importance, these qualities should not be selected haphazardly. Organizations and their clientele are better served if time and care

are taken to identify them through processes that involve staff at all levels.

Coming Full Circle

This journey began with a discussion of various factors that can affect therapy. The most important of these, philosophy, is a primary undercurrent yet one of the most underexplored aspects of therapy. It remains relatively unchartered territory when compared to well-researched factors such as theories, methods, and therapist variables. Philosophy may be considered ambiguous, insignificant, and unnecessary to its detractors; however, it is clear that what therapists believe largely affects what they do. Due to its influence, an ongoing exploration of philosophy is necessary to the success of clients and the growth of individual therapists and their respective affiliations and practice settings. Situated in both research and anecdotal evidence, a strengths-based philosophy provides a way to partner with clients to create hope and possibilities for present and future change.

SUMMARY POINTS

- Just like clients, therapists can become stuck in therapy.
- Four areas or *pathways to impossibility* that contribute to impasses and for which therapists monitor include *the anticipation of impossibility; the theory countertransference; repetition of unhelpful methods, techniques, and practices;* and *inattention to clients' motivation.*
- In addition to employing client feedback strategies, therapists engage in active processes to monitor and address potential stuck points and pathways of impossibility.
- Therapists use *ongoing self-reflection,* setting aside time to reflect on sessions and the elements of those sessions, to review video or audiotapes, and to explore any personal reactions.
- Therapy frameworks can also be used as a way to think about a situation or a client differently.
- *Supervision* provides an excellent forum for self-reflection, identifying unhelpful patterns, and generating new ideas.
- Supervision is a collaborative process and *isomorphic* to those in therapy as supervisors

work to create contexts in which learning can take place, accountability can be ensured, and new ideas can be generated.
- *Reflecting conversations* provide a medium for generating new ideas for therapists who are experiencing impasses.
- Effective therapists engage in activities to increase their knowledge and grow through deliberate practice and ongoing self-evaluation.
- Lack of support and negativity, in particular, can prove devastating to organizations, often leading to "staff infections" in which negativity becomes pervasive, interfering with relationships and spreading through an organization or setting.
- A strengths-based philosophy is not simply a response at a case-by-case, individual level but provides the background for organizational success.
- Organizationally, a culture of feedback allows staff at all levels to better understand the experiences of clients served, including what is working and what is not.
- Process-oriented feedback mechanisms are used at the end of therapy to invite clients to

share their experience with staff at all levels; this feedback is integral to shaping future services.

- The long-term sustainability of programs requires a clearly articulated mission, vision, and principles that drive those entities.
- An organization's core philosophical principles should be timeless and enduring although the means and ways to carry them out may vary.
- For ideas to matter and make a difference, it is necessary that they be put into action and that staff "walk the talk."

DISCUSSION QUESTIONS

1. What are ways that therapists can identify, monitor, and respond to personal views and patterns that may contribute to impasses?

2. What are risks to clients and therapists when therapists fall into pathways of impossibility?

3. In what ways can supervision be helpful to therapists?

4. What are characteristics of effective and successful therapists?

5. What are ways that organizations can begin to develop and incorporate a strengths-based philosophy?

A Brief Exploration of the Evolution of Psychotherapy

Psychotherapy has evolved significantly since its creation in the early 1900s. Rich with tradition, it has been brought to life by prominent figures and their groundbreaking models. It is important to understand and acknowledge such innovators and their approaches without paying allegiance to them. These individuals paved the way for future practice, research, and, ultimately, the evolution of new approaches. Although their contributions are numerous and varied, their theories can be collapsed, in a general way, within or between three different "waves" of psychotherapy (Bertolino & O'Hanlon, 2002; O'Hanlon, 1994, 1999). Each of these movements represents various epistemological viewpoints (in other words, different ways to conceptualize "reality").

The First Wave: A Pathology Focus

The first wave symbolized the "beginning" as it ushered in a major departure in the perception of mental illness. Prior to Sigmund Freud, mental illness was believed to be the result of physical causes (for example, lesions on the brain) or demonic spirit possession. Freud was perhaps the first to develop a "scientific" approach to psychotherapy. As early as 1905, however, he (1905/1953) recognized that psychotherapy had a long, albeit undefined, history, "Let me remind you that psychotherapy is in no way a modern method of treatment. On the contrary, it is the most ancient form of therapy in medicine" (p. 258).

Although Freud maintained a linkage to biological thinking, he reframed the cause and cure of emotional maladjustment in psychological terms. Freud's psychoanalysis became known as an *intrapsychic* approach, identifying mental illness as being within the individual. Freud presumed that symptoms—and hence, pathology—were the result of unresolved emotional material that had been repressed and buried in the unconscious. The analyst's role was to delve into clients' pasts and help them "work through" unresolved unconscious content. Treatment was understood as a cathartic, emotionally expressive process in which patients would reexperience traumatic and/or painful events. It was believed that this "talking cure" would lead to a strengthening of the ego, thereby allowing it to moderate the opposing forces of the id and superego.

Psychoanalysis and first wave approaches are consistent with the medical model, which holds that symptoms (in other words, the pathology or disease) are identified, a prescriptive treatment is administered, and symptom amelioration occurs. In the face of well-documented criticisms, some of Freud's original ideas have been discarded or modified whereas others remain intact, either in principle or as linguistic icons. An example of a model that has maintained analytic roots is *object-relations theory* (Fairbairn, 1954; Kernberg, 1976; Mahler, 1979a, 1979b), which is based on research studying the effects of early relationships and attachment (Bowlby, 1969, 1973, 1980). Several analytic approaches have also been revamped and applied to families (Ackerman, 1958; Boszormenyi-Nagy, 1987; Scharff & Scharff, 1987).

Linguistically, the influence of psychoanalysis and the first wave is easily recognizable in both professional and nonprofessional genres. Terms such as *defense mechanism, ego,* and *complex* are conversational commonplaces. In a more historical sense, the first wave is immortalized for its role in the creation of psychiatric descriptors that are a central part of mental health nomenclature. This is evidenced in the *Diagnostic and Statistical Manual of Mental Disorders* (DSM), which was originally published in 1952 and is currently in its fourth edition (DSM IV-TR) (APA, 2000).

The Second Wave: A Problem Focus

As psychology and psychotherapy continued to evolve, a transformation characterized by a series of progressions took place in the early to mid-twentieth century. One transformation was represented by a movement away from pathology in favor of "problems." Not simply a semantic element, this transition brought with it the view that clients did not have be "cured" but could grow and change by altering thinking or "self-talk" by changing patterns of action and interaction, by examining reinforcement contingencies, or by learning new skills.

During this time, *behaviorism* gained prominence and offered a radical departure from psychoanalysis. Behaviorists maintained that people were conditioned by external factors and downplayed psychological processes by viewing problems as the result of maladaptive behaviors (Skinner, 1953). Consistent with earlier theories, in its infancy, behaviorists were held as the only experts in the therapeutic milieu, responsible for designing interventions and programs to modify problematic behaviors. This resulted in criticisms of behaviorism as depersonalizing and inhumane: People were treated like machines.

As the second wave evolved, a host of approaches began to gain notoriety. As with behaviorism, these models maintained the focus on the individual while drawing attention to change in the "here and now." Several of these models also emphasized the role of behavioral interventions in facilitating change but focuses on cognitive processes and the development of insight and awareness. Unlike behavioral therapy, the contention was that logical (in other words, rational thought) processes were necessary for lasting change. These approaches included *person-centered therapy* (formerly *client-centered therapy*) (Rogers, 1951, 1957, 1961), *Gestalt therapy* (Perls, 1969, 1973), *cognitive therapy* (Beck, 1976; Beck,1995), and *rational emotive therapy* (later *rational emotive behavior therapy*) (Ellis, 1962, 1973, 1994, 1996).

Another significant development within the second wave was the advent of family therapy, in particular, *family systems theory,* which brought with it new ways to conceptualize problems. Although a variety of approaches had been adapted to work with families (Gurman & Kniskern, 1980, 1990), family systems theory was a unique departure from simply applying models that had been developed for individuals to families. The systemic-relational paradigm held that problems were due to dysfunctional communication and behavioral patterns within relational systems (Cottone, 1992). Born out of a variety disciplines, family theorists relied on cybernetics, the study of how systems use corrective mechanisms to maintain homeostasis (in other words, status quo).

In adopting an *interactional* perspective, family systems therapists hypothesized problems in terms of family structure, hierarchy, rules, roles, and boundaries (Hoffman, 1981; Watzlawick, Weakland, & Fisch, 1974). Constructs such as personality were no longer sealed within the person but were influenced by patterns of communication within family and social relationships. Rather than focusing on content (what was being discussed), family therapists emphasized process (how messages are communicated). This distinction changed every facet of therapy from assessment through intervention.

During this time, clinicians largely maintained responsibility for designing interventions that would alter, interrupt, and ultimately, change patterns of interaction among family members. Influential models included *Bowenian* (Bowen, 1978; Kerr & Bowen, 1988), *strategic* (Boscolo, Cecchin, Hoffman, & Penn, 1987; Haley, 1963, 1987; Madanes, 1981; Selvini Palazzoli, Boscolo, Cecchin, & Prata, 1978; Watzlawick, Weakland, & Fisch, 1974), *structural* (Minuchin, 1974; Minuchin & Fishman, 1981; Minuchin, Rosman, & Baker, 1978), and *experiential family* therapies (Satir, 1964, 1972; Whitaker & Bumberry, 1988; Whitaker & Keith, 1981).

In the 1970s, the concerns that brought families to therapy reflected the growing diversity in society. Family systems theory gained enormous popularity as it offered a viable response to changes in society by situating them in social context. New directions in research were also spawned with increasing attention given to issues such as ethnicity, culture, religion/spirituality, blended families, and disability. This area of concentration became known as *family studies*. The *family life cycle* (Carter & McGoldrick, 1999/2005) was another development that described how families go through developmental phases, within which are various challenges and transitions to be negotiated. Through these ongoing efforts, family therapy gained its own voice, and a handbook was developed as an alternative to the *DSM* to diagnostically classify relational difficulties experienced by couples and families (Kaslow, 1996). Family systems therapy also introduced a distinct syntax of terms, such as *intergenerational, coalition,* and *enmeshment,* emphasizing relational processes. As had happened with the first wave, this terminology became influential.

Not all clinicians were satisfied with the directive, expert stance that had become a trademark of interactional approaches. This resulted in varying degrees of experimentation by therapists in search of different ways to work with couples and families. One idea that injected new life into interviewing processes was *circular questioning*. Arising out of the therapeutic approach of the Milan team (Selvini-Palazzoli, Boscolo, Cecchin, & Prata, 1978) and further articulated by psychiatrist Karl Tomm (1984a, 1984b), circular questioning served as a vehicle for helping clients to see themselves in a relational context. Through persistent process-oriented questioning, clinicians would help clients to contextualize problems, drawing attention to patterns of communication embedded in family structure and relationships. The therapist was encouraged to assume a posture of being active and curious, allowing the therapist's genuineness to become more apparent, contributing to an atmosphere in which new understandings could emerge. It was proposed that circular questioning alone could trigger therapeutic change (Tomm, 1987).

The second wave also proved exciting as a new generation of well-researched individual and systemic hybrids surfaced. These included *dialectical behavior therapy* (DBT) (Dimeff & Koerner, 2007; Linehan, 1993; Miller, Rathus, & Linehan, 2006), *emotionally focused family therapy* (EFT) (Greenberg & Johnson, 1988; Johnson, 2004, 2005), *multisystemic therapy* (MST) (Henggeler & Borduin, 1990), *functional family therapy* (FFT) (Alexander & Parsons, 1982), *internal family systems* (IFS) (Schwartz, 1995), and *medical family therapy* (McDaniel, Hepworth, & Doherty, 1992). These models brought more breadth to the second wave with several maintaining fundamental principles of systems theory.

The first two waves dealt primarily with the "discovery" of pathology and problems with the concept of reality as knowable by the therapist (Bertolino & O'Hanlon, 2002). This "modernist" template considered mental health professionals as experts who, through their respective theoretical models, could explain or determine truths about people and their problems. Mental health professionals were in charge of virtually every aspect of therapy from assessment to formulating hypotheses to developing interventions. Although first and second wave approaches shared many common features, there was considerable competition between theorists who posited that there were "right" ways to work with people. It was assumed that if the correct method were determined, universal principles could be discovered to explain and change all human behavior and relationships.

The Third Wave: Becoming Strengths Based

The contributions of first and second wave theorists, researchers, and clinicians provided psychotherapy the momentum from which to grow and gain legitimacy. This progression also led to questions about shortcomings associated with psychotherapy as a field and what were considered highly coveted models. First and second wave assumptions that had gone relatively unchallenged for many years became the subject of inquiry (Gergen, 1982, 1985, 1991; Shotter, 1993; Watzlawick, 1984). At the forefront were practitioners, many of whom experienced personal discomfort between what they had been taught, what they believed, and what they were practicing. Bertolino and O'Hanlon (2002) commented:

> In the late 1970s and early 1980s, mental health practitioners and, in particular, family therapists, began to take notice of their biases and blinders. Therapists were finding holes in their theories and prejudices (e.g., sexism and cultural biases) that had gone unacknowledged and without challenge for years (p. 3).

One of the most important explications of these concerns was the feminist critique, which emphasized the importance of gender-related and sociocultural issues that had been downplayed during the first 100 years of psychotherapy (Gilligan, 1982; Goldner, 1985; Hare-Mustin, 1978, 1987; McGoldrick, Pearce, & Giordano, 1982). The Women's Project in Family Therapy was particularly instrumental in the reexamination of systems theory and its inadvertent power differentials, gender stereotyping, and marginalization of females (Walters, Carter, Papp, & Silverstein, 1988).

Following the development of family studies initiated in the second wave, research on issues affecting couples and families continued to mature. The breadth of these studies grew exponentially, reflecting contextual influences and changes in families, culture, society, and technology (Coleman & Gangong, 2003; Milardo, 2000). This further exposed the bounds of quantitative inquiry with regard to couples and families. As a means of capturing the essence of interpersonal experience, the qualitative paradigm (for example, ethnographic or single case studies) offered an alternative research methodology. This methodology presented a different kind of dilemma, however, given the lower ability to generalize the findings from qualitative studies.

As the role of interpersonal experience became increasingly apparent, alternative philosophical pathways, which had been explored only to a limited degree, began to make inroads in psychotherapy. These avenues drew further attention to the concepts of objective reality, language, and dialogic discourse, all of which are elemental to talk therapies, and were exemplified through three concepts: *postmodernism, constructivism,* and *social constructionism.*

Postmodernism, Constructivism, and Social Constructionism

The assumption that social reality is objective and knowable contributed to various forms of bias emphasized in theoretical schemas. The third wave was marked by a response to this notion through a radical epistemological shift known as postmodernism. Usually associated with the writings of philosophers such as Jacques Derrida, Michel Foucault, Jean-François Lyotard, and Ludwig Wittgenstein, postmodernism represents an intellectual trend and challenge to the ideas of objective reality, fixed scientific knowledge, and universal truths.

It suggests that there are multiple, subjective realities and ways to view the world with context, culture, language, experience, and understanding as primary influences. Knowledge is viewed as subjective and continuously evolving through one's interpretations of experience and subsequent reinterpretations of those interpretations.

Not an era but a critique, postmodernism in psychotherapy accentuated constructivism and social constructionism. *Constructivism* is a philosophical stance rooted in biology and the physical properties of individual perception. Constructivists emphasize the subjectivity of knowledge, disputing the view that knowledge represents the "real world." The subjective constructions of the world that people hold are not the same as the physical reality that is "out there." External objective reality cannot be known, and no one perspective is considered more true or correct than another (Maturana, 1978). Early constructivists such as George Kelly (1977) posited that people are active participants in organizing what they perceive and in constructing what they know.

Social constructionism is grounded in philosophy, relationships, and community and represents a wider domain of interpretation (Berger & Luckmann, 1966). Social constructionists emphasize how meaning emerges from complex webs of interaction, relationships, and social processes. The generation of meaning occurs as individuals interrelate and talk with others or with themselves. Consequently, social realities are continually renegotiated and never truly set. Although a physical reality exists (for example, if you touch fire, it will burn you), social realities are created and recreated through language and interaction. Therapy is a matter of finding what fits best with the environment given ethical and ecological factors including, but not limited to, age, gender, race, class, ethnicity, religion, and family background. Language and interaction are the primary vehicles for facilitating change with each therapeutic dialogue or interaction leading to the creation of something new—a *reauthoring* or *rewriting* of stories (White & Epston, 1990).

The realization that therapists cannot maintain complete objectivity also meant acknowledging that they are influenced within the therapeutic milieu. Referred to as *second-order cybernetics* or *cybernetics of cybernetics*, therapists went from being seen as outside observers to being viewed as part of the therapeutic system. This proposition validated what many had already been thinking and experiencing: Clinicians, like clients, are in an ongoing, recursive process of influencing and being influenced. Clinicians also have constructed realities or stories that are more or less useful depending on the situation but are no more or less true. This conceptualization resulted in the revamping of a variety of first and second wave approaches with theorists incorporating aspects of constructivism and social constructionism (Mahoney, 2003; Neimeyer & Mahoney, 1995).

Collaboration, Competency, and Change

Inspired by new ideas for practice, practitioners began to explore the multitude of ways that clients' preferences and motivations could be accentuated in therapy. This idea was evidenced by *collaboration, competency,* and *change. Collaboration* meant including clients wherever possible so that their preferences and ideas about the scope of and focus on services, goals, and methods for achieving those goals could be heard and incorporated. The notion of shared expertise between clinicians and clients underscored collaboration.

A second embodiment was a *competency or strengths base*. Instead of focusing predominately on pathology or problems—which often obscures resources and solutions within clients—therapists began to more actively elicit clients' internal strengths and abilities and those within their social networks. By acknowledging clients' capacities, therapists no longer had to accept what their theories were saying—that clients were in some way "damaged" and/or incapable of positive change. This idea had been explored years earlier by theorists such as Milton H. Erickson, who was adept at eliciting and evoking his patient's abilities, strengths, and resources (O'Hanlon & Hexum, 1990; Rossi, 1980). His *utilization approach*, which used what the patient brought to the therapeutic encounter, was central to his way of doing therapy. According to Erickson (1954a), "The purpose of psychotherapy should be the helping of the patient in that fashion most adequate, available, and acceptable. In rendering the patient aid, there should be full respect for and utilization of whatever the patient presents" (p. 127). He believed that people already possess—within themselves or their social systems—what they need to resolve their problems.

The final part of the equation involved a focus on *change*. Following a trend established in the second wave, clinicians began to deemphasize therapists' explanations and learn more about change as a constant process. Clinicians noticed numerous ways that change affects everyday life and occurs outside of therapy. Miller and colleagues (1997) commented:

Therapeutic time is spent more productively when the therapist and client focus on and enhance the factors responsible for change-in-general rather than on identifying and then changing the factors a theory suggests are responsible or causing problems-in-particular. . . . Indoctrinating clients into a particular model of problem causation might actually . . . [undermine] the very factors responsible for the occurrence of change by drawing clients' attention to whatever a particular theory suggests is causing their suffering (p. 127).

Coinciding with a strengths focus, therapists strived to activate change processes by helping clients to more fully explore and develop previous and potential possibilities. Drawing on the sensibility that clients have abilities and strengths that often go unnoticed in times of trouble was a hallmark of the third wave. Third-wave approaches of note included *solution-focused, solution-oriented,* and *narrative therapies.* Other approaches emerged as well, making additional contributions to the third wave (Hoyt, 1994, 1996, 1998).

Solution-focused therapy's (SFT) primary developer, Steve de Shazer (1985, 1988, 1991), had a background in the Mental Research Institute (MRI) brief therapy model. A former student of Milton Erickson, Bill O'Hanlon is credited with the creation of *solution-oriented therapy* (SOT) (O'Hanlon & Weiner-Davis, 2003). Evolving from different persuasions, both SFT and SOT share common principles. The most fundamental of these is the premise that there are *exceptions* to the "problems" that bring people to therapy. At times things go differently and problems are less apparent or absent altogether. This is highlighted through "solution talk," conversations in which therapists engage clients in conversations about solutions and change as opposed to problems and explanations. Closely aligned with this are several tenets, including (1) if it ain't broke don't fix it; (2) if what you're doing isn't working, do something different; (3) if what you're

doing works, do more of it; and (4) there are exceptions to problems.

SFT and SOT therapies are rooted in the Ericksonian concept of a future orientation. Erickson (1954a) remarked, "Emphasis should be placed more upon what the patient does in the present and will do in the future than upon a mere understanding of why some long-past event occurred" (p. 127). To help resolve patients' problems and develop a sense of the future, he would have his patients envision futures in which their problems were resolved. Erickson would help patients to take action in the present to achieve problem resolution and future goals. Likewise, the *miracle question* in SFT is used as a means to help clients to envision a time in the future when their problems would be resolved and their lives would be better (de Shazer, 1988).

Solution-based therapies have been criticized on several levels. One argument is that they tend to be superficial with little attention given to "deeper" issues. Another contention is that an emphasis on solution-talk can lead to therapists being "solution forced" (Nylund & Corsiglia, 1994). These criticisms indicate two contextual themes. First, they reflect the strongly held traditions of earlier theorists, many of whom believed that solution-based therapies were shallow and did not get to "root" issues. Next, solution-based therapies were developed largely in response to a growing managed care climate as third-party payers stressed efficiency and accountability. The result was a plethora of brief and time-sensitive approaches. Ironically, many traditional models considered to be longer term were also reconstituted as brief models. Although a myriad of these approaches surfaced in rapid fashion, the concepts of "solution based" and "brief" became inextricably linked.

Michael White and David Epston are credited as being the creators of the *narrative* approach to therapy (Epston, 1989; Epston & White, 1992; White & Epston, 1990; White, 1989, 2007). Emerging out of the underpinnings of French philosophy, narrative therapists became interested in how problems become oppressive in people's lives. Problems are shaped by social, cultural, religious, political, and other dominant influences. According to this perspective, when people's stories about themselves and their lives become "problem saturated," problems arise.

A main focus of the narrative approach is the use of *externalizing conversations* whereby people and their problems are separated through conversations. In essence, the *person* is never the problem—the problem is the problem. These types of conversations help people with the identification of *unique outcomes,* which represent alternative stories or aspects of lived experience that run counter to problem-saturated stories. Narrative therapists view people as heroes and heroines who have loosened the grips that problems have tried to maintain over them. This premise aligns narrative therapy with other approaches that tend to emphasize client strengths.

The third wave has proved a fertile ground for a plethora of approaches that share the assumption that ongoing therapist-client conversations pave new roads to change (Anderson, 1993, 1997; Anderson & Goolishian, 1988, 1992; Hoffman, 1993; Madigan & Law, 1998). With an emphasis on collaboration, competency, and change, therapists have experienced a shift from being responsible for change to being facilitators of change. By erasing the boundaries established through previous theoretical constructs, other opportunities for expansion have become apparent. In some instances, what has emerged is not necessarily "new." Most important has been a growing acceptance and respect for perspectives that allow for ideas that had been considered "cutting edge."

Contributions of Note: From Waves to Ripples

Through its evolution, psychotherapy has produced numerous specialized approaches. These methods have spanned the three waves and are noteworthy for their roles in expanding the bounds of talk therapies. Primarily sensory-based (in other words, visual, auditory, kinesthetic, olfactory, gustatory) and facilitating the mind-body connection, these specialized methods have at times brought about remarkable results. Four approaches in particular have been both hailed and criticized: *hypnosis, neuro-linguistic programming* (NLP), *eye movement desensitization and reprocessing* (EMDR), and *energy therapies.*

The roots of hypnosis can be traced back hundreds of years. Freud and many early analytic thinkers used and formalized hypnosis, albeit with limited success. Milton Erickson is considered by many to have had the most significant impact on the technique. His ideas and methods have been interpreted and modified over the years (Bandler & Grinder, 1975; Gilligan, 1987; Grinder, DeLozier, & Bandler, 1977; Lankton & Lankton, 1983; O'Hanlon, 1987; Zeig, 1982, 1985a, 1985b, 1994; Zeig & Lankton, 1988). The transformation of hypnosis since the 1970s is clear: the hypnotherapist's role changed from instructing clients what to do to evoking abilities (Barber, 1996; Dolan, 1985; Flemons, 2002; O'Hanlon & Martin, 1992; Yapko, 1995, 2003). This transformation drew further attention to the role of language in generating therapeutic possibilities. Again, this strengths-based concept assumed that clients had resources within themselves that could be used in the service of change.

NLP was developed in the mid-1970s by Richard Bandler and John Grinder (Bandler & Grinder, 1975; Dilts, 1983; Dilts, Grinder, Bandler, & DeLozier, 1980; Geary & Zeig, 2001; Grinder & Bandler, 1976, 1981; Lankton, 1980) and evolved from the work of Milton Erickson, Fritz Perls, and Virginia Satir. NLP began as an exploration of the relationship between neurology, linguistics, and observable patterns of behavior while maintaining close ties to hypnosis. Today NLP is most frequently known as set of models regarding how communication affects and is affected by subjective experience. Practitioners use techniques rooted in linguistics to change mental states and associations. An emphasis on language as fundamental means of facilitating change is central to NLP.

EMDR and energy therapies have drawn attention and controversy for their uniqueness. Developed by psychologist Francine Shapiro (2001; Shapiro, Kaslow, & Maxfield, 2007) as a method for individuals experiencing the aftereffects of trauma, EMDR combines cognitive, behavioral, and sensory-based (mainly visual, but it can include auditory and kinesthetic modalities) processing. The overarching idea is that deliberate eye movements guided by therapists assist in processing stuck remnants of traumatic experience. Energy therapies, which have been refined in recent years, are based on the thesis that there are perturbations (in other words, blocks) disturbing the body's energy system. It is believed that these must be removed or cleared for the person to achieve psychological balance. Energy therapists use visual (in other words, eye movements), auditory (for example, tones, spoken word, music, various sounds), and kinesthetic (for example, tapping, touch) processes to achieve facilitate change (Gallo, 2000; Phillips, 2000). It is worth noting that both EMDR and energy therapies have drawn sharp criticisms regarding their efficacy (Davidson & Parker, 2001; Devilly & Spence, 1999; Goldstein, deBeurs, Chambless, & Wilson, 2000).

From the large waves to the small ripples, many significant overarching movements and trends have created the foundation of psychotherapy. These contributions can be found in some form in virtually every approach currently employed by therapists. It is therefore important to understand and respect these various theoretical developments and their relative influence on the past, present, and future of therapy.

Ackerman, N. W. (1958). *The psychodynamics of family life*. New York: Basic Books.

Adler, A. (1956). *The individual psychology of Alfred Adler: A systematic presentation in selections from his writings*. [H. L. Ansbacher & R. R. Ansbacher, Trans.].

Albom, M. (1997). *Tuesdays with Morrie: An old man, a young man, and life's greatest lesson*. New York: Doubleday.

Alexander, J. F., & Parsons, B. V. (1982). *Functional family therapy*. Monterey, CA: Brooks/Cole.

Allen, D. M. (2007). The search for a unified metatheory of personality, psychopathology, and psychotherapy: Grand or grand illusion? A book review essay. *Journal of Psychotherapy Integration, 17*(3), 274–286.

American Psychiatric Association. (2000). *Diagnostic and statistical manual of mental disorders IV TR*. Washington, DC: American Psychiatric Association.

APA Presidential Task Force on Evidence-Based Practice. (2006). Evidence-based practice in psychology. *American psychologist, 61*(4), 271–285.

Andersen, T. (1987). The reflecting team: Dialogue and metadialogue in clinical work. *Family Process, 26*, 415–428.

Andersen, T. (Ed.). (1991). *The reflecting team: Dialogues and dialogues about the dialogues*. New York: Norton.

Andersen, T. (1993). See and hear, and be seen and heard. In S. Friedman (Ed.), *The new language of change: Constructive collaboration of psychotherapy* (pp. 303–322). New York: Guilford.

Anderson, H. (1993). On a roller coaster: A collaborative language systems approach to therapy. In S. Friedman (Ed.), *The new language of change: Constructive collaboration in therapy* (pp. 323–344). New York: Guilford.

Anderson, H. (1997). *Conversation, language, and possibilities: A postmodern approach*. New York: Basic Books.

Anderson, H. (2005). Myths about "not knowing." *Family Process, 44*(4), 497–504.

Anderson, H., & Goolishian, H. (1988). Human systems as linguistic systems: Evolving ideas about the implications for theory and practice. *Family Process, 27*(4), 371–393.

Anderson, H., & Goolishian, H. (1992). The client is the expert: A not knowing approach to therapy. In S. McNamee & K. J. Gergen (Eds.), *Therapy as social construction* (pp. 25–39). Newbury Park, CA: Sage.

Arkowitz, H. (1992). Integrative theories of therapy. In D. K. Freedheim (Ed.), *History of psychotherapy: A century of change* (pp. 261–303). Washington, DC: American Psychological Association.

Arredondo, P., & D'Andrea, M. (1995, September). AMCD approved multicultural counseling competency standards. *Counseling Today*, 28–32.

Asay, T. P., & Lambert, M. J. (1999). The empirical case for the common factors in therapy: Quantitative findings. In M. A. Hubble, B. L. Duncan, & S. D. Miller (Eds.), *The heart and soul of change: What works in therapy* (pp. 33–56). Washington, DC: APA Press.

Atkins, D. C., & Christensen, A. (2001). Is professional training worth the bother? A review of the impact of psychotherapy training on client outcome. *Australian Psychologist, 36*(2), 122–131.

Bachelor, A., & Horvath, A. (1999). The therapeutic relationship. In S. D. Miller (Ed.), *The heart and soul of change: What works in therapy* (pp. 133–178). Washington, DC: American Psychological Association.

Baldwin, S. A., Wampold, B. E., & Imel, Z. E. (2007). Untangling the alliance-outcome correlation: Exploring the relative importance of therapist and patient variability in the alliance. *Journal of Consulting and Clinical Psychology, 75*(6), 842–852.

Bandler, R., & Grinder, J. (1975). *The structure of magic: A book about language and therapy*. Palo Alto, CA: Science and Behavior Books.

Barber, J. (1996). *Hypnosis and suggestion in the treatment of pain: A clinical guide*. New York: Norton.

Bateson, G. (1972). *Steps to an ecology of mind*. New York: Ballentine.

Bechtoldt, H., Norcross, J. C., Wyckoff, L. A., Pokrywa, M. L., & Campbell, L. F. (2001). Theoretical orientations and employment settings of clinical and counseling psychologists: A comparative study. *The Clinical Psychologist, 54*(1), 3–6

Beck, A. T. (1976). *Cognitive therapy and the emotional disorders*. New York: International Universities Press.

Beck, J. S. (1995). *Cognitive therapy: Basics and beyond*. New York: Guilford.

Bedi, R. (2006). Concept mapping the client's perspective on counseling alliance formation. *Journal of Counseling Psychology, 53*(1), 26–35.

Berger, P. L., & Luckmann, T. (1966). *The social construction of reality: A treatise in the sociology of knowledge*. New York: Doubleday/Anchor Books.

Bertolino, B. (1999). *Therapy with troubled teenagers: Rewriting young lives in progress*. New York: Wiley.

Bertolino, B. (2001). Lights, camera, action!!! Making new meanings through movies. In H. G. Rosenthal (Ed.), *Favorite counseling and therapy homework assignments: 56 therapists share their most creative strategies Vol. II* (pp. 43–46). Philadelphia, PA: Brunner-Routledge.

Bertolino, B. (2003). *Change-oriented psychotherapy with adolescents and young adults: The next generation of respectful and effective therapeutic processes and practices*. New York: Norton.

Bertolino, B., & Caldwell, K. (1999). Through the doorway: Experiences of psychotherapists in a week-long training intensive. *Journal of Systemic Therapies, 18*(4), 42–57.

Bertolino, B., Kiener, M., Patterson, R. (2009). *The therapist's notebook on strengths-based and solution-based therapies*. New York: Routledge.

Bertolino, B., & O'Hanlon, B. (Eds.). (1998). *Invitation to possibility-land: An intensive teaching seminar with Bill O'Hanlon*. Bristol, PA: Brunner/Mazel.

Bertolino, B., & O'Hanlon, B. (2002). *Collaborative, competency-based counseling and therapy*. Boston: Allyn & Bacon.

Bertolino, B., & Schultheis, G. (2002). *The therapist's handbook for families: Solution-oriented exercises for working with children, youth, and families*. New York: The Haworth Press.

Bertolino, B., & Thompson, K. (1999). *The residential youth care worker in action: A collaborative, competency-based approach*. New York: The Haworth Press.

Beutler, L. E. (1989). Differential treatment selection: The role of diagnosis in psychotherapy. *Psychotherapy, 26*, 271–281.

Beutler, L. E., & Castonguay, L. G. (2006). The task force on empirically based principles of therapeutic change. In L. G. Castonguay & L. E. Beutler (Eds.), *Principles of therapeutic change that work* (pp. 3–10). New York: Oxford University Press.

Beutler, L. E., & Clarkin, J. (1990). Systematic treatment selection: Toward targeted therapeutic interventions. New York: Brunner/Mazel.

Beutler, L. E., Consoli, A. J., & Lane, G. (2005). Systematic treatment selection and prescriptive psychotherapy. In J. C. Norcross & M. R. Goldfried (Eds.), *Handbook of psychotherapy integration* (2nd ed.) (pp. 121–143). New York: Oxford University Press.

Beutler, L. E., & Harwood, T. M. (2000). *Prescriptive psychotherapy: A practical guide to systematic treatment selection*. New York: Oxford University Press.

Beutler, L. E., Malik, M., Alimohamed, S., Harwood, T. M., Talebi, H., Noble, S., & Wong, E. (2004). Therapist variables. In M. J. Lambert (Ed.), *Bergin and Garfield's handbook of psychotherapy and behavior change* (5th ed.) (pp. 227–306). New York: Wiley.

Binswanger, L. (1975). *Being-in-the-world: Selected papers on Ludwig Binswanger*. London: Souvenir Press.

Blatt, S. J., Sanislow, C. A., Zuroff, D. C., Pilkonis, P. A. (1996). Characteristics of effective therapists: Further analyses of data from the National Institute of Mental Health Treatment of Depression Collaborative Research Program. *Journal of Consulting Psychology, 64*(6), 1276–1284.

Blow, A. J., Sprenkle, D. H., Davis, S. D. (2007). Is who delivers the treatment more important than the treatment itself? The role of the therapist in common factors. *Journal of Marital and Family Therapy, 33*(3), 298–317.

Bohart, A. C., Elliott, R., Greenberg, L. S., & Watson, J. C. (2002). Empathy. In J. C. Norcross (Ed.), *Psychotherapy relationships that work: Therapist contributions and responsiveness to patients* (pp. 89–108). New York: Oxford University Press.

Boisvert, C. M., & Faust, D. (2006). Practicing psychologists' knowledge of general psychotherapy research findings: Implications for science-practice relations. *Professional Psychology: Research and Practice, 37*(6), 708–716.

Bordin, E. S. (1979). The generalizability of the psychoanalytic concept of the working alliance. *Psychotherapy: Theory, Research, and Practice, 16*, 252–260.

Boscolo, L., Cecchin, G, Hoffman, L., & Penn, P. (1987). *Milan systemic family therapy*. New York: Basic Books.

Boszormenyi-Nagy, I. (1987). *Foundations of contextual therapy*. New York: Brunner/Mazel.

Bowen, M. (1978). *Family therapy in clinical practice*. New York: Aronson.

Bowlby, J. (1969). *Attachment and loss: Vol. 1. Attachment*. New York: Basic Books.

Bowlby, J. (1973). *Attachment and loss: Vol. 2. Separation*. New York: Basic Books.

Bowlby, J. (1980). *Attachment and loss: Vol. 3. Loss, sadness, and depression*. New York: Basic Books.

Boyle, S. W., Smith, L. L., Farley, O. W., & Hull, G. H. (2008). *Direct practice in social work* (2nd ed.). Boston: Allyn & Bacon.

Breunlin, D., Schwartz, R., & MacKune-Karrer, B. (1992). *Metaframeworks: Transcending the models of family therapy*. San Francisco: Jossey-Bass

Brickman, P., Rabinowitz, V., Karuza, J., Coates, D., Cohn, E., & Kidder, L. (1982). Models of helping and coping. *American Psychologist, 37*, 368–384.

Brown, G. S., Burlingame, G. M., Lambert, M. J., Jones, E., & Vaccaro, J. (2001). Pushing the quality envelope: A new outcomes management system. *Psychiatric Services, 52*(7), 925–934.

Brown, J., Dreis, S., & Nace, D. K. (1999). What really makes a difference in psychotherapy outcome? Why does managed care want to know? In M. A. Hubble, B. L. Duncan, & S. D. Miller (Eds.), *The heart and soul of change: What works in therapy* (pp. 389–406). Washington, DC: APA Press.

Brown, L. S. (2008). *Cultural competence in trauma therapy: Beyond the flashback*. Washington, DC: American Psychological Association.

Bugental, J. F. T. (1987). *The art of the psychotherapist*. New York: Basic Books.

Burlingame, G. B., Lambert, M. J., Reisinger, C. W., Neff, W. L., Mosier, J. (1995). Pragmatics of tracking mental health outcomes in a managed care setting. *The Journal of Mental Health Administration, 22*, 226–236.

Burlingame, G. B., Mosier, J. L., Wells, M. G., Atkin, Q. G., Lambert, M. J., & Whoolery, M. (2001). Tracking the influence of mental health outcome. *Clinical Psychology and Psychotherapy, 8*, 361–379.

Burlingame, G. B., Wells, M. G., & Lambert, M. J. (1996). *Youth Outcome Questionnaire*. Stevenson, MD: American Professional Credentialing Services.

Burlingame, G. B., Wells, M. G., Lambert M. J., & Cox, J. (2004). Youth Outcome Questionnaire: Updated psychometric properties. In M. E. Maruish (Ed.), *The use of psychological testing for treatment planning and outcome assessment* (3rd ed.). Mahwah, NJ: Lawrence Erlbaum.

Cade, B., & O'Hanlon, W. H. (1993). *A brief guide to brief therapy*. New York: Norton.

Carr, A. (Ed.) (2001). *What work with children and adolescents? A critical review of psychological interventions with children, adolescents, and their families*. London: Routledge.

Carter, B., & McGoldrick, M. (Eds.). (1999/2005). *The expanded family life cycle: Individual, family, and social perspectives* (3rd ed.). Boston: Allyn & Bacon. [reprinted 2005]

Castonguay, L. G., & Beutler, L. E. (2006a). Preface. In L. G. Castonguay & L. E. Beutler (Eds.), *Principles of therapeutic change that work* (pp. iii–viii). New York: Oxford University Press.

Castonguay, L. G., & Beutler, L. E. (2006b). Common and unique principles of therapeutic change: What do we know and what do we need to know? In L. G. Castonguay & L. E. Beutler (Eds.), *Principles of therapeutic change that work* (pp. 353–369). New York: Oxford University Press.

Castonguay, L. G., & Beutler, L. E. (2006c). *Principles of therapeutic change that work*. New York: Oxford University Press.

Castonguay. L. G., & Hotforth, M. G. (2005). Change in psychotherapy: A plea for no more "nonspecific" and false dichotomies. *Clinical Psychology: Science and Practice, 12*, 198–201.

Chambless, D. (1996). Identification of empirically supported psychological interventions. *Clinicians Research Digest, 14*(6), 1–2.

Chambless, D. L., & Hollon, S. D. (1998). Defining empirically supported therapies. *Journal of Consulting and Clinical Psychology, 66,* 7–18.

Chiles, J., Lambert, M. J., & Hatch, A. L. (1999). The impact of psychological interventions on medical cost offset: A meta-analytic review. *Clinical Psychology,* 6(2), 204–220.

Christensen, A., & Jacobson, N. S. (1994). Who (or what) can do psychotherapy: The status and challenge of nonprofessional therapies. *Psychological Sciences, 5,* 8–14.

Christophersen, E. R., & Mortweet, S. L. (2001). *Treatments that work with children: Empirically supported treatment strategies for managing childhood problems.* Washington DC: American Psychological Association.

Coleman, M., & Ganong, L. (2003). *Points and counterpoints: Controversial relationship and family issues in the 21st century.* Los Angeles: Roxbury.

Collins, J. (2001). *Good to great: Why some companies make the leap . . . and others don't.* New York: HarperCollins.

Collins, J. (2005). *Good to great and the social sectors: A monograph to accompany good to great.* New York: HarperCollins.

Constantino, M. J., Castonguay, L. G., & Schut, A. J. (2002). The working alliance: A flagship for the "scientist-practitioner" model in psychotherapy. In G. S. Tryon (Ed.), *Counseling based on process research: Applying what we know* (pp. 81–131). Boston, MA: Allyn & Bacon.

Cooperrider, D. L., & Whitney, D. (2005). *Appreciative inquiry: A positive revolution in change.* San Francisco: Berrett-Koehler Publishers.

Cottone, R. R. (1992). *Theories and paradigms in counseling and psychotherapy.* Boston: Allyn & Bacon.

Craighead, W. E., Bjornsson, & A. S., & Amarson, E. O. (2005). Specificity and nonspecificity in psychotherapy. *Clinical Psychology: Science and Practice, 12,* 189–193.

Crits-Christoph, P., & Mintz, J. (1991). Implications of therapist effects for the design and analysis of comparative studies of psychotherapies. *Journal of Consulting and Clinical Psychology,* 59(1), 20–26.

Cummings, N. A. (2007). Treatment and assessment take place in an economic context, always. In S. O. Lilienfeld & W. T. O'Donohue (Eds.), *The great ideas of clinical science: 17 principles that every mental health professional should understand* (pp. 163–184). New York: Routledge.

Cummings N. A., Cummings, J. L., & Johnson, J. N. (1997). *Behavioral health in primary care: A guide for clinical integration.* Madison, CT: Psychosocial Press (an imprint of International Universities Press).

Cummings, N A., O'Donohue, W. T., & Ferguson, K. E. (2002). *The impact of medical cost offset on practice and research: Making it work for you.* Cummings Foundation on Behavioral Health: *Healthcare utilization and cost series, vol. 5.* Reno, NV: Context Press.

Davidson, P. R., & Parker, K. C. H. (2001). Eye movement desensitization and reprocessing (EMDR): A meta-analysis. *Journal of Consulting and Clinical Psychology,* 69(2), 305–316.

De Jong, P., & Berg, I. K. (2007). *Interviewing for solutions* (3rd ed.). Pacific Grove, CA: Brooks/Cole.

De Laszlo, V. S. (1991). (Ed.). *The basic writings of C. G. Jung.* Princeton, NJ: Princeton University. [Originally published in 1959]

DeRubeis, R. J., Brotman, M. A., & Gibbons, C. J. (2005). A conceptual and methodological analysis of the nonspecifics argument. *Clinical Psychology: Science and Practice, 12,* 174–183.

DeRubeis, R. J., & Crits-Christoph, P. (1998). Empirically supported individual and group psychological treatments for mental disorders. *Journal of Consulting and Clinical Psychology, 66,* 37–52.

de Shazer, S. (1985). *Keys to solution in brief therapy.* New York: Norton.

de Shazer, S. (1988). *Clues: Investigating solutions in brief therapy.* New York: Norton.

de Shazer, S. (1991). *Putting difference to work.* New York: Norton.

Devilly, G. J., & Spence, S. H. (1999). The relative efficacy and treatment distress of EMDR and a cognitive-behavior trauma treatment protocol in the amelioration of post traumatic stress disorder. *Journal of Anxiety Disorders, 13,* 131–157.

Dilts, R. (1983). *Applications of neuro-linguistic programming.* Capitola, CA: Meta Publications.

Dilts, R., Grinder, J., Bandler, R., & DeLozier, J. (1980). *Neuro-linguistic programming: Vol. I: The study of the structure of subjective experience.* Capitola, CA: Meta Publications.

Dimeff, L. A., & Koerner, K. (2007). (Eds.). *Dialectical behavior therapy in clinical practice: Applications across disorders and settings*. New York: Guilford.

Dolan, Y. M. (1985). *A path with a heart: Ericksonian utilization with resistant and chronic clients*. New York: Brunner/Mazel.

Drake, R. E., Merrens, M. R., & Lynde, D. (Eds.). (2005). *Evidence-based mental health practice: A textbook*. New York: Norton.

Dreikurs, R. (1954). The psychological interview in medicine. *American Journal of Individual Psychology, 10*, 99–122.

Duncan, B. L., Hubble, M. A., & Miller, S. D. (1997a). *Psychotherapy with "impossible" cases: The efficient treatment of therapy veterans*. New York: Norton.

Duncan, B. L., Hubble, M. A., & Miller, S. D. (1997b). Stepping off the throne. *Family Therapy Networker, 21*(4), 22–31, 33.

Duncan, B. L., Miller, S. D., & Sparks, J. A. (2004). *The heroic client: A revolutionary way to improve effectiveness through client directed, outcome-informed therapy* [Revised paperback edition]. San Francisco: Jossey-Bass.

Duncan, B. L., Miller, S. D., Sparks, J. A., Claud, D. A., Reynolds, L. R., Brown, J., & Johnson, L. D. (2003). The session rating scale: Preliminary psychometric properties of a "working" alliance measure. *Journal of Brief Therapy, 3*(1), 3–12.

Dunn, T. W., Burlingame, G. M., Walbridge, M., Smith, J., & Crum, M. J. (2005). Outcome assessment for children and adolescents: Psychometric validation of the Youth Outcome Questionnaire 30.1 (Y-OQ®-30.1). *Clinical Psychology and Psychotherapy, 12*, 388–401.

Elkin, I. (1994). The NIMH treatment of depression collaborative research project: Where we began and where we are. In A. E. Bergin & S. L. Garfield (Eds.), *Handbook of psychotherapy and behavior change* (4th ed., pp. 114–142). New York: Wiley.

Elkin, I., Shea, M. T., & Watkins, J. T. (1989). National Institute of Mental Health Treatment of Depression Collaborative Treatment Program: General effectiveness of treatments. *Archives and General Psychiatry, 46*(11), 971–982.

Ellis, A. (1962). *Reason and emotion in psychotherapy*. Secaucus, NJ: Lyle Stuart.

Ellis, A. (1973). *Humanistic psychotherapy: The rational-emotive approach*. New York: McGraw-Hill.

Ellis, A. (1994). *Reason and emotion in psychotherapy (Rev. 2nd ed.)*. New York: Kensington.

Ellis, A. (1996). *Better, deeper, and more enduring brief therapy: The rational emotive behavior therapy approach*. New York: Brunner/Mazel.

Emoto, M. (2004). *The hidden messages in water*. Hillsboro, OR: Beyond Words Publishing.

Emoto, M. (2007). *The healing power of water*. Carlsbad, CA: Hay House.

Epston, D. (1989). *Collected papers*. Adelaide, South Australia: Dulwich Centre Publications.

Epston, D., & White, M. (1992). *Experience, contradiction, narrative, and imagination: Selected papers of David Epston and Michael White 1989–1991*. Adelaide, South Australia: Dulwich Centre Publications.

Epston, D., White, M., & "Ben." (1995). Consulting with your consultants: A means to the co-construction of alternative knowledges. In S. Friedman (Ed.), *The reflecting team in action: Collaborative practice in family therapy* (pp. 277–313). New York: Guilford.

Ericsson, K. A., Charness, N., Feltovich, P. J., Hoffman, R. R. (Eds.). (2006). *The Cambridge handbook of expertise and expert performance*. New York: Cambridge University Press.

Erickson, M. H. (1954a). Special techniques of brief hypnotherapy. *Journal of Clinical and Experiential Hypnosis, 2*, 109–129.

Erickson, M. H. (1954b). Pseudo-orientation in time as a hypnotherapeutic procedure. *Journal of Clinical and Experiential Hypnosis, 2*, 261–283.

Erickson, M. H. (1965). The use of symptoms as an integral part of hypnotherapy. *American Journal of Clinical Hypnosis, 8*, 57–65.

Erickson, M. H. (1980). Migraine headache in a resistant patient. In E. L. Rossi (Ed.), *The collected papers of Milton H. Erickson on hypnosis: Innovative hypnotherapy, vol. IV* (pp. 252–254). New York: Irvington.

Fairbairn, W. R. D. (1954). *An object relations theory of personality*. New York: Basic Books.

Farber, B. A., Brink, D. C., & Raskin, P. M. (Eds.). (1996). *The psychotherapy of Carl Rogers: Cases and commentary*. New York: Guilford.

Farber, B. A., & Lane, J. S. (2002). Positive regard. In J. C. Norcross (Ed.), *Psychotherapy relationships that work: Therapist contributions and responsiveness to patients* (pp. 175–194). New York: Oxford University Press.

Fennell, M. J., & Teasdale, J. D. (1987). Cognitive therapy for depression: Individual differences and the process of change. *Cognitive Therapy and Research, 11*, 253–271.

Fisch, R., Weakland, J. H., & Segal, L. (1982). *The tactics of change: Doing therapy briefly*. San Francisco: Jossey-Bass.

Fisher, J. E., & O'Donohue, W. T. (Eds.). (2006). *Practitioner's guide to evidence-based psychotherapy*. New York: Springer.

Flemons, D. (2002). *Of one mind: The logic of hypnosis*. New York: Norton.

Fonagy, P., Target, M., Cottrell, D., Phillips, J., & Kurtz, Z. (2002). *What works for whom? A critical review of treatments for children and adolescents*. New York: The Guilford Press.

Frank, J. D. (1973). *Persuasion and healing*. Baltimore: Johns Hopkins University Press.

Frank, J. D., & Frank, J. B. (1991). *Persuasion and healing: A comparative study of psychotherapy* (3rd ed.). Baltimore: Johns Hopkins University Press.

Frankl, V. (1963). *Man's search for meaning: An introduction to logotherapy*. New York: Pocket Books.

Frankl, V. (1969). *Will to meaning: Foundations and applications of logotherapy*. New York: World Publishing.

Fraser, J. S., & Solovey, A. D. (2007). *Second-order change in psychotherapy: The golden thread that unifies effective treatments*. Washington, DC: American Psychological Association.

Freedman, J., & Combs, G. (1996). *Narrative therapy: The social construction of preferred realities*. New York: Norton.

Freeman, C., & Power, M. (Eds.). (2007). *Handbook of evidence-based psychotherapies: A guide for research and practice*. New York: Wiley.

Freeman, J., Epston, D., & Lobovits, D. (1997). *Playful approaches to serious problems: Narrative therapy with children and their families*. New York: Norton.

Freud, S. (1953). On psychotherapy. In J. Strachey (Ed.), *The standard edition of the complete psychological works of Sigmund Freud, Vol. VII (1901–105): A case of hysteria, three essays on sexuality and other works* (pp. 255–268). London: Hogarth Press. [Originally published 1905]

Friedman, S. (Ed.). (1995). *The reflecting team in action: Collaborative practice in family therapy*. New York: Guilford.

Gabbard, G.O., & Gabbard, K. (1999). *Psychiatry and the cinema* (2nd ed.). Washington, DC: American Psychiatric Press.

Gabbard, G. O., Lazar, S. G., Hornberger, J., & Spiegel, D. (1997). The economic impact of psychotherapy: A review. *American Journal of Psychiatry, 154*(2), 147–155.

Gallo, F. P. (2000). *Energy diagnostic and treatment methods*. New York: Norton.

Garb, H. N. (2008). Judgment research and the dimensional model of personality. *American Psychologist, 63*(1), 60.

Garfield, S. L. (1989). *The practice of brief psychotherapy*. New York: Pergamon.

Garfield, S. L. (1994). Research on client variables in psychotherapy. In A. E. Bergin and S. L. Garfield (Eds.), *Handbook of psychotherapy and behavior change* (4th ed.) (pp.190–228). New York: Wiley.

Geary, B. B., & Zeig, J. K. (2001). *The handbook of Ericksonian psychotherapy*. Phoenix, AZ: The Milton H. Erickson Foundation Press.

Gergen, K. J. (1982). *Toward transformation in social knowledge*. New York: Springer-Verlag.

Gergen, K. J. (1985). The social constructionist movement in modern psychology. *American Psychologist, 40*, 255–275.

Gergen, K. J. (1991). *The saturated self: Dilemmas of identity in contemporary life*. New York: Basic Books.

Gilligan, C. (1982). *In a different voice: Psychological theory and women's development*. Boston, MA: Harvard University Press.

Gilligan, S. (1987). *Therapeutic trances: The cooperation principle in Ericksonian hypnotherapy*. Philadelphia, PA: Brunner/Mazel.

Goldner, V. (1985). Feminism and family therapy. *Family Process, 24*(1), 31–47.

Goldstein, A. J., de Beurs, E., Chambless, D., & Wilson, K. A. (2000). EMDR for panic disorder with agoraphobia: Comparison with waiting list and credible attention-placebo control conditions.

Journal of Consulting and Clinical Psychology, 68(6), 947–956.

Goodheart, C. D., Kazdin, A. E., & Sternberg, R. J. (Eds.). (2006). *Evidence-based psychotherapy: Where practice and research meet.* Washington, DC: American Psychological Association.

Gottman, J. M. (1999). *The marriage clinic.* New York: Norton.

Greenberg, L. S., & Johnson, S. M. (1988). *Emotionally focused therapy for couples.* New York: Guilford.

Greenberg, R. P. (1999). Common factors in psychiatric drug therapy. In M. A. Hubble, B. L. Duncan, & S. D. Miller (Eds), *The heart and soul of change: What works in therapy* (pp. 297–328). Washington, DC: American Psychological Association.

Grinder, J., & Bandler, R. (1976). *The structure of magic II: A book about communication and change.* Palo Alto, CA: Science and Behavior Books.

Grinder, J., & Bandler, R. (1981). Trance-formations: Neuro-linguistic programming and the structure of hypnosis. Moab, UT: Real People Press.

Grinder, J., DeLozier, J., & Bandler, R. (1977). *Patterns of the hypnotic techniques of Milton H. Erickson, M.D. (Vol. 2).* Cupertino, CA: Meta.

Groopman, J. (2007). *How doctors think.* New York: Mariner/Houghton Mifflin.

Gurman, A. S., & Kniskern, D. P. (Eds.). (1980). *Handbook of family therapy (Vol. I).* New York: Brunner Mazel.

Gurman, A. S., & Kniskern, D. P. (Eds.). (1990). *Handbook of family therapy (Vol. II).* New York: Brunner Mazel.

Guthrie, E., Moorey, J., Margison, F., Barker, H., Palmer, S., McGrath, G., Tomenson, B., & Creed, F. (1999). Cost-effectiveness of brief psychodynamic-interpersonal therapy in high utilizers of psychiatric services. *Archives of General Psychiatry, 56,* 19–26.

Haas, E., Hill, R. D., Lambert, M. J., & Morrell, B. (2002). Do early responders to psychotherapy maintain treatment gains. *Journal of Clinical Psychology, 58*(9), 1157–1172.

Haley, J. (1963). *Strategies of psychotherapy.* New York: Grune & Stratton.

Haley. J. (1973). *Uncommon therapy: The psychiatric techniques of Milton H. Erickson, M.D.* New York: Norton.

Haley, J. (1987). *Problem-solving therapy* (2nd ed.). San Francisco: Jossey-Bass.

Hansen, N., Lambert, M. J., & Forman, E. M. (2002). The psychotherapy dose-response effect and its implication for treatment delivery services. *Clinical Psychology: Science and Practice, 9*(3), 329–343.

Hare-Mustin, R. (1978). A feminist approach to family therapy. *Family Process, 17*(2), 181–194.

Hare-Mustin, R. (1987). The problem of gender in family therapy theory. *Family Process, 26*(1), 15–27.

Harmon, C., Hawkins, E. J., Lambert, M. J., Slade, K., & Whipple, J. L. (2005). Improving outcomes for poorly responding clients: The use of clinical support tools and feedback to clients. *Journal of Clinical Psychology, 61*(2), 175–185.

Hays, P. A. (2007). *Addressing cultural complexities in practice: Assessment diagnosis and therapy* (2nd ed.). Washington, DC: American Psychological Association.

Held, B. S. (1991). The process/content distinction in psychotherapy revisited. *Psychotherapy, 28*(2), 207–217.

Held, B. S. (1995). *Back to reality: A critique of postmodern theory in psychotherapy.* New York: Norton.

Henggeler, S. W., & Borduin, C. M. (Eds.). (1990). *Family therapy and beyond: A multisystemic approach to treating the behavior problems of children and adolescents.* Pacific Grove, CA: Brooks/Cole.

Hesley, J.W., & Hesley, J.G. (2001). *Rent two films and let's talk in the morning: Using popular movies in psychotherapy* (2nd ed.). New York: Wiley.

Hoffman, L. (1981). *Foundations of family therapy: A conceptual framework for systems change.* New York: Basic Books.

Hoffman, L. (1993). *Exchanging voices: A collaborative approach to family therapy.* London: Karnac.

Horvath, A. O. (2001). The alliance. *Psychotherapy, 38*(4), 365–372.

Horvath, A. O., & Bedi, R. P. (2002). The alliance. In J. C. Norcross (Ed.), *Psychotherapy relationships that work: Therapist contributions and responsiveness to patient needs* (pp. 37–69). New York: Oxford University Press.

Horvath, A. O., & Greenberg, L. S. (1989). Development and validation of the Working Alliance Inventory. *Journal of Counseling Psychology, 36*(2), 223–233.

Horvath, A. O., & Greenberg, L. S. (1994). *The working alliance: Theory, research, and practice.* New York: Wiley.

Horvath, A. O., & Luborsky, L. (1993). The role of the therapeutic alliance in psychotherapy. *Journal of Consulting and Clinical Psychology, 61*(4), 561–573.

Horvath, A. O., & Symonds, B. D. (1991). Relation between working alliance and outcome in psychotherapy: A meta-analysis. *Journal of Consulting and Clinical Psychology, 38*(2), 139–149.

Houts, A. C. (2002). Discovery, invention, and the expansion of the modern *Diagnostic and Statistical Manuals of Mental Disorders.* In L. E. Beutler & M. L. Malik (Eds.), *Rethinking the DSM: A psychological perspective* (pp. 17–65). Washington, DC: American Psychological Association.

Howard, K. I., Kopte, S. M., Krause, M. S., & Orlinsky, D. E. (1986). The dose-effect relationship in psychotherapy. *American Psychologist, 41*(2), 159–164.

Howard, K. I., Lueger, R. J., Maling, M. S., & Martinovich, Z. (1993). A phase model of psychotherapy outcome: Causal mediation of change. *Journal of Consulting and Clinical Psychology, 61,* 678–685.

Howard, K. I., Moras, K., Brill, P. L., Martinovich, Z., & Lutz, W. (1996). Evaluation of psychotherapy: Efficacy, effectiveness, and patient progress. *American Psychologist, 51*(10), 1059–1064.

Hoyt, M. F. (Ed.). (1994). *Constructive therapies.* New York: Guilford.

Hoyt, M. F. (Ed.). (1996). *Constructive therapies 2.* New York: Guilford.

Hoyt, M. F. (Ed.). (1998). *The handbook of constructive therapies.* San Francisco: Jossey-Bass.

Hubble, M. A., Duncan, B. L., & Miller, S. D. (Eds.). (1999). *The heart and soul of change: What works in therapy.* Washington, DC: American Psychological Association.

Hubble, M. A., & O'Hanlon, W. H. (1992). Theory countertransference. *Dulwich Centre Newsletter, 1,* 25–30.

Ilardi, S. S., & Craighead, W. E. (1994). The role of nonspecific factors in cognitive-behavior therapy for depression. *Clinical Psychology: Science and Practice, 1,* 138–16.

Jenkins, A. (1996). Moving toward respect: A quest for balance. In C. McLean, M. Carey, & C. White (Eds.), *Men's ways of being* (pp. 117–134). New York: Westview Press.

Jensen, J. P., Bergin, A. E., & Greaves, D. W. (1990). The meaning of eclecticism: New survey and analysis if components. *Professional Psychology: Research and Practice, 21*(2), 124–130.

Johansson, F. (2002). *The Medici effect: Break-through insights at the intersection of ideas, concepts, and cultures.* Boston, MA: Harvard Business School Press.

Johnson, S. M. (2004). *The practice of emotionally focused couple therapy: Creating connection* (2nd ed.). New York: Routledge.

Johnson, S. M. (2005). *Emotionally focused couple therapy with trauma survivors: Strengthening attachment bonds.* New York: Guilford.

Kaslow, F. W. (Ed.). (1996). *Handbook of relational diagnosis and dysfunctional family patterns.* New York: Wiley.

Kazdin, A. E. (2000). *Psychotherapy for children and adolescents: Directions for research and practice.* New York: Oxford University Press.

Kazdin, A. E. (2005). Treatment outcomes, common factors, and continued neglect of mechanisms of change. *Clinical Psychology: Science and Practice, 12,* 184–188.

Kazdin, A. E., & Weisz, J. R. (Eds.). (2003). *Evidence-based psychotherapies with children and adolescents.* New York: Guilford.

Kelly, G. A. (1977). *The psychology of personal constructs.* New York: Norton.

Kernberg, O. F. (1976). *Object relations theory and clinical psychoanalysis.* New York: Aronson.

Kerr, M., & Bowen, M. (1988). *Family evaluation.* New York: Norton.

Kivlighan, D. (2001). Patterns of working alliance development. *Journal of Consulting and Clinical Psychology, 47,* 362–371.

Klein, M. H., Kolden, G. G., Michels, J. L., & Chisolm-Stockard, S. (2002). Congruence. In J. C. Norcross (Ed.), *Psychotherapy relationships that work: Therapist contributions and responsiveness to patients* (pp. 195–215). New York: Oxford University Press.

Kopta, S. M., Howard. K. I., Lowry, J. L., & Beutler, L. E. (1994). Patterns of symptomatic recovery in psychotherapy. *Journal of Consulting and Clinical Psychology, 62*(5), 1009–1016.

Koss, M. P., & Butcher, J. N. (1986). Research on brief psychotherapy. In A. E. Bergin & S. L. Garfield (Eds.), *Handbook of psychotherapy and behavior change* (3rd ed.) (pp. 627–663). New York: Wiley.

Kraft, S., Puschner, B., Lambert, M. J., & Kordy, H. (2006). Medical utilization and treatment outcome in mid- and long-term outpatient psychotherapy. *Psychotherapy Research, 16*(2), 241–249.

Lafferty, P., Beutler, L. E., & Crago, M. (1989). Differences between more and less effective psychotherapists: A study of select therapist variables. *Journal of Consulting and Clinical Psychology, 57,* 76–80.

Lakoff, G., & Johnson, M. (2001). Metaphors we live by. In M. J. Gannon (Ed.), *Cultural metaphors: Readings, research, translations, and commentary* (pp. 3–8). Thousand Oaks, CA: Sage.

Lambert, M. J. (1992). Implications of outcome research for psychotherapy integration. In J. C. Norcross & M. R. Goldfried (Eds.), *Handbook of psychotherapy integration* (pp. 94–129). New York: Basic Books.

Lambert, M. J. (2004). Introduction and historical overview. In M. J. Lambert (Ed.), *Bergin and Garfield's handbook of psychotherapy and behavior change* (5th ed.) (pp. 3–15). New York: Wiley.

Lambert, M. J. (2007). Presidential address: What we have learned from a decade of research aimed at improving psychotherapy outcome in routine care. *Psychotherapy Research, 17*(1), 1–14.

Lambert, M. J., & Bergin, A. E. (1992). Achievements and limitations of psychotherapy research. In D. K. Freddheim (Ed.), *History of psychotherapy: A century of change* (pp. 360–390). Washington, DC: American Psychological Association.

Lambert, M. J., & Bergin, A. E. (1994). The effectiveness of psychotherapy. In A. E. Bergin & S. L. Garfield (Eds.), *Handbook of psychotherapy and behavior change* (4th ed.) (pp. 143–189). New York: Wiley.

Lambert, M. J., & Burlingame, G. R. (1996). *Outcome Questionnaire 45.2.* Wilmington, Delaware: American Professional Credentialing Services.

Lambert, M. J., & Burlingame, G. R., Umphress, V., Hansen, N. B., Vermeersch, D. A., Clouse, G. C., & Yanchar, S. C. (1996). The reliability and validity of the Outcome Questionnaire. *Clinical Psychology, 3*(4), 249–258.

Lambert, M. J., & Finch, A. E. (1999). The Outcome Questionnaire. In M. E. Maruish (Ed.), *The use of psychological testing for treatment planning and outcome assessment* (2nd ed.). Mahwah, NJ: Lawrence Erlbaum.

Lambert, M. J., & Ogles, B. M. (2004). The efficacy and effectiveness of psychotherapy. In M. J. Lambert (Ed.), *Bergin and Garfield's handbook of psychotherapy and behavior change* (5th ed.) (pp. 139–193). New York: Wiley.

Lambert, M. J., Okiishi, J. C., Finch, A. E., & Johnson, L. D. (1998). Outcome assessment: From conceptualization to implementation. *Professional Psychology: Practice and Research, 29*(1), 63–70.

Lambert, M. J., Shapiro, D. A., & Bergin, A. E. (1986). The effectiveness of psychotherapy. In S. L. Garfield & A. E. Bergin (Eds.), *Handbook of psychotherapy and behavior change* (3rd ed.) (pp. 157–211). New York: Wiley.

Lambert, M. J., Whipple, J. L., Hawkins, E. J., Vermeersch, D. A., Nielsen, S. L., & Smart, D. W. (2003). Is it time for clinicians to routinely track patient outcome? A meta-analysis. *Clinical Psychology: Science and Practice, 10*(3), pp. 288–301.

Lambert, M. J., Whipple, J. L., Smart, D. W., Vermeersch, D. A., Nielsen, S. L., & Hawkins, E. J. (2001). The effects of providing therapists with feedback on patient progress during psychotherapy: Are outcomes enhanced? *Psychotherapy Research, 11*(1), 49–68.

Lambert, M. J., Whipple, J. L., Vermeersch, D. A., Smart, D. W., Hawkins, E. J., Nielsen, S. L., & Goates, M. (2002). Enhancing psychotherapy outcomes via providing feedback on client progress: A replication. *Clinical Psychology and Psychotherapy, 9,* 91–103.

Lankton, S. (1980). *Practical magic: A translation of basic neuro-linguistic programming into clinical psychotherapy.* Capitola, CA: Meta Publications.

Lankton, S. R., & Lankton, C. H. (1983). *The answer within: A clinical framework of Ericksonian hypnotherapy.* New York: Brunner/Mazel.

Lankton, S. R., & Lankton, C. H. (1986). *Enchantment and intervention in family therapy: Training in Ericksonian approaches.* New York: Brunner/Mazel.

Law, D. D., Crane, D. R., & Berge, D. M. (2003). The influence of individual, marital, and family therapy on high utilizers of health care. *Journal of Marital and Family Therapy, 29*(3), 353–363.

Lawson, D. (1994). Identifying pretreatment change. *Journal of Counseling and Development, 72*(3), 244–248.

Lazarus, A. A. (1992). Multimodal therapy: Technical eclecticism with minimal integration. In J. C. Norcross & M. R. Goldfried (Eds.), *Handbook of psychotherapy integration* (pp. 231–263). New York: Basic Books.

Lazarus, A. A. (2005). Multimodal therapy. In J. C. Norcross & M. R. Goldfried (Eds.), *Handbook of psychotherapy integration* (2nd ed.) (pp. 105–120). New York: Oxford University Press.

Lebow, J. (1997). New science for psychotherapy. *Family Therapy Networker, 21*(2), 85–91.

Lebow, J. (2006). *Research for the psychotherapist: From science to practice.* New York: Routledge.

Lilienfeld, S. O. (2007). Psychological treatments that cause harm. *Perspectives on Psychological Science, 2*(1), 53–70.

Lilienfeld, S. O., Lynn, S. J., & Lohr, J. M. (Eds.). (2003). *Science and pseudoscience in clinical psychology.* New York: Guilford.

Linehan, M. M. (1993). *Cognitive-behavioral treatment for borderline personality disorder.* New York: Guilford.

Lipsey, M. W., & Wilson, D. B. (1993). The efficacy of psychological, educational, and behavioral treatment: Confirmation from meta-analysis. *American Psychologist, 48,* 1181–1209.

Loar, L. (2001). Eliciting cooperation from teenagers and their parents. *Journal of Systemic Therapies, 20*(1), 59–78.

Lorenz, K. (1997). *King Solomon's ring: New light on animals' ways.* New York: Plume.

Luborsky, L., Barber, J. P., Siqueland, L., Johnson, S., Najavits, L. M., Frank, A., & Daley, D. (1996). The revised Helping Alliance Questionnaire (HAq-II): Psychometric properties. *The Journal of Psychotherapy: Practice and Research, 5*(3), 260–271.

Luborsky, L., Crits-Christoph, P., McLellan, T., Woody, G., Piper, W., Imber, S., & Liberman, B. (1986). Do therapists vary much in their success? Findings in four outcome studies. *American Journal of Orthopsychiatry, 56,* 501–512.

Luborsky, L., Diguer, L, Seligman, D. A., Rosenthal, R., Krause, E. D., Johnson, S., Halperin, G., Bishop, M., Berman, J. S., & Schweizer, E. (1999). The researcher's own therapy allegiances: A "wild card" in comparisons of treatment efficacy. *Clinical Psychology: Science and Practice, 6,* 95–106.

Luborsky, L., McLellan, A. T., Diguer, L., Woody, G., & Seligman, D. A. (1997). The psychotherapist matters: Comparison of outcomes across twenty-two therapists and seven patient samples. *Clinical Psychology: Science and Practice, 4,* 53–65.

Luborsky, L., Singer, B., & Luborsky, L. (1975). Comparative studies of psychotherapies: Is it true that "everyone has won and all must have prizes?" *Archives of General Psychiatry, 32*(8), 995–1008.

Lunnen, K. M., & Ogles, B. M. (1998). A multivariate evaluation of reliable change. *Journal of Consulting and Clinical Psychology, 66*(2), 400–410.

Madanes, C. (1981). *Strategic family therapy.* San Francisco: Jossey-Bass.

Madigan, S., & Law, I. (Eds.). (1998). *Praxis: Situating discourse, feminism and politics in narrative therapies.* Vancouver: Yaletown Family Therapy.

Madsen, W. C. (2006). Teaching discourses to sustain collaborative clinical practice. *Journal of Systemic Therapies, 25*(4), 44–58.

Madsen, W. C. (2007). *Collaborative therapy with multi-stressed families* (2nd ed.). New York: Guilford.

Mahler, M. (1979a). *The selected papers of Margaret S. Mahler: Vol. 1. Infantile psychosis and early contributions.* New York: Aronson.

Mahler, M. (1979b). *The selected papers of Margaret S. Mahler: Vol. 2. Separation-individuation.* New York: Aronson.

Mahoney, M. J. (2003). *Constructive psychotherapy: A practical guide.* New York: Guilford.

Martin, D. J., Garske, J. P., & Davis, M. K. (2000). Relationship of the therapeutic alliance with outcome and other variables: A meta-analytic review. *Journal of Consulting and Clinical Psychology, 68*(3), 438–450.

Maslow, A. H. (1943). A theory of human motivation. *Psychological Review, 50*(4), 370–396.

Maturana, H. R. (1978). Biology of language: Epistemology of reality. In G. Miller & E. Leneberg (Eds.), *Psychology and biology of language and thought* (pp. 27–63). New York: Academic.

May, R., Angel, E., & Ellenberger, H. F. (1958). *Existence: A new dimension in psychiatry and psychology*. New York: Simon & Schuster.

McAuliffe, G., & Erikson, K. (2000). *Preparing counselors and therapists: Creating constructivist and developmental programs*. Virginia Beach, VA: Donning.

McBride, J. (1997). *Steven Spielberg: A biography*. New York: Simon & Schuster.

McCoy, H., & McKay, C. (2006). Preparing social workers to identify and integrate culturally affirming bibliotherapy in treatment. *Social Work Education, 25*(7), 680–693.

McDaniel, S., Hepworth, J., & Doherty, W. (1992). *Medical family therapy New York: Basic Books*.

McGoldrick, M., Gerson, R., & Petry, S. (2008). *Genograms: Assessment and intervention* (3rd ed.). New York: Norton.

McGoldrick, M., Pearce, J., & Giordano, J. (1982). *Ethnicity in family therapy*. New York: Norton.

McMillen, J. C., Morris, L., & Sherraden, M. (2004). Ending social work's grudge match: Problems versus strengths. *Families in Society, 85*(3), 317–325.

Meehl, P. E. (1993). Philosophy of science: Help or hindrance? *Psychological Reports, 72*(3), 702–733.

Meichenbaum, D. (1977). *Cognitive-behavior modification: An integrative approach*. New York: Springer.

Messer, S. B. (1992). A critical examination of belief structures in integrative and eclectic psychotherapy. In J. C. Norcross & M. R. Goldfried (Eds.), *Handbook of psychotherapy integration* (pp. 130–165). New York: Basic Books.

Milardo, R. M. (Ed.). (2000). *Understanding families into the new millennium*. Minneapolis: National Council on Family Relations.

Miller, A. E., Rathus, J. H., & Linehan, M. M. (2006). *Dialectical behavior therapy with suicidal adolescents*. New York: Guilford.

Miller S. D., & Duncan, B. L. (2000). *The Outcome Rating Scale*. Chicago: Author.

Miller, S. D., Duncan, B. L., & Brown, G. S. (2006). Using formal client feedback to improve retention and outcome. *Journal of Brief Therapy, 5*, 5–22.

Miller, S. D., Duncan, B. L., Brown, J. S., Sparks, J. A., Claud, D. A. (2003). The Outcome Rating Scale: A preliminary study of the reliability, validity, and feasibility of a brief, visual, analog measure. *Journal of Brief Therapy, 2*, 91–100.

Miller, S. D., Duncan, B. L., & Hubble, M. A. (1997). *Escape from Babel: Toward a unifying language for psychotherapy practice*. New York: Norton.

Miller, S. D., Hubble, M. A., Duncan, B. L. (2007). Supershrinks: What's the secret of their success? *Psychotherapy Networker, November/December*, 27–35, 56–57.

Miller, W. R., & Rollnick, S. (2002). *Motivational interviewing: Preparing people for change* (2nd ed.). New York: Guilford.

Minuchin, S. (1974). *Families and family therapy*. Cambridge, MA: Harvard University Press.

Minuchin, S., & Fishman, H. C. (1981). *Family therapy techniques*. Cambridge, MA: Harvard University Press.

Minuchin, S., Rosman, B., & Baker, L. (1978). *Psychosomatic families: Anorexia nervosa in context*. Cambridge, MA: Harvard University Press.

Mohr, D. C. (1995). Negative outcome in psychotherapy: A critical review. *Clinical Psychology: Science and Practice, 2*(1), 1–27.

Mueller, M., & Pekarik, G. (2000). Treatment duration prediction: Client accuracy and its relationship to dropout, outcome, and satisfaction. *Psychotherapy: Theory, Research, Practice, Training, 37*(2), 117–123.

Nathan, P. E., & Gorman, J. M. (2007). *A guide to treatments that work* (3rd ed.). New York: Oxford University Press.

Neimeyer, R. A., & Mahoney, M. J. (1995). *Constructivism in psychotherapy*. Washington, DC: American Psychological Association.

Ness, M. E., & Murphy, J. J. (2001). Pretreatment change reports by clients in a university counseling center: Relationship to inquiry technique, client and situational variables. *Journal of College Counseling, 4*(1), 20–31.

Norcross, J. C. (2002). Empirically supported relationships. In J. C. Norcross (Ed.), *Psychotherapy relationships that work: Therapist contributions and responsiveness to patients* (pp. 3–16). New York: Oxford University Press.

Norcross, J. C., Beutler, L. E., & Levant, R. F. (Eds.). (2005). *Evidence-based practices in mental health: Debate and dialogue on the fundamental questions.* Washington, DC: American Psychological Association.

Norcross, J. C., & Goldfried, M. R. (Eds.). (2005). *Handbook of psychotherapy integration* (2nd ed.). New York: Oxford.

Norcross, J. C., Karpiak, C. P., & Lister, K. M. (2005). What's an integrationist? A study of self-identified integrative and (occasionally) eclectic psychologists. *Journal of Clinical Psychology, 61*(12), 1587–1594.

Nylund, D., & Corsiglia, V. (1994). Becoming solution-forced in brief therapy: Remembering something important we already knew. *Journal of Strategic and Systemic Therapies, 13*(1), 5–12.

Nylund, D., & Thomas, J. (1994). The economics of narrative. *Family Therapy Networker, 18*(6), 38–39.

O'Hanlon, B. (1994). The third wave. *Family Therapy Networker, 18*(6),18–26, 28–29.

O'Hanlon, B. (1999). What's the story? Narrative therapy and the third wave of psychotherapy. In S. O'Hanlon & B. Bertolino (Eds.), *Evolving possibilities: Selected papers of Bill O'Hanlon* (pp. 205–220). Philadelphia, PA: Brunner/Mazel.

O'Hanlon, W. H. (1987). *Taproots: Underlying principles of Milton Erickson's therapy and hypnosis.* New York: Norton.

O'Hanlon, B., & Bertolino, B. (1998). *Even from a broken web: Brief, respectful solution-oriented therapy for sexual abuse and trauma.* New York: John Wiley & Sons.

O'Hanlon, B., & Bertolino, B. (2002). *Even from a broken web: Brief, respectful solution-oriented therapy for sexual abuse and trauma.* New York: Norton. [Paperback Edition]

O'Hanlon, W. H., & Hexum, A. L. (1990). *An uncommon casebook: The complete clinical work of Milton H. Erickson, M.D.* New York: Norton.

O'Hanlon, W. H., & Martin, M. (1992). *Solution-oriented hypnosis: An Ericksonian approach.* New York: Norton.

O'Hanlon, W. H., & Weiner-Davis, M. (2003). *In search of solutions: A new direction in psychotherapy* (2nd ed.). New York: Norton.

Okiishi, J., Lambert, M. J., Nielsen, S. L., & Ogles, B. M. (2003). Waiting for supershrink: An empirical analysis of therapist effects. *Clinical Psychology and Psychotherapy, 10*(6), 361–373.

Olkin, R. (1999). *What psychotherapists should know about disability.* New York: Guilford.

Orlinsky, D. E., Grawe, K., & Parks, B. K. (1994). Process and outcome in psychotherapy—noch einmal. In A. E. Bergin & S. L. Garfield (Eds.), *Handbook of psychotherapy and behavior change* (4th ed.) (pp. 270–378). New York: Wiley.

Orlinsky, D. E., & Howard, K. I. (1980). Gender and psychotherapeutic outcome. In A. M. Brodsky & R. T. Hare-Mustin (Eds.), *Women and psychotherapy* (pp. 3–34). New York: Guilford.

Orlinsky, D. E., & Howard, K. I. (1986). The psychological interior of psychotherapy: Explorations with the therapy session reports. In L. S. Greenberg & W. M. Pinsof (Eds.), *The psychotherapeutic process: A research handbook* (pp. 477–501). New York: Guilford.

Orlinsky, D. E., Rønnestad, M. H., & Willutzki, U. (2004). Fifty years of process-outcome research: Continuity and change. In M. J. Lambert (Ed.), *Bergin and Garfield's handbook of psychotherapy and behavior change* (5th ed.) (pp. 307–390). New York: Wiley.

Parker, T. S., & Wampler, K. S. (2006). Changing emotion: The use of therapeutic storytelling. *Journal of Marital and Family Therapy, 32*(2), 155–166.

Paul, G. L. (1967). Strategy of outcome research in psychotherapy. *Journal of Consulting Psychology, 31*(2), 109–118.

Percevic, R., Lambert, M. J., & Kordy, H. (2006). What is the predictive value of responses to psychotherapy for its future course? Empirical explorations and consequences for outcome monitoring. *Psychotherapy Research, 16*(3), 364–273.

Perls, F. S. (1969). *Gestalt therapy verbatim.* Moab, UT: Real People Press.

Perls, F. S. (1973). *The Gestalt approach.* Palo Alto, CA: Science and Behavior Books.

Phillips, M. (2000). *Finding the energy to heal: How EMDR, hypnosis, TFT, imagery, and body-focused therapy can restore mind-body health.* New York: Norton.

Pinsoff, W. M. (1995). *Integrative IPCT: A synthesis of biological, individual and family therapies.* New York: Basic Books.

Pinsoff, W. M. (2005). Integrative problem-centered therapy. In J. C. Norcross & M. R. Goldfried (Eds.), *Handbook of psychotherapy integration* (2nd ed.), (pp. 282–402). New York: Oxford University Press.

Piper, W. E., Ogrodniczuk, J. S., Joyce, A. S., McCallum, M., Rosie, J. S., O'Kelly, J. G., & Steinberg, P. I. (1999). Prediction of dropping out in time-limited interpretive individual psychotherapy. *Psychotherapy, 36*(2), 114–122.

Prochaska, J. O., & DiClemente, C. C. (2005). The transtheoretical approach. In J. C. Norcross & M. R. Goldfried (Eds.), *Handbook of psychotherapy integration* (2nd ed.) (pp. 147–171). New York: Oxford University Press.

Prochaska, J. O., DiClemente, C. C., & Norcross, J. C. (1992). In search of how people change: Applications to addictive behaviors. *American Psychologist, 47*, 1102–1114.

Prochaska, J. O., & Norcross, J. C. (2002). *Systems of psychotherapy: A transtheoretical analysis* (5th ed.). Pacific Grove, CA: Brooks-Cole.

Project MATCH Research Group. (1997). Matching alcoholism treatments to client heterogeneity: Project MATCH posttreatment drinking outcomes. *Journal of Studies on Alcohol, 58*(1), 7–29.

Rapp, C. A. (1998). *The strengths model: Case management with people suffering from severe and persistent mental illness.* New York: Oxford University Press.

Ricks, D. (1974). Supershrink: Methods of a therapist judged successful on the basis of adult outcomes of adolescent patients. In D. Ricks, A. Thomas, & M. Roff (Eds.), *Life history research in psychopathology, vol. 3* (pp. 275–297). Minneapolis, MN: University of Minnesota.

Rogers, C. R. (1951). *Client-centered therapy: Its current practice, implications, and theory.* Boston: Houghton Mifflin.

Rogers, C. R. (1957). The necessary and sufficient conditions of therapeutic personality change. *Journal of Consulting Psychology, 21*, 95–103.

Rogers, C. R. (1961). *On becoming a person.* Boston: Houghton Mifflin.

Rokke, P. D. (1999). The role of client choice and target selection in self-management therapy for depression in older adults. *Psychology and Aging, 14*, 155–169.

Rosen, G. M., & Davison, G. C. (2003). Psychology should list empirically supported principles of change (ESPs) and not credentialed trademarked therapies or other treatment packages. *Behavior Modification, 27*(3), 300–312

Rosen, S. (1982). *My voice will go with you: The teaching tales of Milton H. Erickson.* New York: Norton.

Rosenzweig, S. (1936). Some implicit common factors in diverse methods of psychotherapy. *American Journal of Orthopsychiatry, 6*, 412–415.

Rossi, E. L. (Ed.). (1980). *The collected papers of Milton H. Erickson on hypnosis (Vol. I–IV).* New York Irvington.

Roth, A., & Fonagy, P. (2004). *What works for whom? A critical review of psychotherapy Research* (2nd ed.). New York: Guilford.

Ryle, A. (2005). Cognitive analytic therapy. In J. C. Norcross & M. R. Goldfried (Eds.), *Handbook of psychotherapy integration* (2nd ed.) (pp. 196–217). New York: Oxford University Press.

Sachs, J. S. (1983). Negative factors in brief psychotherapy: An empirical assessment. *Journal of Consulting and Clinical Psychology, 51*(4), 557–564.

Sackett, D. L., Straus, S. E., Richardson, W. S., Rosenberg, W., & Hayes, R. B. (2000). *Evidence based medicine: How to practice and teach EBM* (2nd ed.). London: Churchill Livingstone.

Safran, J. D., Muran, J. C., Samstag, L. W., & Stevens, C. (2002). Repairing alliance ruptures. In J. C. Norcross (Ed.), *Psychotherapy relationships that work: Therapist contributions and responsiveness to patients* (pp. 235–254). New York: Oxford University Press.

Safren, S., Heimberg, R., & Juster, H. (1997). Clients' expectancies and their relationship to pretreatment symptomatology and outcome of cognitive-behavioral group treatment for social phobia. *Journal of Consulting and Clinical Psychology, 65*, 694–698.

Saleeby, D. (2006). *The strengths perspective in social work practice* (4th ed.). Boston: Allyn & Bacon.

Satir, V. (1964). *Conjoint family therapy.* Palo Alto, CA: Science and Behavior Books.

Satir, V. (1972). *Peoplemaking.* Palo Alto, CA: Science and Behavior Books.

Scharff, D., & Scharff, J. (1987). *Object relations family therapy.* New York: Aronson.

Schneider, W., & Klauer, T. (2001). Symptom level, treatment motivation, and the effects of inpatient psychotherapy. *Psychotherapy Research, 11*(2), 153–167.

Schwartz, R. C. (1995). *Internal family systems theory*. New York: Guilford.

Seligman, L., & Reichenberg, L. W. (2007). *Selecting effective treatments: A comprehensive, systematic guide to treating mental disorders* (3rd ed.). San Francisco: Jossey-Bass.

Seligman, M. E. P., & Csikszentmihalyi, M. (2000). Positive psychology: An introduction. *American Psychologist, 55*(1), 5–14.

Sells, S. P., Smith, T. E., Coe, M. J., Yoshioka, M., & Robbins, J. (1994). An ethnography of couple and therapist experiences in reflecting team practice. *Journal of Marital and Family Therapy, 20*(3), 247–266.

Selvini Palazzoli, M., Boscolo, L., Cecchin, G., & Prata, G. (1978). *Paradox and counterparadox*. New York: Aronson.

Sexton, T. L., Alexander, J. F., & Mease, A. L. (2004). Levels of evidence for the models and mechanisms of therapeutic change in couple and family therapy. In M. J. Lambert (Ed.), *Handbook of psychotherapy and behavior change* (5th ed.) (pp. 590–646). New York: Wiley.

Sexton, T. L., Ridley, C. R., & Kleiner, A. J. (2004). Beyond common factors: Multi-level process models of therapeutic change in marriage and family therapy. *Journal of Marital and family Therapy, 30*(2), 131–149.

Shadish, W. R., & Baldwin, S. A. (2002). Meta-analysis of MFT interventions. In D. H. Sprenkle (Ed.), *Effectiveness research in marriage and family therapy* (pp. 339–370). Alexandria, VA: American Association for Marriage and Family Therapy.

Shadish, W. R., Ragsdale, K., Glaser, R. R., & Montgomery, L. M. (1995). The efficacy and effectiveness of marital and family therapy: A perspective from meta-analysis. *Journal of Marital and Family Therapy, 21*, 345–360.

Shapiro, F. (2001). *Eye movement desensitization and reprocessing: Basic principles, protocols, and procedures* (2nd ed.). New York: Guilford.

Shapiro, F., Kaslow, F. W., & Maxfield, L. (Eds.). (2007). *Handbook of EMDR and family therapy processes*. New York: Wiley.

Sharpe, D. (1997). Of apples and oranges, file drawers and garbage: Why validity issues in meta-analysis will not go away. *Clinical Psychology Review, 17*, 881–901.

Shotter, J. (1993). *Conversational realities: The construction of life through language*. London: Sage.

Skinner, B. F. (1953). *Science and human behavior*. New York: Free Press.

Skovholt, T. M., & Jennings, L. (2005). *Mastery and expertise in counseling. Journal of Mental Health Counseling, 27*(1), 13–18.

Skovholt, T. M., & Rønnestad, M. H. (1995). *The evolving professional self: Themes in counselor and therapist development*. New York: Wiley.

Skovholt, T. M., & Rønnestad, M. H. (2001). The long, textured path from novice to senior practitioner. In T. M. Skovholt (Ed.), *The resilient practitioner: Burnout prevention and self-care strategies for counselors, therapists, teachers, and health professionals* (pp. 25–54). Boston: Allyn & Bacon.

Smith, C., & Nylund, D. (Eds.). (1997). *Narrative therapies with children and adolescents*. New York: Guilford.

Smith, M. L., & Glass, G. V. (1977). Meta-analysis of psychotherapy outcome studies. *American Psychologist, 32*(9), 752–760.

Smith, M. L., Glass, G. V., & Miller, T. I. (1980). *The benefits of psychotherapy*. Englewood Cliffs, NJ: Prentice-Hall.

Smith, T. E., Yoshioka, M., & Winton, M. (1993). A qualitative understanding of reflecting teams I: Client perspectives. *Journal of Systemic Therapies, 12*(3), 28–43.

Snyder, C. R. (2000). *The handbook of hope: Theory, measures, and applications*. New York: Academic Press.

Solomon, G. (2001). *Reel therapy: How movies inspire you to overcome life's problems*. Lebhar-Friedman Books

Sprenkle, D. H., & Blow, A. J. (2004). Common factors and our sacred models. *Journal of Marital and Family Therapy, 30*(2), 113–129.

Staudt, M., Howard, M. O., & Drake, B. (2001). The operationalization, implementation, and effectiveness of the strengths-based perspective. *Journal of Social Service Research, 27*(3), 1–21.

Steenbarger, B. N. (1992). Toward science-practice integration in brief counseling and therapy. *The Counseling Psychologist, 20*(3), 403–450.

Steering Committee. (2001). Empirically supported therapy relationships: Conclusions and recommendations of the Division 29 Task Force. *Psychotherapy, 38*(4), 495–497.

Stricker, G. (2002). What is a scientist-practitioner anyway? *Journal of Clinical Psychology, 58*(10), 1277–1283.

Stricker, G., & Gold, J. R. (Eds.). (1993). *Comprehensive handbook of psychotherapy integration.* New York: Plenum.

Stuart, R. B., & Lilienfeld, S. O. (2007). The evidence is missing from evidence-based practice. *American Psychologist, 62*(6), 615–616.

Sue, D. W., Arredondo, P., & McDavis, R. J. (1992). Multicultural counseling competencies and standards: A call to the profession. *Journal of Counseling and Development, 70*(4), 477–486.

Sue, D, W., & Sue, D. (2007). *Counseling the culturally different: Theory and practice* (5th ed.). New York: Wiley.

Tackett, J. L., Silberschmidt, A. L., Krueger, R. F., & Sponheim, S. R. (2008). A dimensional model of personality disorder: Incorporating *DSM* Cluster A characteristics. *Journal of Abnormal Psychology, 117*(2), 454–459.

Tallman, K., & Bohart, A. (1999). The client as a common factor: Clients as self-healers. In M. A. Hubble, B. L. Duncan, & S. D. Miller (Eds.), *The heart and soul of change: What works in therapy* (pp. 91–132). Washington, DC: American Psychological Association.

Talmon, M. (1990). *Single session therapy: Maximizing the effect of the first (and often only) therapeutic encounter.* San Francisco: Jossey-Bass.

Talmon, M., Hoyt, M. F., & Rosenbaum, R. (1990). Effective single-session therapy: Step-by-step guidelines. In. M. Talmon, *Single session therapy: Maximizing the effect of the first (and often only) therapeutic encounter* (pp. 34–56). San Francisco: Jossey-Bass.

Task Force on Promotion and Dissemination of Psychological Procedures (TFPP). (1995). Training in and dissemination of empirically-validated psychological treatment: Report and recommendations. *The Clinical Psychologist, 48,* 2–23.

Timko, C., Moos, R. H., Finney, J. W., Moos, B. S., Kaplowitz, M. S. (1999). Long-term treatment careers and outcomes of previously untreated alcoholics. *Journal of Studies on Alcohol, 60*(4), 437–447.

Tohn, S. L., & Oshlag, J. A. (1996). Solution-focused therapy with mandated clients: Cooperating with the uncooperative. In S. D. Miller, M. A. Hubble, & B. L. Duncan (Eds.), *Handbook of solution-focused brief therapy* (pp. 152–183). San Francisco: Jossey-Bass.

Tomm, K. (1984a). One perspective on the Milan systemic approach: Part I: Overview of development, theory and practice. *Journal of Marital and Family Therapy, 10*(2), 113–125.

Tomm, K. (1984b). One perspective on the Milan systemic approach: Part II: Description of session format, interviewing style and interventions. *Journal of Marital and Family Therapy, 10*(3), 113–125.

Tomm, K. (1987). Interventive interviewing: Part I: Strategizing as a fourth guideline for the therapist. *Family Process, 26*(1), 3–13.

Tomm, K. (1988). Interventive interviewing: Part III: Intending to ask lineal, circular, strategic, or reflexive questions? *Family Process, 27*(1), 1–15.

van der kolk, B. A. (1994). The body keeps score: Memory and the emerging psychobiology of post traumatic stress. *Harvard Review of Psychiatry, 1,* 253–265.

van der kolk, B. A., McFarlane, A. C., & Weisaeth, L. (Eds.). (1996). *Traumatic stress: The effects of overwhelming experience on mind, body, and society.* New York: Guilford.

Wachtel, P. L., Kruk, J. C., & McKinney, M. K. (2005). Cyclical psychodynamics and integrative relational psychotherapy. In J. C. Norcross & M. R. Goldfried (Eds.), *Handbook of psychotherapy integration* (2nd ed.) (pp. 172–195). New York: Oxford University Press.

Walters, M., Carter, B., Papp, P., & Silverstein, O. (1988). *The invisible web: Gender patterns in family relationships.* New York: Guilford.

Wampold, B. E. (2001). *The great psychotherapy debate: Models, methods, and findings.* Mahwah, NJ: Lawrence Erlbaum.

Wampold, B. E. (2005). Establishing specificity in psychotherapy scientifically: Design and evidence issues. *Clinical Psychology: Science and Practice, 12,* 194–197.

Wampold, B. E., & Brown, G. S. (2005). Estimating variability in outcomes attributable to therapists: A naturalistic study of outcomes in managed care. *Journal of Consulting and Clinical Psychology, 73*(5), 914–923.

Wampold, B. E., Goodheart, C. D., & Levant, R. F. (2007). Clarification and elaboration on evidence-based practice in psychology. *American Psychologist, 62*(6), 616–618.

Wampold, B. E., Mondin, G. W., Moody, M., Stich, F., Benson, K., & Ahn, H. (1997). A meta-analysis of outcome studies comparing bona fide psychotherapies: Empirically, "All must have prizes." *Psychological Bulletin, 122*, 203–215.

Waters, D. B., & Lawrence, E. C. (1993). *Competence, courage, and change: An approach to family therapy.* New York: Norton.

Watzlawick, P. (Ed.). (1984). *The invented reality: How do we know what we believe we know? Contributions to constructivism.* New York: Norton.

Watzlawick, P., Weakland, J., & Fisch, R. (1974). *Change: Principles of problem formation and problem resolution.* New York: Norton.

Wedding, D., Boyd, M., & Niemiec, R. M. (2005). *Movies and mental illness: Using films to understand psychotherapy.* Cambridge, MA: Hogrefe & Huber Publishing.

Weiner-Davis, M., de Shazer, S., & Gingerich, W. J. (1987). Using pretreatment change to construct a therapeutic solution: An exploratory study. *Journal of Marital and Family Therapy, 13*, 359–363.

Weisz, J. R. (2004). *Psychotherapy for children and adolescents: Evidence-based treatments and case examples.* New York: Cambridge University Press.

Westen, D., Novotny, C. M., & Thompson-Brenner, H. (2005). EBP ≠ STL Reply to Crits-Christophet et al. (2005) and Weisz et al. (2005). *Psychological Bulletin, 131*(3), 427–433.

Whipple, J. L., Lambert, M. J., Vermeersch, D. A., Smart, D. W., Nielsen, S. L., & Hawkins, E. J. (2003). Improving the effects of psychotherapy: The use of early identification of treatment and problem-solving strategies in routine practice. *Journal of Counseling Psychology, 50*(1), 59–68.

Whitaker, C. A., & Bumberry, W. M. (1988). *Dancing with the family: A symbolic experiential approach.* New York: Brunner/Mazel.

Whitaker, C. A., & Keith, D. V. (1981). Symbolic-experiential family therapy. In A. S. Gurman & D. P. Knoskern (Eds.), *Handbook of family therapy, vol. 1* (pp. 187–225). New York: Brunner/Mazel.

White, M. (1989). *Selected papers.* Adelaide, South Australia: Dulwich Centre Publications.

White, M. (1995). *Re-authoring lives: Interviews and essays.* Adelaide, South Australia: Dulwich Centre Publications.

White, M. (2007). *Maps of narrative practice.* New York: Norton.

White, M., & Epston, D. (1990). *Narrative means to therapeutic ends.* New York: Norton.

White, M. B., & Russell, C. S. (1997). Examining the multifaceted notion of isomorphism in marriage and family therapy supervision: A quest for conceptual clarity. *Journal of Marital and Family Therapy, 20*(3), 315–333.

Widiger, T. A., & Trull, T. J. (2007). Plate tectonics in the classification of personality disorder: Shifting to a dimensional model. *American Psychologist, 62*, 71–83.

Wile, D. (1977). Ideological conflicts between clients and psychotherapists. *American Journal of Psychotherapy, 37*, 437–449.

Wolin, S, J., & Wolin, S. (1993). *The resilient self: How survivors of troubled families rise above adversity.* New York: Villard Books.

Yalom, I. D. (1980). *Existential psychotherapy.* New York: Basic Books.

Yapko, M. D. (1995). *Essentials of hypnosis.* New York: Brunner/Mazel.

Yapko, M. D. (2003). *Trancework: An introduction to the practice of clinical hypnosis* (3rd ed.). Philadelphia, PA: Brunner-Routledge.

Zeig, J. K. (Ed.). (1982). *Ericksonian approaches to hypnosis and psychotherapy.* New York: Brunner/Mazel.

Zeig, J. K. (Ed.). (1985a). *Ericksonian psychotherapy: Vol. I: Structures.* New York: Brunner/Mazel.

Zeig, J. K. (Ed.). (1985b). *Ericksonian psychotherapy: Vol. II: Clinical applications.* New York: Brunner/Mazel.

Zeig, J. K. (Ed.). (1994). *Ericksonian methods: The essence of the story.* New York: Routledge.

Zeig, J. K., & Lankton, S. R. (Eds.) (1988). *Developing Ericksonian therapy: State of the art.* New York: Brunner/Mazel.

Index

Page numbers followed by an "f" indicate figures; those followed by a "t" indicate tables.